Legal Support Practitioner Series

CRIMINAL LITIGATION

A TEXT DESIGNED TO SUPPORT THE NVQ IN LEGAL PRACTICE STANDARDS

Endorsed by The Law Society of England and Wales

Cavendish Publishing Limited

London • Sydney

BOOKS IN THE SERIES

CLIENT CARE

RESIDENTIAL CONVEYANCING

COMMERCIAL CONVEYANCING

PRIVATE CLIENT

FAMILY AND MATRIMONIAL

CRIMINAL LITIGATION

CIVIL LITIGATION

SALE AND PURCHASE OF BUSINESSES

LOCAL GOVERNMENT

Legal Support Practitioner Series

CRIMINAL LITIGATION

A TEXT DESIGNED TO SUPPORT THE NVQ IN LEGAL PRACTICE STANDARDS

Endorsed by The Law Society of England and Wales

Jane Tyrer, LLB, MA, Barrister
Principal Lecturer in Law and Field Chair of Law
Buckinghamshire Chilterns University College

David LD Lawton, MA, Solicitor Advocate
Partner, Budd Martin Burrett, Chelmsford

Series Editor
Richard Norrie, Director, The Law Coach

Cavendish Publishing Limited

London • Sydney

First published in Great Britain 2000 by Cavendish Publishing Limited, The Glass House, Wharton Street, London, WC1X 9PX, United Kingdom
Telephone: +44 (0) 20 7278 8000 Facsimile: +44 (0) 20 7278 8080
E-mail: info@cavendishpublishing.com
Visit our Home Page on http://www.cavendishpublishing.com

Tyrer, Jane
Criminal litigation – (Legal support practitioner series)
1 Criminal procedure – England 2 Criminal procedure – Wales
3 Criminal law – England 4 Criminal law – Wales
I Title II Lawton, David
345.4'2'05

ISBN 1 85941 440 0

Printed and bound in Great Britain

DEDICATION

To my parents

JT

To Ursula, Jim and Hilary

DL

FOREWORD

This book is one of a specially written Legal Support Practitioner Series edited by The Law Coach, the first training provider to be accredited by The Law Society to offer solicitors' Continuing Professional Development over the internet. The books have been created to address the *Occupational Standards in Legal Practice* for the National Vocational Qualifications (NVQs). These NVQs in legal practice are endorsed by The Law Society of England and Wales. The level of the qualification is that equivalent to an undergraduate university degree.

Unlike traditional qualifications, NVQs are obtained by those actually engaged in the area of legal practice covered by the Standards. Because such persons taking the qualifications will be assessed through the evidence of the work they are doing in the legal environment, the acquisition of an award denotes the candidate's competence at doing the work. Additionally, an assessment of the law which underpins legal practitioner NVQs will be undertaken through a written test. As such, those gaining the qualification will have won a 'kite mark' as to their competence and so be recognised as having met national standards.

Edexcel Foundation (Edexcel) is the awarding body for the NVQs in legal practice. The role of the awarding body is to ensure that centres (which may be your workplace or an academic institution) assessing candidates' work and legal knowledge do so within national guidelines and policies.

This book is carefully written to reflect the national *Occupational Standards,* and is designed to assist candidates for the NVQs to meet the levels of competence which are expected from those engaged in undertaking legal services for clients. The approach adopted in the writing is essentially practical, whereby the legal support practitioner is 'talked through' the tasks intrinsic to the work, introducing the law and legal points of practice as they occur in real life. In this way, the book is unlike the usual law text, which is often written without regard to how the law is used. You will see that, while the left hand column sets out the various aspects of the legal work, the right hand column is used to carry a number of activity points. These include checklists, self-assessment questions, portfolio exercises, 'think points' and legal points (see Key to Symbols, p ix). The text is, therefore, intended to be more interactive.

This series has its own web page on The Law Coach website (www.law-coach.com/legal_practitioner_support_serie.htm). Here, you will find updates on the law, information about the series and contacts for the NVQs in legal practice.

Because the national *Occupational Standards* represent a statement of competence, the books can be used by law firms and other legal offices beyond the acquisition of a qualification. The books serve as a training guide and, for those employed in the legal office, as a best practice guide or workbook.

Richard Norrie
Director, The Law Coach
Series Editor

KEY TO SYMBOLS

OVERVIEW: the activities that the NVQ unit will be addressing.

OBJECTIVES: a statement of what the reader will be able do on completion of the unit.

DOCUMENT: a reference to a document, legal form, precedent or further reading.

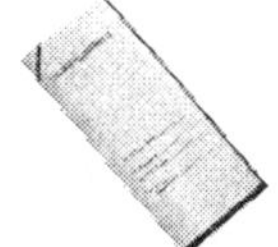

LEGAL POINT: a particular point of law, a case or a particular statutory reference.

PORTFOLIO GUIDANCE: an indication by the author of the type of evidence that the reader needs to draw from his/her work to demonstrate an ability to meet the performance standards in an NVQ.

REMEMBER: the author sets out points or checklists to be remembered.

SELF-ASSESSMENT QUESTION: a question based on a point made in the text. Answers are given in an Appendix to each unit.

THINK POINT: a matter raised by the author requiring careful thought on issues arising from the text.

VERY IMPORTANT POINT: the author draws the reader's attention to a matter of great importance.

SELF-ASSESSMENT TEST: examples of the type of questions to be set by Edexcel, the NVQ awarding body, designed to assess your knowledge and understanding of the law relevant to the NVQ variant covered in the respective unit.

CHECKLIST: a summary of key points at the end of each unit.

ACKNOWLEDGMENTS

I would like to express my gratitude to all those whose support and assistance have enabled this work to come to fruition.

I would especially like to thank: Helene Bellafatto for her hawkeye attention to detail and extreme patience in correcting the draft of the text; Margaret Britt, formerly law librarian of Thames Valley University, for her advice on the research section; Sophie Tarassenko of Thames Valley University for her wise counsel in times of trial; and Professor Malcolm Davies, also of Thames Valley University, for his support and continued encouragement and for instilling in me the confidence to undertake this venture.

Jane Tyrer

Many thanks to my cheerful and efficient secretary Gillian Claydon for all her hard work in translating my part of the text into intelligible script. I would also like to thank Viv Latham for her assistance with authorities, and all my other colleagues both past and present in the litigation department of Budd Martin Burrett for their assistance with criminal work and their support and friendship over the years. I would like to thank Daniel Raphaie for arousing my interest in both prison law and human rights law, Penny Sergeant of Liberty who put me in contact with him, and other people who are prepared to stand up against injustice.

David Lawton

We also wish to thank the following who have kindly given their permission for use of copyright materials:

- the Controller of HMSO for extracts from statutes (PACE 1984 and Codes);
- the CPS for permission to use extracts from the Code for Crown Prosecutors © Crown Copyright 1994;
- the Department of the Lord Chief Justice for permission to reproduce the Mode of Trial Guidelines;
- the Legal Aid Board's Transaction Criteria are copyright works and are reproduced here with the kind permission of the Board. They may not be copied or otherwise reproduced without prior permission of the Legal Aid Board. Note that the transaction criteria are subject to change. As the transaction criteria are used to audit casefiles, they may change where there are changes in law and best practice. The Legal Aid Board will give notice of the introduction of revised issues of transaction criteria in FOCUS – the Board's newsletter.

Jane Tyrer

David Lawton

TABLE OF CONTENTS

TABLE OF CASES

TABLE OF STATUTES

TABLE OF ABBREVIATIONS

actual bodily harm	ABH
assistance by way of representation	ABWOR
Citizens' Advice Bureau	CAB
community service order	CSO
Crime and Disorder Act	CDA
Criminal Justice Act	CJA
Criminal Justice and Public Order Act	CJPOA
Criminal Law Act	CLA
Criminal Procedure and Investigations Act	CPIA
Crown Prosecution Service	CPS
Department of Social Security	DSS
Home Office	HO
Legal Aid Board Transaction Criteria	LABTC
Magistrates' Courts Act	MCA
Offences Against the Person Act	OAPA
Police and Criminal Evidence Act	PACE
Powers of Criminal Courts Act	PCCA
pre-sentence report	PSR
triable either way	TEW

UNIT 1

REPRESENTING CLIENTS AT POLICE STATIONS

OVERVIEW

Six activities comprise this unit:

1.1 assembling information prior to charge;

1.2 consulting with investigating authorities;

1.3 assisting and advising clients at police stations;

1.4 assisting clients with interviews;

1.5 representing vulnerable clients;

1.6 assisting clients with identification procedures.

In Appendix 1, there is a section on preliminary knowledge and understanding for any candidates who may need a general introduction in advance of the specific activities set out above.

OBJECTIVES

To become fully competent in this unit, you will need knowledge and understanding of:

Offences

- identify the components of the following common offences, including their specific defences, the elements which the prosecution must prove, and the likely sentencing tariffs: assault occasioning actual bodily harm; possessing a controlled drug with intent to supply; handling stolen goods; possessing an offensive weapon; taking a motor vehicle; theft; affray;
- distinguish arrestable from serious arrestable offences.

Representative's role

- describe the representative's role in defending clients in relation to:
  - the representative's authority to act for a person detained in a police station;
  - the representative's role and aims when acting for such a client, with regard to probing of the prosecution case, representations to be made to the police, and the purpose of advice to be given to the client;
  - the effect of detention on clients' behaviour in the police station, and appropriate responses to typical behaviour.

Procedure

- describe the basic sequence of events in criminal cases, from clients' arrest/arrival at the police station to conviction and sentence, and the critical factors at each stage;
- state the different ways by which crimes can be tried.

Substantive criminal law

- explain the meaning of the following terms: burden of proof, *actus reus*, *mens rea*, intention, recklessness, maliciousness, dishonesty, knowledge and belief, possession;
- describe the modes of participation in crime of sole and joint principal and accomplice.

Defence

- explain the defence of 'self-defence'.

Police and Criminal Evidence Act (PACE) 1984

- describe the provisions of PACE 1984 in relation to: search of the client's premises; arrest; voluntary attendance at the police station and search upon arrest; duties of custody officer before and after charge; responsibilities in relation to detained persons; detention, time limits and reviews; searches of detained persons; right to have someone informed when arrested; fingerprinting, taking of intimate and other samples; right to legal advice; bail; special treatment of juveniles and other vulnerable persons; keeping of and entitlement to see custody records; cautions; conduct and tape recording of interviews; charging;
- explain the sections of PACE 1984 related to the exclusion of unreliable confessions, evidence obtained unfairly, documentary evidence, and the conduct and tape recording of interviews;
- explain the provisions of PACE 1984 in relation to identification.

Evidence

- explain how facts are proved, including the rule against hearsay and its exceptions;
- explain the evidential consequences of a suspect:
  - remaining silent;
  - remaining selectively silent;
  - sections 36 and 37 special warnings;
  - denying guilt at interviews;
  - making a 'mixed' statement;
  - making a confession;
- explain the evidential value of admissions made by a co-accused.

ASSEMBLING INFORMATION PRIOR TO CHARGE

RANGE

Achievement must cover all the following contexts.

Type of information

Details

As laid down in the Legal Aid Board Transaction Criteria (see Document 4 in Appendix 2).

EVIDENCE

You will need to produce the specific pieces of performance evidence listed below. In addition, you will need to demonstrate that you have achieved the objectives specified at the beginning of this unit. You may do this by producing further pieces of evidence from real and simulated performance, by answering questions posed by your assessor or by passing a written examination.

You will need to provide evidence of:

1 having assembled information as detailed in the **Range** above prior to three clients' charges, one of whom should be a client with a considerable history;
2 having taken full notes of client interviews prior to charge on two occasions;
3 having communicated with officers to exchange necessary information on two occasions;
4 having made special provisions for at least one vulnerable client.

CRITERIA

You will demonstrate achievement if:

(a) all necessary information is collected from clients and recorded accurately in files, in accordance with office procedures;
(b) all necessary information about alleged offences and treatment of clients is collected and recorded accurately in files, in accordance with office procedures;
(c) sustained efforts are made in obtaining all requested information;
(d) your involvement in the cases and authority to act for clients is communicated to officers, clients and any other relevant parties;
(e) all potential conflicts of interest are identified, and action is taken to protect the client's position;
(f) any need for special provisions for vulnerable clients is identified and action is taken to ensure that clients are not disadvantaged.

1.1.1 INTRODUCTION

This unit is concerned with all the matters that might arise in connection with your work with clients at the police station. This is a crucial part of the criminal process for both the police and the suspect, as it might affect the nature of the offence charged as well as whether the client is charged, cautioned, or is not proceeded against at all. It will also affect both the progress of a case and many interim stages, such as the granting or witholding of bail. Because of the importance of this stage, increasing attention has been paid in recent years to the training and expertise of those who deal with clients at the police station, and a police station accreditation scheme has been set up for assessing the competence of new solicitors and representatives attending the police station.

The arrangements under the Duty Solicitor Scheme also limit the categories of people who can attend the police station, and in the case of solicitors' representatives, the scheme dictates who can attend the police station under the legal aid arrangements.

When you deal with clients in the police station, you may be involved in:

(a) assembling information that the client provides;

(b) gaining information from other individuals in order to assist your client;

(c) advising the client on the basis of all available information;

(d) assisting the client in police station procedures;

(e) advising the client on the consequences of other police procedures, such as searches, etc;

(f) communicating with other individuals as to your client's position or intentions;

(g) recording all details in the office files, in accordance with office procedures.

Recording your dealings with your client is important for many reasons:

- to ensure that there is a record of what has happened – you cannot always trust this to memory;
- to provide an *aide-memoire* of matters to be followed up;
- so that others can see what has been advised or done;
- to protect your client if there are irregularities or queries in police actions;
- to protect you if there is a query over your actions;
- to demonstrate work done for the purpose of legal aid or other billing.

These tasks are often interdependent: they do not necessarily arise at separate defined moments, but for the purpose of analysing and learning the tasks it is convenient to break them down into the elements set out in the activities in this unit.

In this section we are looking, therefore, at the task of assembling information before your client is charged. It may be that your client has attended the police station simply to be charged, or it may be that there is to be an interview prior to that stage (see 1.4 below). Very often the client will attend under arrest, but may be attending voluntarily.

The Legal Aid Board Transaction Criteria

These transaction criteria (the LABTC) were prepared and are used by the Board as a quality audit tool in connection with the franchising of legal aid. They are thus a set of benchmarks for criminal practice, and you will have noted in the **Range** above that this activity is specifically linked to the information required by the criteria. Thus, it is essential to be aware that it is against these criteria, as well as those specifically stated in the *Occupational Standards*, that your performance is assessed. Most of the matters referred to in the LABTC are also discussed in the body of this unit, but you should refer to the criteria themselves.

To assist you, a copy of the LABTC is included in Document 4 in Appendix 2.

1.1.2 WHAT IS AN ARREST?

An arrest is usually described as the moment at which detention or custody starts. It is also connected very often to the start of proceedings: arrest followed by a charge. As an arrest is a significant infringement of a person's liberties, the circumstances under which a person can be arrested are circumscribed by the law. These are described below, and include:

(a) arrest under a warrant (when a court specifically gives a power to arrest);

(b) arrest in connection with suspicion of certain offences; and

(c) arrest in order to prevent or end conduct or where practicalities dictate.

An arrest can be carried out either by physical restraint (reasonable force) or by words. As we will see, an arrested person must normally be told that s/he is under arrest: where no physical restraint is being used, then the words themselves will constitute the arrest.

Often, an arrest is followed by a police interview. As a result of the interview, the suspect may well be charged. Once the police have sufficient evidence to charge a suspect, they must do so and all interviewing must then stop. The charge will commence a chain of events that may lead to court proceedings or a caution.

1.1.3 WHEN CAN A PERSON BE ARRESTED?

The police can arrest a person either with or without a warrant, as described below.

1.1.4 ARREST UNDER A WARRANT ISSUED BY A MAGISTRATE OR JUDGE

Most warrants are issued after proceedings have been commenced and a defendant fails to attend on bail or summons. A warrant may then be issued either with or without bail (backed or not backed for bail).

Occasionally, an arrest warrant is issued to commence proceedings, where the defendant is charged with an indictable offence or an offence punishable by imprisonment, or the defendant's address is not sufficiently established for the purpose of service of a summons. Serious offences carry a power of arrest themselves, so a warrant of arrest is unnecessary.

A warrant authorises the arrest of an individual. If backed for bail, the individual will subsequently be released to attend court. If not backed for bail, s/he will be kept in custody until s/he can be brought before a court to ensure his/her attendance on the next occasion.

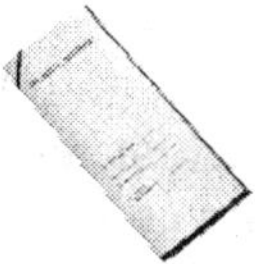

An example of a warrant of arrest is given in Document 1 in Appendix 2 to assist you.

1.1.5 ARREST WITHOUT A WARRANT (SUMMARY ARREST)

The police have a variety of powers of arrest, some relating to the type of offence (arrestable offences, which carry with them an automatic power of arrest), some to specific powers granted or preserved by statute, and others to the circumstances which are provided for under the 'general arrest conditions', where the police have powers to arrest where it is necessary to prevent crime or to ensure the suspect can be dealt with.

Summary of arrest powers:

- arrest without warrant for arrestable offences under Part III (sections 24–33) of PACE 1984;
- arrest without warrant under a list of statutory enactments specifically preserved by PACE 1984, section 26(2) and schedule 2;
- arrest without warrant under specific statutory powers created after PACE 1984 came into force;
- the common law power of arrest for a breach of the peace; anyone (including a police officer) may arrest a person who is committing or about to commit a breach of the peace.

1.1.6 WHEN CAN THE POLICE ARREST SOMEONE FOR AN ARRESTABLE OFFENCE?

Section 24 of the Police and Criminal Evidence Act (PACE) 1984 states that a police officer may arrest, without warrant, anyone who:

(a) is committing an arrestable offence; or

(b) the police officer has reasonable grounds to believe is committing an arrestable offence;

(c) is about to commit an arrestable offence; or
(d) the officer has reasonable grounds to believe is about to commit an arrestable offence.

If the police officer has reasonable grounds to believe that an arrestable offence has been committed (whether it has or not), s/he may arrest without warrant someone s/he has reasonable grounds to believe has committed it.

A person (X) can be arrested by someone other than a police officer (eg, an ordinary person or a store detective (a citizen's arrest)) (Y) if:

(a) X is committing an arrestable offence; or
(b) Y has reasonable grounds to believe that X is committing an arrestable offence; or
(c) an arrestable offence has been committed, and Y has reasonable grounds to suspect that X is guilty of that offence.

There is no power of citizen's arrest for someone about to commit an arrestable offence, nor for someone suspected of an arrestable offence which has not in fact been committed.

A police officer also has the power to arrest someone for any offence, even a trivial one, where the general arrest conditions apply. These give the power to the police to arrest where the other method of commencing proceedings (issuing a summons) is impracticable because the name or address supplied is suspect, or where it is necessary to remove an individual to prevent him/her from causing harm.

Section 25 of PACE 1984:

(1) Where a constable has reasonable grounds for suspecting that any offence which is not an arrestable offence has been committed or attempted, or is being committed or attempted, he may arrest the relevant person if it appears to him that service of a summons is impracticable or inappropriate because any of the general arrest conditions is satisfied.
(2) In this section 'the relevant person' means any person whom the constable has reasonable grounds to suspect of having committed or having attempted to commit the offence or of being in the course of committing or attempting to commit it.

The general arrest conditions are that:

(a) the name of the relevant person is unknown to, and cannot be readily ascertained by, the constable;
(b) the constable has reasonable grounds for doubting whether a name furnished by the relevant person as his/her name is his/her real name;
(c) the relevant person has failed to furnish a satisfactory address for service, or the constable has reasonable grounds for doubting whether an address furnished by the relevant person is a satisfactory address for service;
(d) the constable has reasonable grounds to believe that arrest is necessary to prevent the relevant person:
    - causing physical injury to him/herself or any other person;

- suffering physical injury;
- causing loss of or damage to property;
- committing an offence against public decency; or
- causing an unlawful obstruction of the highway;

(e) the constable has reasonable grounds to believe that arrest is necessary to protect a child or other vulnerable person from the relevant person.

1.1.7 WHAT IS AN ARRESTABLE OFFENCE?

There are various categories by which an offence is termed arrestable. These are offences that are:

(a) punishable by a fixed term of imprisonment or a maximum term of five years or more;

(b) specifically added to the definition, eg, section 24(2) of PACE 1984 adds:

- certain offences under the Obscene Publications Act 1959;
- certain offences under the Protection of Children Act 1978;
- offences in relation to ticket touting;
- carrying offensive weapons or bladed articles;
- offences under Football (Offences) Act 1991;
- going equipped for theft;
- taking a vehicle without the owner's consent;
- attempts to carry out any of the above offences;

(c) the subject of a specific power of arrest preserved by PACE, eg, for:

- a breach of a condition of bail;
- failure to provide a roadside breath test.

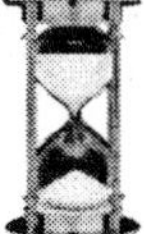

1 What offence is punishable by a fixed term of imprisonment?

2 Is burglary an arrestable offence?

3 Is common assault an arrestable offence?

Schedule 2 to PACE 1984.

1.1.8 DEALING WITH CLIENTS IN THE POLICE STATION

When dealing with a client in a police station, you will need to consider and take account of the fact that s/he may be under pressure: s/he may be anxious, frightened, angry or ashamed. In order to be able to gain the information you require, you may have to reassure and calm the client down. S/he may not realise the need for the information you are seeking, particularly in relation to background material. The client might simply want to 'get on with it' or 'get out of the police station', and may be jeopardising his/her long term position in order to achieve this.

Other clients may have been in the police station more often than you have, and will be content to go along with what they perceive is an inevitable consequence of their activities. Some clients may not understand why they have been arrested, and some may complain about the way they have been treated by the police. Though more clients will complain about their treatment by the police and the wrongfulness of their arrest than have a justified grievance, some will have been wrongfully (as opposed to merely mistakenly) identified, arrested or questioned. Others may have specific worries or special needs (see 1.1.15 and 1.5 below).

You may not know of the particular difficulties of a client before arrival at the police station, but if you are told before arrival, you should try to make arrangements on their behalf beforehand.

4 What constitutes an arrest?

5 When can a police officer arrest someone?

6 When can a store detective arrest someone?

7 John is observed driving a car in an erratic manner at 11 pm . The registration of the car is that of a car reported as stolen earlier that night. He is known to the police to be on bail with a 10 pm to 7 am curfew. He is stopped by the police and asked to provide a breath sample. He refuses, and also refuses to give his name and address. What powers of arrest do the police have?

Consider how the mood of your client might inhibit your ability to represent him/her, particularly at the stage of gathering information.

Who can attend the police station to give advice?

- When the person is a client of your firm, you may attend as a solicitor's representative instructed by your firm to attend the firm's client.
- Under the Duty Solicitor Scheme.
- The duty solicitor arrangements allow for a duty solicitor to arrange for a representative employed by the firm to give advice to a suspect (other than a member of the armed services) at the police station, provided that:
  - the representative can attend within 45 minutes;
  - consent has been given to the use of representatives by the duty solicitor committee; and
  - the person is approved.

Your firm will advise you about seeking accreditation in accordance with the police station

1.1.9 WHAT DO YOU NEED TO DO BEFORE ATTENDING AT THE POLICE STATION TO ADVISE A CLIENT?

When you attend at the police station to assist a client before charge, you will wish to be as well-informed as possible, in order that you can best prepare to advise your client. Sometimes, you will be able to obtain much information before your attendance, but in other situations, time and circumstances will mean that you will have very little information other than the name of the client and a possibly hazy outline of the offence.

You will also need to take certain items with you; most of them are obvious, and it is sensible to have these items together ready for attendance, rather than having to hunt around prior to departure.

If you have been contacted by a third party at the request of the potential client, you should contact the police station (if you are in an urban area served by several police stations, you may first need to verify at which one the person in question is being held) to inform him/her that you have been asked to attend, and that you will be advising the client prior to interview.

Provided that the request for you to attend has not been made against the wishes of the client, no interview should take place prior to your arrival. It is important that your client is able to exercise his/her right to legal advice before the interview goes ahead. Thus, before your arrival, you must ensure that your involvement has been recorded. To confirm this, when you give your name ensure that you note the name of the person to whom you speak, and the time. Normally, this will be the custody officer.

Before setting out, discover what information you can about your client: if the firm has represented the client before, you may be able to check the files, or gain an overview of the client's history from another member of the firm who has dealt with him/her. You may learn that the client is already on bail, is awaiting court appearance on other matters, or has a significant history of involvement with the police. Although you will in any event ask both your client and the police about these matters on arrival

accreditation scheme and the duty solicitor arrangements.

You must always inform the client in such circumstances (as in all dealings with a client) of your status.

PACE 1984, when referring to a solicitor, includes a trainee solicitor, a duty solicitor representative or an accredited representative (PACE 1984, Code C, para 6.12).

What to take when attending at a police station

Essential:

- equipment for taking notes (paper and pen, possibly recording equipment – see below);
- form of identification and firm's cards and authorisation;
- your firm's standard police station attendance note;
- PACE 1984 reference book;
- any other necessary texts.

If possible and if appropriate:

- map of area (for identifying where incidents took place);
- coins for telephone or a mobile phone (not for use when with your client or in the police station);
- camera (for recording appearance where identification is in issue, or where police mistreatment is alleged);
- cigarettes for client (not very healthy but possibly calming).

at the police station, it often helps you to plan how you will approach the client (and to anticipate the police's likely view of your client and the case against him/her) if you are forewarned.

You may have limited information about the suspected offence, or you may have precise details. It is unlikely that the offence will be so unusual that you are completely unfamiliar with its nature, but it is always good practice to mentally check that you understand what the prosecution would have to establish before guilt could be proved, in order that you can properly assess the evidence and advise the client in interview. However, it should be borne in mind that, very often, the offence suspected may not be the one eventually charged, and an offence charged may differ from the offence eventually brought to trial. It is also useful at this stage to be aware of the lesser offences that it might be advisable for your client to plead guilty to at a later stage if s/he accepts part but not all of the police case against him/her.

Always beware, especially when receiving information from a third party, that you do not improperly divulge confidential information: this is a potential problem where a client is known to you to have had previous involvement with the police.

Consider how your approach to your client will be affected if s/he has a long history of involvement with the police.

In addition, you should be aware of the possibility of a caution, which may be canvassed where the offence is not of the greatest seriousness and especially if the alleged offender has no previous convictions. A caution involves the admission of guilt and is recorded, but does not rank as a conviction.

1.1.10 TELEPHONE ADVICE

It may be that you are attending having already spoken to the arrested client personally, in which case you may have given some advice over the phone. If that is the case, you should have advised your client to be circumspect in what s/he tells you as the telephone may be in a public, or at least not private, area.

You can establish the brief details of what the client has been arrested for and the circumstances of the arrest. You should advise the client (unless

8 How will your client's bail position be affected if s/he is already on bail for another matter? (See Unit 2.)

s/he does not wish you to attend, or you advise him/her that it is not necessary) of your approximate arrival time, and that s/he should not answer any questions until s/he has seen you. You should advise him/her, or better, ask to speak to the custody officer directly to inform him/her of your involvement and that your client wishes to take legal advice before interview.

PACE 1984, Code C, para 6 – note for guidance – provides that where a person chooses to speak to a solicitor on the telephone, s/he should be allowed to do so in private unless this is impractical because of the design and layout of the custody area or the location of telephones.

A duty solicitor must give telephone advice before attending at the police station, unless his/her attendance is almost immediate. If you are representing the duty solicitor, discover what advice was given initially.

1.1.11 WHAT SHOULD YOU DO ON ARRIVAL AT THE POLICE STATION?

Inform someone of your arrival: you should tell the person (who may be a police officer or a civilian) on reception duty of your arrival, your position and the client you are representing. Although you cannot always expect to be instantly shown through to the custody area, as there will be other duties to be attended to, you should be dealt with and conveyed to your client as soon as is practicable.

Your client should be informed of your arrival, even if you cannot immediately see him/her. If you are not dealt with expeditiously, you should politely but firmly remind the officer of your presence and that your client is entitled to legal advice: always record the time at which you arrive at the station and the time you are permitted entry to the custody area. You will not wish to see your client immediately, as there is information that you will wish to seek from police officers before you speak to your client (see below).

A suggested checklist for consideration before attending police station

- Client's name?
- Location of police station?
- How was attendance requested?
- Client's history with firm?
- Nature of offence?
- Is client in custody or attending voluntarily?
- Research necessary?
- Is it necessary to inform police station that you are attending?
- Can you gain information from custody officer prior to attendance?
- Has the client been given telephone advice?
- All necessary items gathered? (See above.)

1.1.12 WHAT INFORMATION SHOULD YOU SEEK BEFORE SEEING YOUR CLIENT?

In order to be able to determine the importance of any information your client can provide, you need information before you speak to your client from both:

(a) the custody officer; and

(b) the investigating officer,

so that you understand the nature of the evidence against your client, the police view of the case and the way the investigation is being conducted (see 1.2 below).

1.1.13 GAINING ACCESS TO THE CLIENT

If you attend as a result of a request to assist a client in custody prior to interview and possible charge, as will most often be the case, you will need to establish that you are representing that client's own solicitor or are acting under the Duty Solicitor Scheme. You may need to identify whether you have the authority to act, and you must observe your firm's procedures in this regard.

The right to legal advice

You will need to be aware of your client's rights to legal advice and the circumstances in which this can be delayed.

The position regarding access to legal advice is crucial to the client and to yourself. PACE 1984, section 58 and Code C set out the following principles:

(a) except in certain circumstances, a detained person has a right to seek legal advice;

(b) that advice is confidential, and can be obtained free of charge, by way of the Duty Solicitor Scheme;

(c) a detained person should always be told that s/he is able to seek legal advice at any time and that the legal advice will be free of charge;

(d) the person may seek legal advice after having first said that s/he did not want it;

(e) a detained person can always seek advice from his/her own legal adviser, but if this would cause unreasonable delay, a duty solicitor adviser will be offered;

(f) people attending voluntarily at the police station may also consult a legal adviser at any time;

(g) access to a legal adviser can never be wholly denied, but it can be delayed in the circumstances set out in Annex B to Code C, that is:

Section 58 and para 6.1 of PACE 1984 state that a person arrested and held in custody in a police station or other premises shall be entitled, if s/he so requests, to consult a solicitor privately at any time. Access may only be delayed as set out in 1.2 below.

- if the offence is a serious arrestable offence;
- if the suspect has not yet been charged;
- if an officer of the rank of at least superintendent has reasonable grounds to believe that access would lead to:
  - interference with or harm to evidence, or interference with or injury to people;
  - alerting of other suspects;
  - hindrance to the recovery of property.

Where a suspect has asked for legal advice, and Annex B to the Code does not apply (ie, s/he is permitted to seek legal advice at the time), then no interview should take place, or if one has started, it should not continue, in the absence of a legal adviser unless:

(a) an officer of the rank of superintendent or above authorises an interview to commence because s/he has reasonable grounds to believe that:
- delay would involve the immediate risk of harm to a person, or serious loss of or damage to property;
- awaiting the solicitor's arrival would cause unreasonable delay in the investigation; or

(b) the solicitor chosen cannot be contacted, or has declined to attend, *and* the person has declined the duty solicitor or s/he is unavailable.

Where an interview has been commenced in the absence of a legal adviser because of risk to person or property, once the danger has been averted the interview should be suspended pending the arrival of a legal adviser.

When a person has been permitted to consult a solicitor, s/he should not be interviewed without the solicitor being present if the latter is at the station, on his/her way or is easily contactable by phone.

PACE 1984, Code C, para 6.6.

Definition of a serious arrestable offence

A serious arrestable offence is:

(a) an offence listed in schedule 5 to PACE 1984 (offences which are always, and would be expected to be termed serious);

(b) any arrestable offence which is intended or likely to lead to, has led to or is a threat to lead to:

- serious harm to national security;
- serious interference with the administration of justice;
- death;
- serious injury;

Schedule 5 lists murder, kidnapping, certain sexual offences, etc.

- substantial financial gain;
- serious financial loss (serious to the loser).

The *significance* of the harm to the loser is crucial, not the absolute value of the loss.

Attendance with your client by arrangement

If you attend with your client by arrangement, the information you require will have probably been obtained in the more congenial atmosphere of the office, and there should be no difficulty in obtaining access to your client to assist him/her in the relevant procedures. It will nevertheless be necessary to make it clear to the officers involved that you are the representative of your firm and are representing the client in question.

1.1.14 WHAT FACILITIES DO YOU NEED FOR SPEAKING TO YOUR CLIENT?

See 1.4 below for interviews. If you have to use a room which is not an interview room ensure that:

(a) the furniture is appropriate;

(b) any telephone is switched off or diverted, but that;

(c) you can contact someone when you have completed the interview.

Where should the consultation with the client take place?

A solicitor's interview room should normally be available for use by a solicitor and client: if it is in use, normally the solicitor should be asked if it is possible to wait until the room is free. If this is not acceptable, the interview is urgent or there is no interview room, other facilities may need to be made available. If the police interview room is used, you should verify with the police officer that the taping machine is switched off. In extreme cases, a cell or secure visits room may be offered. If the latter, you should only accept that facility if the screen between you and the client can be removed so as to allow proper confidential instructions to be given. If a cell is offered, you should not accept this unless you are satisfied that you can conduct a professional interview, with due regard to a legal adviser's safety, propriety and ability to take notes, and otherwise conduct a consultation.

1.1.15 WHAT IS THE POSITION REGARDING VULNERABLE CLIENTS?

You may be asked to assist clients who, by age, infirmity, mental or physical ill health or lack of command of English, need special assistance (see 1.5 for particular provisions). But the underlying position in relation to vulnerable clients is the same as with all other clients. The special safeguards are in addition to other rights.

Your portfolio should provide evidence of having made special provision for at least one vulnerable client.

1.1.16 ESTABLISHING YOUR ROLE

You should be aware of your firm's procedures in this respect and comply with them, remembering that you can expect to be visiting the same police station on many occasions and having to build up a professional working relationship with officers. It may well be that at the outset of your practice you attend with a well known member of your firm: you should take advantage, not only of course to observe techniques, but to begin to establish your credibility and authority to act with the officers.

If you attend as the result of a duty solicitor referral, your file should show:

(a) what time you telephoned the police station; and
(b) who you spoke to.

If you gave advice over the phone, your file should show what that advice was.

If you attend at the request of a third party, eg, the client's parent, partner or friend, your file should show:

(a) the name; and
(b) contact details and relationship of that person to the client.

1.1.17 BEFORE SEEING YOUR CLIENT

Before attending at the police station you will probably know only the name of the client, and possibly the broad circumstances under which s/he is there, whether under arrest, attending voluntarily or answering bail, and probably what s/he is suspected of.

Naturally, you will wish to obtain or verify as much information as you can before you attend. It may be that the client is already known to you or your firm. It is always advisable to ascertain whether your firm (and which individual) had represented the client before.

If you take the phone call requesting attendance, you will be able to gather information yourself. If the phone call is from the client, you should be circumspect as to the questions asked as the conversation may be overheard.

If you are able to speak to the custody officer, you may be able to ascertain what the offence suspected is and at roughly what time the police wish to interview.

You should always make it completely clear:

(a) that you are attending to advise the client;

(b) approximately how long this will take, especially if the police are anxious to interview; and

(c) you should tell your client not to answer questions until you arrive.

If it is obvious that an appropriate adult's presence (see 1.5 below) is necessary, you should ascertain whether one has been requested and who it is.

Your portfolio should include evidence of having communicated with officers to exchange information on two occasions.

The mentally ill or juvenile client should not be interviewed in the absence of an appropriate adult.

1.1.18 WHAT INFORMATION DO YOU NEED FROM THE CLIENT PRIOR TO HIM/HER BEING INTERVIEWED BY THE POLICE?

Information on the client's background, as well as the client's treatment whilst in custody, is often necessary at this stage. Often, pressures of time and the understandable concerns of the client may make you wish to focus on the immediate events that have led to his/her attendance at the police station, in particular the reasons for and circumstances of the arrest (if the client is under arrest). Nevertheless, your approach to a police station interview should be the same as you would adopt in an office interview, and the fullest possible picture of events should be obtained.

As with an office interview, you should use the time to assess the emotional state of the client. This is likely to be affected more in a police station than in the office, due to the stress of the situation. The information you require can be categorised as:

(a) preliminary/personal details;

(b) circumstances of arrest (if applicable);

(c) circumstances of this period of custody;

(d) previous contact with police;

(e) previous or pending court proceedings;

(f) client's version of events;

(g) if appropriate, information relevant to bail negotiations (see 2.2 below).

1.1.19 PRELIMINARY INFORMATION FROM YOUR CLIENT

In all cases, you will need to ascertain or verify the following:

(a) the full name of the client;

(b) his/her usual address;

(c) his/her usual phone number or other contact;

(d) his/her age and date of birth.

You will usually wish to ascertain whether the client has already informed someone of his/her whereabouts, or if s/he would like you to do so.

1.1.20 CIRCUMSTANCES OF ARREST IF UNDER ARREST

The client may have been arrested at the scene of an alleged crime, at home or elsewhere, as a result of an investigation, complaint or information received.

It is necessary to ascertain the circumstances because:

(a) it will throw light on the investigation and the evidence;

(b) if the arrest is wrongful, evidence obtained thereafter may be inadmissible;

(c) if the arrest is wrongful, liability, eg, for assault on a constable while trying to carry out the arrest, or for resisting arrest, will not arise.

1.1.21 CIRCUMSTANCES OF THE PERIOD OF CUSTODY

You will need to verify that the requirements of PACE 1984 have been adhered to in terms of the treatment of your client.

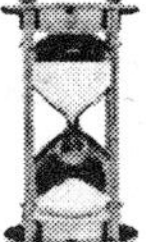

9 List the circumstances in which an officer can arrest a suspect without a warrant.

PACE 1984 checklist based on extracts from Code C: Conditions of Detention

- So far as is practicable, not more than one person shall be detained in each cell.
- Cells in use must be adequately heated, cleaned and ventilated. They must be adequately lit, subject to such dimming as is compatible with safety and security, to allow people detained overnight to sleep. No additional restraints shall be used within a locked cell unless absolutely necessary, and then only suitable handcuffs.
- Blankets, mattresses, pillows and other bedding supplied shall be of a reasonable standard and in a clean and sanitary condition.

- Access to toilet and washing facilities must be provided.
- If it is necessary to remove a person's clothes for the purposes of investigation, for hygiene or health reasons or for cleaning, replacement clothing of a reasonable standard of comfort and cleanliness shall be provided. A person may not be interviewed unless adequate clothing has been offered to him/her.
- At least two light meals and one main meal shall be offered in any period of 24 hours. Drinks should be provided at meal times and upon reasonable request between mealtimes. Whenever necessary, advice shall be sought from the police surgeon on medical or dietary matters.
- Reasonable force may be used if necessary:
  - to secure compliance with reasonable instructions, including instructions given in pursuance of the provisions of a code of practice; or
  - to prevent escape, injury, damage to property or the destruction of evidence.
- Persons detained shall be visited every hour, and those who are drunk, at least every half hour. A person who is drunk shall be roused and spoken to on each visit.
- The custody officer must immediately call the police surgeon (or, in urgent cases, for example, where a person does not show signs of sensibility or awareness, must send the person to hospital or call the nearest available medical practitioner) if a person brought to a police station or one who is already detained there:
  - appears to be suffering from physical illness or a mental disorder; or
  - is injured; or
  - fails to respond normally to questions or conversation (other than through drunkenness alone); or
  - otherwise appears to need medical attention.
- If a detained person requests a medical examination, the police surgeon must be called as soon as is practicable. The detainee may in addition be examined by a medical practitioner of his/her own choice at his/her own expense.
- If a person is required to take or apply any medication in compliance with medical directions prescribed before the person's detention, the custody officer should consult the police surgeon prior to the use of the medication. The custody officer is responsible for the safekeeping of any medication and for ensuring that the person is given the opportunity to take or apply medication which the police surgeon has approved.

PACE 1984, Code C also deals with the access to legal advice. Code C, para 6 includes notes for the guidance of police officers in connection with allowing or preventing legal advisers from seeing clients. It is important to understand what your role is: the police are aware that your role is to protect and advance the legal rights of the suspect, and that this might not assist their task. Appropriate behaviour, recognising the potentially conflicting duties of both parties, will enable a professional relationship to develop. Your duty, however, is not to prevent the police from properly carrying out theirs; you can be removed from an interview if you prevent the proper questioning of a suspect:

(a) a detained person has a right to free legal advice and to be represented by a solicitor. The solicitor's only role in the police station is to protect and advance the legal rights of his/her client. On occasions, this may require the solicitor to give advice which has the effect of his/her client avoiding giving evidence which strengthens a prosecution case. The solicitor may intervene in order to seek clarification or to challenge an improper question to his/her client or the manner in which it is put, or to advise his/her client not to reply to particular questions, or if s/he wishes to give his/her client further legal advice. Paragraph 6.9 (removal of solicitors from interviews) will only apply if the solicitor's approach or conduct prevents or unreasonably obstructs proper questions being put to the suspect or his/her response being recorded. Examples of unacceptable conduct include answering questions on a suspect's behalf and providing written replies for him/her to quote;

(b) in a case where an officer takes the decision to exclude a solicitor, s/he must be in a position to satisfy the court that the decision was properly made. In order to do this, s/he may need to witness what is happening him/herself;

(c) if an officer of at least the rank of inspector considers that a particular solicitor or firm of solicitors is persistently sending non-accredited or probationary representatives who are unsuited to provide legal advice, s/he should inform an officer of at least the rank of superintendent, who may wish to take the matter up with The Law Society;

- If a detained person has in his/her possession or claims to need medication relating to a heart condition, diabetes, epilepsy or a condition of comparable potential seriousness, then the advice of the police surgeon must be obtained.

Your role is to protect and advance the rights of the clients. It is accepted that this might not assist the police case. Proper action by the legal adviser, including proper objection to a line of questioning, and advising a client to remain silent at interview, is never a ground for excluding the adviser from interview.

(d) subject to the constraints of Annex B, a solicitor may advise more than one client in an investigation if s/he wishes. Any question of a conflict of interest is for the solicitor under his/her Professional Code of Conduct. If, however, waiting for a solicitor to give advice to one client may lead to unreasonable delay to an interview with another, the provisions of para 6.6 apply. These allow an interview to take place without legal advice if delay would cause risk to person or property, or if a solicitor cannot or will not attend (see above).

It is essential that you ascertain what has happened since the arrest. For example:

(a) has the client been questioned at all?
(b) if so, did the client make any response?
(c) if so, what was it?
(d) have any searches been carried out?
(e) have any samples been taken?
(f) was consent asked for?
(g) was it given?

Excluding a legal adviser is a serious step, which the police will not take lightly. If they are wrong in excluding a legal adviser, it is very unlikely that a court would accept any evidence obtained thereafter in interview. A suspect should always be offered an alternative legal adviser if exclusion has taken place: Code C, paras 6.10, 6.11.

In circumstances where delay might arise because of advising two clients, it may be necessary to seek assistance from a colleague rather than jeopardise the clients' positions, if interview in the absence of a legal adviser is a likely course. Immediately, however, you should seek to establish the police grounds for stating that the delay would be unreasonable.

A suspect who requests legal advice should not normally be interviewed without the presence of a legal adviser, even in cases of urgency, if the adviser is present in the police station when the interview is to take place or is on his/her way. You should always indicate to the investigating officer in any initial contact that you are going to attend, and your likely time of arrival.

If questioning takes place contrary to PACE 1984, any damaging information obtained from your client is unlikely to be admissible in court.

1.1.22 PREVIOUS CONTACT WITH THE POLICE

You will need to know whether the client has had previous dealings with the police, either in connection with the present matter or generally. This is useful in giving you an overview of more than the present matter: there may have been a long history or investigation, or the incident may have arisen suddenly. It will also give you useful background information to assess how familiar your client is with police station procedures, whether s/he has a justifiable grievance about police behaviour, whether the client's reputation may have led to him/her being wrongly suspected, and whether police identification of him/her is likely to be accurate as s/he is well known.

This information may well lead into the next area you need to be aware of.

This background information will give you an appreciation of the police view of the case, whether there are matters relating to the improper obtaining of evidence by the police, and the state of mind of your client.

1.1.23 PREVIOUS OR PENDING COURT PROCEEDINGS

It is also important to be aware of pending or previous court proceedings, for many of the same reasons as outlined above, but also because this will have an impact on bail decisions and, further, court proceedings may have to be transferred or delayed to allow different matters before different courts or at different stages to be brought together. If your client is kept in custody, s/he may not be able to answer his/her bail on another matter.

1.1.24 CLIENT'S VERSION OF EVENTS

The client may be anxious to tell you his/her version of the events that led to his/her being at the police station. Often, you may wish to deal with these matters early in the interview, but there are many factors involved in settling your client down and assessing his general demeanour that mean that it is often advantageous to you both to deal with the topics set out above before addressing the central issues. As you will see below, it is advisable in any event to explain at the outset to your client the plan or structure you propose to follow. Equally, in eliciting the main information from your client, you need to explain the way or order in which you would like the information to be given.

It is usually best to allow the client a relatively free flow, and probe or question in a minimal way until you have at least a broad outline of the incident, and only then go over the sequence of events in further detail, exploring any contradictions or gaps.

You may thus wish to ask the client to tell you what happened from a given point to the time when s/he was arrested (if immediately in respect of the incident) or until the close of the matter under consideration.

Throughout the assessing of your client's version, you need to be aware of what constitutes the offence for which s/he is under suspicion in order to advise him/her of his/her liability for that offence on his/her version of the events. By way of assistance, Table 1 in Appendix 1 lists the elements of seven very common offences.

1.1.25 IF APPROPRIATE, INFORMATION RELEVANT TO BAIL NEGOTIATIONS

On this subject, you should also see 2.2 below.

Much of the information gathered under the above headings will be relevant to any negotiations or application for bail that might be made. However,

Your portfolio should include evidence of having assembled information in the range prior to charge for three clients, one with a considerable history.

you will wish to make specific enquiries relevant to the likely or actual grounds for refusal if that is expected. For checklists on bail information, see 2.2 below.

1.1.26 HOW DO YOU STRUCTURE THE INTERVIEW WITH THE CLIENT?

Some guidance has been given above, with the important principle being to take as much time as is necessary to:

(a) gather the information required;

(b) assess the client's demeanour;

(c) assess the police case in the light of the client's version;

(d) advise the client of his/her legal situation;

(e) advise the client on his/her safest course of conduct in the interview with the police;

(f) be advised of the client's decisions as to interview;

(g) plan the police interview.

Your interview with the client

1 Just as in the office, you need to greet your client, explain who you are and your role. Always make it clear that you are a representative of your firm and that your role is to protect his/her interests. Never suggest that you are a qualified solicitor if that is not the case.

2 You should then check, by observation and questions, the client's welfare and, in particular, whether s/he has:

   (a) any injuries;

   (b) any obvious mental inability;

   (c) language difficulties.

3 You should ask whether the client has any immediate worries (hunger, thirst, anxiety about relatives) that would affect his/her ability to cope with your questions.

4 Explain the proposed structure and purpose of the interview and that it is confidential.

5 Take the client through the structure.

6 Explain his/her legal position and the advantages and disadvantages of answering police questions.

   Under s 34 of the Criminal Justice and Public Order Act (CJPOA) 1994, a court can draw adverse inferences from the failure of a defendant to reveal, when asked in police interview, a matter which s/he later relies upon in his/her defence at trial. This will only arise when

You must never lead your client to believe that you are a qualified solicitor if, in fact, you are not.

R v Argent [1997] 2 Cr App R 27; *R v Condron* [1997] 1 WLR 827; *R v Cowan* [1995] 3 WLR 881; section 34 of the CJPOA 1994.

it would be reasonable for the defendant to have revealed the matter. Thus, if the suspect did not realise the relevance of a fact, it would be unreasonable to expect him/her to reveal it at interview. The advice of a solicitor is not of itself sufficient ground not to reveal something at interview, but legal advice on the basis that the police case was insufficiently disclosed will often be acceptable.

Merely advising a suspect not to answer questions is not sufficient to prevent adverse inferences being drawn.

It may not be possible or advisable to consider at this stage the likely plea, but if it is, your client will probably wish to be aware of the likely sentence if s/he pleads guilty. You should bear in mind the likely sentence in view of the Magistrates' Association Sentencing Guidelines and case law, as well as the effect of credit being given for an early guilty plea.

7 Explain what you know about the police case. The client's comments on the police evidence and circumstances of arrest, and so on, will then allow you to move on to the next stages of your task, which are to:
   (a) assess the evidence;
   (b) advise the client on his/her options;
   (c) advise the client on his/her safest position and interview;
   (d) advise the client on the interview and take his/her instructions.

8 Once the decision has been made, you should brief the client on the format of the police interview and explain formalities if s/he is unfamiliar with them, namely:
   (a) that the interview will be tape recorded;
   (b) that you will make an opening statement;
   (c) the meaning and wording of the caution;
   (d) how to seek legal advice in the interview;
   (e) explain what you will do in the interview;
   (f) what you will do if you think s/he needs advice during the interview.

9 You should then rehearse the interview as far as possible, to allow the client to appreciate the likely style of questioning and, if the decision has been made not to answer questions, the difficulty of maintaining that stance.

A failure to reveal something in interview or at charge can result in an adverse inference being drawn. A statement on charge may often be advisable as no questions can be asked after charge.

1.1.27 WHAT SHOULD YOUR APPROACH TO THE CLIENT BE AT THIS STAGE?

Throughout the interview you should assess your client's state of mind and health and, whether s/he is:

(a) fit for interview by the police;

(b) likely to be able to withstand police questioning;

(c) able to give coherent and sensible answers (if a reply interview is to be undertaken);

(d) able to give information to the police to prevent adverse inferences being drawn at trial from failure to disclose.

When taking instructions from (or interviewing) any client in any situation, you are expected to be able to:

(a) allow your client to express his/her concerns;

(b) identify the client's own goals;

(c) help the client to determine the most important goals;

(d) elicit relevant information and distinguish between relevant and irrelevant information;

(e) use appropriate questioning techniques;

(f) assist the client to make a decision as to the best course of action;

(g) establish a professional relationship with the client and deal with any ethical problems that may arise when advising a client.

This applies equally to criminal clients and equally whether dealing with clients in the police station or in the office. Of course, there may be constraints when dealing with clients in the police station, and you may be dealing with a client who threatens your personal safety, but these are your objectives.

It is worth remembering at this stage, however, that clients who have been arrested and kept in custody may react in different ways. This will partly, but not entirely, be affected by:

(a) whether the client has been involved with the police and arrested before;

(b) whether the client is or believes him/herself to be guilty or at fault;

(c) the circumstances of arrest, including time and place;

(d) whether other people know or need to know about the arrest, and whether they will be worried, embarrassed or angry;

(e) the client's health, sobriety, temperament, intelligence and mental health.

Any type of client may be confused, having been in custody for some time, and may feel panic or frustration. Clients may make themselves believe that they are completely in the right. Most difficult of all, even though you are there to help, clients may be aggressive, have unrealistic expectations, or may believe (possibly correctly) that they have wider experience than you. Just as in other areas of practice, you may experience a variety of different clients, in age, class and gender, as well as in background and temperament.

It is worth remembering that criminal clients often, even if guilty, have a sense of justice, though this is often misplaced. Your responsibility is to protect and advance the client's legitimate interests at all times.

1.1.28 WHAT SHOULD YOU DO AT THE END OF YOUR CONSULTATION WITH THE CLIENT?

Before letting the police know your client is ready for interview, you should:

(a) confirm the advice you have given and the decision the client has made as to his/her approach in interview;

(b) verify your advice, the client's position, and any procedures that are to take place;

(c) ensure that the client understands the format of the interview and police procedures and has no further queries about it;

(d) explain the bail situation if applicable.

Then you should notify the police that your client is ready for interview.

During interview under caution and during your own consultation with the client, you should always take full and accurate notes.

Your duty to clients is the same, whatever their background and offence. Consider the issues raised in relation to dealing with the following clients: a middle aged woman charged with shoplifting; an 18 year old man charged with a public order offence; a 50 year old man charged with indecent exposure; a 30 year old repetitive burglar.

You will need to provide evidence of having taken notes of two client interviews prior to charge on two occasions.

Summary: consultation with client before police interview

Structure

- Greeting.
- Explain your position and role.
- Outline course of consultation.

Information

- Background.
- Circumstances of arrest and custody.

- Previous dealings with police and courts.
- Client's version.
- Advice on situation and whether to respond.
- Client's decision on whether to answer questions.
- Explain procedures in interview.
- Explain how to seek further help.
- Explain how and when you will advise or intervene and why.
- Practice.
- Inform officer you are ready.

Where client is juvenile or mentally handicapped or disordered:

- Advise client of the role of appropriate adult.

For further reading, see *Becoming Skilled* and *Active Defence*, both published by The Law Society.

CONSULTING WITH INVESTIGATING AUTHORITIES

RANGE

Achievement must cover all the following contexts.

Officers

Custody officers, investigating officers.

Method of consultation

By telephone, in person.

EVIDENCE

You will need to produce the specific pieces of performance evidence listed below. In addition, you will need to demonstrate that you have achieved the objectives specified at the beginning of this unit. You may do this by producing further pieces of evidence from real and simulated performance, by answering questions posed by your assessor or by passing a written examination.

You will need to provide evidence of:

1 having challenged refusals of access to clients on at least one occasion;
2 having documented investigations of custody records on three occasions;
3 having persisted in obtaining information from an investigating officer where it was initially denied, on two occasions;
4 having made representations concerning bail conditions imposed by the police on at least one occasion.

CRITERIA

You will demonstrate achievement if:

(a) officers are informed of the representative's status in relation to the client;
(b) access to clients is sought and refusals challenged;
(c) copy or sight of custody records is sought and refusals challenged;
(d) officers are informed of proposed courses of action following agreement with clients;
(e) sustained efforts are made in cases where investigating authorities refuse representative's requests;
(f) representations concerning bail conditions to be imposed or varied are made to the custody sergeant.

1.2.1 INTRODUCTION

You may be involved in dealing with a client who is already a client of your firm. Alternatively, you may attend under the Duty Solicitor Scheme. Your role in either case is the same, the only differences relating to legal aid matters, your previous knowledge of the client, and assumptions about whether your firm will continue to represent the individual. (For matters relating to legal aid and the Duty Solicitor Scheme generally, see 2.3 below; for assistance with identification, see 1.6 below.)

This activity is concerned with your role and responsibilities in dealing with the investigating authorities. You will need to seek access to your client, and sometimes seek access where this is being prevented or delayed by the police: you will, therefore, need to be clear as to your own and your client's rights in this situation, and how further representations should be made if difficulties arise. It is also important to remember that you should be given appropriate access for advising the client and taking confidential instructions.

You will also almost always require information from the investigating authorities, usually before you see your client. You therefore need to be aware of:

(a) the situations in which such information will be useful;

(b) what that information may consist of; and

(c) when and what you can insist on seeing.

You will also need to be aware of the circumstance where and with whom you might negotiate to assist the client, eg, over bail conditions imposed by the police (see also 2.2 below).

All your negotiations should be recorded, as should any information obtained or supplied. In particular, you must carefully record the requests you made for access in your attendance note, or log all instances of refusal or delay to access to your client, and the reasons given for refusal or delay.

The right of a person in police custody (or voluntarily attending the police station) to seek confidential advice from a legal adviser is safeguarded by PACE 1984, section 58 and Code C. There are limited situations when this can be delayed. Where a client is wrongly not allowed access to a legal adviser, evidence thereafter obtained may be inadmissible in any subsequent trial.

1.2.2 INFORMATION BEFORE ARRIVAL AT THE POLICE STATION

When you or your firm are initially contacted, you may speak to either the custody officer or the investigating officer. The officer may be prepared to give you some information over the telephone, though it is unlikely that much will be divulged. Many custody officers, however, will be willing at this stage to exchange information about obvious vulnerabilities if the suspect is a juvenile, obviously mentally ill or disordered, or suffering from some physical illness or the effects of drugs or alcohol.

If the client is known to you, you may already be aware of the existence of any permanent vulnerabilities, and it may be appropriate to ensure that the custody officer is aware of the position. If the client is unknown to you, or is suffering from abuse of drugs or alcohol, the custody officer may indicate that the client may not yet be fit for interview, and indicate the expected time scale for interview.

You should carefully note in your records any information supplied, not only regarding the condition of your client, but if the investigating or custody officer does give you information, this will help you to consider matters before your attendance at the police station and to compare this information with fuller information supplied later. This may give insight into the police approach to the case.

By virtue of PACE 1984, Code C, para 6.6 and note for guidance 6B, if a legal adviser is requested by the client, no interview should take place in his/her absence unless an interview is necessary to prevent harm (see 1.1 above). If the adviser has indicated that s/he is on the way to the police station, no interview of his/her client should take place until s/he is with the client and has had an opportunity to give advice.

You may need to consider whether you and/or the officer think that there is need for an interpreter or, in the case of a juvenile or mentally ill person, an appropriate adult or interpreter.

1.2.3 ON ARRIVAL AT THE POLICE STATION

Before seeing your client, you should try to obtain as much information as possible from:

(a) the custody officer; and

(b) the investigating officer.

Advising your client on any police interview

Although there is much information that these officers can give you, they are only obliged to give you very limited information. You should develop skills of negotiation in order to gain as much knowledge as possible before advising your client. Naturally, circumstances may vary: if you client has been arrested during an incident, there may well be little background information yet collated; compare this to the situation where the client has been arrested after an investigation. Nevertheless, whenever the police are ready to interview, they will have some information, and of course they will always have information on which the arrest was based.

On arrival at the police station:

- inform the desk officer of your arrival;
- ask that your client is informed of this;
- ask the investigating officer for information;
- ask the custody officer for information;
- check on police perceptions of vulnerability;
- note in your records all matters, including time of arrival and time you see your client;
- consider the case against your client.

See also 1.1 above.

Whenever an officer is unhelpful, either by denying the existence of or knowledge of the information you are interested in or by using tactics to defer your request, you will need to politely but firmly negotiate in order to obtain further facts.

(Detailed further guidance on approaches to all police station procedures are to be found in two Law Society publications, *Becoming Skilled* and *Active Defence*, which give advice on principled negotiation.)

You should be able to stand your ground confidently without being offensive or aggressive:

(a) make it clear that you understand the police's position;

(b) expect that your position is similarly understood;

(c) ask again for the information;

(d) record verbatim what is said by way of refusal or excuse.

If you do not consider that you have full disclosure of the police case so far against your client, you may wish to advise that your client does not answer questions in interview, and you may wish to advise the officer of this. This may occasionally prompt further disclosure. Legal advice not to answer questions on the basis of inadequate disclosure will normally be sufficient to prevent adverse inferences being drawn.

1.2.4 WHAT DO YOU NEED TO KNOW?

The matters listed below are those about which you may require information. In some circumstances, you may already know the answer by virtue of your knowledge of the client or from other information supplied by the police. It is not necessary in those cases to slavishly ask all questions. Similarly, your knowledge of the investigating officer or of the particular procedure in that police station will allow you to frame your questions accordingly. Nevertheless, you will often wish to ask the police (either the investigating officer or the custody officer) for information which will verify the matters you have learned or will learn from your client.

It is important that you understand as much as possible about the police view of and approach to the case. This will put you in a much better position to advise your client.

If you advise your client not to answer questions in interview, and s/he later relies at trial on a fact that could have been revealed in interview, adverse inferences may be drawn against your client (see 1.2.6 below), unless it was not reasonable to reveal such facts. If the client had insufficient information about the police case against him/her, for example, adverse inferences might not be drawn.

1.2.5 WHAT INFORMATION SHOULD YOU REQUEST FROM THE CUSTODY OFFICER?

Even when you have been given some information in advance of attendance at the police station, whether by the police or by your client, it is almost always necessary to confirm the information formally with the custody officer or investigating officer, perhaps both. It may be the case that the custody

A solicitor must be permitted to consult with the custody officer as soon as is practicable after arrival at the police station: PACE 1984, Code C, para 2.4.

officer is not the one you speak to in any event (if the shift has changed), so it is even more important to confirm details.

The information you would be seeking here would cover:

(a) client details;
(b) confirmation or discovering whether the client is voluntarily attending or under arrest;
(c) custody record number;
(d) if arrested:
   - when s/he was arrested;
   - circumstance of and leading up to arrest;
   - course of custody until present (ie, what has occurred since arrest);
   - when the detention was authorised;
(e) whether there has been any other questioning under caution or otherwise, and if so:
   - whether the client has made any significant response;
   - whether s/he has remained silent;
(f) whether the person, in the officer's view, is in need of medical treatment or is vulnerable in some way:
   - if so, what steps have been taken, or what examination or advice has been given;
(g) whether any fingerprints or bodily samples have been taken or are intended to be taken, and if so:
   - what is the legal authority and reason for doing so;
   - has consent been obtained;
(h) whether any identification procedures have been carried out or are intended;
(i) whether an intimate or non-intimate search has taken place or is intended and, if so;
   - what is the legal authority and reasons;
   - has consent been obtained;
(j) whether there are other suspects involved.

In view of the limits on detention without charge, it is important to keep an accurate record of the time at which detention commenced (see 1.3.34 below).

The custody record

You must ask to see the custody record, and are absolutely entitled to do so. This will verify or cast light or doubt on some of the above, and is a fruitful source of information in itself.

It may be that the record will reveal matters in which you are already concerned. These may be your client's condition, whether requests have been made for medical attention, and whether s/he was given access to legal advice at the first opportunity. Further, it might reinforce or undermine what you

Your portfolio should show evidence of having documented investigations of custody records on three occasions.

have been told either by your client or the police, regarding timings of detention or any previous interviews, perhaps if legal advice was not initially requested (or if it was and advice had been denied).

There may, however, be matters recorded, the significance of which are not yet apparent. Perhaps they relate to evidence which is not yet available or made known to you, such as the significance of the suspect's property on arrest. It is thus essential that you see the custody record at an early stage and take a copy for further study when you leave the police station.

An example of a custody record is provided in Document 2 in Appendix 2.

1.2.6 WHAT INFORMATION SHOULD YOU REQUEST FROM THE INVESTIGATING OFFICER?

In many circumstances, you will be asking similar information of the investigating officer as you have asked of the custody officer. The crucial difference, however, is that the custody officer will not normally have access to the full evidence in the case, and the custody record will not record it. The investigating officer is primarily the source of details about the police case so far.

However, after interview, the custody officer is in overall charge of when the interview must stop and whether a charge will be made because the investigating team has sufficient evidence. Once sufficient evidence is obtained, the interview must stop: no further questions can then be asked.

Your portfolio should show evidence of having persisted in obtaining information from both custody officers and investigating officers when it was initially denied on two occasions. As in all cases where information is initially denied, firm probing, recognising that the officer has a different priority to yours, but that s/he recognises that you also have a role, will usually bear fruit. This will very often be determined by your awareness of the information required and the type of information that the police may or may not have. You will also recognise that judgments over disclosure at this stage may have to be made quickly by the police officer. Where information is refused, you should always ask why and record the reasons.

The state of the police's case and the evidence against your client

Prior to gaining access to your client, your consultation with the investigating officer should probe in particular the state of the police's case and the evidence against the client, both of which are set out and explained under the headings below.

The police version of the case against your client

You might want to explore the police version of the case by asking questions in the following areas:

(a) what brought the matter to the attention of the police;

(b) what their initial response to the complaint or incident was;

(c) what their initial actions at the scene were;

(d) what police dealings with the suspect there have been before, during or after the offence.

The evidence against your client

Have the police:

(a) obtained witness statements? If so, from whom? Were the witnesses present at the scene? How many witnesses? How many statements?

(b) obtained any information from informers or covert surveillance?

(c) found any items of evidence:

- at the scene?
- in searches of the suspect, whether special warnings were given?
- in searches of premises (see 1.3 below)?

Under sections 36 and 37 of the CJPOA 1994, special warnings have to be given to the client before adverse inferences can be drawn from the failure to account for his/her presence at the scene or for possession of items. Sections 36 and 37 of the CJPOA 1994 provide that:

(a) where a person is arrested and s/he has with him/her or in the place s/he was arrested:

- any object substance or mark or any mark on an object;
- which is reasonably believed to relate to the person's involvement in a specified offence; and
- after being informed of the officer's suspicions and asked to account for the item, s/he fails to do so,

adverse inferences can be drawn from the failure to account;

(b) where a person is arrested at or near a place where the offence for which s/he is arrested has been committed; and

- his/her presence is reasonably believed to be related to the offence;
- after being informed of the officer's suspicions and asked to account for his/her presence, s/he fails to do so;

adverse inferences can be drawn from the failure to account.

In order for inferences to be drawn at trial from the failure to account (the inference being that s/he had no good reason) when later interviewed, the following guidance is given in PACE 1984, Code C, paras 10.5A and 10.5B. The interviewing officer must tell the suspect:

(a) what offence s/he is investigating;

(b) what fact s/he is being asked to account for (eg, object, mark or presence);

(c) that s/he believes the fact is related to the suspect's involvement in the offence;

(d) that the court may draw a proper inference from his/her failure or refusal to account;

(e) that a record is being made of the interview, and that it may be given in evidence.

This procedure is referred to as giving special warnings.

Whether a description of the suspect has been given

If there has been a description of the suspect, ask:

(a) what the first description was, and whether it has been amended;

(b) if there is more than one description, did the witnesses talk to each other?

Police guidance for dealing with identifications includes the mnemonic of 'ADVOKATE':

A Appearance
D Distance
V Visibility
O Obstruction
K Known or seen before
A Any reason to remember
T Time lapse
E Error or material discrepancy.

The mnemonic is used as a reminder of the points made in *Turnbull*, in terms of how evidence of identification should be assessed (noting that even a very certain witness or number of witnesses could be mistaken), and the necessity of weighing up all the circumstance of the identification, including length of observation, lighting, visibility, whether the witness knew the person or was seeing the person for the first time, etc (see also 1.6.1).

In particular, the mnemonic advises the police to be aware of discrepancies between the descriptions. You may use this both as a checklist for verifying police procedures, as they are advised to consider all the above aspects, and for later use by yourself when assessing the appearance of your client in comparison with the identification given. Identification evidence is inherently suspect evidence due to the possibility of error, the suggestibility of witnesses and the tendency of memories to fade. Courts are therefore wary of relying too much on uncorroborated identification evidence, and rules under PACE 1984 provide some safeguard against procedures that might tend to unsafe evidence. Nevertheless, any identification which may relate or appear to relate to a suspect can be very damaging, and you must be active in safeguarding his/her position, including careful assessment of the value of any such evidence.

R v Turnbull [1977] QB 224 and Code D of PACE 1984 deal with the provisions for and difficulties of relying on identification evidence; see also 1.6 below.

Whether a search of premises has been made or is intended to be made

If either situation applies, you need to discover why.

Where a search has already been carried out, you need to ask:

(a) whether any evidence has been obtained; and

(b) if so, what evidence.

Whether others are likely to be accused in connection with this matter

Legal aid requirements are such that, provided there is no conflict of interest, the Legal Aid Board requires that co-defendants be jointly represented wherever possible.

If this is so, you should ask whether there are others:

(a) under arrest; or

(b) being sought;

(c) if others are under arrest, are they legally represented, and if so, by whom?

Whether the client is vulnerable in the police's view

In this situation, you need to enquire whether an appropriate adult or interpreter has been requested, attended or briefed (see 1.5 below). Specifically, you should ask:

(a) the police's view of client's condition;

(b) what their present intentions are as to charge;

(c) what their present intentions are as to bail;

(d) what their present intentions are as to interview.

If so, you will also need to consult with the appropriate adult/interpreter before police interview.

Whether any questioning has already been carried out

All questioning regarding a person's involvement in an offence constitutes an interview, and should be carried out under caution: PACE 1984, Code C, para 11.1A.

Paragraph 11.1 provides that an interview should be carried out under caution and at a designated police station, unless delay in getting to a police station might lead to interference with evidence, physical harm to others, alerting of other suspects or hindrance to the recovery of property. Once the risk has been averted, the interview should cease until arrival at a designated police station.

You should find out whether your client answered any questions or made any significant responses, and if so, what responses.

Other points to note

Although the investigating officer is advised that s/he must not lie to the solicitor who attends, s/he is under a duty to judge what to disclose, and circumstances and individuals of course vary. A police officer who may be helpful when dealing with a juvenile who is a first time suspect may not be as helpful when dealing with an adult or repeat offender. S/he may have different approaches to different types of offences, and his/her approach may change when s/he is busy or not under pressure, and when s/he is on firm or weak ground evidentially. Often, what is not disclosed, or is left vague or unspecified, may tell you as much as the information actually provided. Careful probing may reveal more information.

After gaining all the information that you can, you are ready to see your client, but allow yourself a little time to digest the information and plan the interview. You should then request that you see your client, first ensuring you have suitable facilities (see 1.1 above).

Note for guidance 6F to Code C of PACE 1984 allows the police to complain to The Law Society about unsuitable advisers.

1.2.7 GAINING ACCESS TO THE CLIENT

If you attend, as will most often be the case, as a result of a request to assist a client in custody prior to interview and charge, you will need to establish that you are representing that client's own solicitor or are present under the Duty Solicitor Scheme. You may need to identify that you have the authority to act and observe your firm's procedures in this regard. You will need to be aware of your client's rights to legal advice and the circumstances in which this can be delayed.

Section 58 of PACE 1984 provides that:

(1) A person arrested and held in custody in a police station or other premises shall be entitled, if he so requests, to consult a solicitor privately at any time.

(2) Subject to subsection (3) below, a request under subsection (1) above and the time at which it was made shall be recorded in the custody record.

Annex B to Code C explains the position:

1 The rights set out in sections 5 or 6 of the Code or both may be delayed if the person is in police detention in connection with a serious arrestable offence, has not yet been charged with an offence, and an officer of the rank of superintendent or above has reasonable grounds for believing that the exercise of either right:

(i) will lead to interference with or harm to evidence connected with a serious arrestable offence or interference with or physical injury to other people; or

(ii) will lead to the alerting of other people suspected of having committed such an offence but not yet arrested for it; or

(iii) will hinder the recovery of property obtained as a result of such an offence.

Clause 8 adds:

> ... or if an officer of the rank of superintendent or above has reasonable grounds for believing that the exercise of access to a solicitor:
>
> (a) will lead to interference with the gathering of information about the commission, preparation or instigation of acts of terrorism; or
>
> (b) by alerting any person, will make it more difficult to prevent an act of terrorism or to secure the apprehension, prosecution or conviction of any person in connection with the commission, preparation or instigation of an act of terrorism.

2 These rights may also be delayed where the serious arrestable offence is either:

(i) a drug trafficking offence and the officer has reasonable grounds for believing that the detained person has benefited from drug trafficking, and that the recovery of the value of that person's proceeds of drug trafficking will be hindered by the exercise of either right or;

(ii) an offence to which Part VI of the Criminal Justice Act 1988 (covering confiscation orders) applies and the officer has reasonable grounds for believing that the detained person has benefited from the offence, and that the recovery of the value of the property obtained by that person from or in connection with the offence, or if the pecuniary advantage derived by him from or in connection with it, will be hindered by the exercise of either right.

1.2.8 WHAT CAN I DO IF I AM PREVENTED FROM SEEING MY CLIENT?

You should ask the reason for the refusal, record the reason given in your own notes, and ask that it be noted in the custody record.

There may be a perfectly reasonable cause for a slight delay, eg, an absence of suitable interview rooms, or the client may be undergoing medical examination.

Other reasons can be dealt with appropriately. For example, if your authority is doubted, you can

Your portfolio should provide evidence of having challenged refusals of access to clients on at least one occasion.

demonstrate with your identification or authority from your firm that you are the appropriate representative.

If an unsatisfactory (ie, non-PACE) reason is given for denying access, you should ask the officer to justify the refusal, assert that it is not a reason provided in the legislation, and, if s/he persists, ask to speak to a senior officer. Always verify what is recorded in the custody record.

If a reason given in PACE 1984 is alleged to be the reason for not allowing you access, you should ask the officer to explain his/her reasons, record them, seek to challenge them and again ask to see a senior officer.

PACE 1984 provides that in certain circumstances access can be properly delayed. If access is delayed, your file should record:

(a) the reason given for the delay;
(b) the extent of the delay;
(c) whether representations were made by you to seek access.

Code C, Annex B and note for guidance B4 provide that the officer may authorise delaying access to a specific solicitor only if s/he has reasonable grounds to believe that that specific solicitor will, inadvertently or otherwise, pass on a message from the detained person or act in some other way which will lead to harm to evidence, injury to a person, alerting of suspects or delay in recovering property coming about. In these circumstances, the officer should offer the detained person access to a solicitor (who is not the specific solicitor about whom s/he has concerns) under the Duty Solicitor Scheme.

Right of access to solicitor: it is an important principle that a suspect being held and questioned by the police is entitled to legal advice, and attempts to deny or delay this right may result in any evidence thereby obtained being ruled inadmissible at trial under sections 76 or 78 of PACE 1984.

10 Can the custody officer prevent a suspect from seeking legal advice?

1.2.9 SHOULD I TELL THE CUSTODY/INVESTIGATING OFFICER ANYTHING AT THIS STAGE?

You should tell the officer:

(a) that you are there to advise your client;
(b) what your role is;
(c) what facilities you require;
(d) that you need to speak to your client before any interview with the police takes place.

11 What facilities will you require for interview?

1.2.10 INFORMING THE POLICE OF YOUR CLIENT'S DECISIONS

After you have consulted with your client and a decision has been made as to whether s/he is going to make a reply or no-reply interview, you may inform the police that you and your client are ready, indicating the approach you are going to take. You may instead, and this is usually preferable, wait until the commencement of the interview to indicate your approach.

1.2.11 AFTER THE POLICE INTERVIEW: CHARGE

Once the police have sufficient evidence to do so, they must charge the suspect and cease interviewing. If they have insufficient evidence on which to charge, they must release the client at the latest on the expiry of the time limits for detention (see 1.3 below).

1.2.12 AFTER THE POLICE INTERVIEW: BAIL

After interview, the client will be released on bail with or without conditions, or remanded in custody and brought before a magistrates' court. Bail conditions can be imposed by the police on the same ground as a magistrates' court, and similar conditions (other than residence in a probation hostel) can be imposed.

The police can sometimes, through an excess of zeal or for other reasons, seek to impose inappropriate, unnecessary or most commonly ineptly worded conditions. You should be alert to these problems and challenge the need for or appropriateness of such conditions (see 2.2 below).

Your portfolio should show evidence of having made representations concerning bail conditions imposed by the police on at least one occasion.

It must be appreciated, however, that for most clients, if the choice is between a remand in custody and a draconian or inconvenient condition, the latter is usually their choice. A balance needs to be struck, remembering that at the next court appearance conditions can be reviewed, but that a court may be influenced in its assessment of the case's seriousness where it sees that very restrictive conditions have been imposed.

ASSISTING AND ADVISING CLIENTS AT POLICE STATIONS

RANGE

Achievement must cover all the following contexts.

Method of communication

By telephone, in person.

Interview

Before interview, after interview.

Rights and obligations

In relation to:

- search of the client's premises;
- arrest or voluntary attendance at the police station and search upon arrest;
- duties of the custody officer before and after charge;
- responsibilities in relation to detained persons;
- detention, time limits of detention and reviews;
- searches of detained persons;
- the right to have someone informed when arrested;
- fingerprinting, photographs, DNA samples, speculative searches;
- taking of intimate and other samples;
- the right to legal advice;
- bail;
- special treatment of juveniles and other vulnerable persons;
- keeping of and entitlement to see custody records.

Professional and ethical standards

Duty to clients, standards of care, protection of interest, conflicts of interest, obligations to the court, client confidentiality.

EVIDENCE

You will need to produce the specific pieces of performance evidence listed below. In addition, you will need to demonstrate that you have achieved the objectives specified at the beginning of this unit. You may do this by producing further pieces of evidence from real and simulated performance, by answering questions posed by your assessor or by passing a written examination.

You will need to provide evidence of:

1 having informed the clients of their **Rights and obligations** as set out in the **Range**, by both **Methods of communication** specified;

2 having produced notes of two meetings with clients both before and after **Interview**.

CRITERIA

You will demonstrate achievement if:

(a) clients are informed of their representative's status and function;
(b) clients are informed if their conversations may not be private;
(c) clients are informed of their legal rights and obligations;
(d) the client's right to silence is explained;
(e) the need for a personal visit and the urgency of the client's needs for legal advice are assessed if contact is by telephone;
(f) clients are informed of the proposed course of action;
(g) advice given is right in fact and law and in accordance with recognised procedures.

1.3.1 INTRODUCTION

This part of the unit deals with the range of situations where you may need to advise a client who is at the police station, other than at interview (which is dealt with at 1.4 below) and identification procedures (dealt with at 1.6 below).

You may be attending to assist a client already known to your firm, or called out under the Duty Solicitor Scheme, to assist with interview or other procedures. In either case, there are various ancillary matters on which the client may need information, advice and reassurance.

1.3.2 WHAT IS THE ROLE OF THE SOLICITOR'S REPRESENTATIVE?

Your role is to protect and advance the legal rights of the client.

Professional conduct and ethics

The conduct of a solicitor's representative must be in accordance with the Solicitors' Code of Professional Conduct and, in particular in this context, you should be conscious always of the need to protect the client's rights and interests (which are your primary functions, in any event), and of the duty of client confidentiality.

The Code of Professional Conduct lays down detailed and sometimes complex provisions. Basically, however, the principles seek to give guidance about the application of fundamental tenets of integrity and professionalism. In a criminal practice, primary concerns involve issues of conflict of interest and client confidentiality.

Although, if unqualified, you are not strictly personally governed by the rules of professional conduct, as a member of your firm you must obey the same rules and standards as a fully qualified member. The solicitors for whom you work are in breach of their professional duty if they allow anyone to do anything on their behalf which infringes a solicitor's duties. If in any doubt, you should consult the Guide to the Professional Conduct of Solicitors (published annually by The Law Society), and/or a member of your firm.

Breaches of professional conduct are bad for the firm, bad for the client and bad for you, and can lead to disciplinary action being taken.

Duty to the client

Standards of care

The solicitor should always carry out work to the proper standard.

Client care

Solicitors' firms all have a system of client care to ensure that clients know about how their case will be dealt with, how to complain if it is not properly dealt with in their view, and the cost implications.

Confidentiality

A solicitor and his/her employees are under a duty to keep confidential the affairs of the client and to ensure that staff do the same. The duty of client confidentiality is linked to, but is not the same as, legal professional privilege.

The latter term refers to the rules that protect the client from disclosure of communications between lawyer and client in court proceedings, and between either of them and a third party in relation to contemplated litigation. However, the principle of client confidentiality is much wider in its ambit and seeks to ensure that all information, requests for advice and advice given are not divulged to anyone without the client's permission.

This means that a solicitor or solicitor's employee should not divulge matters concerning his/her client, without the client's consent, to anyone, including other solicitors outside the firm, co-accuseds, the client's partner, the client's employer, the client's parents, or other relations.

When dealing with several family members, where a parent or partner may have a legitimate and genuine concern over the client, it is important to remember who your client is, that your duty is to that client, and that information, even of an apparently trivial nature (such as the address of the client), should not be disclosed without clear instructions from your client.

The duty of confidentiality can be overridden where the client is using the solicitor to commit a

Where a young client (under 16) is concerned, it may be that the client consults you with and through his/her parents. For those between 16 and 18, you must consider whether the child is old enough to instruct you him/herself. Over 18s are, of course, adults.

crime or in some circumstances involving terrorism or child abuse. Consult the Guide to the Professional Conduct of Solicitors.

The rules of confidentiality apply to any information given you by the client, even regarding previous convictions, in that you should not disclose previous convictions without the client's consent. However, you may not allow a court to be misled. There is an exception in relation to information relevant to legal aid eligibility: if the client's eligibility changes, there is a duty to the Legal Aid Fund such that the client must be asked for consent to inform the Legal Aid Board of the change (alternatively, the client should inform the Legal Aid Board him/herself), or else the firm must cease to act.

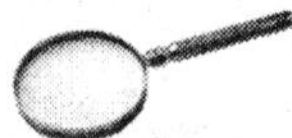

You must not allow a court to be told incorrectly that a client has no previous convictions.

Protecting clients' interests

The solicitor's duty is always to act in the best interests of the client, subject only to his/her duty to act in the interest of the proper administration of justice.

Avoiding conflicts of interest

Often, you or your firm may be approached by two or more defendants in the same proceedings, or indeed asked to represent another client to save legal aid costs. This will often be perfectly proper: the two defendants can properly be represented by the same firm or individual in the firm. This can be the case whether the clients are pleading guilty or not guilty, and whether they both plead the same way or not. The situation may arise, however, that the two cases are in conflict, so that it would be improper for one firm to act for them both. This may arise where each blames the other for the offence or each claims that the other took the major role. Essentially, a conflict arises whenever the proper defence of one client may compromise or damage that of the other. The firm should never be in the position that it has information from one client (or ex-client) that can be to the advantage of another.

When two co-accused approach you, they should be interviewed separately so that any conflict can be dealt with by refusing to take instructions from the second client before interview. Otherwise, if interviews have been conducted with both clients and a conflict of interest is later revealed, neither client can be accepted: thus, two clients will be lost to the firm. However, it occasionally happens that, despite separate interviewing, it is not until after the second client has given instructions that the conflict of interest is revealed. In those circumstances, you must withdraw from both cases. You may have confidential information, or an insight into the one case that may assist the other accused. As the knowledge gained by one member of the firm is deemed to be held by the firm in its entirety, a conflict cannot be resolved by two accused being represented by different solicitors, or even by different branches within the firm. Issues of conflict may arise between co-accused who are friends or members of the same family, as well as those who are clearly antagonistic towards each other from the outset.

Duty to the court

Your overriding duty is not to mislead the court. This means that you must not in any circumstances give the court information (or allow the court to be given information by an advocate, etc) which you know to be wrong. Against this must be set the legal principles which provide that neither a defendant nor a solicitor always has to volunteer information.

1.3.3 WHAT IS THE POSITION OF THE CLIENT WHO IS ATTENDING THE POLICE STATION VOLUNTARILY?

Persons may voluntarily attend the police station, perhaps because they:

(a) are asked to do so by the police; or

(b) learn that the police want to interview them.

It may be that on attendance, the person is arrested, in which case s/he is treated as – and has the rights of – an arrested person.

If, however, the person remains a voluntary attender, s/he:

(a) should be treated no less favourably than an arrested person;

(b) is free to leave, and should be told that they are free to leave, at any time.

1.3.4 WHAT IS THE POSITION OF THE CLIENT UNDER ARREST?

Anyone arrested has certain rights, mostly to be found in PACE 1984, which determine how the arrested person should be treated and dealt with at the police station, including provisions as to interview (see 1.4 below), identification procedures (see 1.6 below) and the length of time a person can be detained. Before we consider those aspects, however, it is essential to examine the concept of arrest itself, what constitutes an arrest and when it can be carried out.

1.3.5 WHAT IS AN ARREST?

An arrest is usually described as the moment at which detention or custody starts. It is also connected very often to the start of proceedings: arrest being followed by a charge, which may lead to court proceedings. As an arrest is a significant infringement of a person's liberties, the circumstances under which a person can be arrested are circumscribed by the law. These are described below, and include arrest under a warrant (when a court specifically gives a power to arrest), arrest in connection with suspicion for certain offences and arrest in order to prevent or end criminal conduct.

The police also have the power to arrest people where there would be no other way of ensuring that they could be proceeded against. At first sight, the legal rules surrounding arrest can seem complicated, but you will soon become familiar with the general legal approach. Your main concern will be to ensure that someone who seeks your advice after arrest has been properly arrested. Improper arrest, where the police have detained someone without power to do so, may mean that:

(a) the client has a right of action against the police;
(b) any evidence obtained against the client during, or as a consequence of, the improper arrest, will be excluded in any trial.

You will, therefore, need to know:

(a) what constitutes an arrest;
(b) when someone can be arrested: usually this will be performed by the police, but there are powers of arrest in certain circumstances where anyone has a power to arrest (the citizen's arrest). You are most likely to have to deal with the circumstances of a citizen's arrest in the context of arrest by a store detective, though this in itself is comparatively rare: usually the police are asked to attend after a suspected shoplifter has been 'requested to accompany the detective to the shop manager's office', and the arrest is thereafter made by a police officer;
(c) what must be done on arrest.

By virtue of section 78 of PACE 1984, evidence can be excluded at trial in the exercise of the court's discretion, if the admission of the evidence upon which the prosecution seeks to rely would be adverse to the fairness of the proceedings. In coming to a decision, the court may take into account the circumstances in which the evidence was obtained. This section is often used in applications to the Crown Court for the exclusion of evidence obtained in breach of any of the provisions of PACE 1984. However, a breach of PACE 1984 does not of itself require exclusion of subsequent evidence: it is merely a consideration that the court will take into account.

1.3.6 HOW IS AN ARREST CARRIED OUT?

As stated above, someone is arrested if stopped from leaving a place by any means.

An arrest can be carried out either by physical restraint, where only reasonable force necessary for the circumstances should be used, or by words alone. As we will see, arrested persons must normally be told that they are under arrest: where no physical restraint is being used, then the words themselves will constitute the arrest. The arrested person should also be cautioned.

1.3.7 WHEN CAN A PERSON BE ARRESTED?

The police can always arrest someone when they have an arrest warrant issued by a court. Most warrants are issued after proceedings have been commenced and a defendant fails to attend on bail or summons: a warrant may then be issued either with or without bail (backed or not backed for bail), in order to ensure his/her attendance on the next occasion.

Otherwise, the police can only arrest someone if a power to arrest exists: eg, all serious offences carry a power of arrest, making a warrant unnecessary. These, however, arise in a variety of ways and it is important to understand them.

Where a warrant is backed for bail, the person mentioned in it is arrested and then released again to attend court as directed. This means that the person is now under a compulsion to attend court and, if s/he fails, s/he will be re-arrested (and usually kept in custody until s/he can be taken to court).

1.3.8 WHEN CAN SOMEONE BE ARRESTED WITHOUT A WARRANT?

Summary of situations

Arrest without a warrant is possible in the following situations:

(a) the police and all individuals have power to arrest in relation to arrestable offences, but the powers of the police are exercisable in wider circumstances than those of the ordinary citizen;

(b) arrest by a police officer or other person to prevent or stop a breach of the peace;

(c) powers of arrest preserved in PACE 1984, even though the offence is not within the definition of an arrestable offence;

(d) powers of arrest given in Acts of Parliament passed after PACE 1984 where new offences are created;

(e) where the general arrest conditions apply;

(f) where a person has been required to attend a police station for fingerprinting and has failed to do so;

(g) where statute provided powers to officials other than police officers, eg, Customs and Excise officials or immigration and transport police (not covered in this book).

1.3.9 WHAT IS THE POWER TO ARREST FOR AN ARRESTABLE OFFENCE?

You will most commonly be dealing with people arrested in connection with arrestable offences. The definition of an arrestable offence is twofold, comprising serious offences defined by their possible sentences, and certain additional offences deemed serious but which do not carry such onerous sentences.

The arrest power for such offences depends on whether the arresting person is a police officer or any other person. The powers are defined in terms of whether an arrestable offence has been committed or is suspected to have been committed, and whether the person under arrest has committed or is suspected of having committed it. Effectively, this means, as you would expect, that the citizen's arrest can usually only be safely carried out where a suspect is caught virtually 'red-handed'.

Anyone has a power to arrest where:

(a) the person arrested is committing an arrestable offence; or

(b) the arresting person has reasonable ground to believe the arrested person is committing an arrestable offence;

(c) an arrestable offence has in fact been committed, and the arresting person has reasonable grounds to suspect the arrested person is guilty of the offence.

Additionally, a police officer can arrest without warrant:

(a) in respect of offences that are being committed:
   - a person who is committing an arrestable offence; or
   - a person the police officer has reasonable grounds to believe is committing an arrestable offence;

(b) in respect of suspected offences, whether or not an arrestable offence has actually been committed, but the police officer has reasonable grounds to believe that it has been committed;
   - any person s/he has reasonable grounds to believe has committed it;

An arrestable offence is one where the sentence is:

(a) fixed by law (eg, murder);

(b) carries at least five years' imprisonment (eg, burglary); or

(c) is an offence specifically made arrestable by PACE 1984 (section 24(2)), including:
   - taking a motor vehicle without authority;
   - going equipped for theft;
   - using violence to secure entry (Criminal Law Act 1977, section 6);
   - ticket touting;
   - certain sexual offences;
   - offences under the Football (Offences) Act 1991;
   - offences involving publication of obscene or racially offensive matters;
   - carrying offensive weapons;
   - having a bladed article in a public place;
   - having a bladed article on school premises.

See section 24 for the full definition of arrestable offence.

There is no power of citizen's arrest for someone about to commit an arrestable offence, nor for someone suspected of an arrestable offence which has not in fact been committed.

(c) in respect of anticipated offences:
- any person who is about to commit an arrestable offence; or
- any person whom the officer has reasonable grounds to believe is about to commit an arrestable offence.

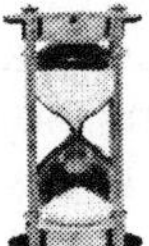

12 Which offence is punishable by a fixed term of imprisonment?

13 Is robbery an arrestable offence?

14 Is driving with excess alcohol an arrestable offence?

15 Is being drunk and disorderly an arrestable offence?

16 Is common assault an arrestable offence?

1.3.10 WHAT ARE THE POWERS OF ARREST WHEN THE OFFENCE ITSELF IS NOT ARRESTABLE?

Powers of arrest are specifically preserved by section 26 and schedule 2 of PACE 1984, which include loitering for the purpose of prostitution and the power of arrest where a breach of bail occurs or is thought likely to happen. Other legislation has also created new powers of arrest, such as for failure to provide a roadside breath test, failing a breath test, possession of alcohol at sporting events, involvement in a rave, squatting and public order offences, including conduct likely to cause harassment, alarm or distress.

Additionally, the police have power to arrest for any offence if the general arrest conditions apply.

See: schedule 2 to PACE 1984; sections 4 and 5 of the Public Order Act 1986; Part V of the CJPOA 1994.

1.3.11 WHAT ARE THE 'GENERAL ARREST CONDITIONS'?

Section 25 of PACE 1984 provides that, where a police officer has reasonable grounds for suspecting that any offence has been committed or attempted, or is being committed or attempted, s/he may arrest the relevant person if it appears to him/her that service of a summons is impracticable or inappropriate because any of the general arrest conditions is satisfied.

The general arrest conditions are as follows:

(a) the name of the relevant person is unknown to, and cannot be readily ascertained by, the constable;

(b) the constable has reasonable grounds for doubting whether a name furnished by the relevant person as his/her name is his/her real name;

(c) the relevant person has failed to furnish a satisfactory address for service, or the constable has reasonable grounds for doubting whether an address furnished by the relevant person is a satisfactory address for service;

Whether someone is lawfully under arrest will be relevant not only in relation to evidence obtained from him/her, but also whether s/he can be charged with escaping, obstructing, assaulting a police officer, etc.

(d) the constable has reasonable grounds to believe that arrest is necessary to prevent the relevant person from:
- causing physical injury to him/herself or any other person;
- suffering physical injury;
- causing loss of or damage to property;
- committing an offence against public decency; or
- causing an unlawful obstruction of the highway;

(e) the constable has reasonable grounds for believing that arrest is necessary to protect a child or other vulnerable person from the relevant person.

This means that in any situation where, for practical reasons, it is unlikely that proceedings can be started without the arrest of the person (false name or address) or where arrest is thought to be necessary to deal with an immediate problem (public decency or obstruction) or to protect people, then this section can be used. It can also be a fallback provision for police officers where it is unclear whether or not there is a right to arrest. Wide as the provision might appear, though, it can only be deployed where one of the above conditions exist.

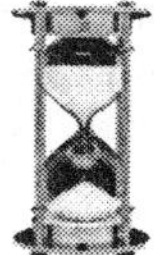

17 List the categories where an arrest can be made by a police officer.

18 On your arrival at the police station, your client informs you that s/he was arrested for no reason at all and s/he wants to make a complaint. S/he tells you that s/he was outside a public house where a fight had taken place, and when the police arrived, they arrested a friend of your client. On trying to prevent the arrest, your client was him/herself arrested. Had the police a valid reason to arrest your client?

1.3.12 IS YOUR ADVICE TO THE CLIENT AT THE POLICE STATION CONFIDENTIAL?

The client has a right to confidential legal advice: the right to confidentiality is the client's, so s/he is free to disclose your advice to anyone, if they so wish. You are not at liberty to disclose your advice to anyone (other than other employees of your firm, consistent with good practice, and the need to inform, record and take advice) without the client's permission.

You must be very clear, particularly when dealing with clients at the police station, as to whether the client wishes information (and, if so, what information) to be given to others as to his/her whereabouts and circumstances. Difficulties can arise in connection with family members and co-accuseds or potential co-accuseds.

At the police station, however, although the advice from a legal adviser is supposed to be confidential, it is sometimes the case that advice is given in inappropriate surroundings where it can be overheard. This is usually avoidable, merely by waiting for a free interview room, but care should be taken, especially when giving advice over the telephone.

1.3.13 IS ANY INFORMATION GIVEN TO YOU BY YOUR CLIENT CONFIDENTIAL?

As above, just as the advice you give to your client is confidential, so is any information given you by your client, and the same warning applies as in 1.3.12 above.

1.3.14 WHAT IS THE POSITION OF A CLIENT WHO IS UNDER ARREST?

On arrival at the police station, an arrested person is entitled to:

(a) have someone informed of his/her arrest and whereabouts;

(b) seek legal advice privately (and to obtain free legal advice under the Duty Solicitor Scheme);

(c) consult the Codes of Practice under PACE 1984;

(d) be informed and given written notice of the above rights.

Vulnerable clients must be treated appropriately: in particular, there may be a need to contact an appropriate adult or interpreter (see 1.5 below).

1.3.15 WHO CAN THE ARRESTED CLIENT INFORM?

The arrested client can inform any one person s/he wishes to of his/her arrest and whereabouts. This is in addition to his/her right to seek legal advice, and is often referred to as the right not to be held incommunicado.

Such notification can only be delayed up to 36 hours and only in the circumstances set out in 1.3.16 below.

If the client is transferred to another station, s/he has a right to have someone notified (whether the same person or another person).

If the person that the client wishes to notify cannot be contacted, the client may choose up to two alternatives. If they too cannot be contacted, the custody officer has discretion to allow further attempts until the information has been conveyed.

The client is also entitled to talk by telephone for a reasonable length of time to one person, but, except when the telephone call is to a solicitor, the

Section 56 of PACE 1984 provides that an arrested person on arrival at the police station has the right on request, as soon as is practicable, to have one friend, relative or other person who is known to him/her or who is likely to take an interest in his/her welfare, told of his/her arrest and the place where s/he is being detained.

police officer may listen and intervene if the right is being abused. The phone call, except when to a solicitor, is, therefore, not confidential and its contents can in theory be given in evidence. This right is in addition to the right to inform someone of the detained person's whereabouts and the right to seek legal advice (which may be by telephone), but often tends to be combined with one or the other.

1.3.16 CAN THE RIGHT TO NOTIFY SOMEONE BE DELAYED?

Delay in allowing notification can only take place if:

(a) the offence concerned is a serious arrestable offence (see 1.3.35 below) or the special provisions in relation to terrorism offences apply;

(b) an officer of the rank of superintendent or above authorises delay;

(c) the officer concerned has reasonable grounds for believing that allowing communication will lead to:

- interference with, or harm to, evidence connected with a serious arrestable offence;
- interference with, or physical injury to, other persons;
- the alerting of other persons suspected of having committed such an offence but not yet arrested for it; or
- will hinder the recovery of property obtained as the result of such offence;

(d) the offence is a drug trafficking offence, and;

- the officer has reasonable grounds for believing that the detained person has benefited from drug trafficking; and
- the recovery of the value of that person's proceeds of drug trafficking will be hindered by notification of the person in question; or

(e) the offence is one where a confiscation order could be made under Part VI of the Criminal Justice Act (CJA) 1988, and the officer has reasonable grounds for believing that the detained person has benefited from the offence, and that the recovery of the property obtained by that person from or in connection with the offence or of the pecuniary advantage derived by him/her from or in connection with it will be hindered by notifying the chosen person in the exercise of the right.

The right to notify someone can only be delayed in serious arrestable offences other than those covered by (d) and (e), opposite, when (a), (b) and (c) are present together.

1.3.17 CAN THE RIGHT TO NOTIFY SOMEONE BE PREVENTED ALTOGETHER?

The right to notify someone can only be delayed for up to 36 hours.

1.3.18 CAN SOMEONE CONTACT A POLICE STATION AND ASK WHETHER A PERSON IS UNDER ARREST?

If a friend or relative of a detainee, or a person with an interest in a detainee's welfare, asks where the detainee is, the information must be given, provided that the detainee agrees and provided that the case is not one involving a serious arrestable offence, and the detainee is lawfully being held incommunicado.

This effectively means that anyone may enquire as to whether a person has been arrested. The information cannot be given if the detainee does not wish it. Otherwise, unless the situation described at 1.3.16 above applies, the information must be provided.

If you are attending to advise the client, then either the client has been allowed to contact you to obtain legal advice, or you will have been contacted on behalf of the client by a friend with whom contact has been allowed. Nevertheless, you should check the custody record and seek the client's instructions as to whether s/he was permitted any other communication that s/he was entitled to, or indeed if the client wants to contact someone or have such a person informed now.

Being unable to contact those who might be concerned, or those who are needed to take over child care, business or other domestic responsibilities (even a matter such as feeding a pet) can seriously affect the client's well being in custody, his/her ability to withstand interview or other procedures and to respond appropriately, and generally can create a feeling of isolation. It is therefore important as one of your tasks in protecting the client's interests that you ensure as far as possible that such matters are dealt with.

Conversely, clients may be concerned lest a partner, parent or indeed employer discovers the client's arrest: police may sometimes play on these fears. You should always be careful that you have clear instructions. There are, of course, situations where an appropriate adult must be involved.

1.3.19 CAN YOU INFORM SOMEONE ON BEHALF OF THE CLIENT?

If the client asks you to let someone know of his/her whereabouts, then the client is explicitly giving you permission to reveal confidential information. Police officers may only prevent the client from informing someone of his/her whereabouts where the consequences set out at 1.3.16 above are thought likely to result.

Very rarely is access to a solicitor denied on such a basis, as it is thought unlikely that a solicitor would be inveigled into criminal behaviour or duped into providing information to an accomplice. It is therefore important that you are not unwittingly involved. Care should be taken when passing on messages other than simple information as to the whereabouts of the client and that you are advising him/her. For example, 'Tell Fred to hide the loot' should be treated with suspicion, and the message declined!

1.3.20 CAN THE CLIENT INSIST ON SEEING OR SPEAKING TO A SOLICITOR?

Under PACE 1984, a person under arrest (or helping the police voluntarily) is entitled by section 58 to consult privately with a solicitor if s/he so wishes, and no interview by the police should normally be conducted without legal advice if the suspect wishes to be given legal advice.

There are, however, certain exceptions where legal advice may be delayed:

(a) the offence is a serious arrestable offence (see 1.3.36 below); and

(b) the delay is authorised by a superintendent;

(c) because it is felt that contact with a solicitor might lead to:

- the interference with or harm to evidence; or
- the interference with or physical injury to other person; or
- the alerting of other suspects; or
- the hindrance of the recovery of property.

An interview may also commence in the absence of a solicitor in urgent cases (see 1.2 above).

In this context, a solicitor includes (see Code C, para 6.12 of PACE 1984) a trainee solicitor, a duty solicitor and a representative or accredited representative. If a solicitor wishes to send a non-accredited or probationer representative, that person shall be admitted unless an officer of the rank of inspector or above believes that such a visit will hinder the investigation. If access is thus refused, the solicitor sending the refused person must be notified, as must the client, and the custody record must be so endorsed.

1.3.21 IF YOU ARE TELEPHONED BY A CLIENT WHO IS AT A POLICE STATION, MUST YOU ATTEND THE POLICE STATION?

If your firm is telephoned by a client from the police station and asked for advice, the discussion will indicate whether attendance is needed or requested. Sometimes, it will be sufficient to give the client straightforward advice over the telephone. However, you must remember that the telephone call may not be confidential, in that it may be overheard in the police station.

The client may indicate that s/he would like immediate simple advice or confirmation of his/her legal position, or s/he may want assistance in a forthcoming interview. If you speak to the custody officer yourself over the telephone, you will usually be able to obtain an indication of when the interview is likely to take place.

Under the rules of the Duty Solicitor Scheme, a telephone discussion might take place with the duty solicitor, and this might resolve the matter without a visit to the police station. Telephone advice should usually be provided to the client under the Duty Solicitor Scheme by the duty solicitor, unless the duty solicitor is at or near the station and can give advice directly. Initial advice can be postponed if the client is incapable of seeking advice due to violence or drunkenness.

The client should then also be told that the solicitor (or the solicitor's representative) will attend to assist and advise at the police station. A representative can attend to advise at the police station after initial advice from the duty solicitor.

In the following situations, a suspect should always be attended at the police station so that advice and assistance can be given:

(a) after arrest for an arrestable offence and an interview is intended;

(b) where there is an identification procedure to be carried out;

(c) where the suspect complains of mistreatment by the police.

Where the suspect is a juvenile or is otherwise vulnerable, attendance will be usual. In other cases, the duty solicitor, after advising initially by phone, will make a judgment as to whether attendance is necessary.

1.3.22 WHAT SHOULD YOU DO IF THE CLIENT IS IN A PARTICULARLY VULNERABLE CATEGORY?

Clients may need to have special considerations and special arrangements made on their behalf if they are in one of the following groups:

(a) juveniles;

(b) mentally disadvantaged;

(c) ill or injured;

(d) non-English speaker;

(e) deaf;

(f) under the influence of drugs or alcohol.

This may involve arrangements for the attendance of an appropriate adult or interpreter, consultation or referral to a doctor, social worker or psychiatrist and, in particular, the awareness of the special provisions

You must produce evidence of having informed clients of their rights and obligations in all matters covered, both by telephone and in person.

for these categories of people by PACE 1984 (see 1.5 below).

1.3.23 CAN THE CLIENT BE SEARCHED WHEN S/HE IS ARRESTED?

You may be asked to advise on your client's position in regard to a number of police procedures, including giving advice on whether the police were acting within the law by taking certain steps, and advising on the consequences for the client of these procedures. In addition, you will need to be aware of the propriety of the measures taken, as contraventions may affect the admissibility of evidence thereby obtained. The police have a variety of powers to search, including stopping and searching, searching on arrest and on arrival at the police station, and the search of premises.

'Prohibited articles' means offensive weapons or articles for burglary, property obtained by theft, a vehicle taken without permission or property obtained by deception.

A person or vehicle can be stopped and searched for stolen or prohibited articles if the officer has reasonable grounds for suspecting that such items are on the person or in the vehicle.

If your client has been arrested somewhere other than at the police station, s/he may be searched (section 32 of PACE 1984):

(a) if the police officer has reason to believe that s/he may present a danger to him/herself or others;

(b) for anything which that person might use to escape from lawful custody; or

(c) for anything which might be evidence in relation to an offence.

Evidence of any offence, not merely the one in question, can be retained.

Items found may be kept, and the officer may seize and retain any object found which s/he believes might be used in that way.

Such a search does not allow the removal of more than outer garments in public, but allows for the search of an arrested person's mouth, and is confined to such searches as are reasonable.

Provided the arrest itself was lawful, it is unlikely that any successful challenge to the discovery of evidence could be mounted on the ground that a search was carried out in breach of these provisions, but it is nevertheless important to know the precise limit of the police's powers in the rare cases that such an objection may be made. It is also necessary, on occasion, to reassure clients where officers were acting within their powers.

1.3.24 CAN THE ARRESTED CLIENT'S PREMISES BE SEARCHED?

The police can enter and search premises without a search warrant:

(a) to enter and search, to execute an arrest warrant, to arrest for an arrestable offence or to prevent personal injury or damage to property (section 17 of PACE 1984); and

(b) if the premises are occupied or controlled by a person arrested for an arrestable offence, if there are grounds to suspect that there is evidence of the offence or a connected offence on the premises (section 18 of PACE 1984).

If your client has been arrested, the police also have powers to enter and search any premises where the client was when arrested or just before s/he was arrested, in order to look for evidence in connection with the offence in question (section 32 of PACE 1984).

This only allows a search where the officer has reasonable grounds to believe that evidence might be on the premises. This, of course, will be affected by the nature of the alleged offence and the recent behaviour of the client. Where the premises consist of more than one dwelling, the power to search is limited to the dwelling either where the arrest took place or where the person was immediately before the arrest and also parts of the premises occupied in common.

It is important to note that the power to search for evidence arises where the officer has reasonable grounds to believe that there is evidence on the premises in connection with the offence in question, but, if evidence of any offence is discovered, the items discovered can be retained, as can items that might have been obtained as a result of the commission of an offence.

These powers, of course, relate to search without a warrant. If the officer has a search warrant, s/he does not need any of the statutory grounds for a search, though they will have been asserted before a magistrate to obtain the warrant.

Your client is arrested in a street outside his/her house on suspicion of dealing in class A drugs.

19 What powers of search do the police have (including power to search premises)?

20 If s/he had just left the flat in which friends of his/hers lived, what powers do the police have to search those premises?

21 Can the police retain any of the following if discovered in the search?

(a) class B drugs?

(b) firearms?

(c) large quantities of money?

(d) scales?

1.3.25 CAN THE ARRESTED CLIENT'S CAR BE SEARCHED?

Section 23 of PACE 1984.

Any reference in PACE 1984 to premises includes any vehicle, vessel, tent or moveable structure. Hence, the power to search premises extends to cars and any of the other matters specified as coming within the definition.

The power to stop and search referred to above relates also to vehicles, but is limited to stolen or prohibited items.

1.3.26 CAN THE POLICE TAKE AWAY ITEMS FOUND IN A SEARCH?

Material is subject to legal professional privilege if it is any material (eg, a letter or other document, including an electronic document) which is a communication:

(a) between the client and a legal adviser for the purpose of giving of legal advice; or

(b) between the client and legal adviser, or between either of them and a third party, in relation to contemplated legal proceedings.

The police have powers of seizure, as they are called, so long as the police were legally on the premises and the items are not subject to legal privilege.

In addition, the officer must have reasonable grounds for believing that the items:

(a) were obtained as a result of the commission of an offence; or

(b) constitute evidence in relation to this or any other offence; and

(c) it is necessary to seize them to prevent them being lost, concealed, altered or damaged.

1.3.27 CAN THE POLICE HAVE ACCESS TO COMPUTER INFORMATION?

Increasingly, information is stored in computers, and so the police would wish to have access to such matters: this is not confined to high tech or fraud offences, as more people are used to communicating by electronic means. Additionally, with the high rate of computer theft, documents on a computer may sometimes indicate the computer's origin.

Where a police officer has reasonable grounds to believe that there is information in a computer which is accessible from the premises:

(a) which might be evidence in relation to any offence; or

(b) might have been obtained as a result of the commission of an offence; and

(c) that it might be lost, damaged, altered or concealed,

s/he can require that the information be produced in a form in which it can be viewed and taken away, again provided that it is not privileged information.

1.3.28 CAN THE POLICE KEEP THINGS FOUND DURING A SEARCH?

Provided the search is lawful, the police may keep items seized until trial, if they consider that the items might be used as evidence in a trial, or for forensic examination in connection with an investigation. Where goods are believed to be stolen, they can be retained with a view to establishing their rightful owner.

However, this provision is subject to certain limitations:

(a) if a photograph or copy would be sufficient for the purpose specified, the police should return the actual item after making such a copy or photograph;
(b) items seized because they might cause injury, damage, interfere with evidence, or assist in escape, must be returned to the individual if s/he is released from detention;
(c) the occupier of premises which have been searched or the person from whom an item was seized can ask for a record of what was taken, and can request supervised access to the items.

It may happen that evidence is seized that your client would like returned for his/her legitimate business or personal needs: often, the evidential significance, if any, can be adequately conveyed by a photograph. If the evidence is documentary, it may be that your client's need of the document is itself satisfied by having a copy returned (the original, if relevant, may be needed as evidence).

1.3.29 SEARCHES UNDER A SEARCH WARRANT

A search warrant granted by a court allows entry and search:

(a) for the purpose for which it was granted;
(b) at a reasonable hour, unless this would frustrate its purpose;
(c) within one month of the date of issue (dated and timed); but
(d) it does not allow access to excluded, special procedure or legally privileged materials for which special authorisation must be applied from a circuit judge.

An example of a warrant to enter and search premises is given in Document 3 in Appendix 2.

Excluded material applies to:

- records acquired in a trade or profession for health matters;
- human tissue or fluid for medical diagnosis or treatment;
- confidential journalistic records.

Special procedure material relates to other confidential material acquired in the course of a trade, business or profession.

Legal professional privileged material is defined at 1.3.26 above.

A search warrant granted by a court will be dated and timed to prevent it from being obtained after a search has been carried out.

1.3.30 CAN THE CLIENT BE SEARCHED AT THE POLICE STATION?

As the custody officer has a duty to record in the custody record everything the arrested person has with him/her when s/he is either brought to the police station under arrest or is arrested at the police station, a search may therefore be carried out, if it is deemed necessary, by an officer of the same sex as the arrested person.

Any item may be taken and retained by the police, but clothing and personal effects may only be taken if the custody officer believes they may be used:

(a) to cause injury;

(b) to damage property;

(c) to interfere with evidence;

(d) to assist in escaping; or

the custody officer has reasonable grounds to believe that they may be evidence relating to an offence.

Intimate searches (ie, of the body orifices other than the mouth) may only be carried out under the authority of a superintendent or above, where it is believed that the arrested person has concealed:

(a) a class A drug that s/he intended to supply to others or to export; or

(b) something that could cause injury to him/herself or others.

1.3.31 CAN SAMPLES BE TAKEN FROM THE CLIENT?

Bodily samples can be asked for in connection with any imprisonable offence, but the taking of intimate samples requires the written consent of the person involved. However, failure to give consent to the taking of such a sample may lead to adverse inferences being drawn at trial from the failure to give consent. The authority of a superintendent or officer of higher rank is required for the taking of such samples.

Non-intimate samples do not require consent of the person if the authority of superintendent or above is given.

What is an intimate sample?

An intimate sample is one of blood, semen or other tissue fluid, urine, pubic hair, a swab from a body orifice or a dental impression.

What is a non-intimate sample?

A sample of hair from parts of the body other than the pubic area, a nail sample or an under-nail sample, a swab from parts of the body other than a body orifice, saliva and footprints constitute non-intimate samples.

What about DNA samples?

DNA information may be obtained from hair, blood, saliva, etc. Where such samples are taken and no conviction or caution results, the sample itself should be destroyed, but in some situations the DNA profile can be retained.

Samples can be used to make what is called a 'speculative search'. This means that they can be checked against other records held by the police. Suspects should be informed that a speculative search might be carried out (PACE 1984, Code D, para 5.11A).

What about fingerprints?

Fingerprinting can only be done with the person's consent, unless:

(a) a superintendent authorises it; or
(b) the suspect is charged with or informed that s/he will be reported for a recordable offence; and
(c) has not had his/her fingerprints taken in the course of investigation; or
(d) s/he has been convicted of a recordable offence.

Where fingerprints are taken during an investigation and no conviction or caution of the suspect results, the prints should be destroyed.

Reasonable force can be used to take fingerprints.

Fingerprints can be used to make what is called a speculative search. This means that the prints can be checked against other records held by the police. Suspects should be informed that a speculative search might be carried out (PACE 1984, Code D, para 3.2A).

1.3.32 CAN THE ARRESTED CLIENT BE PHOTOGRAPHED?

A photograph of an arrested person can be taken at a police station if:

(a) the person consents in writing;
(b) s/he is arrested with others or in circumstances where it is necessary to establish who was arrested, at what time and at what place; or

(c) s/he has been charged with or reported for a recordable offence and has not yet been released or brought before a court;

(d) s/he has a conviction for a recordable offence and no photograph has been taken, or an officer of superintendent or above authorises it because the person is suspected of a crime and there is identification evidence in relation to it (PACE 1984, Code D, para 4).

Photographs taken should be destroyed if the matter does not result in conviction or caution.

Force cannot be used in order to take a photograph.

1.3.33 WHAT IS THE ROLE OF THE CUSTODY OFFICER?

As the role of the custody officer is central to what happens in the police station and effectively what happens to the client, it is important to recognise what this officer's specific duties are before and after charge, remembering that this officer is responsible, throughout the period of custody, for the client, for his/her conduct while in custody and for its recording in the custody record.

Prior to charge

Before charge, the custody officer has a role in assessing whether there is sufficient evidence against the arrested person to charge him/her.

The officer must:

(a) decide whether there is sufficient evidence to charge; or

(b) release the arrested person on bail unless s/he is to be detained in order to secure or preserve evidence or to obtain it by questioning (the latter being the most usual reason for detention before charge).

If the officer authorises detention, s/he must make a written record of the grounds for detention in the presence of the arrested person, who should be informed of those grounds unless s/he is incapable of understanding, is violent or likely to become so, or is in urgent need of medical attention.

If it is decided that there is sufficient evidence to charge, the arrested person shall be charged or released without charge. If, however, the arrested person is not fit to be dealt with, s/he can be kept in custody until fit to be dealt with.

If the arrested person is released without charge pending a decision on whether to prosecute, the custody officer shall inform him/her of this.

On arrival at the police station, the custody officer has to assess the state of the evidence: if it is already sufficient, then a charge should be made without an interview being carried out.

As soon as the custody officer considers that there is sufficient evidence to charge, interviewing must stop (or, indeed, not be commenced), and the arrested person must be charged or released without charge (which is unlikely, but this allows for situations where, although there is evidence, a decision is made not to proceed, or a charge is to be preferred later).

After charge

Once the arrested person has been charged, the custody officer has to release him/her on bail, unless one of the following reasons exists to keep the person in custody:

(a) the name or address given is suspect;

(b) there are grounds for believing that the person will fail to appear in court in answer to bail;

(c) where the charge is an imprisonable offence, to prevent the person from committing an offence;

(d) if not imprisonable, it is thought necessary to prevent the person from causing injury or damage;

(e) it is necessary to prevent interference with administration of justice;

(f) it is necessary for the charged person's own protection; or

(g) if a juvenile, it is in his/her or her own interests.

If detention is authorised, a written record must be made of the ground and the person informed unless s/he is incapable of understanding, is violent or is likely to become so, or is in urgent need of medical attention.

If a juvenile is detained, arrangements must be made for him/her to go to local authority accommodation.

These are the grounds for witholding bail, which are effectively the same as the grounds applicable in a court. The police can take into account the same matters as a court in arriving at the decision that one of these grounds is applicable.

1.3.34 HOW LONG CAN THE CLIENT BE DETAINED WITHOUT CHARGE?

As we have already seen, an arrested person can be interviewed in order to obtain evidence about the charge, but once enough evidence has been obtained, s/he must be charged with the offence. At that point, interviewing must cease and the person must be released on bail or held in custody and taken before a magistrates' court.

Before charge, there are limits as to how long a person can be held in custody. Within the overall period, a series of reviews must be carried out, as laid down by PACE 1984, to ensure that the need for detention is constantly evaluated. These time limits, particularly the overall limits on detention *prior to charge,* are often referred to as the 'custody clock'.

22 On what grounds can a detainee be refused bail by the police after charge?

23 When must a suspect be charged?

24 What is the role of the custody officer?

25 When must the custody officer inform the detainee of the grounds for detention?

The custody clock

The overall detention time limits are as follows:

(a) maximum detention without charge for an arrestable offence, other than a serious arrestable offence, is 24 hours;

(b) where a serious arrestable offence is concerned, up to a further 12 hours of detention without charge can be authorised by an officer of the rank of superintendent or above if s/he believes that:

- the investigation is being carried out expeditiously and diligently; and
- continued detention is necessary to secure or preserve evidence for the relevant offence, or to obtain evidence by questioning the suspect;

(c) if the person is released after 24 hours, s/he cannot be re-arrested for the same offence without a warrant, unless there is new evidence (section 41(9) of PACE 1984);

(d) after 36 hours, a warrant of further detention must be obtained from a magistrates' court, or the person must be released (or charged).

Whether an offence is a serious arrestable offence is only of significance in relation to detention in the police station and the power to delay contact: it has no significance in relation to the powers to arrest. See 1.3.35 below.

1.3.35 WHAT IS A SERIOUS ARRESTABLE OFFENCE?

Arrestable offences have been defined above (see 1.3.9 above). A serious arrestable offence is an arrestable offence which falls into one of two categories.

Serious arrestable offences are either:

(a) offences which are always serious (such as murder, manslaughter, rape, kidnapping, certain sexual offences, causing death by dangerous driving or by careless driving under the influence of drink or drugs); or

(b) any arrestable offence which is deemed serious because it has or is intended to have the result of:

- serious harm to national security or public order;
- serious interference with the administration of justice or the investigation of an offence;
- death or serious injury;
- substantial financial gain;
- serious financial loss (serious to the loser).

See section 116 and schedule 5 of PACE 1984.

R v McIvor [1987] Crim LR 409: the amount of loss was held not to be substantial when shared amongst them.

1.3.36 REVIEW OF DETENTION

Within the overall time limits, there is a regular timetable of reviews to ensure the need for continued detention.

The sequence of reviews that must be carried out is as follows:

(a) the first review shall not be later than six hours after the detention was first authorised;

(b) the second review shall be not later than nine hours after the first; ie, a maximum of 15 hours after detention;

(c) subsequent reviews shall be at intervals of not more than nine hours.

A review can be postponed if it is not practicable or if the suspect is actually in mid-interview, or no review officer is available, but it must be carried out as soon as is practicable and the reason for any delay must be recorded.

Who must carry out the review?

The review must be carried out by the review officer, namely, an officer of at least the rank of inspector who has not been directly involved in the investigation.

What does a review involve?

The officer (the review officer) must be satisfied that:

(a) there is insufficient evidence at that stage to charge the suspect;

(b) further detention is necessary to secure or to preserve evidence relevant to the offence for which the person has been arrested, or to obtain evidence by questioning the suspect.

It is usually the case that detention is required for further questioning, but occasionally, it is to prevent the alerting of other actual or potential suspects by the person in police custody, or to prevent the suspect from disposing of or concealing evidence. Thus, such detention may be associated with the search of premises, other arrests and delay in informing people of the arrest.

Do you have a role in the review?

The suspect must be given the reasons for continued detention, which must be recorded and, unless the suspect is asleep or unfit (whether medically or because of unruly behaviour), at each review s/he must be given the opportunity to make representations as to whether or not s/he should continue to be detained.

In addition, you are permitted, if available at the time of the review, to make such representations. You therefore have a role to seek to limit the period of detention and to verify (whether you are present or through the custody record) that the proper procedures have been observed.

When making representations about continued detention, there are many occasions when you will be able to argue that there is no danger of evidence being lost, etc. It is more difficult to deal with situations where the police want to interview further. However, if some interviewing has been carried out, you may be able to argue that all the information is now available. However, it may be that your client's interests are best served (if s/he is making a no comment interview) by waiting until the expiry of the detention period.

1.3.37 WHAT HAPPENS AFTER 36 HOURS HAVE EXPIRED?

To detain your client further, a warrant of further detention (for up to another 36 hours) must be obtained from a magistrates' court. If this is to be done, your client may be present and be represented: you should, therefore, arrange representation as required.

Magistrates can grant a warrant for up to a further 36 hours if they are satisfied that:

(a) a serious arrestable offence is involved;

(b) the investigation is being carried out expeditiously and diligently;

(c) continued detention is necessary to secure or preserve evidence for the relevant offence or to obtain evidence by questioning the suspect.

One further application can be made, and magistrates can grant up to a total of 96 hours in total continued detention.

26 What must the police do on arrest?

27 When can the police search an arrested person?

1.3.38 CONSULTING WITH YOUR CLIENT CONFIDENTIALLY

When you deal with a client at the police station, you and your client are entitled to discuss his/her situation – for you to take instructions – confidentially, and then for you to advise the client.

PACE 1984, Code C, para 6.1 states that anyone in police detention should be able to, and should be informed that s/he is able to, consult and communicate privately with a solicitor.

This is reiterated from time to time (eg, in Home Office Circular 24/1998, which recognises that lack of consultation facilities is often the cause of delay in proceedings), and guidelines remind police officers that arrested people are entitled in interview to:

(a) privacy, which means that the interview should not be overheard;

(b) security for the solicitor, with some alarm system. It is also required that the interview be capable of being monitored without impinging upon the privacy of the conversation;

(c) suitable facilities, which include a desk, chairs, adequate heating, lighting and ventilation.

A solicitor's interview room should normally be available for use by the solicitor and client: if it is in use, normally the solicitor should be asked if it is possible to wait until the room is free. If this is not acceptable, the interview is urgent or there is no interview room, other facilities may need to be made available.

If the police interview room is used, you should verify with the police officer that the taping machine is switched off. In extreme cases, a cell or secure visits room may be offered. If the latter, you should only accept that facility if the screen between you and the client can be removed to allow proper confidential instructions to be given. If a cell is offered, you should not accept this unless you are satisfied that you can conduct a professional interview.

You need to provide evidence of having informed clients of their rights and obligations by telephone and in person.

1.3.39 TAPE RECORDING OF INTERVIEWS

Since the introduction of tape recording of interviews, there has been little cause to challenge what is said at interview by clients. How they came to say it may still be a cause of concern (see section 76 of PACE 1984), and the consequences of what they say or do not say is a complex issue.

If you attend with the client at interview, you will have a general recollection of the type of response s/he made, but it may be that the detail of any answers gains importance in the light of other information or evidence. If you did not attend at interview, you may have little appreciation of what was said, except for:

(a) your client's own recollection;

(b) the balanced summary provided by the police under the advance disclosure rules.

PACE 1984 provides (by Code E, para 4.16) that the suspect must be provided with a copy of the tape as soon as is practicable, either after being informed that s/he will be prosecuted, or indeed after being charged.

Section 76 of PACE 1984 provides that evidence of confessions shall not be admissible in trial unless the prosecution proves beyond reasonable doubt that the confession was not obtained by oppression or in consequence of anything said or done that made the confession unreliable. In addition, as mentioned above, section 78 provides an exclusionary discretion to the court where evidence is obtained unfairly.

Some police stations may be able to provide facilities for fast copying of tapes, but this seems rarely to be done. Unless there is a specific reason why this will prejudice their investigations, the police should allow you to make your own audio recording if you wish, using your own equipment, but it is important to recognise that time taken in copying and supplying tapes can be a cause of significant delay. However, it may not be in your client's interest to hasten proceedings, nor may you wish to be involved in the procedure and expense of self-taping.

Whichever process is adopted, unless you were present at interview *and* it is a simple case where the client's wishes and best course is clear, you will normally wish to obtain a copy of and examine the tape before the client is advised on plea.

Police station assistance checklist

- Have all procedures been carried out properly?
- Have I checked the custody record?
- Have I asked for a copy of any interview tape?
- Does my client understand the follow-up procedures?
- Have I made a full note of my interview with the client?

You will need to provide evidence of notes of two meetings with clients before and after interview.

ASSISTING CLIENTS WITH INTERVIEWS

RANGE

Achievement must cover all the following contexts.

Types of interview

Reply interviews, no-reply interviews.

Improper behaviour

- Oppressive/bullying conduct, improper questioning.
- Giving misleading or insufficient information.

Location

- Advising by telephone.
- Participation in the interview.

EVIDENCE

You will need to produce the specific pieces of performance evidence listed below. In addition, you will need to demonstrate that you have achieved the objectives specified at the beginning of this unit. You may do this by producing further pieces of evidence from real and simulated performance, by answering questions posed by your assessor or by passing a written examination.

You will need to provide evidence of:

1 having attended with clients at both **Types of interview** in the **Range** and having produced detailed notes;

2 having monitored questioning and challenged **Improper behaviour** (as described in the **Range**) on two occasions;

3 having given advice to two clients in both **Locations** in the **Range**.

CRITERIA

You will demonstrate achievement if:

(a) the representative's presence at interview is arranged;

(b) the representative's role in interviews is explained to clients and officers;

(c) attempts are made to ensure that clients understand and are allowed to answer freely;

(d) objections are made to improper behaviour by investigating authorities;

(e) interviews are stopped whenever consultation in private is necessary;

(e) full and accurate records are made of interviews.

1.4.1 INTRODUCTION

An interview takes place when your client is:

(a) under arrest:

- having been arrested during the course of an incident, eg, a public order incident or suspicion of burglary; or
- after police investigation following the report of an incident;

(b) voluntarily attending the police station to assist with enquiries.

See also 1.2.6 above and 1.4.16 below regarding questioning.

The custody officer is commonly a police officer of the rank of sergeant (s/he must be at least of this rank). Such an officer, who is attached to 'designated police stations' (ie, those where interviews of arrested persons can take place), has responsibility for the person in custody and anything which happens to the detainee in that time, including during questioning. In particular, it is the custody officer's responsibility to ensure that the provisions of PACE 1984 are complied with, the custody record is fully and accurately completed, and the time limits on and reviews of detention are applied (see 1.3 above).

Assisting a client at a police station, particularly when it involves advising on interview, is a very important task, dealing as it does with a vital point in the process for both sides: what transpires in interview and the course the client decides to take will often determine the course the proceedings will take. This is not limited to, but includes, cases where the client at an early stage decides to plead guilty and makes a full confession. Assisting a client also involves decisions on whether to answer questions where there is an intention to plead not guilty, dealing with oppressive interviewing, and generally helping the client to deal with a difficult and stressful situation.

If you are called out to attend a police station to assist a client in custody, unlike dealing with a client by pre-arranged appointment, you will not have much time to prepare. However, you should have had opportunities to observe procedures and techniques, and no employee should be asked to attend on such matters unless competent to do so.

Before arriving at the police station you will know the name of the client. Normally, your firm will have been telephoned by either a police officer or by the client directly (the latter happens only occasionally). If your firm has been contacted by the client directly, this will usually be because s/he has had prior dealings with your firm, so you may be able to arm

The provisions of PACE 1984 apply equally to voluntary attenders and those under arrest.

You will, however, usually have some time to prepare: in your conversation with the custody or investigating officer you should ascertain when the police intend to interview, and ensure that the officer is aware that you will be attending to advise the person in question. Once a legal adviser is asked to attend, interviewing should not take place before his/her arrival, unless to await the solicitor would involve unreasonable delay in the investigation. The solicitor should be allowed to be present at the interview if easily available (Code C, paras 6.6, 6.8). Although you must act promptly and appropriately, this means that you will usually at least have the opportunity to gather items and check matters of law and practice.

yourself with background material before you attend (crucial information would be whether s/he is already involved in other proceedings – perhaps on bail and due in court). If your firm is approached because you are the rostered duty solicitor firm, it may well be someone with whom you have had no previous dealings.

Occasionally, you may be contacted by a friend or a family member who has been contacted by the arrested person, under the arrested person's right to inform someone of the arrest. That individual may be able to tell you very little of the circumstances, or may have been told an 'edited' version of the events by the arrested person. Always check which police station is involved – it is too easy to be told that X is 'at the police station' and to assume that you are both referring to the same station. If the person informing you does not know which station is involved, you may have to telephone the various possibilities.

Keep a record of the telephone calls you make to demonstrate (if necessary) that enquiries were made, and of the time at which your involvement was notified to the police.

If you speak to your client over the telephone, you should limit the information you seek, in view of the fact that the conversation may be overheard in the police station. In most cases (see 1.3), you will be attending the police station to advise the client prior to and during interview. You will need some basic information from the client which should be solicited by questions requiring only a yes or no answer, or simple factual information such as confirmation of his/her name.

There is, however, information that can be conveyed to the client:

(a) advise the client that you will be attending and your expected time of arrival. Explain that on your arrival you will ask that s/he should be notified, but that you will have inquiries to make of the police before you see him/her. When you do see him/her, you will be asking questions of him/her about the arrest, his/her background and the circumstances which led to the arrest, so explain that s/he should be thinking over any matters which might be of assistance;

(b) reassure your client that the reason for your attendance is to advise him/her and investigate whether there are any immediate problems relating to his/her confinement or his/her treatment in the police station;

A person detained in the police station has the right not to be held incommunicado: Code C, para 5 provides that a detained person can have contacted someone concerned with his/her welfare, at public expense and as soon as practicable, except where such contact might lead to interference with evidence, the alerting of suspects and so on, and the offence is a serious arrestable offence (as at 1.4.4 below).

Remember to indicate your likely time of arrival and confirm that no interview will take place until you are in attendance and have given the detainee legal advice.

Your portfolio should show that you have given advice to clients over the telephone and have participated in a police interview.

(c) find out whether s/he has been questioned in any way, and has made any response;

(d) remind him/her that s/he should not answer questions of any kind, even ones that are stated to be off the record or appear to be casual, until s/he has discussed the matter fully with you. Invite him/her, if asked, to simply state that s/he is not answering questions until s/he has received legal advice.

1.4.2 PREPARATION FOR THE POLICE INTERVIEW

When you deal with a client at the police station, you and your client are entitled to discuss the client's situation – for you to take instructions – confidentially.

PACE 1984, Code C, para 6.1 states that anyone in police detention should be able to and should be informed that they are able to consult and communicate privately with a solicitor. Recent Home Office guidelines have recognised that a lack of consultation facilities is often the cause of delay in proceedings and remind police officers that arrested people are entitled in interview to:

(a) privacy – which means that the interview should not be overheard;

(b) security for the solicitor, with some alarm system. It is also required that the interview be monitored without impinging upon the privacy of the conversation;

(c) suitable facilities, including a desk, chairs, adequate heating, lighting and ventilation.

1.4.3 WHAT IS THE ROLE OF THE SOLICITOR'S REPRESENTATIVE?

Note for guidance 6D to Code C of PACE 1984 notes that it is accepted that the effect of legal advice might be that the suspect does not answer police questions: this is not a ground to prevent the client from having access to an adviser.

The role of the solicitor or of the solicitor's representative at the interview is very clear and is enshrined in PACE 1984, namely, to protect and advance the legal rights of the client.

Your role in interview (after preparing the client and taking instructions) is to:

(a) monitor the interview;

(b) object to and prevent improper questioning or behaviour;

(c) object to and prevent improper disclosure during interview by the police.

The police should not, eg, misrepresent the law or wrongly claim to have information. Your primary role, indicated in the ways set out above, is to protect and advance the legal interests of your client. It is not to answer for the client, nor is it to prevent questions from being put to the client.

1.4.4 CAN YOU INSIST ON BEING PRESENT?

If the client wants legal advice, whether under arrest or helping the police voluntarily, s/he is entitled to it, unless there are grounds for delaying the advice. Delay in legal advice is only possible under PACE 1984 if:

(a) the offence is a serious arrestable offence; and

(b) delay is authorised by a superintendent because consulting with a legal adviser would, in the superintendent's view, result in:
- interference with or harm of evidence or interference with or physical injury to another person;
- the alerting of other suspects;
- the hindrance of the recovery of property; or

(c) the offence is one of drug trafficking or one where a confiscation order could be made and notification would prevent the proceeds of the crime from being recovered; or

(d) a superintendent believes that delay in interviewing will involve an immediate risk of harm to people or damage to property.

It is very difficult for the police to show that consultation with a legal adviser will result in one of the above outcomes, but you must ensure that there is no lack of professionalism on your part that might lead to one of those consequences being anticipated.

Under Code C, para 6, where a person has been permitted legal advice and the adviser is available (that is, s/he is at the station, on his/her way or is easily contactable), the adviser must be allowed to be present at the interview. The adviser can only be required to leave the interview if his/her conduct makes it impossible for the investigator to put the questions properly. Advising a client to remain silent or asking the officer to rephrase questions (where that is appropriate) is not a ground for exclusion. Removing a solicitor in these circumstances, as the Code states, is a serious step and requires a senior officer's authority. Most officers, when dealing with professionally behaved solicitors and representatives, will accept that they have a job to do, as you will usually accept that the police have. Improper behaviour by a legal adviser will include giving a client's responses for him/her and improperly challenging legitimate questioning techniques.

If it suggested that you are not able to see the client for one of the reasons listed here, you should ask what the reason is and invite the police to justify this. Record the reason given and ask for the custody record to show this. Also, note the identity of the officers concerned: you may also need to make representations to the custody officer or the superintendent as to the position.

It occasionally happens that you are asked to take something to or from the client in police custody or to convey a message from your client. You should be very circumspect about even the most innocent matters and, if in doubt, refuse.

28 When can a client be refused access to a solicitor?

29 When can an interview take place without a solicitor?

30 When can a solicitor be removed from an interview?

1.4.5 HOW CAN YOU ASSERT YOUR ROLE AT INTERVIEW?

Before the interview, you will have consulted with the officers, and may have already indicated what is going to happen in the interview, namely, whether your client is going to answer questions or not.

At the outset of the interview, you should make an opening statement on the tape explaining your role and, if it is the case that you are advising your client to make no comment, the reason for this. If your client is going to answer questions, you should also state the circumstances in which you will intervene in the questioning, which are explained below. You should be firm and clear as to your role, but not aggressive or diverted from your purpose. Remember that the overarching role of the representative at the police station is to advance and protect the legal rights of the client.

In your consultation with the interviewing officer, you will already have been able to establish your role as protecting the rights of your client by probing the police case. In making an opening statement, you are again able to assert your role. The statement of what will happen and when you will intervene is a statement that the police must allow to be made and will be recorded – this will stamp your authority on the interview. It is also an opportunity to set the tone and pace to a certain extent.

1.4.6 CAN YOU OBJECT TO QUESTIONING?

You can intervene during the interview and object to improper questioning. Questioning may be improper either in its content and subject matter or in its style and manner.

Your portfolio should show that you have monitored questioning and challenged improper behaviour on two occasions.

Guidelines as to what might constitute improper questioning

Questions should not be asked about undisclosed information.

If new information, including documents, witness statements or statements from potential co-accuseds, is produced or referred to for the first time in the interview, you are entitled to intervene. You may ask for time to discuss these matters with your client in private, prior to his/her answering questions concerning the new matters.

Questions should be capable of being properly answered

For this reason, multiple, unclear or hypothetical questions should not be asked. If they are asked, you are entitled to intervene to ask for clarification, rewording or withdrawal of any such questions.

In particular, if multiple questions (a string of questions asked together, which require separate answers) are posed, you can ask that they be put one question at a time.

Questions can be unclear and give rise to intentional or unintentional misunderstandings very easily, particularly over the identification of individuals and timings. A simple example is where a number of people are being described as involved in an incident. For example, '... and did he hit him?' might require clarification of which person was which. Similarly, the use of the word 'then' can be intended to mean at that time, or next.

The use of slang or jargon by either a police officer or the interviewee may need clarification.

Hypothetical questions, which usually invite the client to speculate on a course of action as being likely or not, should be discouraged.

Questions should not be asked in an oppressive or bullying manner

This can be difficult to judge: firm questioning is proper, and questions can be repeated until the client gives a full enough answer or states that s/he will not answer. Discrepancies can be put to the client. What is not permitted, and where you should intervene, is where the questioning contravenes section 76 of PACE 1984.

A breach of section 76(2) means that any confession obtained thereby would be held inadmissible by a court if the prosecution sought to rely on it. It is for the prosecution to prove (beyond reasonable doubt) that any confession was not obtained by oppression of the person who made it, or in consequence of anything said or done which was likely, in the circumstances existing at the time, to render unreliable any confession so made.

See the case of *R v Paris and Others* (1992) 97 Cr App R 99 where, despite the presence of a solicitor, the police conducted what was described as a hectoring and bullying interview, in which the defendant made 300 denials of the offence of which he was suspected. On appeal, this was held to infringe section 76 of PACE 1984, and that the resulting confession should not have been admitted at trial.

Section 76(2) of PACE 1984 provides as follows:

> If in any proceedings where the prosecution proposes to give in evidence a confession made by an accused person, it is represented to the court that the confession was or may have been obtained –
>
> (a) by oppression of the person who made it; or
>
> (b) in consequence of anything said or done which was likely, in the circumstances existing at the time, to render unreliable any confession which might be made by him in consequence thereof,
>
> the court shall not allow the confession to be given in evidence against him except insofar as the prosecution proves to the court beyond reasonable doubt that the confession (notwithstanding that it may be true) was not obtained as aforesaid.

Your role at the interview is to prevent a breach of section 76 or to complain if the section is breached, but it is important at this stage to recognise the possible consequences for the police if improper conduct or, under subsection (b), actions or words leading to unreliable confessions, take place. The consequence that a resulting confession may not be admitted in evidence is usually sufficient disincentive for the police to discontinue such an approach.

If the police apply pressure or offer inducements (such as early release on bail, dropping of more serious charges) in return for a confession, it is likely that this would constitute a breach of section 76, which would render the confession inadmissible.

1.4.7 WHAT CAN YOU DO IF THE OFFICER CONTINUES?

If you have asked the officer to rephrase a question which you consider to be improper, or to desist from an approach which you think contravenes PACE 1984, and the officer persists, you should intervene in a clear and firm manner, indicating the reason and that you are now advising your client to answer no further questions. This intervention will be recorded on the tape and should be clearly stated.

1.4.8 CAN YOUR CLIENT DISREGARD YOUR ADVICE?

As with all matters in which you deal with clients, you are giving them advice which they are at liberty to accept or reject: the choice is ultimately theirs.

When you advise the client before interview, you will have advised him/her on the advantages and disadvantages of making a reply or no-reply (no comment) interview. After explaining these, you will decide together what strategy to adopt and practise it (see 1.3 above). Even if your advice is that one course of action is clearly better than another for the client (eg, in situations where your advice is that a no comment interview will not result in adverse inferences), the client may wish to disregard that advice. You should make a careful record of both your advice and the client's decision, but then your role is still to support your client in the course adopted, and to protect and advance his/her legal rights. Similarly, in the situation envisaged in the paragraph opposite, if, because of a police officer's conduct, you are advising the client to stop answering questions, the client is still at liberty to disregard your advice. It is always advisable, however, if you wish to change or reinforce your advice, to ask for the interview to be stopped so that you can advise your client in private.

If the client is becoming flustered as a result of the interview or as a result of the disorientating effect of being in custody, it may be advisable to slow the interview down and calm the client by an intervention to offer legal advice.

1.4.9 CAN YOUR ADVICE CHANGE DURING THE INTERVIEW?

If you have initially advised your client to answer questions, and the interviewing technique or content falls into one of the categories described in the guidelines above, you can and should, after initially voicing a complaint to the officer, then indicate that you wish to advise your client further in private, or directly indicate as described above that you are now advising your client to cease answering questions.

1.4.10 WHEN SHOULD YOUR CLIENT ANSWER QUESTIONS?

Your client should answer questions:

(a) when s/he has a defence that is clear and supportable, and the client is able to deal with the questioning; or

(b) when s/he wishes to make a full confession.

Credit for a confession

If your client wishes to confess and your advice is to accept guilt, it can be an important point for mitigation that this was accepted at the earliest opportunity.

Formal credit (ie, a reduction of the sentence) for an early guilty plea relates primarily to entering the plea at the earliest stage of the court proceedings. However, the client is entitled to know what the evidence against him/her is, before making a decision. This may be obvious to the client if arrested in the course of an offence, but it may still be necessary to assess the level of offence indicated by the evidence.

When it is safe/unsafe for your client not to answer questions

You should always consider what is the safest procedure for the client. It is safe not to answer questions when there is little or no risk of an adverse inference being drawn, eg, where the information disclosed by the police to you and the client is insufficient to warrant a response, or where the client's physical, mental or emotional state is such that it would be unreasonable to expect answers.

It should, of course, be remembered that adverse inferences (see 1.4.12 below) only arise from a failure to disclose a matter later relied on at trial, and not from silence itself, or from a failure to account under sections 36 and 37 of the CJPOA 1994.

It is unsafe to answer questions, despite the risk of adverse inferences (see 1.4.12 below), if the client is not able to answer coherently, is easily suggestible or confused, is liable to be misled or has no satisfactory response.

Insufficient disclosure will normally minimise the risk of adverse inference: the court will not think it reasonable to fail to disclose a matter later relied on at trial if the exact allegation, evidence or nature of the case was not clear.

1.4.11 WHEN SHOULD YOUR CLIENT REFUSE TO ANSWER?

Your client should refuse to answer questions when your advice is not to answer because:

(a) there has been insufficient disclosure; or

(b) your view is that the client is unable to deal with an interview,

only after you have given advice as to the possible consequences of failure to answer.

1.4.12 WHAT ARE THE CONSEQUENCES OF FAILURE TO ANSWER?

The circumstances which allow for adverse inferences

Under the CJPOA 1994, inferences (eg, that the client had something to hide or had no sufficient answer) may be drawn against a defendant at trial if s/he fails to disclose some matter at interview that s/he later relies on at trial. This can happen only if it was reasonable to expect the information to be given. So, if, eg, the client is not aware of the time the offence is alleged to have been committed, it would not be reasonable to expect disclosure of an alibi for that time.

Adverse inferences can also be drawn against a defendant (provided that s/he has been given a special warning of the consequences of failing to answer) who:

(a) fails, when asked upon arrest, to account for the presence of an object, substance or mark: section 36 of the CJPOA 1994;

(b) fails, when asked upon arrest, to account for his/her presence at a particular place: section 37 of the CJPOA 1994.

The following should also be noted:

(a) a conviction, or indeed a decision that there is a case to answer at trial, cannot be on the basis only of an inference from silence: there must be other evidence;

(b) legal advice to remain silent is not of itself sufficient to prevent an inference arising;

(c) a client may have to waive confidentiality and legal professional privilege so that a solicitor may give evidence as to the reason for the advice, in support of an argument that an adverse inference should not be drawn.

R v Condron [1997] 1 Cr App R 185.

Possible disclosure of the reason for silence

Where a client is in danger of an adverse inference being drawn, it may be necessary not only to disclose that s/he was advised to remain silent, but also to disclose the reasons for that advice. In order to explain the position, the client and/or legal adviser may be required to give evidence on that matter. As stated above, for the legal adviser to do so requires the client to waive legal professional privilege and the duty of confidentiality, which would otherwise prevent disclosure in court of communications between client and adviser.

1.4.13 WHAT SHOULD YOU DO IF YOUR CLIENT NEEDS ADVICE DURING THE INTERVIEW?

Before the interview starts, explain to your client how s/he can ask you for advice, or how you will indicate that you consider advice to be necessary. For example, to the client who begins to answer during a no-reply interview, you might say: 'My advice to you has been to answer no comment. Do you wish for the interview to be suspended so that I can give you further advice?' It is advisable to practise both your intervention and your client's ability to seek advice, which might be done by stating: 'I would like further advice from my adviser.'

Even when you are sure that your client has made a decision on your advice as to the course to follow and is clear as to the process, anxiety or confusion can sometimes lead to the client apparently changing course. It may be that the client has in fact rationally reconsidered and changed his/her mind, but this is unlikely, given the situation. If the client does want to re-assess the situation, and change from a no-reply interview to a reply interview, this should be done calmly, without pressure and after considered legal advice. The client will need to be alerted and reassured either by a statement such as: 'My advice to you has been, and remains, not to answer questions at this time. Do you wish for the interview to be suspended so that you can seek further advice from me?'

Rehearsal before the interview, showing the client how to seek or how to respond to advice, is helpful in alerting the client to the meaning of the comments.

1.4.14 WHEN MIGHT A CLIENT NEED ADVICE DURING AN INTERVIEW?

A client will need advice when s/he diverges from the agreed course, or where the interviewer is using inappropriate techniques, or in any case where s/he is uncertain of the best course to follow.

1.4.15 CAN THE CLIENT CHANGE APPROACH DURING THE INTERVIEW?

The client may wish to change his/her approach during an interview, but this should be done after consideration, not as a result of pressure. Selective silence, answering some but not other questions, can give rise to inferences, and so should not be made. If the client accidentally slips into a response in a no-response interview, s/he should revert back to the agreed method of reply, usually 'no comment', rather than silence, unless after consideration with the adviser the client decides that s/he wishes to reply.

In interview, if the client makes mixed responses – mixing acceptance of some matters (confessions) and denial of others – all matters are admissible (subject to sections 76 and 78 of PACE 1984), so too if the suspect is selectively silent – answering some questions but refusing to answer others. All answers are admissible. It is likely that adverse inferences will be drawn from the refusal to answer.

1.4.16 HOW DO THE POLICE RECORD THE INTERVIEW?

There is a requirement for interviews to be tape recorded. This is done by means of a double taping on unused tapes overlaid with a time signal. Since the introduction of the tape recording of interviews, there has been little cause to challenge what is actually said at interview by clients. How they came to say it may still be a cause of concern (see, eg, under section 76 or section 78 of PACE 1984), and the consequences of what they say or do not say is a complex issue. If you attend with the client at interview, you will have a general recollection of the type of response which s/he made, but it may be that the detail of any answers gains in importance in the light of other information or evidence.

An interview which includes any questioning of a suspect in order to ascertain his/her involvement in an offence should only be carried out (except in cases of emergency) at a designated police station in accordance with the prescribed procedures and taped as described here. If questioning is conducted by a police officer on the way to the police station, this will usually be improper and will not of itself yield admissible material. It may, however, have the effect of making the suspect feel he has already admitted the offence and, therefore, that he might as well repeat his/her admissions at interview. You should, therefore, verify with your client before the taped interview that s/he has not made any 'informal admissions'. If s/he has, these will taint the recorded interview and all damaging matters may be inadmissible.

1.4.17 SHOULD YOU RECORD THE INTERVIEW?

It is important that you take accurate detailed notes of the interview and that you ask for a copy of the interview tape or make your own recording.

If you do not attend at interview, you may have little appreciation of what was said, except for:

(a) your client's own recollection;

(b) the balanced summary provided by the police under the advance disclosure rules, which, however, is often inaccurate, so tapes should be sought.

Your portfolio should show that you have attended with clients at reply and no-reply interviews, and have produced detailed notes.

1.4.18 DO YOU OR YOUR CLIENT HAVE ACCESS TO THE TAPE RECORDING OF THE INTERVIEW?

Some police stations may be able to provide facilities for fast copying of tapes, but this seems to be done rarely. Unless there is a specific reason why this will prejudice their investigations, the police should allow you to make your own audio recording if you wish, using your own equipment, recognising that time taken in copying and supplying tapes can be a cause of significant delay. However, it may, of course, not be in your client's interests to hasten proceedings, nor may you wish to be involved in the procedure and expense of doing the taping yourself.

Whichever process is adopted, unless you were present at interview *and* it is a simple case where the client's wishes and best course is clear, you will normally wish to obtain a copy of and examine the tape before the client is advised on plea. The importance of responses in interview may have a different sense once other evidence is available.

1.4.19 CAN YOUR CLIENT BE INTERVIEWED AGAIN?

Once the police have sufficient evidence to charge your client, s/he must be charged and all interviewing must stop. However, your client may be interviewed again if:

(a) s/he is released without charge; or

(b) kept in custody (within the detention time limits: see 1.3.34 above) without charge; or

(c) re-arrested on a new matter.

1.4.20 WHAT ABOUT SPECIALLY VULNERABLE CLIENTS?

See 1.5 below:

(a) a juvenile or mentally disordered suspect should not be interviewed in the absence of an appropriate adult;

(b) a person who is deaf or who has an insufficient command of English should not be interviewed without an interpreter being present.

You have a role in respect of both of these situations.

1.4.21 PSYCHOLOGICAL FACTORS

Whether the client is particularly vulnerable or not, arrest, custody and interrogation can have profound effects. People can become disorientated, highly distressed and very susceptible to suggestion. Even the stress of being confined, having limited access to washing or toilet facilities, exercise, rest or refreshments can induce panic to a lesser or greater degree. This can result in the suspect being at a low ebb in a situation when s/he needs his/her wits about him/her. It can also result in inappropriate behaviour to the police, in recognising the need to concentrate or to treat the matter seriously, or in recognising your role and allowing you to perform it. In some cases, the client may become aggressive, not only to the police but also to you. This can be very difficult for a representative to deal with, but a professional approach, along with a recognition that these factors are precisely why the need for legal help at such a time is so essential, will usually enable the representative to continue. Never put yourself at risk.

1.4.22 WHAT SHOULD YOU DO AFTER INTERVIEW?

Before leaving the police station:

(a) you should confirm whether your client is going to be charged, and with what offence (this may happen in any event at the end of the interview);

(b) you may have decided with your client to make a defence statement after charge. The advantage of making a defence statement is that no questions can be asked, and it may minimise the risk of an adverse inference arising;

(c) your client may have decided to make other disclosure after charge;

(d) you should determine the police's intention as to any procedures (identification (see 1.6 below), searches, taking of samples, etc) that are going to take place after the interview, and explain them to your client. Only identification procedures are likely to involve your attendance;

(e) you must establish whether there is to be an objection to bail and, where appropriate, make representations on bail conditions or denial of bail. Explain the implications of bail conditions to your client and verify the date of attendance at court or of return to the police station;

(f) if your client is to be taken in custody to court, take instructions and make arrangements for representation;

(g) if you have not already done so, check the custody record;

(h) make any necessary arrangements with your client about attending at your office (if on bail) for further instructions;

(i) make a full and careful note of all information, and of any matters to be followed up;

(j) have a final consultation with your client to confirm or explain next steps.

After charge, your client is permitted and may be well advised to make a statement setting out his/her defence. This is a statement on charge. The advantages of making such a statement are that:

- no further questions can be asked; and
- the risk of adverse inferences being drawn is minimised.

The statement should be prepared in writing with your advice and read out by your client.

The custody record should record all incidents of detention, including whether legal advice was requested or refused. Even where matters are recorded on the custody record, you should make your own notes of requests made and information sought and supplied (or refused). You need to have your own record, and there may be matters where you wish to challenge the custody record. If this is obvious at the time, or if you have a matter of complaint, you should always raise the matter and request that the custody record be noted with your point. Record the name, number and rank of the officer with whom you deal. Be sure also to record the timing of incidents (important for the reasons mentioned above, and in respect of legal aid claims).

REPRESENTING VULNERABLE CLIENTS

RANGE

Achievement must cover all the following contexts.

Vulnerability

Inability to understand English, physical disability or injury, mental disability, age.

Agencies

Police surgeon, independent surgeon, interpreter, social worker.

EVIDENCE

You will need to produce the specific pieces of performance evidence listed below. In addition, you will need to demonstrate that you have achieved the objectives specified at the beginning of this unit. You may do this by producing further pieces of evidence from real and simulated performance, by answering questions posed by your assessor or by passing a written examination.

You will need to provide evidence of:

1 having appraised client and appropriate adult of their respective roles in writing or verbally in two cases;

2 having advised a client and preserved client confidentiality in the presence of an appropriate adult.

CRITERIA

You will demonstrate achievement if:

(a) the nature of the client's vulnerability is accurately assessed;

(b) where there is doubt regarding a client's vulnerability, expert advice is sought;

(c) client's vulnerabilities are communicated to officers and efforts made to ensure that the client is not disadvantaged;

(d) persons are advised of their role and the need for impartiality and confidentiality;

(e) clients are advised of the role of any assisting person and the need for confidentiality.

1.5.1 INTRODUCTION

This activity is concerned with the recognition of, identification of and response to vulnerable clients. You should also refer to 1.1, 1.3 and 1.4 above, as those sections apply to such clients. You may recognise that certain clients are particularly vulnerable or have special needs: in those circumstances, you may have to seek further assistance for them. Some of these needs are specifically recognised by the law; in other circumstances you may need to negotiate special help for a client.

List the particular types of vulnerable clients that you might be involved in assisting. What special needs might be apparent at this stage? How do you think these needs can be addressed?

1.5.2 WHAT IS MEANT BY A 'VULNERABLE CLIENT'?

Those who are not yet 17 are juveniles for the purposes of police station procedures. The adult court is for those of 18 and over. Children under 10 have no criminal responsibility.

A vulnerable client is any client whose age, condition or disability requires that special provision be made for him/her in the legal process. Two categories – young people and people who are mentally ill or mentally handicapped – are especially recognised in law and are treated in a special way throughout the legal process, including, in certain situations, the recognition or apportionment of criminal responsibility. Others are recognised as requiring particular consideration during the investigation and court process owing to difficulties of understanding. Juveniles (those aged under 17) and the mentally ill are again included here, as are those who cannot freely communicate or understand, either because of lack of hearing or lack of command of the language.

As PACE 1984 requires reading and writing to be carried out by the suspect as a matter of practice, assistance is also usually sought for illiterate suspects.

Other categories are recognised as requiring consideration because of often temporary and sometimes self-induced problems, such as intoxication through drink or drugs, or illness which may affect the client's ability to deal with criminal processes, which also pose a risk to their safety. Your concern, therefore, is initially and primarily for the legal consequences of the vulnerability, but inevitably there will be occasions that your concern will be affected by humanitarian considerations. It is worth considering in this context your own strategies for dealing with advising clients who – guilty or not guilty – have particular problems in dealing with the legal process.

1.5.3 HOW WILL YOU KNOW IF THE CLIENT IS VULNERABLE?

Vulnerability due to age will usually be obvious, but with all clients, especially younger clients (whether in the police station or not), you should ask their age.

Vulnerabilities due to lack of ability to communicate will usually very soon be apparent. These can arise where there is a language difficulty between you and the client, and/or when there is a language difference between the police officer and your client, and/or you or the police officer and any appropriate adult. Furthermore, you should remember that those whose command of English is perfectly suitable for normal situations, may find that the precision sometimes needed for consultation with a legal adviser or in police interview (or later in court), or the stress of the situation, may result in language difficulties that are not normally present. It is also often the case that those whose hearing or lip reading skills are sufficient for normal purposes need help in the peculiar circumstances of a police interview.

The most difficult situations of all to assess arise concerning clients who have a mental illness or a mental disability. Extreme cases will be obvious, but it can be difficult to differentiate between someone who is ordinarily distressed or nervous, someone intoxicated by drink or drugs, someone who is not particularly intelligent, someone who is avoiding facing reality, and someone who has a psychological or psychiatric problem. If you are in doubt, you should seek advice.

1.5.4 WHERE CAN YOU SEEK ADVICE?

If necessary, you should seek advice from a police doctor. If the client is known to the social, health or probation services, they may be able to advise and, indeed, the custody officer may share your concern. Most custody officers will be helpful in this regard: they do not want to have an arrestee's health problems rebound on them, nor do they wish it to be said that they disregarded the needs of vulnerable groups. Having said this, however, it is your responsibility to protect the client's interests and you cannot divest yourself of that responsibility to the custody officer. It may be only in conversation with your client that it becomes apparent that there is a difficulty.

Very occasionally, in refugee or travelling communities, you may be dealing with a client who is or claims to be uncertain as to his/her age. Very often, they may have other vulnerabilities as well, but if in doubt seek advice. As far as PACE 1984 is concerned, a person who appears to be under 17 should be treated as a juvenile (Code C, para 1.5) until there is clear proof to the contrary.

1.5.5 APPROPRIATE ADULTS

There are certain situations where the law (in PACE 1984) provides that an 'appropriate adult' should be involved where a suspect is to be interviewed by the police. These are in relation to:

(a) the mentally ill client;

(b) the juvenile client.

1.5.6 WHO IS AN APPROPRIATE ADULT?

In the case of a person who is mentally disordered or mentally handicapped, the 'appropriate adult' means:

(a) a relative, guardian or some other person responsible for his/her care or custody;

(b) someone who has experience of dealing with mentally disordered or mentally handicapped people, but who is not a police officer or employed by the police; or

(c) failing either of the above, some other responsible adult aged 18 or over who is not a police officer or employed by the police.

Persons who are victims, witnesses or suspects in the offence should not be appropriate adults.

An appropriate adult in the case of a person who is or appears to be a juvenile is:

(a) his/her parent or guardian (or, if s/he is in care, a representative of the care authority or voluntary organisation);

(b) a social worker;

(c) failing either of the above, another responsible adult aged 18 or over who is not a police officer or employed by the police.

If the person is under a supervision order (ie, a court order on a juvenile), reasonable steps must be taken by the police to notify the supervising officer (PACE 1984, Code C, para 3.8).

A lay visitor or solicitor attending the police station should not act as responsible adult (Code C, para 1.7).

Lay visitors are volunteers who undertake duties in relation to police station procedure.

1.5.7 WHAT IS THE ROLE OF THE APPROPRIATE ADULT AT THE POLICE STATION?

The role of the appropriate adult is to enhance communication between the police and the suspect and between the suspect and yourself, and to aid the suspect's understanding of the procedures in the police station and of his/her position. It is not to speak for the client, nor to side with the client or with the police. The role of appropriate adult may be particularly difficult where the adult is actually responsible for the client, a parent being the most obvious and difficult example.

Parents may be angry, humiliated or culpable when attending with their offspring.

Although the adult may advise the suspect, that advice might not always be in the best interests of the suspect. It is your role to protect the client's interests, and the adult's role is to help the suspect understand the advice. The adult should be briefed by the police about his/her role, but may have been inadequately briefed or have misunderstood the situation: you must ensure that the appropriate adult is clear about his/her role.

1.5.8 DEALING WITH THE APPROPRIATE ADULT

When your client is to be assisted by an appropriate adult, you should:

(a) assess the appropriate adult's suitability;
(b) gauge his/her understanding;
(c) brief the adult on his/her role;
(d) ensure the adult understands the confidentiality of the discussion.

Briefing appropriate adults on their role

You should brief the appropriate adult yourself as to his/her role, after checking what s/he has been told by the police. You should also seek to gauge the adult's suitability for the role. This will be affected by his/her ability to relate to the role you describe, but may also be affected by their relationship to the suspect. The adult may very well have very intense or confused feelings about the plight of the suspect, feeling responsible for, afraid for, protective of or angry towards the suspect, or be frightened about his/her own position, perhaps because, rightly or wrongly, the adult feels involved and complicit in the offence.

Even social workers as appropriate adults may not be completely independent if they feel a personal responsibility for a child or a mentally ill person. They may feel let down by their charge, or that they themselves have let the vulnerable person down. These feelings must be put to one side if the adult is going to assist effectively in the process. Social workers, despite experience in their field, may not be particularly experienced in the police station context: do not assume that they are familiar with procedures and their role. You should also ascertain the proposed appropriate adult's knowledge and understanding of any of the suspect's difficulties and of the suspect's contact with the police. (You should also inquire tactfully from the adult as to the adult's own contacts with the police, which may indicate his/her own awareness of and attitude to the police.) It is also possible that the adult may need an interpreter because of deafness or language difficulties.

An estranged parent whom the juvenile does not wish to communicate with is unsuitable as an appropriate adult.

Your portfolio should show that you have appraised the client and the appropriate adult of their roles in writing or verbally in two cases.

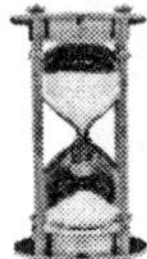

31 What is the role of the appropriate adult?

Confidentiality

You should explain very carefully the confidentiality principle: that things said in the presence of the appropriate adult, to and by the client, are confidential.

Irrespective of whether the appropriate adult is a member of the suspect's family or a professional, such as a social worker, s/he may not understand his/her role or the need for confidentiality. Particularly, but not exclusively, when the attending adult is the suspect's parent, s/he may feel that disclosure of information, including the client's instructions to the police, would be beneficial, that it would be for the child's own good, and would foster beneficial treatment from the police. Sometimes that view will be correct. Often it is not. The appropriate adult's role is to aid communication and understanding, to monitor fair procedures in the police station, and to advise the vulnerable person. Your role is to protect and advance the vulnerable person's legal interests, which includes advising on the issue of confidentiality. If you determine that the appropriate adult does not understand and accept that the role is governed by the principle of confidentiality, you should advise the adult that you will speak alone to the client and that you will, if your client agrees, ask the adult to rejoin the consultation between you and the client.

Although this point is often difficult to grasp, even for those genuinely concerned about the welfare of the individual, involving the appropriate adult in a combined defence of the client, with both playing their separate roles, can often be effectively achieved. However, your role in any subsequent interview with the police may be further complicated when an appropriate adult is involved, as you will have to monitor not only the client's behaviour and responses but also the appropriate adult's behaviour and responses to ensure that s/he is able to properly fulfil the role.

Often, of course, the appropriate adult will have been called to the police station first and have requested legal advice. If that is the case, the need for legal advice and the difference of your roles will be easier to explain.

Your role is to protect the interests of the client, which may include advising a no-reply interview or advising as to liability or procedure. An adult should understand that s/he must not inform the police or anyone else of that advice, nor of any confession made or other information divulged by the client, whether to the police or in conversation with you.

Your portfolio should show evidence of having advised a client and preserved confidentiality in the presence of an appropriate adult.

The appropriate adult checklist

- Is the adult capable of understanding and suitable in terms of their relationship with your client?
- Does the adult understand his/her role?
- What briefing has been given by police?
- Have you briefed the adult?
- Have you explained confidentiality?

1.5.9 WHAT SHOULD YOU TELL THE CLIENT?

You should carefully explain:

(a) the difference between your role and that of the appropriate adult;

(b) the situation as to confidentiality;

(c) that the client is entitled to consult in private with the solicitor if the client wishes (PACE 1984, Code C, para 1.EE).

The client can always consult privately with the appropriate adult (PACE 1984, Code C, para 3.12).

Though you will have explained this to the proposed appropriate adult, you must also explain very carefully to the client both your differing roles and the requirement of confidentiality. Your client should be aware that s/he may consult with you or the appropriate adult in the absence of the other and in the absence of the police. You should also make it clear to the client that, just as you are bound by the rules of confidentiality, so too is the appropriate adult.

As mentioned above at 1.5.8 (confidentiality), in your consultation with the adult you will have been able to assess their familiarity with and understanding of the role of an appropriate adult. If you have any cause for concern about the adult's acceptance of the fact that what passes between the client, you and the adult is entirely confidential, you should make this clear to the client and advise both parties that you will initially take instructions from the client privately as to whether the adult should be present throughout the rest of the consultation.

1.5.10 WHAT OTHER ASSISTING PERSON MIGHT BE NEEDED?

If your client *or* the appropriate adult has difficulty in understanding English, wishes to have an interpreter, appears to be deaf, or if there is any doubt about either party's ability to hear or speak to the extent that it prevents the police officer from communicating with the client satisfactorily about his/her rights, an interpreter should be called.

Someone who can converse in English under normal circumstances may still need an interpreter when under stress or when dealing with technical or detailed matters.

Remember the need to communicate between you and the client, between the client and the police, and, if an appropriate adult is required, between you, the client, the adult and the police.

An interpreter must be able to translate between the necessary languages or to sign for deaf suspects (see below).

1.5.11 ROLE OF THE INTERPRETER

An appropriate adult must not also be the interpreter involved. This is because the roles are different.

The interpreter must be impartial and accurate.

Difficulties may arise with interpreters in a variety of ways. If they are called by the police, they may identify with the police, and seek to bring that to bear in the consultation or interview. Others may identify with the suspect and have an antipathy towards the police, or indeed towards legal advisers. To defend or judge the suspect is inappropriate, as is the tendency of some interpreters to attempt to mediate between the suspect and an appropriate adult where one is also involved.

If you need the services of an interpreter between you and client, consider whether there is a need to appoint your own interpreter rather than use one appointed by the police. In any event, the interpreter should be informed or reminded as to the need for confidentiality.

Occasionally, interpreters may try to defend or explain the suspect's behaviour from a cultural perspective, or alternatively blame the suspect for behaving contrary to his/her community's standards. Either stance is inappropriate and unhelpful on the part of an interpreter, and this must be firmly and tactfully made clear.

1.5.12 THE YOUNG CLIENT

Where your client is (or appears to be) a juvenile, s/he should not be interviewed or asked to give or sign a statement without the presence of an appropriate adult, unless there is an urgent need for an interview.

It will not usually be necessary for you to contact an appropriate adult for a juvenile, as this will be done by the police, but you may need to advise on the availability of an appropriate adult where the client is known to you. You will also need to liaise with the person to ensure that s/he understands the role of the appropriate adult. Occasionally, an adult may attend who is not suitable, eg, where the parent attends, and the juvenile is in real fear of or estranged from that adult. You have a role in considering the suitability of the appropriate adult.

PACE 1984, Code C, Annex C provides that, when an interview is to take place in a police station or other authorised place of detention, vulnerable suspects can be interviewed or interviewed without an appropriate adult, if, and only if, an officer of the rank of superintendent or above considers that delay will lead to interference with or harm to evidence or other people, the alerting or other suspects, or hinder the recovery of property,

The appropriate adult's role is to assist communication. If the juvenile is fearful (rather than just worried about being in trouble), communication will not be enhanced.

1.5.13 THE MENTALLY ILL CLIENT

If you know or suspect that your client is mentally disordered, or has a mental disability that will inhibit your ability to take instructions and more importantly the client's ability to deal with the police interview, you should alert the custody officer, who has a responsibility to arrange for the attendance of an appropriate adult to assist the client. (On who can be an appropriate adult, see 1.5.6 above.)

With such clients, the attendance of an appropriate adult does not relieve you of your responsibility. In fact you will have an additional responsibility to ensure that the appropriate adult is aware of and fulfils his/her role.

Such a person should not be interviewed or asked to sign or make a statement in the absence of an appropriate adult, unless there is need for an

PACE 1984, Code C, para 1.4 provides that, if an officer has any suspicion, or is told in good faith, that a person of any age may be mentally disordered, mentally handicapped or mentally incapable of understanding the significance of questions put to him/her or his/her replies, then that person shall be treated as mentally disordered or mentally handicapped.

urgent interview to safeguard people or evidence (Code C, para 11.1) or where Annex C applies (where an officer of rank of superintendent or above certifies that such a consequence may arise).

It is sometimes difficult to differentiate between clients who are mentally disordered or handicapped and those who are confused, panicking, shocked or suffering from the effects of drugs or alcohol. The approach taken by PACE 1984, which will guide the police, is the approach you should follow: if you have a concern, assume that there may be a problem, and seek help. This may, of course, necessitate the use of some tact when explaining to your client why you are seeking the attendance of another person, but very often clients will readily inform you where they have problems or are already receiving treatment for psychological or psychiatric problems, or problems associated with stress, depression, anxiety or substance abuse. It should be noted, however, that a client's description of the nature or causes of the problem, or of its methods of treatment, might not always be accurate.

As always, your file should record your concerns, and any information provided to or arrangements made for the attendance of an appropriate adult.

1.5.14 THE CLIENT WHOSE ENGLISH IS LIMITED

See PACE 1984, Code C, para 11.1 and Annex C.

Except where there is reason to interview a vulnerable suspect urgently (as at 1.5.12 above), a client who:

(a) has difficulty in understanding English;

(b) does not speak the same language as the interviewing officer;

(c) wishes an interpreter to be present,

should not be interviewed in the absence of an interpreter. Police are advised as to how to obtain the services of interpreters, but you have a role in satisfying yourself that the interpreter can act appropriately and arranging for other assistance if s/he does not.

The role of the interpreter is to interpret, not to advise, protect or expand on or sift information. Translating in the important and stressful arena of the police station, either between you and the client or between you, the client and the police officer, is a particularly challenging role (see 1.5.11 above).

You must be aware that certain concepts do not translate exactly: it is important that the exact ambit of your questions and the client's answers is clear, and that the effect of any advice you give through an interpreter is also clear. It is difficult to ensure this, but you must be ready to pick up clues of misunderstandings in tone of voice, manner of speech and body language. In particular, you should immediately stop any conversations that appear to be going on between interpreter and client between question and answer. You should inform the interpreter that if s/he realises that there is a misunderstanding, then the interpreter should tell you and you will clarify it by further questions.

1.5.15 THE CLIENT WHO IS ILL OR INJURED

It may be that your client is exhibiting symptoms of illness: these may be clear to you as a lay person, or something may vaguely give you cause for concern. You may need to be aware of these matters for a variety or combination of reasons:

(a) Does the client need urgent medical treatment?

If so, you should contact the custody officer, who should arrange for the client to be examined by a police surgeon, or if necessary, admitted to hospital.

(b) Is the client fit to be interviewed?

If not, you should protect the client's interests by bringing this to the attention of the custody officer, and the client should not undergo interview unless and until fit.

(c) Does the condition affect the client's liability for the offence?

If this might be the case, your advice to the client will need to take account of this fact, and you may need to conduct further legal and medical research.

(d) Was the condition/injury caused or contributed to by the offence?

If so, this may be relevant to your assessment of the evidence and your client's liability for the offence.

(e) Was it caused by any part of the arrest/custody procedure?

If so, this may explain your client's behaviour or confirm any allegations about the police's behaviour.

Conditions that affect the client's mental capacity, perception, or ability to control his/her movements may all have a bearing on his/her legal culpability.

32 How might injuries sustained by your client support or undermine a defence of self-defence?

All injuries sustained during the arrest or custody should be assessed very carefully: sometimes they will be caused by your client's behaviour/condition, and in other cases may support allegations made by the client about police misbehaviour. Serious injuries should always be treated appropriately. Even minor matters should be carefully noted, and

(f) Does the client's condition, even if s/he is fit for interview, affect the advice you will give him/her about responding to questions?

It may simply be that the client requires access to their regular medication (eg, an asthma inhaler or hay fever medication), which may be:

(a) among the client's possessions;
(b) obtainable in some circumstances via the police surgeon; or
(c) something you can arrange to have brought to the station from the client's home, after consulting with the police.

It is important, not only for the client's well being and your own peace of mind, but also as part of your role in protecting the client's interests, that you alert the officer and record the matter in your file. The police will not normally be unhelpful in such matters – they have no wish for those in their custody to come to serious harm or injury – but sometimes you may have to be firm where there is a difference of opinion over the genuineness of the complaint. Even the recording of your concern will provide some protection of your client's interests.

Special problems are very often encountered in the drug user suffering from withdrawal symptoms: medical advice might vary depending on the nature of the drug in question.

If the client has injuries, your file should record:

(a) a description of the injury;
(b) the client's explanation of the cause;
(c) whether there were any witnesses to the injury;
(d) whether you asked for the police surgeon;
(e) whether the injury affects the client's fitness to be interviewed;
(f) whether the injury has been recorded on the custody record;
(g) whether you should have, or have already had, the injury photographed.

recorded in your notes and on the custody record. The police are entitled to use reasonable force in dealing with a lawful arrest: what is reasonable may be affected by the client's conduct.

The mental or physical condition of the client may be a reason for advising that the client does not answer questions in interview, and may provide a reason for the court not to draw adverse inferences under the CJPOA 1994 (see 1.4 above).

If the client is suffering from a medical condition relevant to fitness for interview or his/her safe custody, the file should show:

(a) the nature of the condition;

(b) the client's explanation of the effect of the condition, eg, risk of nausea or dizziness or visual disturbance;

(c) name and address of client's doctor;

(d) whether you needed to call the police surgeon;

(e) whether the condition has been recorded on the custody record.

If you or the police officer think the client is unfit to be interviewed by reason of a medical condition or drink/drugs, your file should record:

(a) what your assessment is; and

(b) whether the police surgeon has been called or has attended (there is no obligation to call a surgeon for simple drunkenness, though the detainee should be regularly checked).

Fitness for interview assessment checklist

- Can the client withstand the stress of an interview?
- Has the client got his/her wits about him/her?
- Are the client's perceptions clear?
- Is the client coherent?
- Might the interview inhibit or delay urgent medical attention?

PACE 1984 provides that, in such cases, the custody officer must immediately call the police surgeon (or in urgent cases – for example, where a person does not show signs of sensibility or awareness – must send the person to hospital or call the nearest available medical practitioner) if a person brought to a police station or already detained there:

(a) appears to be suffering from physical illness or a mental disorder; or

(b) is injured; or

(c) fails to respond normally to questions or conversation (other than through drunkenness alone); or

(d) otherwise appears to need medical attention.

This applies even if the person makes no request for medical attention and regardless of whether s/he has already had medical treatment elsewhere (unless brought to the police station direct from hospital).

1.5.16 THE CLIENT WHO IS DEAF

The custody officer should ensure that a deaf person must not be interviewed in the absence of an interpreter, unless s/he so agrees in writing.

This also applies where an appropriate adult who is deaf is called to assist a juvenile, or where the adult has hearing or speaking difficulties.

1.5.17 THE CLIENT WHO IS VISUALLY HANDICAPPED OR UNABLE TO READ

This problem may be associated with others referred to above, but if this is the only vulnerability experienced by your client, special care should be taken in ensuring that all documentation is carefully checked and explained; and in particular, where written consent or signature is required, the client may wish that you sign on his/her behalf.

Though not mentally disordered, an illiterate person is often treated as though he is, and an appropriate adult may thus be involved.

1.5.18 GENERAL

Dealing with vulnerable clients requires care in any situation: in the stress of the police station, particular attention should be given, to ensure not only that the legal protection provided by PACE 1984 is observed, but also that all the people involved understand and can cope with the situation. Your role is to ensure as far as possible that this occurs, where that is consistent with your duty to your client.

The term 'vulnerable client' can be used to apply to all the situations covered in this section, but is primarily used to refer to juveniles, the mentally ill and those who need the services of a translator.

ASSISTING CLIENTS WITH IDENTIFICATION PROCEDURES

RANGE

Achievement must cover the following contexts.

Identification procedures

Identification parades, group identifications, electronic imaging, confrontation.

EVIDENCE

You will need to produce the specific pieces of performance evidence listed below. In addition, you will need to demonstrate that you have achieved the objectives specified at the beginning of this unit. You may do this by producing further pieces of evidence from real and simulated performance, by answering questions posed by your assessor or by passing a written examination.

You will need to provide evidence of:

1 having obtained full information regarding witnesses' descriptions on two occasions;
2 having met with clients to explain their rights in relation to two of the **Identification procedures**;
3 having made full written records of at least one identification parade;
4 having made representations to relevant officers to attempt to ensure that two types of **Identification procedures** are fair.

CRITERIA

You will demonstrate achievement if:

(a) information about witnesses' descriptions of suspects is obtained;
(b) representations are made to ensure that identification procedures are fair;
(c) clients are advised of their right to request an identification parade, and of the advantages and disadvantages of doing so;
(d) clients are advised of the consequences of not agreeing to participate in an identification parade;
(e) clients are advised of the advantages and disadvantages of different identification procedures and of specific procedures chosen;
(f) full written records are made of the identification procedure.

1.6.1 INTRODUCTION

An identification procedure may take place when the identity of the perpetrator of an offence is in doubt. Where the police do not have a suspect in mind, they might show a witness photographs or take them to the site of the incident to determine whether a possible suspect can be found. Where there is a suspect, a number of differing identification procedures can be used to determine whether s/he can be identified by one or more witnesses.

You may be involved in advising a client who is a suspect and wishes or is asked to take part in a procedure by the police. Identification evidence is considered by the courts as being particularly worthy of cautious consideration, because it can be very unreliable. For this reason, and despite its uncertainty, it can appear very cogent. PACE 1984 provides a complex set of provisions for the protection of those undergoing identification procedures, designed also as far as possible to protect the integrity of the evidence.

If the case comes to trial and any identification evidence is used in the trial, the court will be guided by the case of *R v Turnbull* [1977] QB 224. The guidelines *Turnbull* (see opposite) should be considered when assessing the value of possible identifications in order to assess the strength of any case against your client. As we saw at 1.2.6, the police have developed the very useful mnemonic of 'ADVOKATE' to remind interviewers of the point made in *Turnbull,* and you may well recognise these prompts as having been used when you read a witness description.

You should be aware, therefore, that evidence in court will be treated circumspectly. However, it is not sufficient to rely on the prospect of a court ruling evidence inadmissible, or placing little weight on it. Safeguarding the client's position before trial, by ensuring that appropriate procedures are used, and that the safeguards laid down are properly followed, may prevent a case ever coming to court, or ensure that any weaknesses in the evidence of identification are fully understood. By explaining the process to a client and advising him/her appropriately, you will further help the client to deal effectively with the procedure and understand its advantages and disadvantages.

In *Turnbull,* the Court of Appeal commented on the dangers of cases based substantially on identification evidence, that such evidence should be treated with extreme caution and should not be the main evidence upon which a conviction is based without more.

This case also laid down guidelines for juries and magistrates in assessing identification evidence. It stated that they should have regard to a number of points: a mistaken witness can be a convincing one; and a number of witnesses can all be mistaken, and listed the circumstances that should be examined closely: the time length of the observation; the distance from which the observation was made; lighting, whether there was an obstruction; whether the witness knows/had seen the suspect before; whether the witness has any special reason for remembering the accused; the length of time between the original observation and later identification to the police, and so on.

1.6.2 IDENTIFICATION PROCEDURES

The available procedures where the police have a suspect (ie, your client) are as follows:

(a) the identification parade;

(b) video identification;

(c) group identification; and

(d) confrontation.

It is often in a client's interests to undergo an identification procedure, provided that the appropriate safeguards are observed. It is usually in a client's best interests to take part in a parade, and to avoid a confrontation at all costs.

1.6.3 WHEN MIGHT AN IDENTIFICATION PROCEDURE TAKE PLACE?

An identification procedure, in terms of an identification parade, a group identification, a video identification or a confrontation, can take place when the police suspect an individual of an offence, and there is a witness who may be able to identify the suspect. The procedures are all described and controlled by Code D of PACE 1984.

These are alternative forms of identification listed in order of preferability, both in legal terms (a parade should be held unless the suspect refuses, then a group identification, unless impracticable or the suspect refuses, and so on) and in terms of the likely advantage to your client. The identification officer will be in charge of all procedures, and should not be the investigating officer in the case.

1.6.4 THE IDENTIFICATION PARADE

Can the police insist on holding an identity parade?

Your client does not need to participate in an identification parade unless s/he wishes to: the parade can only be held with the consent of the suspect. If the police request a parade and the client refuses, then one of the other forms of identification procedure, which do not require consent, might be held. As these are less advantageous to the client, it may be preferable to consent to the parade. It is usually the case that it is in your client's interest to take part in a parade, and it is certainly not in your client's interests to be subject to one of the other forms of identification procedure, so you should seek to avoid these on your client's behalf.

Can the client insist on taking part?

If the client feels that it would be advantageous, he/she can insist on a parade being held. The police must then arrange one, unless it is impracticable to do so. Impracticability usually arises where it is difficult to arrange suitable other members of the parade: perhaps because the suspect is of unusual circumstances, it is possible, and proper, for you to help to find other people to take part in the parade if you and your client think that a parade would be advantageous.

What does an identification parade consist of?

An identification parade (sometimes called a line-up, which expresses how it is done) is governed by Code D under PACE 1984 and must comply with its provisions.

Procedure for the identification parade

1 Before the parade, the suspect will have the procedures explained to him/her by the police, will be cautioned and will be asked whether s/he has any objection to the arrangements or any participant. If there are reasons for objection, either on the part of you or the suspect, s/he is entitled to have legal advice and to have the objection dealt with, if possible.

If there are grounds for objection, these are noted by you and by the investigation officer, especially if your objection is not dealt with, and these matters should be recorded on the identification record (see below).

2 It must be conducted by an officer of the rank of inspector or above.

3 It must consist of at least eight people, other than the suspect, who must look similar to the suspect in age, height, appearance and position in life. If two suspects are included in the parade, they must both look similar.

No more than two suspects can be included in any parade (Code D, Annex A, para 8) and both must look similar to the suspect in age, height, appearance and position in life.

4 The members of the parade will stand in line and each will be numbered. The identifying witness will be brought in and should be told that the person may or may not be present, but if the witness believes that s/he can identify the person, the witness should indicate him/her by stating the number.

5 If there is more than one witness, they should be brought into the parade area individually, and should not be told whether an identification has been made.

If the procedure is flawed, and results in an identification, that evidence will not normally be admissible at trial, and any conviction based on improper procedure will be quashed. See *R v Quinn* [1995] 1 Cr App R 480.

6 A video or colour photograph must be taken of the parade.

7 The parade may take place in an ordinary room or in one equipped with a one-way screen, but if with a screen, it can only take place when the suspect's solicitor, friend or appropriate adult is present or is recorded on video.

8 Everything in the parade must be in the presence and hearing of the suspect and solicitor, friend or appropriate adult, unless a screen is involved which prevents only the suspect from hearing and observing.

9 The suspect may select his/her own position in the line, and may change position (and should

be told that s/he can change position by the identification officer) between each witness if there is more than one.

10 When a witness enters the parade area, s/he should be told that the person may or may not be there, and that the witness should say so if s/he cannot make a positive identification, but should look at each witness twice before trying to identify anyone.

11 If the witness makes an identification after the end of the parade, the suspect should be informed and consideration given to allowing the witness a second opportunity to make an identification.

12 A suspect must have a reasonable opportunity to have a solicitor or friend present.

13 If photographs or other material have been released to the media, each witness, after his/her participation, should be asked if s/he had seen any such material.

14 At the end of the parade, the suspect should be asked by the officer if s/he has any comments.

15 A colour film or video must be taken and a copy supplied to you or the client within a reasonable time. (If the suspect is not convicted or cautioned, the photographic record should be deleted or destroyed.)

16 A record on the appropriate form must also be made. (This is the document, equivalent to the custody record, upon which all incidents during, and complaints about, the parade must be recorded.)

Many suspects think that there is some magic in their position in the line. There is no evidence that any position is more or less dangerous than any other. More important is the conduct of the suspect and the fact that he should be as relaxed as possible.

Any objections should be recorded at this stage.

Can the members of the parade be asked to move, speak or adopt a particular stance?

This can be done if the witness requests it, provided that the officer first asks the witness to see if an identification can be made on appearance only. If the request is to hear the members speak, the officer should remind the witness that the members have been chosen on the basis of appearance only, but then the request may be complied with.

If your client is asked to speak, you should point out that all members of the parade should speak.

1.6.5 GROUP IDENTIFICATION

What is a group identification?

This procedure consists of the police taking the witness to a public place where there can be expected to be a number of people. The witness is then located in a suitable viewing position and asked to survey the people present from a suitable vantage point. Your client (the suspect) will be among the public. This can be done without the client's consent, which means that it can be carried out without notice, without the presence of a solicitor/solicitor's representative, and without the client being aware. It also means that the procedure and the certainty or otherwise of the identification is not recorded by an independent party.

The location is a matter for the identification officer, but you or your client can make representations about it. Other people should be passing by or waiting informally, as in a bus queue, shopping centre or so on.

If the client does not consent, and the identification is done covertly, then of course it will be at a place which the suspect is known to frequent and where other people are present.

The number, race, age, sex, appearance and dress of the other people in the group should be considered by the identification officer, and the circumstances should be considered so that the identification procedure is fair, but inevitably such a process is far less satisfactory and safe for your client.

Although Code D and Annex E suggest that the group identification replicates as far as possible the circumstances to safeguard the parade, this is only true, however, when the client consents and co-operates with the procedure, so that his/her and your views and advice can be taken into account.

When can it be held?

A group identification can be held when the suspect refuses to take part in an identification parade, or agrees and fails to attend, or where a parade is impracticable (Code D, para 2.6). It can take place with your client's consent (and thus in circumstances when you can assist and minimise the dangers) or covertly.

It can also take place where the investigating officer thinks that it would be more satisfactory than a parade, perhaps because a witness is in fear of someone involved in the matter (Code D, para 2.7).

The suspect should be asked for his/her consent (which, if given, means that you can then be involved), but if s/he refuses the procedure can go on unless impracticable. Annex E covers this procedure and lays down detailed rules to cover consent and absence of consent, moving and stationary procedures. The most important points are mentioned below.

If the identification is with the consent of your client

The following need to be borne in mind:

(a) you will usually be able to present (Annex E, para 13) and you and any attending appropriate adult can be concealed from the rest of the group;

(b) the officer must not indicate whether a previous witness has made an identification;
(c) you should hear anything said by the witness;
(d) the witness should not see the suspect, other members of the group or other witnesses before the identification;
(e) witnesses should be brought one at a time;
(f) group identifications should only take place in police stations if necessary for reasons of safety, etc.

If the procedure is without the consent of the suspect

In this situation, although, according to para 33 of Annex E, the police should as far as possible follow the same procedures, this will not always be applicable and, of course:

(a) the suspect will have no right to have a solicitor or other assisting person present;
(b) any number of suspects can be identified at one time.

In all cases

At the end of the procedure, the officer should ask the suspect if s/he has any comments and inform him/her of any identifications made.

A video or colour film should be taken of the general scene after the identification.

1.6.6 VIDEO IDENTIFICATION

What is it?

A video identification is like an identification parade, but is on video, so that there are shots of each member of the parade compiled on a tape. At least eight people similar to the suspect should be included and filmed doing a similar activity. If two suspects of similar appearance are to be included, the video should include at least 12 others.

The suspect and solicitor must be given a reasonable opportunity to see the film before it is shown. If there are grounds for objection, steps should be taken as far as possible to remove them.

You should object if the other people appearing in the video are not sufficiently similar to your client, if the video does not conform with Code D, Annex B or if the video in any way unfairly indicates or draws attention to your client. If the objection is not removed, ensure that you and the identification officer note the records.

You should be given an opportunity to attend the viewing of the video, though the suspect may not. If no solicitor is present, the video identification should itself be videoed.

Similar provisions apply by virtue of Annex B (safeguarding the reliability of witness identification in video procedure) as to procedures with group identifications, eg, ensuring that witnesses do not communicate with each other, the destruction of tapes in the event of an acquittal, and documenting the procedure.

The recording of identification procedures conducted when you were not present enables you to assess in part what that procedure was, but is very limited: it is far safer for your client if you attend.

When may it be carried out?

The procedure may be carried out when the suspect refuses to take part in a parade or group identification, or the officer considers it to be the most satisfactory procedure.

1.6.7 WHAT IS A CONFRONTATION?

This is literally the suspect being faced with the witness, on a one to one basis, with the witness being fully aware that the other person is the suspect, and being asked: 'Is this the person?'

This is the least acceptable and most dangerous type of identification procedure, and there is considerable pressure, whether intended or not, on the witness to confirm the identity of the suspect.

Confrontation procedure is governed by Annex C to Code D, which is the shortest Annex. The brevity of the Annex is an indication of the dearth of protection for the suspect who is involved.

The procedure must be carried out in the presence of the solicitor, unless this would cause unreasonable delay, and normally in the police station.

You must try to avoid your client being involved in a confrontation at all costs. The confrontation does not need consent, but should not be carried out unless all other procedures are impracticable. You should, therefore, seek to persuade the police that another procedure is possible and practicable.

1.6.8 SHOULD THE CLIENT UNDERTAKE AN IDENTIFICATION PARADE IF ASKED?

As indicated above, there are more safeguards against wrong identification in an identification parade than in any of the other procedures. It is for this reason that, if identification is disputed, it is often in your client's interests to consent to a parade if asked.

If a suspect refuses, then the police may carry out one of the less safe procedures which can be performed without consent and without the suspect's

In view of the difficulties of identification evidence and the likelihood of memories fading, it could be said that the parade militates even against correct identification.

co-operation. Furthermore, evidence can be given of the refusal to take part, and inferences can be drawn from that refusal.

It is also worth undertaking a procedure if the descriptions you have been provided with are significantly different from your client's appearance. Even if your client is identified, the credibility of the identification will be questionable, bearing in mind the discrepancies.

1.6.9 SHOULD A SUSPECT REQUEST AN IDENTIFICATION PARADE?

If your client wishes to take part in an identification parade, s/he can insist, unless it is impracticable to hold one. S/he might wish to take part in an identification parade when s/he is confident of not being identified. If an identification at the scene has already been made, even if that identification is challenged, there is little point in allowing the same witness to repeat the identification. If your client is of distinctive appearance (and this is a distinction referred to in the original description), it may be difficult for the police to provide a suitable number of similar candidates.

33 What are the advantages of an identification parade over other procedures?

1.6.10 WHAT IS MY ROLE?

As in any situation when you are attending your client at the police station, your role is to protect and advance your client's interests. This may include:

(a) ensuring that the parade is carried out in accordance with PACE 1984 so that your client is not in anyway disadvantaged;
(b) apprising your client of the format (which is described above);
(c) advising the client on his/her conduct during the procedure;
(d) reassuring your client so that s/he conducts him/herself appropriately;
(e) explaining that you will monitor the conduct of the procedure and object if anything inappropriately affects the client's position;
(f) advising your client that s/he must leave such objections to you;
(g) taking a thorough and detailed note as to exactly what happens at the procedure, in case of subsequent dispute.

The other members of the parade will not know which of them is the suspect. If the suspect draws attention to him/herself so that they are aware of his/her position, this might make the suspect uneasy or subtly affect their manner towards him/her.

1.6.11 WHAT INFORMATION DO YOU NEED BEFORE THE PROCEDURE IS CARRIED OUT?

One of the most important aspects of the police case may well be the description or descriptions given of the alleged offender. It may be that this description is what has led the police to your client, or that they suspect him/her for other reasons but wish to see if a witness can make an identification.

It is essential that you are aware of the original description or descriptions given of the alleged offender, and you should be informed of these before any procedure. You may have found out about these already, if you assisted at any police interview of your client, from your consultation with the officers then or in the interview. It may be that additional witnesses or additional statements have since been made.

Discrepancies between witnesses or between the statements of individual witnesses should always be noted carefully as these may point to a weakness or unreliability in the evidence. It is particularly important in cases involving a number of offenders, such as in a multiple fight, that care is taken to establish which description refers to which alleged perpetrator: it is often the case that a witness confuses several individuals.

You will, as stated above, also wish to know the circumstances of the description.

You will need to provide evidence of having obtained full information about witness's descriptions in two occasions.

1.6.12 ASSESS YOUR CLIENT'S APPEARANCE

You should consider dispassionately how your client could be described, consider whether your client is of unusual appearance that would make a parade (ie, the choice of members) problematic (in any event, you should, at the time of the parade, consider the appearance of the other members of the parade vis à vis your client).

You should also consider whether any of the identifying features are transitory and whether they were present at the time of the offence.

If your client comes to the procedure from any period in custody, particularly if the identification procedure takes place soon after the event followed by a period in police cells, you should ensure that s/he has adequate opportunity to freshen up. Looking unkempt may not only draw attention to your client as a likely culprit, but may also diminish the client's self-esteem and ability to cope with the procedure.

1.6.13 WHAT SHOULD YOU DO BEFORE THE PARADE OR OTHER PROCEDURE?

There are various stages before an identification procedure is carried out. Occasionally, the procedure will be carried out soon after the offence, but most often, particularly in the case of an identification parade, this will take place some time, possibly weeks, after the offence. This means that accurate identification is inherently less likely to take place in any event, as memories fade. You should always be provided with:

(a) the details of the first description given by the witness who is to attend;

(b) any identification material released to the media if that has been done (Code D, Annex A, para 2A).

Information to be given to the suspect

The client who is a suspect must be given certain information. Before a parade or group or video identification, the officer must, under Code D, para 2.15, notify the suspect of the following matters, and this information must be contained in a written notice handed to the suspect, which s/he should sign:

(a) the purposes of the parade, or group identification or video identification;

(b) s/he is entitled to free legal advice (see Code C, para 6.5);

(c) the procedures for holding the procedure (including his/her right to have a solicitor or friend present);

(d) where appropriate, the special arrangements for juveniles;

(e) where appropriate, the special arrangements for mentally disordered and mentally handicapped people;

(f) s/he does not have to take part in a parade, or co-operate in a group identification or with the making of a video film and, if it is proposed to hold a group identification or video identification, s/he is entitled to a parade if this can practicably be arranged;

(g) if s/he does not consent to take part in a parade or co-operate in a group identification or with the making of a video film, his/her refusal may be given in evidence in any subsequent trial, and the police may proceed covertly without his/her consent or make other arrangements to test whether a witness identifies him/her;

- if s/he should significantly alter his/her appearance between the taking of any photograph at the time of his/her arrest or after charge and any attempt to hold an identification procedure, this may be given in evidence if the case comes to trial, and the officer may then consider other forms of identification;

- a video or photograph may be taken of him/her when s/he attends for any identification procedure;

(h) whether the witness had been shown photographs, photofit, identikit or similar pictures by the police during the investigation before the identity of the suspect became known;

(i) if s/he changes his/her appearance before a parade, it may not be practicable to arrange one on the day in question or subsequently, and, because of his/her change of appearance, the identification officer may then consider alternative methods of identification;

(j) s/he or his/her solicitor will be provided with details of the description of the suspect as first given by any witnesses who are to attend the parade, group identification, video identification or confrontation.

There are various stages where you might be involved before, during and after an identification procedure:

(a) discussions with your client as to the procedure to be adopted;

(b) discussions with the police as to the procedure to be adopted;

(c) briefing your client as to his/her conduct in the procedure;

(d) monitoring the pre-procedure events (in particular, ensuring that no inappropriate contact with witnesses is made by the police, that witnesses do not communicate before the procedure, or see your client or other members of the parade/procedure before it takes place);

(e) monitoring the procedure;

(f) making representations about the conduct of the procedure.

1.6.14 INFORMATION FROM THE POLICE

Before the procedure, you should be aware of the initial description given of the suspect, and of any subsequent ones. You may learn about this in connection with an interview under caution carried out earlier, or in discussion with the investigating officer in connection with the identification procedure proposed. It is essential that you note in particular any discrepancies in a witness's description or between one witness and another. An assessment

34 What does *R v Turnbull* say about identification evidence? What does the mnemonic, 'ADVOKATE', stand for?

of the value and reliability of descriptions in accordance with the case of *Turnbull* (above) should be made at this stage.

1.6.15 CONSULTING WITH AND BRIEFING YOUR CLIENT

As explained above, it will normally be in your client's interest to consent to an identification procedure and resist the less favourable procedures, particularly the covert group identification (by consenting to it) and, above all, the confrontation. When you have fully considered the situation, you should enable your client to make an informed decision on the procedures, then you should brief him/her on what will happen. This will include briefing a client on their conduct. Guidance is given below in terms of conduct on an identification parade; a similar approach should be used for a group identification.

You must provide evidence of having met with clients to explain their rights in relation to two of the identification procedures.

1.6.16 BRIEFING ON CONDUCT

An identification parade can be a very nerve wracking and stressful undertaking, even for those who are familiar with police station procedure (even indeed for non-suspects who take part in the parade). Nervousness may attract the attention of the identifying witness: knowing that this is the case may further unsettle the suspect.

It is, therefore, worth reminding your client of the uncertainty of eye witness identification.

In advising him/her how to behave, you should encourage him/her to relax, by reassuring him/her of the above and of your presence and role, and that:

(a) s/he should try to look straight ahead;
(b) if the witness looks at him/her, s/he should look back, but not take undue notice of the witness by following his/her movements about the room;
(c) s/he should not look at you if you are in the room;
(d) s/he should adopt the same stance as the others on the parade;
(e) if there is a screen, s/he should assume that there might at any time be a witness present;
(f) s/he should not change position and thus identify him/herself as a suspect to the volunteers, unless s/he has been identified, and then only if s/he wishes to;
(g) s/he should not protest at procedures or instructions because you will ensure that his/her position is protected.

1.6.17 CAN YOU INSIST ON BEING PRESENT?

You will normally be able to be present at a parade or group identification with consent. You must be present at a confrontation, and if not present at a video identification, the identification procedure should itself be videoed.

1.6.18 WHAT MIGHT YOU OBJECT TO?

Annex A to Code D covers identification parades: you should be familiar with its provisions, which are designed to protect the integrity of evidence. Any deviation from the procedure should be objected to.

Some of the more important matters are:

(a) presence of the investigating officer: it is the *identification* officer who is in charge of the parade and the investigating officer should not be present in the area;
(b) presence of a police officer where they could influence a witness's reaction to the parade;
(c) where there is any improper communication (verbal or otherwise) between police officers and witnesses;
(d) where witnesses communicate;
(e) where witnesses see any of those participating before the parade takes place;
(f) if any unauthorised person enters the parade area and could have informed the witness of the location of the suspect;
(g) where incorrect procedures are adopted;
(h) where the other members of the parade are insufficiently like your client;
(i) where a voice identification is expected and the voices are insufficiently alike.

You must provide evidence of representations to officers to attempt to ensure that two types of procedures are fair.

1.6.19 HOW DO YOU OBJECT?

How you object will depend on whether the parade has started or is in the process of preparation, and whether an adjustment can be made or the whole procedure is compromised. You should consider first of all whether the matter can be rectified without disadvantage to your client. If so, then objection should be made to the identification officer with the expectation that the matter will be adjusted.

You should ensure that your objection and its cause and result are noted in the identification record. If the matter is not rectified, you should make further representations about the safety of the parade and ask that the procedure be aborted, whilst remembering that usually the parade will be the best option for your client. Seriously compromised procedures are unlikely to provide admissible evidence.

Ensure also that you record in your own notes your objection and the result.

After the parade, your client should be asked if s/he has any views: objections must be made then, even if they have already been made.

1.6.20 OBJECTING TO OTHER PROCEDURES

If involved in any of the other procedures, you should object in the same way if the relevant provision of the Code or Annex is not adhered to, or if anything takes place that will disadvantage your client unfairly.

1.6.21 RECORDING THE PROCEDURE

You should make a detailed note of every aspect of the procedure (not confined solely to matters upon which you make representations), including:

(a) positions of all those taking part;

(b) witnesses' reactions, questions, uncertainties;

(c) all officers' activities in the parade.

You must provide evidence of having made full written records of at least one identification parade.

APPENDIX 1: PRELIMINARY KNOWLEDGE AND UNDERSTANDING

INTRODUCTION

In order to become fully competent in this unit, you will need to be aware of and thoroughly understand a wide variety of basic criminal law and procedure. It will be convenient to set some of these out in general terms in this appendix for reference purposes.

At the police station, you will be dealing with clients who are suspected of any type of criminal offence. We will examine the general principles and explain the concepts involved, largely by reference to seven very common offences, which will demonstrate their application and effect:

(a) assault occasioning actual bodily harm;

(b) possession of a controlled drug with intent to supply;

(c) handling stolen goods;

(d) possessing offensive weapons;

(e) taking a motor vehicle without the owner's consent;

(f) theft;

(g) affray.

CRIMINAL OFFENCES

For an act or omission to be categorised as a criminal offence, it must contravene some aspect of the criminal law. The criminal law is found in both case law and statute law. Although most criminal offences are created or defined by statute, there are still some important offences, notably murder and manslaughter, which are common law offences: that is, they are defined only by case law.

All offences have case law which explain their meaning and effect, and you will, from time to time, need to research and consider some of the decisions on interpretation. The essential meanings are, however, for the most part well established.

All criminal offences are composed of a number of elements: these are the constituent parts of an offence, which a defendant must be proved to have engaged in, in order to be found guilty of the offence.

Actus reus and *mens rea*

The elements of the offence are usually divided into elements that relate to the thing done, such as the taking of goods (appropriation) in theft, the driving and its manner (in dangerous driving) and so on, and to elements that relate to the mind of the alleged offender – what might be termed the mental element of the crime. The former is referred to as the *actus reus* and the latter as the *mens rea* of the offence.

Obviously, what constitutes the guilty act (*actus reus*) can vary infinitely with what comprises the elements of the offence, but there is also a great deal of variation in what can be involved in the guilty mind (*mens rea*).

Participation: principals and accessories

Those involved in crimes may commit them individually or with others, and may have varying levels of involvement. All the parties to a crime are accomplices, but a defendant may be charged on his own as a *principal offender*, which means that s/he would be solely responsible for the offence if found guilty. If involved with other offenders, those responsible may be equally involved as joint principles, or some may be involved in a lesser way.

In either case, offenders may be tried together as co-accused or co-defendants in the same case. Lesser offenders may not be primarily responsible for the offence complained of but may have contributed to the offence by helping in some way, either before or after the event in question. Thus, a robbery may be carried out by one person, but a second person may have driven the 'getaway' car, and a third may have helped with the planning. The secondary parties could be liable as accessories. Some may accept guilt and plead guilty; others may plead not guilty and go on to trial.

Level of involvement will be important in the establishment of liability and, of course, sentence in the event of a guilty verdict. Whilst all involved in any level with the offence are liable to be sentenced equally, secondary parties will usually receive a lighter sentence.

WHAT ARE THE ELEMENTS OF OFFENCES?

Table 1 below lists some commonly encountered offences and the elements involved, together with the statutory provision creating the offence. This is not intended to be a complete definition of the offences, as many of the terms set out in the offence are further defined or explained in the relevant Act. You should always consult the appropriate sources (see also 2.4 below) in order to fully understand the meaning and application of the provisions.

As you will see, some of the offences are easily defined and break down very simply and obviously into constituent parts. Others are more complex in definition, hence greater care needs to be taken in identifying their elements.

The importance of understanding what constitutes the elements of offences will be readily understood when we consider the impact of the burden of proof and what the prosecution has to prove in order to secure a conviction. From your client's point of view, if there is no or insufficient evidence on one or more elements of the offence, s/he is entitled to be acquitted. This will obviously also affect advice on plea.

TABLE 1: ELEMENTS OF SEVEN COMMON OFFENCES

Name of offence	Provision defining offence	Elements
Assault occasioning actual bodily harm (ABH)	Section 47 of the Offences Against the Person Act 1861	• assault (ie, intentionally or recklessly causing the apprehension of immediate unlawful violence) • causing actual bodily harm
Possession of a controlled drug with intent to supply	Section 5 of the Misuse of Drugs Act 1971	• possession of a controlled drug with • intent to supply another
Handling stolen goods	Section 22 of the Theft Act 1968	• dishonestly *either*: • receiving stolen goods, • knowing or believing the goods to be stolen; *or*: • undertaking or assisting in their retention, removal, disposal or realisation (or arranging to do so), • by or for the benefit of another, • knowing or believing the goods to be stolen
Possessing an offensive weapon	Section 1 of the Prevention of Crime Act 1953	• having, • in a public place, • an offensive weapon (as defined in the Act), • without lawful authority or reasonable excuse.* * Note: This part of the offence is not an element of it in the same way as the others, as the defendant has to prove (by virtue of the statute) that he had lawful authority, etc. Thus, this falls within one of the exceptions to the rule in *Woolmington* (see proof of offences below).
Taking a motor vehicle without the owner's consent	Section 12 of the Theft Act 1968	• without having the consent of the owner or other lawful authority, *either*: • taking any conveyance for his own or another's use; *or*: • knowing that any conveyance has been taken without such authority, • driving it or allowing him/herself to be carried in or on it
Theft	Section 1 of the Theft Act 1968	• dishonest • appropriation • of property belonging to another, • with the intention of permanently depriving the other of it
Affray	Section 3 of the Public Order Act 1986	• using or threatening unlawful violence towards another, • such as would cause a person of reasonable firmness to fear for his personal safety.

INTENTION

In many criminal offences, the level of intention, or type of intention, involved in the offence plays a crucial role in its definition. Generally speaking, the more deliberate the offence and its outcome, the more serious and culpable the offence will be regarded. At the lowest end of intentionality are those offences which are called offences of strict liability, which do not require any *mens rea* at all: these are mostly, but not exclusively, offences created by statute to regulate trade and industry and to protect the public. Thus, food and drugs, weights and measures and environmental legislation create offences that can be committed by doing the relevant act (selling short weight or food unfit for human consumption), despite not knowing that that was the case. Most statute-created offences of strict liability (or absolute offences, as they are sometimes known) create defences to relieve the offender of liability where the offence is either:

(a) the fault of someone other than the accused; or

(b) was committed despite the accused taking all reasonable steps to prevent it.

MENS REA

Where the offence is not one of strict liability, some element of *mens rea* is necessary. This can be specifically included in the statement of the offence. For example, there may be reference to *dishonesty* and *knowing or believing*. Both of these phrases, which will be further explained below, relate to the specific level and type of *mens rea* necessary for someone to have committed the offence. Without that *mens rea*, and without the person being proved to have that *mens rea*, then s/he is not guilty in law of the offence.

Where the offence does not include a specific and clear reference to a mental element, the courts will normally interpret the section as requiring the act to have been committed knowingly in order for an offence to have been committed (*Sweet v Parsley* [1970] AC 132).

This is exemplified in the interpretation of the word 'possession'. In many offences, such as those involving the possession of a prohibited item (eg, drugs or an offensive weapon), the courts have held that a person should not be found to be in possession of something s/he did not know s/he had, or in the case of drugs, did not know were prohibited drugs.

Knowledge, intention, etc

Sometimes one of the elements of the offence, part of the *mens rea*, is specifically set out, very often by use of one of the following terms:

(a) intentionally;

(b) recklessly;

(c) maliciously;

(d) dishonestly;

(e) knowing or believing.

All of these have caused problems to the court in interpretation, and the following points can be made.

Intention

Offences may involve intention, whether the offence is a common law offence (example: murder is the unlawful causing of another person's death *with the intention of causing death or really serious harm*) or a statutory offence (section 18 of the Offences Against the Person Act (OAPA) 1861): causing grievous bodily harm with intent to do grievous bodily harm or to resist arrest.

Intention, intent or intentionally is used to refer to appreciation of the outcome or consequences of the act in question. Intention does not involve motive, or necessarily involve planning (though evidence of either may demonstrate intent).

Recklessly

Recklessness is a part of many offences that can be committed either intentionally or recklessly (such as the assault element of actual bodily harm in Table 1 above), and may involve realising a risk inherent in an action but going on to do it anyway, or failing to spot an obvious risk. The precise definition of recklessness for particular offences varies, and careful consideration must be given to the appropriate meaning.

Maliciously

Malice or maliciously is used in the definition of some offences, such as in sections 18 and 20 of the OAPA 1861. The word requires an intent to do the relevant harm or injury, or foresight of some harm.

Dishonestly

The case of *R v Ghosh* [1982] QB 1053 sets out the general test for whether conduct is to be regarded as dishonest, and this will be a matter of fact for the jury or the magistrates to decide. This case sets a two part test:

(1) Is the conduct to be regarded as dishonest, according to the ordinary standards of reasonable and honest people? Only if the answer to that question is 'yes' is the second part of the test to be applied. If the answer is 'no', then the conduct is not dishonest.

(2) Did the defendant realise that what s/he was doing was dishonest by such standards?

In addition, the Theft Act 1968 provides a list of circumstances where conduct is not to be regarded as dishonest for the purpose of that Act.

The Theft Act 1968, section 2, states:

> **(1) A person's appropriation of property belonging to another is not to be regarded as dishonest –**
>
> (a) if he appropriates the property in the belief that he has in law the right to deprive the other of it, on behalf of himself or a third person; or
>
> (b) if he appropriates the property in the belief that he would have the other's consent if the other knew of the appropriation and the circumstances of it; or
>
> (c) (except where the property came to him as trustee or personal representative) if he appropriates the property in the belief that the person to whom the property belongs cannot be discovered by taking reasonable steps.
>
> **(2) A person's appropriation of property belonging to another may be dishonest notwithstanding that he is willing to pay for the property.**

Knowing or believing

Knowing or believing may occur as alternate ways of committing an offence, as in the offence of handling stolen goods (above). 'Knowing' has its ordinary meaning, but can include the situation often referred to as 'wilful blindness': almost a refusal to acknowledge the obvious. *R v Taaffe* [1984] AC 539: belief is less than knowledge and can be similar to the wilful blindness referred to above.

PROOF OF OFFENCES

What needs to be proved

In order to be found guilty of an offence, either:

(a) the defendant must plead guilty to the offence; or

(b) the prosecution must prove the defendant guilty of the offence on the basis of admissible evidence. The prosecution must prove the case beyond reasonable doubt, so that the lay magistrates, stipendiary magistrates (in the magistrates' court) or the jury (in the Crown Court) are satisfied of the guilt of the defendant. This means that the prosecution has to satisfy the jury or magistrates of every element of the offence to that standard.

How it is proved

Evidence that is presented to the court will usually be oral evidence, by a witness giving evidence from the witness box. In some circumstances, written evidence can be put before the court and, often, exhibits will be produced to demonstrate the existence or appearance of articles. Written evidence can be produced. This may be to show the existence of a document. If the document is introduced as a way of proving the truth of its contents, it will usually be what is called hearsay evidence. Hearsay is normally not admissible as evidence, unless a particular provision allows its introduction in a trial.

In relation to such documents, the following are the most common situations allowing for the introduction of documents. Reference should be made to the full terms of the legislation referred to:

(a) those produced in the course of a trade or business can be adduced if they comply with sections 23–25 of the Criminal Justice Act (CJA) 1988;

(b) computer produced documents can be produced under section 69 of PACE 1984;

(c) witness statements can be read under section 9 of the CJA 1967 in the magistrates' court if accepted by all parties and provided and served in the required form;

(d) under the Criminal Procedure and Investigations Act (CPIA) 1996, statements tendered at committal proceedings can be produced and relied on at trial in the Crown Court unless the judge excludes them or the defendant objects within 14 days of committal (so it is important to consider documents at committal and object within the time limit if the original maker of the statement is required for cross examination at the trial);

(e) under section 23 of the CJA 1988, hearsay documents may be permitted to be adduced in court when the original maker is:
   - dead, or cannot attend court because of their bodily or mental condition;
   - outside the UK and it is not reasonably practicable for him/her to attend; or
   - where all reasonable steps have been taken to find them and cannot be found; or
   - where the statement was made to the police and the maker is in fear of giving evidence or is being kept out of the way;

(f) maps and diagrams are often produced in court to aid explanation: they will need to be proved by the party producing them. This means that if a witness wishes to explain the location of an incident by means of a map s/he provides, s/he will need to produce the map and explain its relevance. The opposing party will be given an opportunity to challenge it.

The standard to which it must be proved

The standard of proof in a criminal case is generally expressed as being 'beyond reasonable doubt', though it can be stated in terms of being satisfied so that the triers of fact are so satisfied as to be 'sure'. Triers of fact are entitled to draw conclusions or make inferences from evidence adduced.

Who has the burden of proof?

Prosecution

The prosecution must prove its case by adducing relevant evidence that is not excluded.

The prosecution is said to have the burden of proof of all elements of the offence in a criminal case except:

(a) in the case of insanity and allied defences;

(b) where a statute provides an exception expressly;

(c) in the case of implied statutory exceptions.

The leading case is *Woolmington v DPP* [1935] AC 462, in which Lord Sankey said: 'Throughout the web of the English criminal law, one golden thread is always to be seen: that it is the duty of the prosecution to prove the prisoner's guilt ... subject to the defence of insanity and to statutory exceptions.'

An example of a statutory exception is in the Prevention of Crime Act 1953, where the burden is expressly placed on the defence. Section 1 makes it an offence for someone to have with him/her an offensive weapon in a public place without lawful authority or reasonable excuse, the proof of which shall lie with the defendant (see Table 1 above).

Thus, in such a case the prosecution must prove that:

(a) the defendant (and no other);

(b) had with him/her;

(c) in a public place;

(d) a weapon;

(e) which was offensive (within the definition in the statute).

However, the prosecution does not have to prove the absence of authority or excuse. The defendant has to prove that s/he had lawful authority or reasonable excuse.

Defendant

Whenever the defendant has the burden of proving something because s/he is relying on a defence of insanity or because statute places a burden on him/her, his/her standard of proof is on the 'balance of probabilities'. This means that the defendant must prove that it is more likely than not that s/he was insane, or s/he had the excuse referred to.

A particular statutory provision which places the burden on the defendant is section 101 of the Magistrates' Courts Act 1980, which provides that any party seeking to rely on an exception, exemption, proviso, excuse or qualification must prove that s/he comes within the proviso or excuse. It has been held, however, that the courts will be slow to place any such burden on the defendant, unless the words of the statute are clear and the burden is one that the defendant can shift relatively easily (*R v Hunt* [1987] AC 352). An example of this is where the defendant is charged with driving without a licence. Once the prosecution has established that a request for a licence to be produced was made, it is for the defendant to establish s/he did have the licence, not for the prosecution to show that s/he did not.

The evidence and possible responses by the defence:

(a) the evidence must persuade the person or persons charged with deciding on the facts of the guilt of the defendant before s/he can be convicted;

(b) the evidence can be direct evidence of the facts, or can be circumstantial leading to an inference of the relevant matter. For example, in a prosecution for theft, the prosecution must prove that the defendant:

- dishonestly;
- appropriated;
- property belonging to another;
- with the intention of permanently depriving the other of it.

Evidence may be given in court that Mrs Brown (the defendant) was seen putting a bottle of whisky in her coat pocket in a supermarket and leaving without paying.

If this evidence is accepted by the magistrates or jury as true, they will probably be satisfied that Mrs Brown has appropriated (ie, taken) the goods (the bottle of whisky) belonging to another (ie, the supermarket proprietor). The prosecution must also, of course, establish that it was the defendant (Mrs Brown) who committed the offence (ie, the identity of the offender).

What of the *mens rea* of the offence? This includes both dishonesty and the intention of permanently depriving that other of it, though the evidence and meaning of both these elements is often the same.

The evidence that the defendant was dishonest and intended permanently to deprive the supermarket of the whisky is circumstantial or inferential:

(a) it was Mrs Brown who put the item in her pocket, instead of in the appropriate basket;

(b) she left without paying or attempting to pay.

The defence need do nothing: there is no burden of proof for the defence unless one of the exceptions to the rule in *Woolmington* applies.

In our example above, Mrs Brown may, of course, accept that she is guilty, or she may not and thus plead not guilty. She may 'put the prosecution to proof': wait and see if the evidence the prosecution has can hold up. She may directly seek to weaken, refute or undermine the evidence: eg, by suggesting that the witness did not see (or could not have seen) what she described or is otherwise unreliable. She may herself advance evidence that prevents the implication or inference from the evidence being made (the items were put in her coat pocket because her basket was full and she was afraid the bottle would break, and that she subsequently forgot to pay, quite innocently, at the checkout). If the latter is the position, the defendant does not have to prove this explanation: the burden of proof is on the prosecution. The prosecution has to persuade the fact finders that that explanation is not true.

Alternatively, the defendant might advance a defence, such as insanity, where she alleges that her mental capacity was such that she was unable to understand that what she was doing was wrong: here, she would have to prove her insanity, on the balance of probabilities.

Where the burden exceptionally lies on the defendant, the standard is only on the balance of probabilities, which means the defendant only has to prove that something is more likely than not.

In other types of offence, the defendant may contest the charge in other ways:

(a) by a mere denial: putting the prosecution to proof, which may include the challenging of the validity of some of the evidence; or

(b) by adducing evidence that itself challenges the evidence or assumptions made on the basis of the evidence.

In other cases, the defendant might adduce a positive defence, which effectively means that s/he is saying, 'Yes, I did what you say, but for certain reasons I am not guilty'. This would include cases where the defendant relies on the assertion, in a case involving an allegation of violence, that s/he was acting in self-defence (or defence of another or of property). Thus, s/he would seek to suggest, on the basis of the prosecution or defence evidence, that in committing the assault s/he was not acting unlawfully, because s/he was defending him/herself from an assault or threat of assault from the alleged victim.

The defendant relying on self-defence still bears no burden of proof, so all s/he has to do is to raise the issue: in other words, suggest in evidence or by cross-examination of the prosecution witnesses that s/he was acting in lawful self-defence. It is still then for the prosecution to prove that this was not the case. Self-defence is a defence if the amount of force used was in proportion to the perceived threat. If the defendant wrongly believed that s/he was under threat and acted proportionately to defend him/herself or another from the threat, s/he can still rely on the defence.

Other positive defences, where the defendant is relying on some other fact or argument to render him/herself not liable for the offence, are:

(a) duress – this can provide a defence to all crimes (except murder) where death or very serious injury is threatened unless the defendant carries out the crime;

(b) duress of circumstances – allowed, eg, when the defendant 'had' to act in a criminal way in order to avoid very serious consequences;

(c) provocation – a partial defence that reduces murder to manslaughter in certain circumstances where the defendant's self-control is suddenly overborne;

(d) diminished responsibility – a partial defence that reduces murder to manslaughter in certain circumstances;

(e) intoxication – only a defence where the intoxication vitiates a specific intent required by the offence in question.

EVIDENCE AND ADMISSIBILITY

The elements of the offence must be proved on the basis of admissible evidence. Any evidence is admissible if relevant to the proof of the offence, unless excluded by a rule of law or by the exercise of the court's discretion to exclude.

Evidence is excluded by rules of law if it is:

(a) hearsay evidence, unless an exception applies allowing hearsay evidence to be admitted;

(b) evidence about the previous convictions or offences of the accused, unless an exception applies;

(c) opinion evidence, except where the opinion of an expert is given or where it is a matter of common judgment.

A note on hearsay evidence

Hearsay evidence is evidence, whether in writing or oral, of statements which were made outside of the court (ie, not during the trial as part of the evidence), in order to prove the truth of the statement (not the fact that the statement was made).

Where there are two co-accuseds, the statement of one which may implicate both him/herself and the other accused is only evidence against the maker. It cannot be evidence against the other party unless it is made in his/her hearing and accepted by him.

The most important exceptions where hearsay is admitted are in relation to:

(a) confession evidence, if it complies with section 76 of PACE 1984, ie, it is not obtained by oppression or in consequence of something said or done which renders the confession unreliable;

(b) documentary hearsay, if complying with sections 23–25 of the CJA 1988, which provide that documents produced in the course of a business, from information provided originally by someone with direct knowledge of that information, are admissible. If the document is produced specifically for criminal proceedings or investigations, additional safeguards must also be complied with.

Evidence can also be excluded at the discretion of a judge. The court has a discretion to exclude evidence that has been unfairly obtained. Section 78 of PACE 1984 states that, in any proceedings, the court may refuse to allow evidence to be given on which the prosecution proposes to rely, if it appears to the court that, having regard to all the circumstances, including the circumstances in which the evidence was obtained, the admission of the evidence would have such an adverse effect on the fairness of the proceedings that the court ought not to admit it.

Very often, breaches of PACE 1984 and the Codes of Practice made under it may lead to the exclusion of evidence obtained as a result of the breach. Also, the court has a discretion to exclude evidence where the evidence is more prejudicial than probative.

OVERVIEW OF PROCEDURE

You will also need to consider procedure at various stages in some detail, but it is useful at this stage if we take an overview, picking out critical stages in the process. It should be understood, of course, that additional steps, such as further investigations or second interviews, may take place in the pre-court procedure, and additional adjournments or the addition of extra charges or other defendants may complicate the process in court. Overall, however, the process applicable is shown in the following steps.

Pre-charge

The stages are:

(a) complaint or incident that brings matter to police notice;

(b) investigation by police;

(c) arrest of suspect, or summons to court;

(d) if arrest is made, the suspect may be interviewed; leading to

(e) charge;

(f) suspect is then either bailed or kept in custody;

(g) attendance at court.

At court

Questions of legal aid and legal representation may need to be determined.

The procedure in court will depend on the nature of the offence. All offences are either:

(a) *summary only*, meaning they can only be tried in the magistrates' court;

(b) *triable only* on indictment (at the Crown Court); or

(c) *triable either way* (TEW), meaning that they can be tried in either court.

Further explanation is given in Unit 2, but the general procedures are identified here and will depend on the type of offence.

Summary procedure

If the case is summary:

(a) the defendant's plea is taken;

(b) *if his plea is guilty*, the defendant is sentenced after a pre-sentence report (PSR), if necessary;

(c) *if his plea is not guilty*, there is an adjournment for trial with possible a pre-trial review beforehand.

Sentences for summary offences

With the exception of some trading and environment offences, the overall maximum sentence that can be imposed in the magistrates' court is six months' custody and/or a £5,000 fine, but many summary only offences carry a lower maximum. Nevertheless, it should be remembered that just because an offence is summary only, eg, common assault, in many cases a custodial penalty or a community penalty can and will be imposed.

Procedure in offences triable either way (TEW)

The stages here are:

(a) advance disclosure;

(b) indication of plea;

(c) *if guilty*, proceed to sentence (adjournment for PSR may be necessary);

(d) *if not guilty or will not indicate plea*, a decision is taken on mode of trial;

(e) *if decision is summary trial*, the plea is verified as not guilty or taken (if not previously indicated);

(f) the case is adjourned for trial at later date;

(g) *if the decision is trial on indictment*, the case is adjourned for committal/transfer proceedings.

Distinguish summary offences from TEW offences tried summarily, which all carry a maximum six months and/or £5,000 penalty, but in which magistrates can impose up to a year's imprisonment for two or more offences heard together, and which can be committed to the Crown Court for higher sentencing.

Procedure for indictable only offences

The stages are:

(a) adjournment for committal proceedings;

(b) committal.

Note: when the Crime and Disorder Act 1998 is fully implemented, these matters will go straight to the Crown Court without committal proceedings.

SENTENCING

In order to be able to advise clients on the seriousness of offences and the likely outcome, you should always assess offences in terms of:

(a) the category of offence (summary/TEW/indictable only). Some types of offence, particularly assaults and public order crimes, have blurred boundaries between the different offences in the hierarchy. This, together with the tendency of the CPS to down charge and be willing to accept pleas to lesser offences, means that very often a client's case will be resolved at a lower level and in a lower category than that initially expected or indeed merited by the facts. This is a point which should be borne in mind when advising on plea;

(b) the maximum sentence available for this offence, which you can determine from the relevant statute;

(c) if the case will be or is likely to be tried in the magistrates' court, have regard to the Magistrates' Association Sentencing Guidelines. These give the likely sentence for an average offence of the type, together with a list of aggravating and mitigating factors that the sentencing court will have regard to.

Most magistrates' courts follow the guidelines, and your local knowledge will soon confirm the likely course they will take in average cases. In cases in the Crown Court, reported Court of Appeal decisions will provide guidance.

AVAILABLE SENTENCES

The bind over

This is a common law power which provides the possibility of binding over an offender to 'keep the peace and be of good behaviour' for a specified period, on pain of forfeiting a specified sum if s/he fails to abide by the bind over. The bind over, as well as being a sentence, is also available without proof of guilt.

It is much used by magistrates in cases such as neighbour disputes, where both parties can be bound over. Binding over can only be done with the consent of the person to be bound who is invited to 'show cause why s/he should not be bound over'. The only sanction for someone who refuses to be bound over is imprisonment.

Discharges

These can be absolute or conditional and are available when the court has found the defendant guilty, or s/he pleads guilty, and the court feels that punishment is not expedient (Powers of Criminal Courts Act (PCCA) 1973, section 7). An absolute discharge has no effect save in the proceedings. Its imposition suggests technical guilt. A conditional discharge can be imposed for a period of up to three years. Breach (ie, commission of any other offence during the period of discharge) means that the subsequent court may sentence in some other way for the original offence (any way in which the original court could have sentenced).

Fines

These are the most frequently imposed sentence, and account for virtually all sentences in the magistrates' courts. The maximum is £5,000 for most offences in the magistrates' courts, but certain business and environmental offences carry a greater maximum. There is no maximum fine in the Crown Court.

Compensation

This can be imposed as a sentence in its own right, or in addition to another sentence. Compensation can be paid in respect of loss or damage caused by an offence, other than motoring offences. The magistrates' maximum is £5,000, and compensation must always be considered where appropriate and reasons must be given if it is not awarded. There must be sufficient evidence, however, to establish the level of compensation, which can include compensation for the damage in a criminal damage offence, for the goods stolen (and not recovered) in theft, or for injury in an assault.

Community sentences

The range of community sentences is as follows:

(a) *probation*: can be imposed for a period between six months and three years;

(b) *probation with additional requirements* (Powers of Criminal Courts Act (PCCA) 1973, section 2): extra requirements can be added, such as to attend drug or alcohol dependency unit, live at a probation hostel, etc. See the CJA 1991, section 2(1)(a);

(c) *community service order* (*CSO*) (PCCA 1973, section 14): a CSO requires the offender to undertake unpaid work for the community under the direction of the probation service. The work must be completed within one year, and the order can be from 40–240 hours;

(d) *combination order* (CJA 1991, section 56): this is an order created by the CJA 1991, combining one to three years' probation with 40–100 hours community service. This is the only way the two sentences can be combined. Additional requirements can be added, as with a probation order;

(e) *curfew order* (CJA 1991, section 12): an order restricting the defendant's movements for between two to 12 hours per day for a period up to six months. It must not interfere with work, religious observance or attendance at a school;

(f) *attendance centre order* (for those under age 21): this requires the offender to attend in a particular place for a number of hours.

Custodial sentences

These include sentences of imprisonment and suspended sentences. The magistrates' court has power to impose up to six months for one offence and 12 months for two or more TEW offences. Some summary offences carry a lower maximum, whilst others are not imprisonable at all. Maximum custodial sentences in the Crown Court are set by the governing statute.

Sentences limited to motoring offences (including taking without owner's consent)

These are:

(a) penalty points on the driving licence;

(b) disqualification from driving.

Ancillary sentences

The possibilities are:

(a) forfeiture: property in the defendant's possession when arrested which is in connection with the crime may be ordered to be forfeited (eg, tools for burglary, etc);

(b) destruction order: property such as weapons or dangerous drugs may be ordered to be destroyed;

(c) confiscation: the Crown Court may confiscate the proceeds of crime, where the proceeds exceed £10,000. (Usually used for fraud or drugs related crime.)

Deportation

This can be ordered in certain circumstances involving foreign nationals.

Deferred sentence

Sentence can be *deferred* under the PCCA 1973, section 1 for up to six months. This power is used occasionally, where there seems to be a real prospect of the defendant making reparation or 'turning over a new leaf' and s/he is at risk of a custodial sentence. A change in attitude may persuade the sentencing court (which will usually be composed of the same magistrates or judge as the deferring court) to impose a non-custodial sanction.

Note: committal for sentence

The magistrates' court may, instead of sentencing, commit the defendant to the Crown Court for sentence where it does not have sufficient powers (TEW offences only).

WHEN CAN THESE SENTENCES BE IMPOSED?

Sentences are imposed in relation to the seriousness of the offence or offences. The statutory criteria are as follows.

Community sentences

The offence, or the combination of the offence and other associated offences, must be serious enough to warrant it.

The sentence(s) chosen from the possible community sentences must be:

(a) suitable for the offender;

(b) commensurate with the seriousness of the offence or offences in terms of the order's restriction of the offender's liberty:

- *probation order* – any offence (the object is to rehabilitate the offender, protect the public or prevent offences);
- *community service* (offence must be imprisonable, offender must be suitable and work must be available);
- *combination order* (the offence must be imprisonable; the object is to rehabilitate the offender and protect the public or prevent offences);
- *curfew order* (any offence other than murder).

Custodial sentence: CJA 1991, section 1

This can be an immediate sentence where:

(a) *either* the offence(s) is/are so serious that only a custodial sentence is justifiable; *or*

(b) the offence is one of sex or violence and only a custodial sentence is adequate to protect the public from serious harm from the defendant; *or*

(c) the offender refuses to consent to a community sentence where consent is required.

In the case of a suspended sentence (PCCA 1973, sections 22 and 23, as amended by the CJA 1991):

(a) a criterion for imprisonment must exist – only the first will be relevant; *and*

(b) exceptional circumstances exist so that the sentence can be suspended.

The length of custodial sentence is determined as either: the term that is commensurate with the seriousness of the offence; *or* in sex/violence cases, such longer term (up to the maximum for the offence) as is necessary to protect the public from serious harm by the defendant.

SENTENCING IN THE MAGISTRATES' COURT

In coming to an assessment of seriousness, magistrates rely heavily on the Magistrates' Association Sentencing Guidelines, which indicate, as mentioned above, the factors to be taken into account.

For the offences you are primarily concerned with, the sentencing guidelines specify an expected sentence for average offences as follows:

(a) assault occasioning actual bodily harm – custody;

(b) possessing a controlled drug with intent to supply – custody;

(c) handling stolen goods – community penalty;

(d) possessing an offensive weapon – custody;

(e) taking a motor vehicle – community penalty;

(f) theft – discharge or fine, unless in breach of trust, in which case custody;

(g) affray – custody.

Guidelines also exist, not only as to the category of sentence, but where the sentence is likely to be a fine, or in motoring cases likely to involve penalty points or disqualification. Guidelines are given as to the number of points or size of the fine. You should consult the guidelines in all cases.

Where they are considering a custodial or community penalty, magistrates will almost always seek a pre-sentence report from the probation service first.

If the case is to be tried in the Crown Court because of its seriousness, in other words if it is a serious TEW offence or it is only triable on indictment, the most common penalty is a custodial one. However, community penalties and even fines and discharges are imposed in the Crown Court where there is considerable mitigation.

APPENDIX 2: DOCUMENTS

DOCUMENT 1: EXAMPLE OF A WARRANT OF ARREST

WARRANT OF ARREST AT FIRST INSTANCE

(Bail Act 1976, s 3; Magistrates' Courts Act 1980, ss 1, 13, 14, 117; Magistrates' Courts Rules 1981, rr 95, 96)

.... Magistrates' Court (Code:)

Date:

Accused:

Address:

Alleged offence:	[short particulars and statute]
	Information having been laid before me on [oath] [affirmation] by [name of informant] on [date of information] that the accused committed the above offence
Direction:	You, the constables of [County] Police Force, are hereby required to arrest the accused and bring the accused before the magistrates' court at [place] immediately [unless the accused is released on bail as directed below]
*Bail:	On arrest, after complying with the condition(s) specified in Schedule I hereto, the accused shall be released on bail, subject to the condition(s) specified in Schedule II hereto, and with a duty to surrender to the custody of the above Magistrates' Court on [date] at [time] am/pm.

Justice of the Peace

*Delete if bail not granted

SCHEDULE I

Conditions to be complied with before release on bail

To provide suret[y][ies] in the sum of £ [each] to secure the accused's surrender to custody at the time and place appointed.

SCHEDULE II

Conditions to be complied with after release on bail

DOCUMENT 2: EXAMPLE OF A CUSTODY RECORD

CUSTODY RECORD Police and Criminal Evidence Act 1984

Police Station.. Force/Station reference..

ARREST

Reason (Offence/Date/Place)..............................

Where arrested..

Arrested by:

Name...

Rank/No .... Station..........................

Time of Arrest.......... Date................

Time of arrival at Station .... Date ....

Commencement of detention period:
(if applicable and if different to arrival at Station)

Time...................... Date................

Suspect's volunteered comment on details of arrest:-

....

....

DETAINEE

Surname...Mr/Mrs/Miss

Forenames..

Former Surname......................................

Address..

....

....

....

....

Occupation...

Age................. Date of birth.......................

Place of Birth...

Nationality...

Height..................... Sex Male/Female

Ethnic Appearance: White, Dark European, Afro-Caribbean, Asian, Oriental, Arab, Unknown

DETENTION AUTHORISED FOR

Preparation of Charges
Secure or preserve evidence relating to the offence
Obtain further evidence by questioning
Warrant/Court
Other specify..

....

Grounds for detention......................................

....

....

Detention not authorised

Reason..

....

Suspect's volunteered comment on detention decision

....

....

....

Custody Officer

Name .... Rank/No.........................

Signature.................. Time........... Date...........

Officer in the case Name..........................

Rank/No......................

Station.........................

Officer opening record Name..........................

Rank/No......................

Signature.....................

		Time Called	Time Arrived
Appropriate Adult	Yes/No	....	....
Interpreter	Yes/No		
Solicitor	Yes/No		

STATUS OF SOLICITOR ATTENDING

Own Solicitor
Own Solicitor's Representative
Duty Solicitor
Duty Solicitor's Representative

MEDICAL DETAILS

Are you currently:- receiving medication Yes/No
suffering any illness/injury Yes/No
suffering any infirmity Yes/No

Time...............

Signature............................

Date............

If any of the above questions are answered positively full details to be recorded by the Custody Sgt on the Custody Record Continuation Sheet and to be signed by the prisoner..

DETAINED PERSONS RIGHTS ***Complete A in all cases then either B or C***

A. My rights have been read to me and I have been given a copy of the Notice to Detained Person and a copy of the Notice of Entitlements

Signature.................................... Time.................. Date..........................

B. Legal Advice requested.

I want to speak to a solicitor. Name............................ Tel: No.................

Signature....................................

C. Legal Advice declined

I do not want to speak to a solicitor.

Signature.................................... Time.................. Date..........................

I have been informed that the right to speak to a solicitor includes the right to speak with a solicitor on the telephone.

I do not want to do so.

Signature.................................... Time.................. Date..........................

Reasons (if given) for declining legal advice..

....

APPROPRIATE ADULT **INTERPRETER**

Name..........................Tel: No..................... Name.......................... Tel: No.................

Rights and grounds for detention explained and Notices served in presence of Appropriate Adult/Interpreter.

Signature of Appropriate Adult............................ Signature of Interpreter......................................

Time............ Date............................ Time................................Date.....................

INDEPENDENT COMMONWEALTH AND FOREIGN NATIONALS

High Commission/Embassy/Consulate informed Yes Not applicable

Country..

OTHER PERSON REQUESTED TO BE NOTIFIED

I do I do not require anybody to be informed of my arrest.

Signature................................... Time...............................Date.....................

Details of nominated person..

Address/contact no...

....

CUSTODY RECORD Continuation Sheet

Last Review of detention conducted at……………………… Force/Station Ref………………………………

……………………………………………………………………… Name………………………………………………

DATE	TIME	Full details of any action/occurrence involving detained person (include full particulars of all visitors/officers) Individual entries need not be restricted to one line All entries to be signed by the writer

DOCUMENT 3: EXAMPLE OF A WARRANT TO ENTER AND SEARCH PREMISES

WARRANT TO ENTER AND SEARCH PREMISES

(Police and Criminal Evidence Act 1984, s 15)

.... Magistrates' Court (Code:)

Date

On this day an application supported by an information was made by: [specify name of applicant]
for the issue of a warrant under: [state enactment under which warrant is to be issued]
to enter and search the premises at: [specify premises]
and search for: [identify, so far as is practicable, the articles or persons to be sought].

Authority is hereby given for any constable [accompanied by ....]
to enter the said premises on one occasion only within one month from the date of issue of this warrant and to search for the articles or persons in respect of which the above application is made.

Justice of the Peace

ENDORSEMENT

(to be made by constable executing the warrant)

1 [The following articles or persons sought were found: (list)] or [no article or person sought was found]
2 [The following articles other than articles which were sought were seized: (list)] or [no other article was seized]

Signature of constable..................................

Date..

DOCUMENT 4: LEGAL AID BOARD TRANSACTION CRITERIA

GENERAL POINTS

Linked Files

If an organisation wishes to rely upon information or advice on another file for compliance, any such file(s) must be clearly cross-referenced and provided at audit. For criminal matters, where separate files are often opened for different stages of the same matter (advice at police station, magistrates' court, etc), all files must be provided and all files must be closed.

Incomplete Matters

Where a matter concludes before reaching all stages covered by the Transaction Criteria (a case settles, client instructions cease, etc), the file may still be audited, although only up to the stage the file closes.

File Transfer *from* Another Organisation

Where the case has been transferred from another organisation, the file should only be audited where the referral records and information sent by the previous organisation (eg, their file) are available at audit. Compliance should be given for all advice and information on the file, including that of the previous organisation.

File Transfer *to* Another Organisation

Where the case has been transferred to another organisation, the file should only be audited where the complete file of the auditee is available at the audit.

The file should only be audited however, up to the stage at which the referral was made. Compliance should only be given for advice and information on the file of the auditee.

Answer Option Boxes

Where a N/a option box does not appear alongside a question in the transaction criteria, it is an indication that the question should be answered either Yes or No only. There may, however, be instances when, due to the exceptional circumstances of the case and any justification noted by the adviser, a question should be treated as not being applicable. This will be marked, together with a brief note of the reasons, onto the paper copy of the transaction criteria. Such instances are likely to be extremely rare.

Lead Questions

Where a lead question is answered in the negative, all sub-questions should be answered in the negative.

Multiple Questions and Partial Compliance

Some questions require more than one factor to be considered or sought for compliance to be given. These questions have bold linking words.

Attempts to Comply

Where it is clear that the adviser has attempted to meet the requirements of the criteria, record compliance. Where an adviser asks the client for information that the client fails to supply, the adviser has addressed the issue and compliance should be given.

Checklists

A tick against a checklist is not sufficient to demonstrate advice given. If a checklist is used to record advice, the content of the advice and the date must be apparent. Furthermore, where a checklist is used to record information gathering or factual details, where there is no mark against an item on a checklist, the auditor will not assume that the matter has been addressed.

CRIME

This set of criteria covers advice, assistance and representation in all criminal matters. However, it would not be appropriate to audit files which only relate to:

- advice given over the telephone to a client at the police station;
- advice/assistance/representation as a court duty solicitor;
- initial advice outside the police station where charges are not brought against the client; and where the adviser has no further involvement in the matter.

I GETTING INFORMATION

This section must be audited in all cases. Information may be gathered from anywhere on the file, excluding a PSR.

		Yes	No	N/a
(i)	**General information**			
1	Does the file show the following details:			
1.1	The client's name?	[ ]	[ ]	
1.2	The client's address?	[ ]	[ ]	
1.3	The client's telephone number?	[ ]	[ ]	
1.4	The client's date of birth?NFG	[ ]	[ ]	
1.5	The client's National Insurance number?NFG	[ ]	[ ]	[ ]
1.6	Whether the client is married/cohabiting?NFG	[ ]	[ ]	[ ]
1.7	Whether the client has dependants and if so their age(s) and relationship to the client?NFG	[ ]	[ ]	[ ]
1.8	The amount of income and its source?NFG	[ ]	[ ]	[ ]
1.9	The amount of capital owned by the client?NFG	[ ]	[ ]	[ ]
1.10	Whether the adviser has addressed the issue of need for welfare benefits advice?NFG	[ ]	[ ]	[ ]

NFG 1.4 The client's actual date of birth is required for compliance.

NFG 1.5 Establishing that the client has none will give compliance. Only where the client is under 16 is not applicable an option.

NFG 1.6 Only answer n/a if the client is under 16.

NFG 1.7 A dependant is anyone under the age of 18 or anyone who receives Attendance Allowance, or anyone who receives high or middle rate Disability Living Allowance care premium. Where dependants are identified, the age and relationship of each is required for compliance. The n/a option should only be used where the client is under 16.

NFG 1.8 This may be the client's wages, benefits or a combination of the two. As a minimum the client's total income and the source of that income must be given. The file must confirm that there is no other source of income. A signed Application for Advice and Assistance (eg, Green Form) or a signed means form on file and where the amount of income is also noted will give compliance. The n/a option is only available where the client is under 16 or is advised only at the police station.

NFG 1.9 The n/a option is only available where the client is under 16 or is advised only at the police station.

NFG 1.10 As a minimum there must be evidence on the file that a referral to a specialist welfare benefits adviser has been considered. This includes specialist advisers within the same firm. Compliance will also be given where an adviser is able to give appropriate advice themselves. This must be specific advice regarding the client's individual entitlement to a benefit/s or a benefit calculation. The n/a option is only available where the client is under 16 or is advised only at the police station.

II INITIAL INSTRUCTIONS AT POLICE STATION

This section should be audited in all cases in which the adviser takes initial instructions at the police station. Evidence for compliance will only be taken from documents produced or obtained contemporaneously, as well as completed form DSPS1 and letter confirming instructions. Where initial instructions are taken outside the police station, section III, should be audited.

	Yes	**No**	**N/a**
Getting information			
Source of instructions/Access to client			
2 Where the case was a Duty Solicitor telephone referral, does the file show:	N/a	[ ]	
2.1 What time the adviser telephoned the police station?	[ ]	[ ]	
2.2 Who the adviser spoke to?	[ ]	[ ]	
2.3 Where the adviser spoke directly to the client by telephone:		N/a	[ ]
2.3.1 Does the file record the advice given?	[ ]	[ ]	
3 Where the adviser was attending at the request of a third party does the file show.		N/a	[ ]
3.1 The name and contact details of the third party?	[ ]	[ ]	
3.2 The relationship of the third party to the client?	[ ]	[ ]	
4 Where access to the client was delayed, does the file record:[NFG]		N/a	[ ]
4.1 The reason given for the delay?	[ ]	[ ]	
4.2 The extent of the delay?	[ ]	[ ]	
4.3 Whether representations were made by the adviser?	[ ]	[ ]	

Information obtained from the police on arrival at the police station.

Normally, for questions 5–7, evidence for compliance will only be given for information gathered from the police **before the interview,** whilst the adviser is in attendance at the police station. Evidence can be taken from a copy of the custody record if the adviser notes that this has been seen or that a copy has been obtained **at the time of the police station attendance**. Evidence will not normally be taken from a transcript of an interview.

	Yes	**No**	**N/a**
5 Does the file show whether the adviser has obtained or seen a copy of the client's custody record?	[ ]	[ ]	
6 Does the file show that the following information has been gained **from the police**:			
6.1 Whether the client is attending voluntarily or under arrest? and if arrested;	[ ]	[ ]	
6.1.1 When the client was arrested?	[ ]	[ ]	
6.1.2 When detention was authorised?	[ ]	[ ]	
6.2 The nature of the allegation/s or charges?[NFG]	[ ]	[ ]	
6.3 The police version of events/evidence?[NFG]	[ ]	[ ]	

NFG 4 Under certain circumstances, the police have the power to delay access to the client under s 8 Police and Criminal Evidence Act 1984.

NFG 6.2 Eg, theft, assault, criminal damage.

NFG 6.3 Ie, the alleged circumstances of the offence and any evidence, such as being caught in the act or in the vicinity stolen goods found, etc.

		Yes	No	N/a
6.4	Whether there has been a previous interview or any questioning?NFG	[]	[]	
6.5	Whether the client has kept silent or made any significant statements?NFG	[]	[]	
6.6	Where another person has been arrested or is being sought in connection with the alleged offences:		N/a	[]
6.6.1	Their name/s?	[]	[]	
	and, if there are co-accused **in custody:**		N/a	[]
6.6.2	Whether they have instructed other advisers?	[]	[]	
6.7	Where a search of premises has occurred or is intended:		N/a	[]
6.7.1	The reason for the procedure?			
	and, if the search of premises has already occurred:		N/a	[]
6.7.2	Whether evidence has been gathered as a result?	[]	[]	
6.8	Where a body sample has been taken or is intended to be taken:NFG		N/a	[]
6.8.1	The legal authority and reasons for the procedure?	[]	[]	
6.8.2	Whether consent has been obtained?	[]	[]	
6.9	Where an intimate or non intimate search has taken place or is intended to take place:NFG		N/a	[]
6.9.1	The legal authority and reasons for the procedure?	[]	[]	
6.9.2	Whether consent has been obtained?	[]	[]	
	and, if the search has already occurred:		N/a	[]
6.9.3	Whether evidence has been gathered as a result?	[]	[]	
6.10	Where the police or the adviser suspect that the client is unfit to be interviewed by reason of medical condition, injury or drink or drugs:		N/a	[]
6.10.1	Whether the adviser has assessed the client's fitness for interview?	[]	[]	
6.10.2	Whether the police surgeon has been called or attended?NFG	[]	[]	
7	Where the client is a juvenile (under 17) or mentally handicapped or disordered, does the file show:		[]	[]
7.1	The relationship of an appropriate adult to the client?NFG	[]	[]	
7.2	The name and contact details of an appropriate adult?NFG	[]	[]	

NFG 6.4 An interview should be defined as any questioning regarding involvement/suspected involvement in a criminal offence where this is carried out under caution. Questioning should be defined as any questioning regarding involvement/suspected involvement in a criminal offence that is not carried out under caution. Compliance should be given where the adviser has addressed whether any questions have been put to the client and whether or not the client has been cautioned.

NFG 6.5 To be significant, a statement or silence must be capable of being used in evidence against the client, eg, a comment in particular, a direct admission of guilt or a failure or refusal to answer a question put by police or failure to answer it satisfactorily. For compliance, the adviser must positively address whether anything has been said or whether the client has kept silent.

NFG 6.8 This refers to intimate and non-intimate body samples. Do not include fingerprints, photographs, handwriting samples or samples in road traffic cases.

NFG 6.9 Non-intimate search refers to a search where item/s of clothing are removed.

NFG 6.10.2 There is no obligation on the police to call the police surgeon if the client is simply drunk, however, if there is any question whether there may be other factors disorientating the client beyond mere drunkenness or that the client is under the influence of drugs/withdrawal, the surgeon should be called. It is sufficient for compliance to note whether or not the surgeon has been called – it is not necessary for the file to show that the adviser requested that the surgeon be called.

NFG 7.1 An appropriate adult can either be a parent/guardian, social worker or another responsible adult.

NFG 7.2 Compliance in respect of contact details will be given where the file records an address or telephone number of the person or where applicable their service/organisation.

	Yes	No	N/a
7.3 Whether the police have contacted or attempted to contact the appropriate adult?	[]	[]	

Instructions from the client, prior to an interview

For questions 8–14, evidence for compliance must be gained **from the client** while the adviser is in attendance at the police station, **prior to any interview**, unless a private interview is denied.

	Yes	No	N/a
8 Does the file show:			
8.1 Where a social worker/probation officer is involved with client:	N/a	[]	
8.1.1 The name and contact details for the social worker/officer?[NFG]	[]	[]	
8.2 Whether the client is the subject of any current criminal proceedings?	[]	[]	
and if so;		N/a	[]
8.2.1 Whether the client is subject to bail?	[]	[]	
8.3 Whether the client has any previous convictions?			
9 Does the file show whether instructions have been obtained **from the client** on the events of the alleged offence?	[]	[]	
and, where there are witnesses in support of the client		N/a	[]
9.1 The name(s) of the witnesses?[NFG]	[]	[]	
10 Where there is an alibi, does the file show:		N/a	[]
10.1 Details of the alibi?[NFG]	[]	[]	
10.2 Where there are witnesses in support of the alibi;		N/a	[]
10.2.1 The name(s) of the witnesses?	[]	[]	
11 Does the file show that the adviser has confirmed **with the client** what has taken place since the client's arrival at the police station, in particular:			
11.1 Whether there has been an interview or any questioning?[NFG]	[]	[]	
11.2 Whether the client has kept silent or made any significant statements?[NFG]	[]	[]	
11.3 Where procedures for the recovery of evidence have taken place:[NFG]		N/a	[]
11.3.1 Whether the client's consent was obtained?	[]	[]	

Medical problems

	Yes	No	N/a
12 Where the client is suffering from a medical condition which is relevant to the fitness for interview or safe custody of the client, does the file show:[NFG]		N/a	[]

NFG 8.1.1 Either a telephone number or address or contact name of service/voluntary organisation is sufficient.

NFG 9.1 This does not relate to any co-accused.

NFG 10.1 Ie, where, when.

NFG 11.1 An interview should be defined as any questioning regarding involvement/suspected involvement in a criminal offence where this is carried out under caution. Questioning should be defined as any questioning regarding involvement/suspected involvement in a criminal offence that is not carried out under caution. Compliance should be given where the adviser has addressed whether any questions have been put to the client and whether or not the client has been cautioned.

NFG 11.2 To be significant, a statement or silence must be capable of being used in evidence against the client, eg, a comment in particular, a direct admission of guilt, or a failure or refusal to answer a question put by police or failure to answer it satisfactorily. For compliance, the adviser must positively address whether anything has been said.

NFG 11.3 Procedures for the recovery of evidence refer to intimate and non-intimate searches, body samples but not fingerprints, photographs, handwriting or samples in road traffic cases.

NFG 12 Medical condition refers to any physical or mental condition, illness or disability which affects the client. This includes alcohol or drug addiction but is not applicable where the client is simply under the influence of drink or drugs. The question should only be addressed where the adviser notes that there is a relevant medical condition.

	Yes	No	N/a
12.1 That the adviser has noted the nature of the medical condition?NFG	[ ]	[ ]	
12.2 The client's explanation of the effect of the medical condition?NFG	[ ]	[ ]	
12.3 The name and address of the client's doctor or consultant?	[ ]	[ ]	
12.4 Whether the client is under or prescribed any medication?	[ ]	[ ]	
12.5 Whether it was appropriate to call the police surgeon?NFG	[ ]	[ ]	
12.6 Whether it was appropriate to have an entry made in the custody record?NFG	[ ]	[ ]	
Clients with injuries			
13 Where the client has suffered an injury during the course of the alleged offence, arrest, or detention, does the file show:		N/a	[ ]
13.1 A description of the injury?	[ ]	[ ]	
13.2 The client's explanation of the cause?	[ ]	[ ]	
13.3 Whether there are any witnesses to the injury?	[ ]	[ ]	
13.4 Whether it was appropriate to call the police surgeon?NFG	[ ]	[ ]	
13.5 Whether the injury affects the client's fitness to be interviewed?	[ ]	[ ]	
13.6 Whether it was appropriate to have details of the injury entered on the custody record?NFG	[ ]	[ ]	
13.7 Whether it was appropriate to have the injury photographed?NFG	[ ]	[ ]	
Co-accused			
14 Where there are co-accused, does the file show:		N/a	[ ]
14.1 Whether any co-accused is known to the client?	[ ]	[ ]	
14.2 The client's version of the co-accused's role in the offence?	[ ]	[ ]	
14.3 Where the adviser is requested to act for any co-accused does the file show:		N/a	[ ]
14.3.1 Whether there is any conflict of interest?	[ ]	[ ]	
Interview			
15 If the adviser attended an interview does the file show:		N/a	[ ]
15.1 The adviser's own notes of the interview?	[ ]	[ ]	
15.2 Any interventions made by the adviser or confirmation that it was unnecessary to intervene?NFG	[ ]	[ ]	

NFG 12.1 Eg, asthma, heart condition drug addiction.

NFG 12.2 Ie, symptoms such as dizziness/nausea or risks such as fits, coma, etc.

NFG 12.5 If the adviser notes that the police surgeon has been called this is sufficient for compliance. If the police surgeon has not been called, it is sufficient for the adviser to note that this was unnecessary.

NFG 12.6 If a note has been made on the custody record, then this is sufficient for compliance. Where no note has been made, it is sufficient for the adviser to note either that this was unnecessary or that the adviser requested that an entry be made.

NFG 13.4 If the adviser notes that the police surgeon has been called, this is sufficient for compliance. If the police surgeon has not been called, it is sufficient for the adviser to note that this was unnecessary.

NFG 13.6 If a note has been made on the custody record, then this is sufficient for compliance. Where no note has been made, it is sufficient for the adviser to note either that this was unnecessary or that the adviser requested that an entry be made.

NFG 13.7 If photographs are present on file or a note has been made on the custody record that photographs have been taken, this is sufficient for compliance. If it is unclear whether photographs have been taken, it is sufficient for the adviser to note that they were unnecessary.

NFG 15.2 Compliance should also be given where the adviser has later obtained a tape of the interview.

	Yes	No	N/a
On leaving the police station			
16 Does the file show the outcome of the client's detention or voluntary attendance?	[]	[]	
17 Where the client has been charged, does the file show:		N/a	[]
17.1 Date and time and venue of the court hearing?	[]	[]	
17.2 Whether the client has been released on bail?NFG	[]	[]	
and, if not, does the file show:		N/a	[]
17.2.1 Whether the adviser made any representations to the custody officer?	[]	[]	
17.2.2 The place of the client's detention?	[]	[]	
17.2.3 Whether brief instructions on a bail application have been taken?NFG	[]	[]	
18 Where police bail has been imposed, does the file show:NFG		N/a	[]
18.1 Bail date **and** time?	[]	[]	
18.2 The name of the police station to which they must surrender?	[]	[]	
(ii) Advising the client			
19 Where the client is a juvenile (under 17) or mentally handicapped or disordered, was the client advised:		N/a	[]
19.1 On the role of the appropriate adult?	[]	[]	
20 Where **non-intimate samples** are to be or have been taken, was the client advised: N/a []			
20.1 Of their rights regarding the retention/destruction of such samples?	[]	[]	
and, if samples are intended to be taken;			
20.2 Whether to consent to the taking of the sample?	[]	[]	
21 Where **intimate samples** are to be or have been taken, was the client advised:NFG		N/a	[]
21.1 Of their rights regarding the retention/destruction of such samples?	[]	[]	
and, if samples are intended to be taken;		N/a	[]
21.2 Whether to consent to the taking of the sample?	[]	[]	
21.3 Of the implications of any refusal to provide a sample?	[]	[]	

Advising the client prior to interview N/a []

Do not audit this section where the client is not denying the offence. The advice should be given prior to interview. Do not audit this section if no prior interview with the adviser took place.

	Yes	No
22 Does the file show whether the client was given advice in respect of:		
22.1 Whether to answer questions put by the police?	[]	[]

NFG 17.2 Compliance should be given where the file shows either that the client has been released or that the client has been detained in custody.

NFG 17.2.3 It is sufficient for compliance for the adviser to note that the client wishes to instruct other/own solicitor to make the application or to arrange with the client to take instructions at a later date.

NFG 18 Police bail refers to bail issued by police prior to charge whilst further evidence is gathered witnesses interviewed or an ID procedure is planned etc. Questions 17 and 18 are mutually exclusive.

NFG 20 These do not include samples in road traffic cases or samples of handwriting.

NFG 21 Do not include samples in road traffic cases or samples from the mouth.

	Yes	No	N/a
22.2 The implications of failure to raise any facts that they may later seek to rely upon in their defence, when being questioned under caution or being invited to make any statement or reply after charge?	[ ]	[ ]	
23 Where the client is alleged to have made a significant statement or kept silent, was the client advised:NFG		N/a	[ ]
23.1 Whether to make any comment regarding the alleged significant statement or silence?	[ ]	[ ]	
24 Where there is an alibi, was the client advised of the implications of:		N/a	[ ]
24.1 Failure to raise any facts that they may later seek to rely upon when being questioned under caution?	[ ]	[ ]	
25 Where, on arrest, any objects, substances or marks were found on the client or in the place of arrest and the presence of these is in issue:		N/a	[ ]
25.1 Was the client advised or the implications of failure to account for the presence of these when questioned?	[ ]	[ ]	
26 Where on arrest the client was found at a material place, at or about the time the offence was committed and the presence is in issue:		N/a	[ ]
26.1 Was the client advised as to the implications of failure to account for this when questioned?	[ ]	[ ]	
Advice on leaving the police station			
27 Has the adviser confirmed to the client:			
27.1 The outcome of the client's detention?	[ ]	[ ]	
and where the client has indicated cause for complaint against the police:		N/a	[ ]
27.2 The procedure for making a complaint and whether to make any complaint prior to leaving the police station.	[ ]	[ ]	
28 Where bail is granted **after charge**, was the client advised of:		N/a	[ ]
28.1 The importance of answering to bail?NFG	[ ]	[ ]	
28.2 Any conditions, security or surety imposed?NFG	[ ]	[ ]	[ ]
and where conditions have been imposed:		N/a	[ ]
28.3 The consequences of breaching bail conditions?	[ ]	[ ]	
29 Where police bail is granted, was the client advised of:NFG			
29.1 The importance of answering to bail?NFG		N/a	[ ]
30 Where bail is refused, has the client been advised of:		N/a	[ ]
30.1 The procedure for future bail applications?NFG	[ ]	[ ]	
30.2 The prospects of success?	[ ]	[ ]	

NFG 23 Refer to question 6.5 and notes for guidance. If question 6.5 has been answered no, then answer this question no.

NFG 28.1 Give compliance if the client is advised to report when required or advised to inform the authorities or the solicitor if unable to attend.

NFG 28.2 Where no conditions, security or surety has been imposed answer n/a.

NFG 29 Police bail refers to bail issued by police prior to charge whilst further evidence is gathered, witnesses interviewed or an identification procedure is planned for example. Questions 28 and 29 are mutually exclusive.

NFG 29.1 Compliance should be given where the client was advised to report when required or advised to inform the authorities or the solicitor if unable to attend.

NFG 30.1 As a minimum the client must be advised in a letter or attendance when a bail application may be made on their behalf.

	Yes	No	N/a
III INITIAL ATTENDANCE OUTSIDE THE POLICE STATION		N/a	[]

This section should be audited in all cases in which the adviser takes initial instructions outside the police station. If section II has been audited do not audit this section but continue at section IV.

(i) Getting information

	Yes	No	N/a
31 Where the client is a juvenile (under 17), or has a mental disorder, does the file show:		N/a	[]
31.1 The name **and** contact details of the appropriate adult?NFG	[]	[]	
31.2 The relationship of the appropriate adult to the client?NFG	[]	[]	
32 Does the file show:			
32.1 Where a social worker/probation officer is involved with client prior to initial instructions:		N/a	[]
32.1.1 The name and contact details of the social worker/officer?NFG	[]	[]	
32.2 Whether the client is the subject of any other current criminal proceedings?	[]	[]	
and, if so:		N/a	[]
32.2.1 Whether the client is subject to bail?	[]	[]	
32.3 Whether the client has any previous convictions?	[]	[]	

Initial instructions on the alleged offence

	Yes	No	N/a
33 Does the file show:			
33.1 The nature of the allegation/s or charges?NFG	[]	[]	
33.2 The events of the alleged offence?	[]	[]	
33.3 Where there are witnesses in support of the client;		N/a	[]
33.3.1 The name(s) of the witnesses?	[]	[]	
34 Where there are is an alibi does the file show:		N/a	[]
34.1 Details of the alibi?NFG	[]	[]	
34.2 Where there are witnesses in support of the alibi:		N/a	[]
34.2.2 The name(s) of the witnesses?	[]	[]	

NFG 31.1 Either telephone number or address or contact name of service/voluntary organisation is sufficient.
NFG 31.2 An appropriate adult can either be a parent/guardian, social worker or another responsible adult.
NFG 32.1.1 Either a telephone number or address or contact name of service/voluntary organisation is sufficient.
NFG 33.1 Eg, theft, assault, criminal damage.
NFG 34.1 Ie, when and where.

	Yes	No	N/a
Co-accused			
35 Where there are co-accused, does the tile show:		N/a	[ ]
35.1 Whether any co-accused is known to the client?	[ ]	[ ]	
35.2 The client's version of the co-accused's role in the offence?	[ ]	[ ]	
35.3 Where the adviser is requested to act for any co-accused, does the file show:		N/a	[ ]
35.3.1 A note of whether it is appropriate to act?NFG	[ ]	[ ]	
Medical condition			
36 Where the client is suffering from a medical condition that could be relevant to the offence, does the file show:		N/a	[ ]
36.1 The nature of the medical condition?NFG	[ ]	[ ]	
36.2 The effect of the medical condition on the client?NFG	[ ]	[ ]	
36.3 The name and address of the client's doctor or consultant?	[ ]	[ ]	
36.4 Whether the client is under or prescribed any medication?	[ ]	[ ]	
and, if the client attended the police station:		N/a	[ ]
36.5 Whether the client was suffering from the effects of the medical condition at the time of the police station attendance?NFG		[ ]	[ ]
and, if so:		N/a	[ ]
36.5.1 Whether the client was examined by the police surgeon?	[ ]	[ ]	
Events at the police station		N/a	[ ]
This section should be audited when the client has attended the police station prior to consulting the adviser. If the adviser subsequently obtains a copy of the custody record, then this can be used as evidence for compliance.			
37 Does the file show:			
37.1 Whether the client attended the police station voluntarily or under arrest?	[ ]	[ ]	
and where no legal advice was received:		N/a	[ ]
37.2 Whether the client received legal advice?NFG			
37.2.1 Whether legal advice was requested?	[ ]	[ ]	
and where legal advice was received:		N/a	[ ]
37.2.2 Contact details of the former adviser?	[ ]	[ ]	
37.3 Whether the client was interviewed or questioned?NFG	[ ]	[ ]	
37.4 Whether the client kept silent or made any significant statements?NFG	[ ]	[ ]	

NFG 35.3.1 As a minimum the adviser should note whether there is a conflict of interest.

NFG 36.1 Eg, asthma, heart condition, drug addiction.

NFG 36.2 Ie, symptoms such as dizziness/nausea or risks such as fits, coma, etc.

NFG 36.5 This refers to the condition or the symptoms that affected the client at the time of the police station attendance including from alcohol or drug addiction or from any medication taken by the client.

NFG 37.2 If this question is answered no, then question 37.2.1 should be answered no and question 37.2.2 answered n/a.

NFG 37.3 An interview is any questioning regarding involvement/suspected involvement in a criminal offence. This must be carried out under caution. Questioning refers to any questioning regarding involvement/suspected involvement in a criminal offence that is not carried out under caution. Compliance should be given where the adviser has addressed whether any questions have been put to the client and whether or not the client has been cautioned.

NFG 37.4 To be significant, a statement or silence must be capable of being used in evidence against the client, eg, a comment, in particular a direct admission of guilt or a failure or refusal to answer a question put by police or failure to answer it satisfactorily. For compliance the adviser must positively address whether anything has been said.

	Yes	No	N/a
37.5 Where the client was suffering from an injury sustained during the course of the alleged offence, arrest, during or after detention:		N/a	[]
37.5.1 Whether the client was examined by the police surgeon?	[]	[]	
37.6 Where the client has made a complaint against the police:		N/a	[]
37.6.1 Whether the client was advised on making such a complaint?	[]	[]	
38 Where procedures for the recovery of evidence have taken place?NFG		N/a	[]
38.1 Whether the client's consent was obtained?	[]	[]	
39 Where the adviser is instructed before the client's first attendance at court, does the file show:		N/a	[]
39.1 Whether the client has been charged?	[]	[]	
and, if so:		N/a	[]
39.1.1 The date and time and venue of the next hearing?	[]	[]	
40 Where the client has not been charged, does the file show:NFG		N/a	[]
40.1 What stage has been reached in the investigation?	[]	[]	
40.2 Whether police bail has been imposed?NFG	[]	[]	
and, if so:		N/a	[]
40.2.1 Bail date and time?	[]	[]	
40.2.2 The name of the police station to which they must surrender?	[]	[]	

(ii) Advice to client

	Yes	No	N/a
41 Where the adviser was requested but did not attend the client at the police station:		N/a	[]
41.1 Did the adviser give advice directly over the telephone to the client?	[]	[]	
41.2 Does the file record the advice given?	[]	[]	
42 Where **non-intimate samples** are to be or have been taken, was the client advised:NFG		N/a	[]
42.1 Of their rights regarding the retention/destruction of such samples?		[]	[]
and, if samples are intended to be taken:		N/a	[]
42.1.1 Whether to consent to the taking of the sample?	[]	[]	
43 Where **intimate samples** are to be or have been taken, was the client advised:NFG		N/a	[]
43.1 Of their rights regarding the retention/destruction of such samples?	[]	[]	
and, if samples are intended to be taken:		N/a	[]

NFG 38 Procedures for the recovery of evidence refer to intimate and non-intimate searches and body samples but not fingerprints, photographs, handwriting samples in road traffic cases or searches of premises.
NFG 40 Questions 39 and 40 are mutually exclusive.
NFG 40.2 Police bail refers to bail issued by police prior to charge whilst further evidence is gathered, witnesses interviewed or an ID procedure is planned, for example.
NFG 42 Do not include samples in road traffic cases or samples of handwriting.
NFG 43 Do not include samples in road traffic cases or samples from the mouth.

	Yes	No	N/a
43.1.1 Whether to consent to the taking of the sample?	[ ]	[ ]	
43.1.2 Of the implications of any refusal to provide a sample?	[ ]	[ ]	
Advice to client prior/subsequent to an interview		N/a	[ ]
Questions 44–46 should be answered only where the client is denying the offence.			
44 Where the client has been or is to be subject to interview or questioning, does the file show:		N/a	[ ]
44.1 Whether the client has been advised of the implications of failure to raise any facts that they may later seek to rely upon in their defence when being questioned under caution or being invited to make any statement or reply after charge?	[ ]	[ ]	
and where there is an alibi, was the client advised of the implications of:		N/a	[ ]
44.2 Failure to raise any facts that they may later seek to rely upon when being questioned under caution or charge?	[ ]	[ ]	
and, where on arrest, any objects, substances or marks were found on the client or in the place of arrest and their presence is in issue:		N/a	[ ]
44.3 Was the client advised of the implications of failure to account for the presence of these when questioned by police?	[ ]	[ ]	
and where on arrest the client was found at a material place, at or about the time the offence was committed and their presence is in issue:		N/a	[ ]
44.4 Was the client advised of the implications of failure to account for their presence when questioned by police?	[ ]	[ ]	
45 Where the client kept silent or made a significant statement does the file show:NFG		N/a	[ ]
45.1 Whether the client was advised to make any comment regarding the alleged significant statement or silence?	[ ]	[ ]	
46 Where there is to be an interview, does the file show:		N/a	[ ]
46.1 Whether advice was given in respect of whether to answer questions put by police?	[ ]	[ ]	
and where the adviser attends the interview:		N/a	[ ]
46.2 The adviser's own notes of the course of the interview?NFG	[ ]	[ ]	
46.3 Any interventions made by the adviser or confirmation that it was unnecessary to intervene?	[ ]	[ ]	
47 Where bail has been granted after charge, was the client advised of:		N/a	[ ]
47.1 The importance of answering to bail?NFG	[ ]	[ ]	

NFG 45 To be significant, a statement or silence must be capable of being used in evidence against the client, eg, a comment, in particular a direct admission of guilt or a failure or refusal to answer a question put by police or failure to answer it satisfactorily. For compliance the adviser must positively address whether anything has been said or whether the client has kept silent.

NFG 46.2 A full transcript of the interview need not be taken by the solicitor for compliance, a summary of the course of the interview is sufficient.

NFG 47.1 Give compliance if the client was advised to report when required or advised to inform the authorities or the solicitor if unable to attend.

	Yes	No	N/a
47.2 Any conditions, security or surety imposed?NFG	[ ]	[ ]	[ ]
and, where conditions have been imposed:		N/a	[ ]
47.3 The consequences of breaching bail conditions?			
48 Where police bail has been granted, was the client advised of:NFG		N/a	[ ]
48.1 The importance of answering to bail?NFG	[ ]	[ ]	

IV IDENTIFICATION PROCEDURES

N/a [ ]

This section should only be audited when an identification procedure takes place. If none takes place go to section V.

	Yes	No	N/a
49 Does the file show that the adviser has explained to the client:		N/a	[ ]
49.1 The method of identification to be used and the procedure involved?	[ ]	[ ]	
49.2 The rights of the client?	[ ]	[ ]	
50 Where there is to be an identity parade has the client been advised:		N/a	[ ]
50.1 On the implications of refusal to co-operate with an identification parade?	[ ]	[ ]	
50.2 Whether to consent?	[ ]	[ ]	
51 Where the procedure was not an identity parade, does the file record:		N/a	[ ]
51.1 The reasons for the alternative method?	[ ]	[ ]	
51.2 Whether representations were made on the choice of identification method?	[ ]	[ ]	
52 Does the file show:		N/a	[ ]
52.1 The time and date of the procedure?	[ ]	[ ]	
52.2 What occurred during the procedure?	[ ]	[ ]	
52.3 The outcome of the procedure?	[ ]	[ ]	
53 Where the adviser did not attend the identity procedure:		N/a	[ ]
53.1 Have the reasons been noted?	[ ]	[ ]	

V COSTS AND FUNDING

This section must be audited in all cases.

	Yes	No	N/a
54 Where the case is funded by advice and assistance/block funding does the file show that the client has been given advice about:		N/a	[ ]
54.1 What the relevant form of legal aid funding will cover?NFG	[ ]	[ ]	
55 Where a legal aid order is made does the file show that the client was given advice about:		N/a	[ ]

NFG 47.2 Compliance should be given where the client is advised that bail is unconditional. Where there is no indication on the file of conditions, security or surety being imposed answer n/a.

NFG 48 Police bail refers to bail issued by police prior to charge whilst further evidence is gathered, witnesses interviewed or an identification procedure is planned, for example. Questions 47 and 48 are mutually exclusive.

NFG 48.1 Give compliance if the client was advised to report when required or advised to inform the authorities or the solicitor if unable to attend.

NFG 54.1 The client must be given an explanation at the outset of the case. For advice and assistance work the client must be advised that work is limited (in duration/cost) and the limitations on representation. Compliance should be given where the client is advised that there is a 2–3 hour limit or where the client is advised of the financial limit and the hourly rate. Compliance should not be given where the client is advised of the financial limit only.

	Yes	No	N/a
55.1 Whether or not the client will have to make any contribution to the case?NFG	[ ]	[ ]	
and, if there is a contribution:		N/a	[ ]
55.1.1 The duration of payments?NFG	[ ]		[ ]
55.2 The duty to report any changes in financial circumstances and that these may affect eligibility and/or contribution status?	[ ]	[ ]	
55.3 The nature and consequence of withdrawal/revocation?NFG	[ ]	[ ]	
56 If the application for legal aid is refused, does the file show that the client has been advised:		N/a	[ ]
56.1 Of rights of appeal or of renewing the application to the court?	[ ]	[ ]	
56.2 Of prospects of success of the submitting an appeal/ renewing the application?	[ ]	[ ]	
56.3 That a new application can be made if their financial circumstances change?NFG	[ ]	[ ]	[ ]

VI BAIL

		N/a	[ ]

(i) Getting information

Audit this section only if it is clear that a contested bail application has been made, including where the client has been brought to court following a breach of bail, otherwise go to section VII.

Unless otherwise indicated, only notes made in preparation for the application or a brief to counsel/solicitor/advocate can be taken as evidence of compliance.

	Yes	No	N/a
57 Where a contested bail application in court is to be made, does the file show:		N/a	[ ]
57.1 The client's proposed address for bail?	[ ]	[ ]	
57.2 If the client is employed:		N/a	[ ]
57.2.1 Details of employment?NFG	[ ]	[ ]	
57.3 If the client is unemployed:		N/a	[ ]
57.3.1 Details of any trade, profession or last employment?NFG	[ ]	[ ]	
57.4 Whether the client has any previous convictions?NFG	[ ]	[ ]	
57.5 Whether the client has previously been subject to bail:	[ ]	[ ]	
and, if so:		N/a	[ ]
57.5.1 The client's record of offending whilst on bail?	[ ]	[ ]	
57.5.2 The client's record of answering to bail?	[ ]	[ ]	
58 Does the file show the outcome of the application?	[ ]	[ ]	

NFG 55.1 This advice must be given by the time the offer is accepted. If there is no contribution, they should be advised of this.

NFG 55.1.1 This advice must be given by the time the offer is accepted. Where a contribution is due from income, the client must be advised that the payments will last for the length of the case. Where a contribution is due from capital, the client must be advised that this is a one-off payment.

NFG 55.3 A legal aid order can be terminated by withdrawal or revocation. As far as the client is concerned there is no difference. As a minimum the advice must include how the legal aid order may be terminated and how the client would be affected should this occur. It is not necessary to use the actual words 'withdrawal' and 'revocation' in that explanation.

NFG 56.3 N/a is only an option where the application is refused on merits.

NFG 57.2.1 As a minimum for compliance the client's occupation and the name of the employer must be recorded.

NFG 57.3.1 A note that the client has never had gainful employment would also be sufficient for compliance.

NFG 57.4 It will be sufficient for compliance that there is a list of the client's previous convictions on file, otherwise previous convictions or the fact that the client has no previous convictions must be noted.

	Yes	No	N/a
and where bail is withheld does the file show:		N/a	[]
58.1 The reasons for refusal?	[]	[]	
58.2 The address at which the client is to be held?	[]	[]	

(ii) Advising the client

	Yes	No	N/a
59 Was the client advised of the likely outcome of a bail application?	[]	[]	
60 Where the client was advised that bail conditions may be imposed, does the file show:		N/a	[]
60.1 That the adviser has confirmed with the client what conditions may be acceptable to the client and the court?	[]	[]	
61 Where bail has been granted, was the client advised of:		N/a	[]
61.1 The importance of answering to bail?[NFG]	[]	[]	
61.2 Any conditions, security or surety imposed?[NFG]	[]	[]	[]
and where conditions have been imposed:		N/a	[]
61.3 The consequences of breaching bail conditions?	[]	[]	
62 Where bail is withheld, has the client been advised of:		N/a	[]
62.1 The possibility of an appeal or future application?	[]	[]	
62.2 Prospects of success of an appeal or future application?	[]	[]	

VII PREPARING FOR CRIMINAL PROCEEDINGS

This section must be audited in all cases in which criminal proceedings are instituted against the client.

(i) Getting information

	Yes	No	N/a
63 Does the file show that the adviser has obtained a proof of evidence from the client?[NFG]	[]	[]	
64 Does the file show that the adviser has requested or obtained:			
64.1 Details of charges, evidence and witness statements?	[]	[]	
64.2 Copies of previous convictions?	[]	[]	
64.3 A copy of the custody record?[NFG]	[]	[]	[]
65 Where the prosecution has provided any documents or disclosure, does the file show:		N/a	[]
65.1 Has the adviser contacted the client to give them the opportunity to comment?	[]	[]	
66 Where there are witnesses in support of the client:		N/a	[]
66.1 Has the adviser taken proof/s of evidence?	[]	[]	
67 Where medical records are to be sought:		N/a	[]
67.1 Has the adviser obtained a signed authority from the client?	[]	[]	

(ii) Advice on proceedings

	Yes	No	N/a
68 Where the client has not admitted the offence:		N/a	[]
68.1 Has the adviser explained to the client what the prosecution will have to prove and discussed the evidence?	[]	[]	

NFG 61.1 Give compliance if the client is advised to report when required or advised to inform the authorities or the solicitor if unable to attend.

NFG 61.2 Where there is no indication on the file of conditions, security or surety being imposed answer n/a.

NFG 63 This would be in the form of a statement by the client in the first person. Compliance should not be given merely for notes of an attendance with the client where the facts of the case are discussed.

NFG 64.3 N/a is only an option where the client is not arrested and is issued with a summons to appear.

	Yes	No	N/a
68.2 Has the client been advised as to how they should plead?	[ ]	[ ]	
69 Where the client has admitted the offence but disputes the prosecution evidence:		N/a	[ ]
69.1 Has the adviser explained to the client the procedure for a *Newton* hearing and discussed the evidence?	[ ]	[ ]	
70 Has the client been advised which court will deal with the offence?	[ ]	[ ]	

Mode of trial		N/a	[ ]

This should only be audited where the offence is triable either way.

Do not audit this section where the matter is heard by the youth court.

	Yes	No	N/a
71 Does the file show:			
71.1 Whether the client has been advised of the implications of any plea to be made before venue?[NFG]	[ ]	[ ]	
71.2 Whether the adviser explained mode of trial procedure to the client?[NFG]	[ ]	[ ]	

(iii) Advice on progress of the case

	Yes	No	N/a
72 Does the file show that the client has been given advice about the progress of the case? In particular:			
72.1 Advice about how long the case is likely to take?[NFG]	[ ]	[ ]	
72.2 An explanation of the steps that the adviser is going to take on the client's behalf?	[ ]	[ ]	
72.3 Written confirmation of the advice given (or justification for not providing confirmation in writing in exceptional circumstances)?	[ ]	[ ]	
72.4 Advice about the strength of the client's case?[NFG]	[ ]	[ ]	
72.5 Information about when and in what form the next contact will take place?[NFG]	[ ]	[ ]	
72.6 In circumstances where the adviser is unable to represent the client at hearings, information about alternative sources of representation and/or assistance?[NFG]	[ ]	[ ]	[ ]

VIII BRIEF TO COUNSEL/SOLICITOR ADVOCATE

Do not audit this section in relation to instructions for bail applications or pleas in mitigation, but include Newton *hearings.*

	Yes	No	N/a
73 Where there is a brief to counsel, does this include:		N/a	[ ]
73.1 A summary of the evidence?	[ ]	[ ]	
73.2 Available witnesses statements?[NFG]	[ ]	[ ]	

NFG 71.1	Eg, on discount for guilty pleas, the magistrate's decision on mode of trial.
NFG 71.2	As a minimum for compliance the adviser must give an outline of committal and transfer procedure, or note that this is unnecessary.
NFG 72.1	A broad indication of the time estimated to resolve from start to finish will be sufficient.
NFG 72.4	This may be an indication of the prospects of success, or of whether the client is likely to be satisfied with the outcome of the case.
NFG 72.5	It is important from the client's perspective to know when they should expect further contact, and whether they should anticipate a letter, telephone call, or need to attend an appointment.
NFG 72.6	Alternative sources could include: Law Centre, CAB, Advice Centre, Free Representation Unit, McKenzie friend, Solicitor (if the audit is of a non-solicitor agency). Where the adviser represents the client on a *pro bono* basis, answer n/a.
NFG 73.2	Alternatively, compliance should be given where the brief notes that no witness statements are available.

	Yes	No	N/a
73.3 Comment on which witnesses should attend court?NFG	[ ]	[ ]	
73.4 Details of witnesses in support of the client?NFG	[ ]	[ ]	[ ]
73.5 Details of previous convictions?NFG	[ ]	[ ]	
73.6 The date of primary disclosure by the prosecution?	[ ]	[ ]	
73.7 Details of any disclosure already made by the defence?	[ ]	[ ]	

IX MAGISTRATES'/CROWN COURT TRIAL N/a [ ]

This section should be audited in cases where a plea of not guilty is entered and taken to trial. This includes cracked trials.

(i) Advice

	Yes	No	N/a
74 Has the client been advised as to:			
74.1 The date **and** time **and** venue of the trial?	[ ]	[ ]	
74.2 Court procedure?NFG	[ ]	[ ]	
74.3 Whether or not to give evidence?	[ ]	[ ]	
75 Where the client is to give evidence, does the file show:		N/a	[ ]
75.1 Whether the adviser attempted to meet with the client to discuss the evidence?NFG	[ ]	[ ]	
76 Where the client is not to give evidence:		N/a	[ ]
76.1 Was the client advised of the implications of failure to give evidence?	[ ]	[ ]	
77 Where the case is to be tried summarily and the prosecution has made primary disclosure has the client been advised:		N/a	[ ]
77.1 On the implications of making a defence statement to the prosecution?	[ ]	[ ]	
77.2 Whether to make a defence statement to the prosecution?	[ ]	[ ]	
78 Where the case is to be tried in the Crown Court and the prosecution have made primary disclosure has the client been advised:		N/a	[ ]
78.1 On the implications of failure to provide a defence statement?	[ ]	[ ]	
78.2 On the implications of providing a statement which is inconsistent or which differs from any defence made out at trial?	[ ]	[ ]	

(ii) Procedure

	Yes	No	N/a
79 Where there is to be a defence statement, does the file show:		N/a	[ ]
79.1 That this has been served on the prosecution?	[ ]	[ ]	
80 Where defence witnesses are to appear at trial, have they been advised of:		N/a	[ ]
80.1 The date **and** time **and** venue of the trial?	[ ]	[ ]	
80.2 Court procedure?NFG			

NFG 73.3 This refers to both prosecution and defence witnesses with a view to agreeing with the CPS which witnesses will be required to attend. If no witnesses are required, this should be noted.
NFG 73.4 Only answer n/a where there are no witnesses in support of the client.
NFG 73.5 Or confirmation that the client has no previous convictions.
NFG 74.2 A note that such advice was felt to be unnecessary will be sufficient for compliance.
NFG 75.1 Where the adviser confirms that counsel will meet the client in conference to discuss the evidence, this will be sufficient for compliance.
NFG 80.2 A note that such advice was felt to be unnecessary will be sufficient for compliance.

	Yes	No	N/a
81 Where counsel/solicitor advocate is instructed, does the file show:		N/a	[ ]
81.1 Whether a conference was held prior to the hearing/trial?	[ ]	[ ]	
82 Where it is known in advance that the defence is unable to proceed on the date given by the court, does the file show:		N/a	[ ]
82.1 That the court was given notice of this?	[ ]	[ ]	

X SENTENCING

N/a [ ]

This section should be audited in all cases were the client is sentenced. Do not audit this section where the client is only bound over by the court. Unless specifically stated, evidence for compliance can only be gained from the ***pre-sentence report, brief to counsel/solicitor advocate to mitigate or notes/checklist made in preparation for a plea in mitigation.***

Factors relevant to the offence

	Yes	No	N/a
83 Where others were involved in the commission of the offence does the file show:		N/a	[ ]
83.1 The extent of the client's role?NFG	[ ]	[ ]	
84 In relation to the commission of the offence, does the file show:			
84.1 Any mitigating factors?NFG	[ ]	[ ]	
84.2 Any aggravating factors?NFG	[ ]	[ ]	

General factors

	Yes	No	N/a
85 Where a guilty plea was made does the file show:		N/a	[ ]
85.1 At what stage in proceedings this was made?	[ ]	[ ]	
85.2 Any subsequent distress and remorse shown at the commission of the offence?NFG	[ ]	[ ]	
86 Does the file show the length of time spent:			
86.1 On remand?NFG	[ ]	[ ]	[ ]
86.2 Awaiting sentence?NFG	[ ]	[ ]	[ ]
87 Does the file show whether this was the client's first conviction?NFG	[ ]	[ ]	
and where the client has previous convictions does the file show:		N/a	[ ]
87.1 The client's record in discharging sentences received?	[ ]	[ ]	

NFG 83.1 Eg, main protagonist, gang leader, getaway driver, unwilling accessory.

NFG 84.1 Compliance should be given where the adviser identifies such factors as any provocation that the client may have been subject to; that the offence was not premeditated; that the client acted in self-defence; that the offence was not committed for personal gain, etc. This does not include drunkenness/being under the influence of drugs.

NFG 84.2 Compliance should be given where the adviser identifies such factors as a vulnerable victim, use of weapons, premeditation or that a breach of personal trust occurred such as a theft from an employer, etc.

NFG 85.2 If the file is silent, answer no. The adviser or the pre-sentence report should note that remorse has or has not been shown or that this is not an applicable factor for a plea in mitigation.

NFG 86.1 If the file shows that the client spent time on remand, a note of the time spent is required. If it is unclear from the file whether the client spent any time on remand, then answer no. Only answer n/a where the file shows that no time was spent on remand.

NFG 86.2 If the file shows that the matter was adjourned for sentence, a note of the time awaiting sentence is required. If this is unclear from the file, then answer no. Only answer n/a where the file shows that no time was spent awaiting sentence.

NFG 87 Evidence of compliance can be gathered from anywhere on the file. Compliance should be given if there is a list of the client's previous convictions on file, otherwise previous convictions or the fact that the client has no previous convictions must be noted. If this question is answered no, then question 87.1 should be answered no and question 87.2 answered n/a.

	Yes	No	N/a
or, where the client has no previous convictions, does the file show:		N/a	[]
87.2 The availability of any character witnesses?	[]	[]	
88 Does the file show the size of the client's income and its source **at the time of sentencing?**[NFG]	[]	[]	[]
89 Does the file show whether the commission of the offence has had any effect on the client's employment?[NFG]	[]	[]	[]
90 Where the client has a relevant medical condition,[NFG] does the file show:[NFG]		N/a	[]
90.1 The nature of the condition?[NFG]	[]	[]	
90.2 The effect of the condition on the client?[NFG]	[]	[]	
90.3 Treatment received/sought?[NFG]	[]	[]	
91 After sentence, has the client been advised whether or not to appeal either against conviction or sentence?[NFG]	[]	[]	

XI CLOSING THE CASE

This section must be audited for all files.

92 Before closing the file, has the adviser written to the client confirming the outcome?[NFG]	[]	[]	[]

XII TRANSFER OF FILES AND REFERRALS

N/a []

This section must be audited in all cases where a file is transferred or a referral is made.

93 Where the file is transferred to another office, department or fee-earner within the same firm, does the file show:[NFG]		N/a	[]
93.1 That the client has been given an explanation of the reasons for the transfer?	[]	[]	
93.2 That the client has been given the name of the person taking over the case?	[]	[]	
93.3 That the client has been given an opportunity to comment or raise any issues?	[]	[]	
94 Where the client is referred to another organisation for advice, assistance or representation in the same matter, does the file show:[NFG]		N/a	[]

NFG 88 Only answer n/a where the client is under 16. It is not sufficient for the adviser or the pre-sentence report to note that the client's income has not changed. The amount and source of income must be noted.

NFG 89 Answer n/a where the client is unemployed or a juvenile.

NFG 90 Medical condition refers to any physical or mental condition, illness or disability which affects the client, including alcohol or drug addiction.

NFG 90 Ie, asthma, heart condition, drug addiction, etc.

NFG 90.2 Ie, symptoms such as dizziness/nausea or risks such as fits, coma, etc.

NFG 90.3 Eg, where the client is under/prescribed any medication, undergoing a programme of rehabilitation, receiving counselling (eg, group therapy; anger management); psychiatric assessment.

NFG 91 For guilty pleas, compliance should also be given where the client has been advised that the sentence was reasonable in the circumstances.

NFG 92 Answer n/a, only where the adviser has noted on the file that there is no forwarding address for the client. Where the client has been sentenced, this should include an explanation of sentence.

NFG 93 This question must be audited in all cases where the file has been transferred within the firm.

NFG 94 This question must be audited in all cases where the case has been referred to another organisation from the organisation being audited, eg, cases initially dealt with by a non-profit sector agency then referred to a solicitor for further advice and assistance and/or representation; and to cases that are referred to another agency, another solicitor, or from a solicitor to an agency (to obtain specialist advice). Note: a change of solicitor where the client is unhappy with the services of a firm is not a referral.

		Yes	No	N/a
94.1	That the adviser has given the client reasons for the referral and the name of the adviser or organisation to whom they are being referred?	[ ]	[ ]	
94.2	That the client has been given an opportunity to comment or raise any issues?	[ ]	[ ]	
94.3	That the adviser has contacted the other organisation on behalf of the client to make an appointment?	[ ]	[ ]	
94.4	That the adviser has confirmed to the other organisation that the client has received legal aid funding and provided details of the advice given and action taken to date?[NFG]	[ ]	[ ]	[ ]
94.5	That the adviser has asked the other organisation to provide feedback (at various intervals or on conclusion of the case)?	[ ]	[ ]	
94.6	Where that referral is from a non-solicitor agency to a solicitor's practice for advice on any stage, does the file show that the adviser:[NFG]		N/a	[ ]
94.6.1	Assessed and advised the client about whether or not they would have to pay a contribution?	[ ]	[ ]	

NFG 94.4 This is only relevant where the client is referred to a solicitor for further advice, assistance or representation which will be funded by the legal aid scheme in the same matter.

NFG 94.6 This advice must be given before any referral.

APPENDIX 3: ANSWERS TO THE SELF-ASSESSMENT QUESTIONS

SAQ ANSWERS: 1.1

1 The offence that is punishable by a fixed term of imprisonment is the offence of murder: it can only be followed by life imprisonment.

2 Burglary is an arrestable offence because it is punishable by a term of imprisonment of five years or more: it is punishable by up to 10 years' imprisonment for non-dwellings and 14 years for dwellings.

3 Common assault is not an arrestable offence: it is not punishable by a fixed term or by five years or more, and is not one of the offences specified under section 24 of PACE 1984.

4 An arrest is carried out when someone is no longer at liberty. Someone under arrest should be informed of that fact and the reason for the arrest.

5 A police officer can arrest someone:
   (a) with an arrest warrant;
   (b) without warrant for arrestable offences:
   - someone who is committing or about to commit an arrestable offence; or
   - someone whom the police officer has reasonable grounds to believe is committing or about to commit an arrestable offence; or
   - someone whom the police officer has reasonable grounds to believe has committed an arrestable offence, which s/he reasonably believes has been committed (whether it has or not);

   (c) arrest without warrant under preserved powers;
   (d) arrest without warrant under specific statutory powers arising after PACE 1984;
   (e) arrest for a breach of the peace;
   (f) where the general arrest conditions apply.

6 A store detective can arrest someone:
   (a) if the person is committing an arrestable offence; or
   (b) if s/he has reasonable grounds to believe s/he is committing an arrestable offence;
   (c) if an arrestable offence has been committed, someone who is or whom s/he has reasonable grounds to suspect is guilty of the offence;
   (d) for breach of the peace.

7 The police may have the following powers of arrest in John's case:
   (a) for breach of bail (preserved power of arrest);
   (b) for failure to provide roadside breath test (preserved power of arrest);
   (c) under the general arrest conditions (see 1.3.11 above);
   (d) on suspicion (reasonable ground to believe s/he has committed the offence) of taking a vehicle without the owner's consent (made an arrestable offence under section 24).

8 If your client is already on bail, his/her bail position will be affected in that:
   (a) s/he has no right to bail if s/he is alleged to have committed an indictable offence whilst already on bail;
   (b) the police (and court) may consider that there are grounds to refuse bail on the basis that there are grounds to believe that s/he will commit offences whilst on bail (in the light of the new matter).

9 Arrest without warrant by the police can take place:
   (a) for arrestable offences;

- someone who is committing or about to commit an arrestable offence; or
- someone whom the police officer has reasonable grounds to believe is committing or about to commit an arrestable offence;
- someone whom the police officer has reasonable grounds to believe has committed an arrestable offence which s/he reasonably believes has been committed (whether it has or not);

(b) under preserved powers;
(c) under specific statutory powers arising after PACE 1984;
(d) for a breach of the peace;
(e) where the general arrest conditions apply (see 1.3.11 above).

SAQ ANSWERS: 1.2

10 No, it can only be delayed.

11 You will require a private room for consultation with facilities to allow you to:
(a) conduct a professional interview;
(b) have some way of notifying the officer when you have finished.

SAQ ANSWERS: 1.3

12 Murder.

13 Yes, it is punishable with more than five years' imprisonment.

14 No, but special powers of arrest are given.

15 No, but the general arrest conditions might apply.

16 No, but the general arrest conditions might apply.

17 The categories for which an arrest can be made by a police officer are:
(a) with a warrant;
(b) to prevent or stop a breach of the peace;
(c) powers of arrest preserved in PACE 1984, even though the offence is not within the definition of an arrestable offence;
(d) powers of arrest given in Acts of Parliament passed after PACE 1984 where new offences are created;
(e) where the general arrest conditions apply;
(f) where a person has been required to attend a police station for fingerprinting and has failed to do so.

18 There is a possible breach of the peace or public order offence, or a general arrest condition (preventing injury) might apply.

19 The police would have the power to carry out:
(a) a search on arrest;
(b) a search at the police station;
(c) a search of the premises under the control of the suspect or where the suspect has just been.

20 The police can search premises where the client was just before arrest.

21 Yes, as all may be evidence of an offence.

22 If the suspect fails to give a name and address, or the address given is suspect, or where the police officer considers it necessary to prevent interference with the investigation or with justice; or to prevent absconding or the commission of further offences; or for the protection of the defendant.

23 When there is sufficient evidence to charge the suspect.

24 To be responsible for the person in custody, to assess whether there is sufficient evidence to charge, to make decisions on bail.

25 When the decision is made, unless the detained person is incapable of understanding, violent or in need of medical attention.

26 The person must be told that they are under arrest and the reason for their arrest, and must be cautioned and taken to a designated police station. S/he can be searched if arrested.

27 At a police station. If not arrested at a police station, s/he can be searched for dangerous items, for items useful for escape and for any items relevant as evidence.

SAQ ANSWERS: 1.4

28 It cannot be denied, only delayed if:

(a) the offence is a serious arrestable offence;

(b) delay is authorised by superintendent because consulting with a legal adviser would, in the superintendent's view, result in:

- interference with or harm to evidence or interference with or physical injury to other person;
- the alerting of other suspects; or
- the hindrance of the recovery of property.

29 An interview without a solicitor can take place if the client does not want legal advice; or if s/he has asked for legal advice but the above situation applies; or when waiting for a solicitor would result in damage or injury or unnecessary delay to the investigation (see 1.4.4 above).

30 A solicitor can be removed from an interview only when the conduct of the solicitor is such that it prevents the proper questioning of the suspect.

SAQ ANSWERS: 1.5

31 The role of the appropriate adult is to advise and help the individual to understand advice or questions by aiding communication.

32 The position or nature of injuries may support (though not necessarily prove) an allegation of an attack on him/her, to which s/he responded, or may undermine it. Minor injuries to which s/he is alleged to have responded with a severe attack may undermine an argument of self-defence, and vice versa.

SAQ ANSWERS: 1.6

33 An identification parade is the most advantageous procedure for your client because it involves more safeguards for a suspect, and can only be carried out with his/her consent.

34 The case of *Turnbull* pointed out the dangers of relying on uncorroborated identification evidence and set down guidelines for the assessment by juries of identification evidence which was in dispute. In summary, the guidelines underline the need for careful assessment of the identification evidence with regard to the length of time of the observation, the distance from which the observation was made, lighting, whether there was an obstruction, whether the witness knows/had seen the suspect before, whether the witness has any special reason for remembering the accused, the length of time between the original observation and later identification to the police, etc.

ADVOKATE = Appearance; Distance; Visibility; Obstruction; Known or seen before; Any reason to remember; Time lapse; Error (see 1.2.6 above).

APPENDIX 4: SELF-ASSESSMENT TESTS

WRITTEN TEST 1

You are asked by Jim's mother to attend at the police station to advise Jim who has been a client of your firm for some time, and who has a series of previous convictions for theft. Jim is under arrest for theft from a shop.

1 What should you do before attending the police station?

2 If Jim is under 17, what further step(s) will you be involved in?

Assume for the remainder of this question that Jim is over 18.

3 What should you do on arrival at the police station?

4 The investigating officer tells you that Jim was arrested as he left a supermarket, having been seen by a store detective to place a bottle of whisky in his coat pocket and leave without paying. You are denied access to your client, Jim: what should you do?

5 Having been allowed to consult with Jim, you are interrupted after five minutes on the ground that the room is needed for another interview. What do you do?

6 The consultation is allowed to continue. Jim informs you *inter alia* that he had been drinking before the alleged incident and that he went into the shop in question and in error placed the bottle in his coat pocket, as he had forgotten to pick up a wire basket. What other matters should your consultation cover?

7 You notify the officer that your client is ready for interview. What do you say at the outset of the interview?

8 At the end of the interview, your client Jim is charged with theft from the shop. In what circumstances would you advise your client to make a statement on charge?

9 In this case, is there likely to be an identification procedure carried out?

10 What should you do before leaving the police station?

WRITTEN TEST 2

Fred Lader is charged with possessing an offensive weapon in a public place. The item in question is alleged to have been a screwdriver with a sharpened point found in his car. Fred tells you that he carried this item in his car as occasionally the boot sticks and he uses it to open it.

He is also charged with assault causing actual bodily harm on Aldred Hollingswood in a separate incident as a result of a fracas outside a public house.

1 What will the prosecution have to prove in order for him to be convicted?

2 What will the procedure be in court to determine mode of trial?

3 Explain briefly the factors that will be taken into account when sentencing and the likely range of sentence.

4 If during the police interview Fred had stated that he carried the screwdriver in case he met 'that bastard Hollingswood', under what circumstances would that be admissible at his trial?

APPENDIX 5: ANSWERS TO THE SELF-ASSESSMENT TESTS

WRITTEN TEST 1

1 You should:
   (a) telephone police station and if possible speak to your client Jim;
   (b) speak to the custody officer and advise that you will be attending and that no interview should take place before you arrive;
   (c) gather information from office/files, etc;
   (d) remind yourself of the issues in theft and police interview procedure (if necessary)
   (NB: what are the elements of theft (see Appendix 1)? What category of offence is it (see Appendix 1)?);
   (e) verify Jim's age.

2 An appropriate adult should be involved: you will (at the station) need to explain to the appropriate adult his/her role in assisting Jim's understanding and to the client, Jim. You will also have to assess the suitability of the adult to perform the role.

3 You should:
   (a) inform officers of arrival;
   (b) consult with custody officer;
   (c) consult with investigating officer;
   (d) then take instructions from your client Jim.

4 You should:
   (a) ascertain alleged reason;
   (b) check whether it is acceptable reason (very few circumstances where this is likely);
   (c) know what is a serious arrestable offence (see Appendix 1);
   (d) assert your client's right to legal advice;
   (e) complain to a senior officer;
   (f) ensure that the custody record is noted.

5 You should:
   (a) firmly point out that your client is entitled to confidential legal advice, that your duty is to protect and advance the legal interests of your client and that the consultation has not finished;
   (b) give an estimate of how long you require, if that is possible, and tell the officer that you will alert him when you are ready.

6 In your consultation, you should also cover:
   (a) background, personal information;
   (b) any information relevant to the obtaining of bail;
   (c) an exploration of the client's version;
   (d) discussion of and your advice on his safest course in any interview, namely, whether to answer questions or not and, in particular, what the consequences are of failing to answer questions in a police interview.

7 At the outset of the interview:
   (a) explain the role of a solicitor's representative and the circumstances when you will intervene;
   (b) if the client is to give a no-reply interview, state why.

8 If he had made a no-reply interview and you advise that a defence statement may minimise the adverse inferences, and one has been prepared.

9 No, there is no identification dispute

10 Prior to leaving the police station:

(a) arrange next steps with your client;

(b) obtain a copy of the custody record;

(c) deal with any bail matters.

WRITTEN TEST 2

1 The prosecution will have to prove:

(a) Regarding an offensive weapon:

- that Fred had the item; and
- that the car was in a public place.

The prosecution does not have to prove that the possession was without lawful authority or reasonable excuse: Fred has to prove the reasonable excuse. It is a matter of fact for the magistrates to determine: (i) whether they accept the excuse; and (ii) whether they believe Fred.

(b) Regarding the assault causing actual bodily harm:

- that Fred committed an assault (intentionally or recklessly caused someone to fear immediate unlawful violence); and
- it resulted in some physical or mental injury to the aggrieved.

2 For TEW offences such as ABH:

(a) after advance disclosure;

(b) the defendant will be asked whether he wishes to indicate a plea and the procedure will be explained (NB: you should be able to explain the procedure in detail (see Unit 2));

(c) if he wishes to plead guilty, there will be no further mode of trial decision;

(d) if the plea is not guilty, there will be a mode of trial decision on the basis of representations from both sides, the magistrates' decision, and the defendant's view if the magistrates accept jurisdiction.

3 The factors that will be taken into account for sentence are:

(a) the plea (discount for guilty plea);

(b) previous convictions;

(c) circumstances of offence: whether people were put in fear;

(d) vulnerability of victim;

(e) whether the assault was provoked;

(f) group action or by an individual.

4 The statement would be admissible at his trial unless there were:

(a) any circumstances that contravened section 76 of PACE 1984, eg, by applying pressure; or

(b) circumstances that persuaded the court to exclude matters in its discretion under section 78 of PACE 1984, eg, improper procedure, failure to comply with PACE 1984 or the Codes of Practice thereunder.

CHECKLIST SUMMARY OF UNIT 1

At the end of this unit, you should be able to:

- assemble relevant information from your client prior to charge;
- take notes of interviews with clients;
- deal appropriately with the representation of vulnerable clients;
- obtain and challenge police refusals to see clients;
- gain information and access to records from the police;
- advise and assist clients effectively in the police station;
- assist clients effectively in police interviews and protect their interests;
- assist clients with identification procedures and advise them on the best course of action.

TAKING INITIAL INSTRUCTIONS IN CRIMINAL LITIGATION CASES AND GIVING PRELIMINARY ADVICE

OVERVIEW

This unit does not cover situations where initial instructions are taken at a police station, which are discussed in Unit 1.

There are six activities making up this unit:

2.1 assembling and managing information related to cases;

2.2 arranging initial bail proofs;

2 3 dealing with the funding of cases;

2.4 researching the law;

2.5 advising clients on available and likely procedures and plea;

2.6 assisting clients with ancillary matters.

OBJECTIVES

To become fully competent in this unit, you will need knowledge and understanding of:

Obtaining and disclosing information

- identify information to which the defendants are entitled and the extent to which this has been made available in individual cases, including primary and secondary disclosure under the Criminal Procedure and Investigations Act 1996;
- identify when forensic, medical or other expert evidence is required;
- identify the relevant organisations and/or departments to approach in relation to the supply of information;
- locate authorities for the purpose of conducting legal research;
- outline the prosecution and defence duties of disclosure of information.

Substantive

- describe the hierarchy and organisation of police, courts and prosecution authorities;
- describe the broad categories of information contained in and the significance of:
  - the Code for Crown Prosecutors;
  - the cautioning guidelines;
  - National Mode of Trial guidelines;
  - Magistrates' Association Sentencing Guidelines;
- distinguish lawful from unlawful arrest/search by investigating officers.

Offences

- distinguish between summary, either way and indictable-only offences;
- identify the elements which constitute an offence;
- state the statutory requirements of custody time limits in relation to summary or either way offences.

Bail

- explain statutory provisions for bail in relation to:

police station:

- appeals against imposition of conditions/ variations to a second custody sergeant;

magistrates' court:

- appeals against police conditions;
- applications for unconditional bail;

Crown Court:

- appeals against refusal from a magistrates' court (defence);
- appeals against grant of bail (prosecution);

High Court:

- appeals against refusal from the Crown Court;
- applications to vary bail conditions imposed in a magistrates' court.

Funding

- state the circumstances in which it is appropriate to submit an application for legal aid funding;
- describe the procedures for appeals against legal aid refusal;
- describe the extent of cover of legal aid funding and the circumstances in which it can be extended in relation to:
  - prior authority expenditure;
  - representation by counsel in a magistrates' court;
  - enlargement on committal/transfer;
  - legal aid through orders;
  - the need to obtain legal aid for fresh offences;
  - describe the professional obligations in relation to costs for privately funded clients;
- explain the liability of defendants in relation to the payment and recovery of costs at the conclusion of proceedings.

Procedure

- describe the distinguishing features of the following different types of tribunal: Crown Court, magistrates' court, *Newton* hearings.

Evidence

- identify situations in which a challenge to the admissibility of prosecution evidence is appropriate.

ASSEMBLING AND MANAGING INFORMATION RELATED TO CASES

RANGE

Achievement must cover all the following contexts.

Environment

Any location, except a police station.

Cases

Any potential/criminal case.

Information from client

Personal details as laid down in transaction criteria; any outstanding court actions or bail commitments; contact information, including emergency contact.

Information about the offence

As laid down in the Legal Aid Board Transaction Criteria.

Types of information

Medical, forensic and other expert information; character references; prosecution witness antecedents; antecedents of linked defendants; interview tape; custody records; conviction records; search warrant; search record.

Sources of information

Prosecuting authorities; probation services; employers/potential employers; parents/guardians; schools; social services.

Professional and ethical standards

Duty to clients, standards of care, protection of interest, conflicts of interest, obligations to the court, client confidentiality.

EVIDENCE

You will need to produce the specific pieces of performance evidence listed below. In addition, you will need to demonstrate that you have achieved the objectives specified at the beginning of this unit. You may do this by producing further pieces of evidence from real and simulated performance, by answering questions posed by your assessor or by passing a written examination.

You will need to provide evidence of:

1 having obtained and recorded **Information from clients** on three occasions;
2 having obtained details or copies of prosecution evidence in two cases;
3 having obtained two of the types of third party information;

4 having made all necessary provision for at least one client with special needs, eg, retained interpreter or appropriate adult;

5 having made continued oral and written representations to prosecuting authority for provision of information about the offence in two cases;

6 having obtained information from two of the **Sources of information**.

CRITERIA

You will demonstrate achievement if:

(a) all necessary information is collected from clients and recorded accurately in files;

(b) advance information is called for before plea or mode of trial in all cases where it is available;

(c) clients' previous conviction records are applied in all cases;

(d) sustained efforts are made to obtain any information which may assist the conduct of the defence;

(e) return date or court hearing date is recorded and representation is arranged;

(f) all information to which clients are entitled is requested from the available sources;

(g) candidate's involvement with cases is placed on record with police and all other relevant parties;

(h) all necessary information is provided to clients in writing unless otherwise requested;

(i) all potential conflicts of interest are identified and action taken to protect clients' positions;

(j) any need for special provisions for vulnerable clients or those requiring interpretation facilities is identified and action taken to ensure that clients are not disadvantaged;

(k) the time used to obtain documents is appropriate to the nature and complexity of the case.

2.1.1 INTRODUCTION

There is a wide array of tasks associated with gathering information from the client and from other people (other than at the police station, which has been covered in Unit 1).

You could be dealing with a client who has already been advised by you or someone else in your firm at the police station, or someone who has not been previously represented either at all, or by your firm.

Where a client has been previously dealt with by another firm, you will need to obtain information from that firm.

Information gathering is a vital stage in the proceedings: in fact, it should not be described as a separate stage because it is essential throughout your involvement with the client.

It can include:

(a) gathering background personal information about the client;

(b) gathering information about the offence from him and from potential witnesses;

(c) obtaining advice from experts to interpret the evidence;

(d) getting supporting statements from character witnesses or employers, or in the case of juvenile clients, from school, parents or social services;

(e) obtaining information from the prosecution, such as:
   - antecedents of the defendant, co-accused or prosecution witnesses;
   - witness statements;
   - custody and search records/search warrants;
   - copies of interview tapes or summaries, or statements under caution;

(f) liaising with probation;

(g) liaising with co-accused's solicitors;

(h) liaising with other services;

(i) appraising need for special support:
   - for juveniles;
   - for those who are not fluent in English;
   - for those whose physical or mental condition may require special help.

This activity is thus concerned with a variety of situations in which you will need to assemble information. The information may be necessary for pre-trial procedures (and in this connection see also 2.3 below) for advising the client, for court stages of the case, whether in defence or in mitigation after a plea of guilty, or for post trial matters. In order to do this, you will need to consider the information you (or your client) require at different stages and how the information can be obtained. This may mean that you will need to contact your client, or someone else, to gather the information. It may be that you are legally entitled to certain information, eg, from the prosecution or the police. In other circumstances, other bodies will wish to assist you voluntarily and to provide you with information. You will need to liaise with other solicitors or with the probation service or social services. But there are other times when you are seeking information from the reluctant or unwilling. There are still other circumstances when you will need to find out whether information exists and where it can be obtained from: there might be other witnesses to contact and interview. You may also need to consider whether your client needs special assistance because of vulnerability – this is partly governed by the law and partly a matter of judgement.

Your client is entitled to advance disclosure in triable either way cases and to disclosure under the Criminal Procedure and Investigations Act 1996. You must be familiar with these provisions and their effect.

It is also necessary that you are aware of when you or your client needs to provide information to others (eg, under the disclosure regime of the Criminal Procedure and Investigations Act (CPIA) 1996) and the effect of non-disclosure and the applicable time limits.

Failure to disclose in accordance with this Act can lead to 'adverse inferences' being drawn against your client.

You will also need to record the information accurately and in a form in which it can be used as appropriate. Your firm will probably have standard forms for most common situations, and have systems for recording time limits by which matters have to be dealt with or attendances made. It is essential that you note time constraints and are aware of their importance.

The checklists given later in this section are provided to give a guide to the information you should consider in a variety of situations.

2.1.2 PERSONAL DETAILS OF CLIENT

You will need to obtain various personal details from any client, usually on the first occasion you have dealings with him/her. Sometimes, these will need to be updated, verified or supplemented by reference to other agencies. The need for most of the details is self-explanatory, and their necessity will not cause any concern to many clients. However, it should be borne in mind that some of the questions are of a sensitive nature or may be sensitive to that particular client. In any event, some clients may not see the need for such matters, being anxious to get on with explaining their problem to you, or to get advice as to what they should do or a prediction of what will happen next. Interviews must therefore be handled sensitively, with due concern for:

(a) the state of mind;

(b) experience; and

(c) level of understanding of the client.

You must also consider:

(d) the stage of proceedings reached;

(e) whether your client needs to be given advice in order to make a decision;

(f) whether you need to obtain further information in order to advise him/her;

(g) whether you need to provide information to others to safeguard the client's interests or to make arrangements for the same purpose;

(h) the different environments where interviews with clients might take place.

Suggested lists for gathering information are given later in this section. The minimum personal details in most dealings with a client are as follows. These will need to be supplemented as explained below:

- client's full name;
- client's address and telephone number;
- client's date of birth;
- client's marital status;
- age and relationship to client of dependants;
- client's employment or unemployment history.

Increasingly, for example under the CPIA 1996, information has to be provided by a certain date. As courts become more concerned about delay, pressure (sometimes welcome, sometimes not) will be placed on solicitors to deal with stages in cases more speedily and adjournments may be refused.

The Crime and Disorder Act (CDA) 1998 is gradually being brought into effect and also contains a variety of anti-delay provisions.

35 List the specific factors that might affect the way you deal with a criminal client, considering his/her state of mind, and the various types of offences and alleged or actual offenders you might have to deal with.

36 List the places, apart from the police station and the office, where you might have to take instructions from a client. What special factors need to be considered when interviewing in different places? Consider:

- the facilities;
- the time available;
- the state of mind of the client.

The Legal Aid Board Transaction Criteria set out, in a standard format, benchmarking criteria for the amassing of information in criminal cases. See Document 4 in Appendix 2.

However, as suggested below, there may be other matters which you will need to canvass with your client in relation to his/her background or offending history as well as about the alleged offence and proceedings, as appropriate. Before we consider these, it is necessary for you to be familiar throughout your dealings with clients with matters of professional conduct.

2.1.3 PROFESSIONAL CONDUCT

Whether or not you are a solicitor, as a member of The Law Society, you must observe the same rules of professional conduct in all your work for and on behalf of your firm.

Solicitors and barristers are governed by their codes of professional conduct, which lay down detailed and sometimes complex provisions. Basically, however, the principles seek to give guidance about the application of fundamental tenets of integrity and professionalism. In a criminal practice, primary concerns involve issues of conflict of interest, and client confidentiality. Although, if you are not already a member of a legal profession, you are not strictly personally governed by the rules of professional conduct, as an employee of your firm you must obey the same rules and standards as a fully qualified member. The solicitors for whom you work are in breach of their professional duty if they allow anyone to do anything on their behalf which infringes the solicitors' duties. If in any doubt, you should consult The Law Society's *Guide to the Professional Conduct of Solicitors*, and/or a member of your firm.

Breaches of professional conduct are bad for the firm, bad for the client and bad for you, and can lead to disciplinary action being taken.

Duty to the client

Standard of care

The solicitor should always carry out work to the proper standard. What the proper standard of care is, is difficult to define. In the criminal sphere, it can be encapsulated by remembering that your role is to protect and advance the client's legal rights. This necessitates being aware of what they are.

Client care

Solicitors' firms all have a system of client care to ensure that clients know how their case will be dealt with, how to complain if it is not properly dealt with in their view, and the cost implications.

If you are not fully aware of it, identify the client care procedure in your firm and find out who deals with complaints.

Confidentiality

A solicitor and his/her employee are under a duty to keep confidential to the firm the affairs of the client and to ensure that staff do the same. The duty of client confidentiality is linked to, but is not the same as, legal professional privilege. The latter term refers to the rules that protect the client from disclosure in court or to the other party of communications between lawyer and client, and between either of them and a third party in relation to contemplated litigation. However, the principle of client confidentiality is much wider in its ambit and seeks to ensure that all information, requests for advice and advice given are not divulged to anyone without the client's permission. This means that a solicitor or employee should not divulge matters concerning his/her client without his/her consent to anyone, including:

- other solicitors outside the firm;
- others accused in the same proceedings;
- the client's partner (business or domestic);
- the client's employer;
- the client's parents* or other relations.

* Where a young client (under 16) is concerned, it may be that the client consults you through his/her parents. For those between 16–18, you must consider whether the child is old enough to instruct you him/herself. Over 18s are, of course, adults.

When dealing with several family members, where a parent or partner may have a legitimate and genuine concern for the client, it is important to remember who that client is, that your duty is to the client, and that information, even of an apparently trivial nature, including the client's address, should not be disclosed without clear instructions from your client.

The duty of confidentiality can be overridden where the client is using the solicitor in order to commit a crime or in some circumstances involving terrorism or child abuse. Consult the *Guide to the Professional Conduct of Solicitors* for full details.

The rules of confidentiality apply to any information given to you by the client, even to information relating to his/her previous convictions. You should not, therefore, disclose previous convictions without the client's consent, but, at the same time, you should not allow a court to be misled.

There is an exception in relation to information relevant to legal aid eligibility: if the client's eligibility changes, there is a duty to the legal aid fund such that the client must be asked for permission for you to inform the Legal Aid Board of the change (or s/he must inform the Legal Aid Board him/herself), or the firm must cease to act.

Protecting the client's interests

The solicitor's duty is always to act in the best interests of the client, subject only to his/her duty to

Legal professional privilege allows the client not to reveal information that they might otherwise have to.

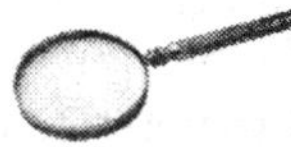

A person over 17 can be interviewed without an appropriate adult. Under 17s should not.

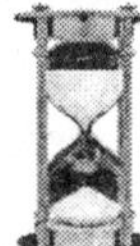

37 You answer the telephone in your office. The caller says she is ringing on behalf of her husband, who is a client of your firm, to ask whether he has been convicted in proceedings that have taken place that morning. What is your response?

Later, another client's mother arrives, asking for her son's latest address. He has been remanded to a bail hostel and she has post for him, but does not know the address. What do you do?

38 In court, the CPS erroneously states that your client has no previous convictions. What should you do?

the public interest in the proper administration of justice.

Avoiding conflict of interest

Often, you or your firm may be approached by two or more defendants in the same proceedings, or indeed be asked to represent another client to save legal aid costs. This will often be perfectly proper: the two defendants can properly be represented by the same firm or individual in the firm. This can be the case whether the clients are pleading guilty or not guilty, and whether they both plead the same way or one pleads guilty and one not guilty. The situation may arise, however, that the two cases are in conflict, so that it would be improper for one firm to act for them both. This may happen where each blames the other for the offence, or each claims that the other took the major role. Essentially, a conflict arises whenever the proper defence of one client may compromise or damage that of the other. The firm should never be in a position where it has information from one client (or ex-client) that can advantage another.

When two co-accused approach you, they should be interviewed separately, so that, in the event of there being a conflict of interest, the second client's instructions can be declined before interview. Otherwise, if interviews have been conducted with both clients and a conflict of interest is later revealed, neither client can be accepted: thus, two matters will be lost to the firm. However, it occasionally happens that, despite separate interviewing, it is not until after the second client has given instructions that the conflict of interest is revealed. In that circumstance, you will normally have to withdraw from both cases. You may have confidential information, or an insight into the one case that may assist the other accused party. As the knowledge gained by one member of the firm is deemed to be held by the firm in its entirety, a conflict cannot be resolved by two accused being represented by different solicitors or even by different branches within the firm, though minor conflicts can be resolved by instructing separate counsel. Issues of conflict may arise between co-accuseds who are friends or members of the same family, as well as those who are clearly from the outset antagonistic to each other.

What is in issue is conflict of interest, not minor differences between the evidence of two co-accused.

Duty to the court

Your overriding duty is not to mislead the court. This means that you must not in any circumstances give the court information (or allow the court to be given information by an advocate or the client) which you know to be wrong. Against this must be set the legal principles that provide that a defendant does not always have to volunteer information; neither does a solicitor on his/her behalf.

The following examples provide particular situations where this principle can cause a problem.

Example

You know that the client has previous convictions, but the court does not because the CPS record is incomplete.

There is no duty to divulge the previous convictions, but you cannot assert the good character of the defendant, either in trial or in sentencing, nor assert that s/he has no convictions for a particular type of offence, eg, for violence when you are aware of a previous unrecorded assault.

If you allow the court to come to a conclusion (for example, on bail or sentencing) on the basis of this being a first incident, when you know of previous convictions, you may be in breach of your duty.

Example

The client has given false details (name, address or date of birth) to the court to avoid discovery of a previous record.

You must advise the client to give the true information to the court, or authorise his/her advocate to do so, or your firm must withdraw from the case: to do otherwise would involve you in misleading the court.

39 Your client has told you that s/he 'did the deed'. Can s/he advance an alibi at trial?

Example

The client has told you/his/her advocate that s/he is guilty of the offence (and you are satisfied in law that s/he is guilty), but states that s/he wishes to plead not guilty.

The prosecution may be 'put to proof' and witnesses cross-examined, the admissibility of a confession or other evidence challenged and a submission of no case to answer made. All of this is within your duty to probe the prosecution case. However, s/he must not be permitted to give evidence which the representative knows to be false.

2.1.4 COLLECTING INFORMATION FROM THE CLIENT

As indicated above, you will be required to gather, record and manage information in a variety of situations in criminal litigation. In order to do this, you will need to understand what information is required in given circumstances and the information's use and purpose. That will necessitate you being familiar with the incidents of criminal litigation covered in the rest of this book and thus being able to identify circumstances in which information is required. The following checklists may be used in most circumstances. Your firm may have

Your portfolio should contain evidence of obtaining and recording information in three cases.

a standardised form. You must, however, be able to determine whether and when the matters are of relevance in any particular case.

For example, family background may be relevant to bail applications. Employment history may also be relevant, as it may be to sentencing.

2.1.5 CLIENT'S BACKGROUND

Although the basic personal details needed in every case have been referred to in 2.1.2 above, it is often useful to have more detailed information, particularly in order to contact clients, especially clients that are very mobile or who may need to be contacted in an emergency.

This is not to suggest that you have to keep 'tabs' on your client, but contact is all important. Your client should be told that s/he must keep in touch.

2.1.6 VULNERABLE CLIENTS

Where the client has special problems that might affect the conduct of the proceedings, these should be noted at the earliest opportunity. These are matters that may affect the way the case progresses, because of their legal effect (eg, youth or mental disability) or the practical arrangements for advising and representing the client, such as his/her deafness or lack of command of English.

You may need to arrange for the attendance of an interpreter or appropriate adult (see also 1.5).

You will need to make all necessary provisions for at least one client with special needs, eg, by arranging for an interpreter or the attendance of an appropriate adult, in at least one case.

CHECKLIST: BACKGROUND

Surname and first names

- Any previous names or aliases

Current address for contact

- Is that a permanent address?
- How long at that address?
- Who else lives there?

Is there another reliable person or address for emergency contact? (Check whether person knows of proceedings and whether s/he can be informed of confidential matters)

Telephone number

- Where is this? Above address? Mobile? Work? Home? Other contact?

Age

Date of birth

Single/married/separated/divorced/living with dependants?

Employed/unemployed/in education/houseperson?

Health (sickness benefit or not)

Type of accommodation (owned/renting, etc)

Has legal aid been granted/applied for? (See 2.3 below)

CHECKLIST: CONSIDERATIONS OF SPECIAL NEEDS

Is there a medical condition relevant to the offence?

Nature and effect on client

Names and addresses of GP and other doctors or hospital involved in treatment

Has the client a sufficient command of English:

- to deal with matters in writing?
- to deal with matters orally?

If not,

- should you advise to attend with a friend or other supporter?
- is there a need for a translator:
  - for office interview?
  - with police?
  - in court?

If so, have arrangements been made?

Juvenile client:

- is s/he able to instruct you him/herself?
- is there a need for an appropriate adult in police interview?
- attendance at court of adult?
- any social service involvement?
- have arrangements been made?

Deafness:

- is a signer necessary?
- have arrangements been made?

Known mental impairment:

- is a carer or appropriate adult needed?
- have arrangements been made?

Is there any other disability that might require alerting of court/prosecution, etc, or special consideration in process?

2.1.7 THE OFFENDING HISTORY, IF ANY, OF THE CLIENT

The offending history of the client will be required in a variety of circumstances (see also bail) in relation to defending a case or for a plea in mitigation.

At various stages of proceedings, it will be necessary to gather or update information in relation to progress. The following will serve as a checklist as to the matters necessary to be considered and recorded. Some of the information may already have been gathered at a different point in the proceedings, but is repeated for completeness.

You will, occasionally, be dealing with a person who is for the first time involved with the courts. Usually, however, there will be a history to take account of. This is extremely important for bail and sentencing, and may also have some significance for the conduct of the trial.

CHECKLIST: INFORMATION ON OFFENDING HISTORY

Has the client any cautions?

Has s/he any previous convictions?

NB: verify details with firm's records if there have been previous dealings with this client, and always with prosecution.

Has the antecedent record been applied for/checked?

Is the client currently on bail?

- Is this court or police bail?
- When is the return date?
- Are there any conditions?

Verify with court documents.

Is the client currently serving any court orders?

Is he currently paying any fines?

- Are payments up to date?

Are there any other criminal proceedings pending?

- What is the relevant date/stage/offence?

Verify as soon as possible with court/prosecution what these dates are.

Apply for records of previous convictions in every case. Clients may deliberately or genuinely forget offences, and very often be mistaken about dates and details. Previous offending history is very important when considering bail and sentencing decisions.

You must have obtained information from two of the sources.

Multiple proceedings can cause difficulties over how best to proceed. Delaying transfer or disposal needs consideration.

CHECKLIST: DETAILS OF PROCESS CHARGE

Has the client been charged?

Has the charge sheet been seen?

What are the details of the charge?

When is the next hearing?

If not charged, what stage has been reached in the proceedings?

Bail or custody history

Has the client been in custody?

Is so, for how long?

Has the custody record been asked for/seen?

If still in custody, when was s/he taken into custody?

If in custody and conditional bail is likely:

- names and addresses of persons willing to stand as sureties (see 2.2 below);
- security that could be given on subsequent bail application (see 2.2 below);
- alternative address or bail hostel.

Has s/he been on bail throughout, or is s/he now on bail?

Is this police bail or court bail?

Are there any conditions attached? (Specify)

Have there been any changes to the bail conditions?

Court appearances

Has the client already appeared in court? if so, where and when?

Was s/he given bail? Were conditions attached?

When is the return date? Is representation arranged?

What is to happen?

Are there co-accuseds?

Who are they represented by?

If by other firms, are they aware of you or your firm's involvement?

Remember the custody time limits in police station for those not charged prevent long detention before charge (see 1.3.34 above).

You need to produce evidence of gaining two of the types of information from third parties.

Clients often do not appreciate the detail of bail conditions and it is important to verify them with firm or court records.

You need to demonstrate the recording of the court or return date and the provision of representation.

You need to demonstrate that your involvement is placed on record with all relevant parties.

Has the client to return to the police station?

Is s/he to be accompanied by a legal adviser?

Have arrangements been made?

Is s/he to return for interview?

Is s/he to return for an identity parade?

Are police aware of your firm's/your involvement?

You must ensure that the police and all other relevant agencies are aware of your firm's involvement.

Has the client to return to the court?

If so:

- name of court;
- date and time.

What is expected to happen?

- who is to represent the client?
- have arrangements for representation been made?

Is the court aware of your firm's/your involvement?

What needs to be done before next hearing?

Has legal aid been granted/applied for?

You must record the making of arrangements for representation and make the parties aware of your involvement.

2.1.8 INFORMATION ABOUT THE ALLEGATION/OFFENCE

You will, of course, also need to consider the information to be gathered in the case in relation to the alleged offence.

The information will naturally vary from case to case, and will be affected by your client's intentions as to plea. However, s/he may not be able to be advised as to plea until certain information is available:

(a) Your starting point will be the offence charged; you should always examine the charge sheet, which will give information as to the alleged offence.

(b) You will then need to ascertain the client's account of the matter and consider your advice.

(c) If s/he is relying on an alibi, what was s/he doing at the time? Are there witnesses?

(d) What is the client's intention as to plea?

(e) Has the client made a statement to the police?

(f) If so, what was said?

(g) Has a copy of the statement/tape been requested/received?

Your portfolio should show that you have obtained details of the prosecution evidence in two cases.

With TEW offences, the client has a right to advance information about the evidence before decisions are made about plea. Other disclosure provisions apply, particularly in the Crown Court under the CPIA 1996. Your portfolio should also show that you have obtained details of the prosecution evidence in two cases.

(h) What is the offending history?
- previous bail record
- breach of existing order
- cautions, court appearances, previous convictions, other court disposals
- have antecedents been applied for?
- has custody record been applied for?

(i) Is any probation officer or social worker involved with the client?

(j) Are there any co-defendants?
- if so, names, ages and addresses
- client's view of their role in offence
- co-defendants' previous convictions if known by client
- have they been applied for to prosecution?
- are co-defendants represented by this firm?
- if by separate solicitors, name of firm

(k) Has the client received advice and assistance or seen the duty solicitor at the police station, and if so, who?

(l) Was a search carried out? Has search warrant/record been examined?

(m) Are there any witnesses to the offence?
- are names and addresses known? If so, specify, if not, can they be discovered?

(n) If the defendant is relying on an alibi witness:
- name and address of witness, or if not known, can these be discovered?

(o) If this is a TEW case, has advance information been applied for/received?

(p) Is this a matter where specialist evidence will be required?
- is legal aid available/applied for?
- type of expert?
- name and address

(q) If the client was identified
- have details of original description by identification witness, if any, been requested from the police?

(r) Are character witnesses to be relied on?
- names and addresses?

(s) Is there other evidence required/available that might assist the client?

Write to the client with an outline of your advice.

All necessary information must be supplied in writing unless otherwise requested.

You must show the request for antecedents.

Be vigilant that there is no issue of conflict.

Your client is entitled to advance information before plea in all TEW cases. Your portfolio should show continued representation for information in two cases.

Original descriptions must be supplied, under the Police and Criminal Evidence Act (PACE) 1984, when requested.

2.1.9 RECORDING THE INFORMATION

After gathering information, throughout your dealings with the matter you will need to record and transmit the information as appropriate. It is essential that the file accurately records work done and advice given, and indeed notes matters to be done in the future, not only as a record of the information for future reference, but also in connection with billing and legal aid.

You should, therefore, check the following at all stages:

(a) Have you recorded all the information correctly?

(b) Have you given any information necessary to the client, in writing unless otherwise requested?

(c) Does the file show, where relevant, requesting and obtaining of:

- charge sheet/custody record?
- police interview record/statement under caution?
- list of previous convictions?
- advance information?
- original description?

(d) Have you noted court return dates, etc?

You will, of course, be aware that an advocate or other adviser may need to rely on your notes when there is pressure of time, or in court to make an application. It is essential, therefore, that your notes can be easily understood by others. Your firm may have a pro forma for most simple information: detailed case background will usually be set out as a proof of evidence.

You need to demonstrate both the recording of information and the supply of this to your client. The content will often show other areas of achievement.

ARRANGING INITIAL BAIL PROOFS

RANGE

Achievement must cover all the following contexts.

Environment

In court, at police station.

Agencies

Bail information scheme officers, community psychiatric nurses, probation services, police, Crown Prosecution Service, clerk to the court, court ushers, co-accused's legal representatives, sureties.

EVIDENCE

You will need to produce the specific pieces of performance evidence listed below. In addition, you will need to demonstrate that you have achieved the objectives specified at the beginning of this unit. You may do this by producing further pieces of evidence from real and simulated performance, by answering questions posed by your assessor or by passing a written examination.

You will need to produce evidence of:

1 having assessed available information and passed relevant information and copy documents to advocates in a coherent form in two cases;
2 having explained to the client his entitlement or lack of entitlement to bail on two occasions;
3 having explained in writing to one potential surety the implications of acting as such;
4 having passed necessary information to at least four **Agencies** in the **Range**.

CRITERIA

You will demonstrate achievement if:

(a) entitlement to bail or otherwise is explained to the client;
(b) all relevant information is provided to advocates and verified where possible;
(c) all relevant information is provided to all relevant agencies with due expedition;
(d) objections to bail are ascertained and counter arguments prepared;
(e) family and other relevant third parties are kept informed of developments;
(f) implications of standing as surety are explained to those proposing to stand;
(g) procedure to be followed if bail is not granted or a variation is sought is explained to clients;
(h) prosecution right to appeal a grant of bail is explained.

2.2.1 INTRODUCTION

At any stage in proceedings before a case is finally disposed of, a court will need to make a decision about whether to keep the accused in custody or release them on bail. This will involve adjournments and remands. These two terms tend to be used interchangeably, but strictly a *case* is adjourned, whereas a *person* is often remanded on bail or in custody. If a case is simply adjourned and the defendant is not placed on bail (or in custody), there is no actionable requirement to attend. Bail is therefore a means of securing attendance. The length of the adjournment might be affected by whether the defendant is remanded on bail or in custody.

There are limitations on the remand length for those in custody, imposed by law. Additionally, many courts have local practices agreed with the CPS as to usual adjournment lengths.

Thus, a decision as to whether the client is to be on bail may arise:

(a) after arrest;

(b) in early court appearances;

(c) during trial;

(d) post-conviction before sentence; and

(e) occasionally after sentence pending appeal.

On first being arrested, a police officer (the custody officer) will have to decide whether to release that individual on police bail to reattend the police station or to attend court. The provisions relating to court bail and police bail are broadly similar, but there are important differences, which will be referred to below, as will the differences for those charged with imprisonable and non-imprisonable offences.

You will need to understand the law and practice relating to bail in order to:

(a) advise the client on the likelihood of his/her being granted or refused bail by a court or police officer;

(b) deal with custody officers in the police station when a client has been arrested;

(c) give information to advocates representing a client in court when there may be an objection to bail;

(d) deal with clients in custody who are seeking bail;

(e) liaise with other agencies such as the probation service, who may have a role in the bail arrangements.

You will need to explain a client's entitlement to bail, or otherwise, on two occasions.

You will need to assess all relevant information and pass it and documents to advocates concerned with a bail application in two cases, in a coherent form.

You will, therefore, need to be familiar with both the law and the practice in relation to the granting and withholding of bail, the imposition of conditions on bail, and the situations where it is possible to challenge decisions made about bail.

Issues of bail are important not only because they affect the liberty of your client, but also because they may have a subtle effect on how the case

When a person appears in court from custody, it always – or often – imbues the case with a greater seriousness, even though that might not be the reason for the custodial remand.

proceeds after the decision is made. Further, a client remanded unexpectedly in custody may not be the best advertisement for your firm.

2.2.2 WHAT IS BAIL?

If a person is on bail, it means that s/he is under a duty to return to (surrender to) the court or police station at a particular time and date. Failure to comply may (and usually will, unless the person has a valid excuse) result in:

- a warrant being issued for his/her arrest;
- an information being laid for breach of bail as a separate offence;
- the unlikelihood of bail being subsequently granted;
- any surety (see below) being forfeited.

Though bail breaches rarely result in significant penalties, they have a considerable impact on later applications for bail.

The CDA 1998 has created quicker and more certain forfeiture of sureties.

Bail can be contrasted with a remand in custody, and also with a simple adjournment where no specific compulsion is placed on the defendant to attend court. Bail, if granted, can be conditional or unconditional.

2.2.3 WHAT IS UNCONDITIONAL BAIL?

Unconditional bail refers to the situation where the client is granted bail without any limitations being placed on his/her activities. S/he is nevertheless under a compulsion to surrender to custody at the specified time, date and place, and failure to do so without a valid excuse will constitute the commission of an offence.

However, it should also be noted that offending whilst on bail is seen as an aggravating feature of any new offence, even if the client is eventually acquitted of the original one. In some circumstances (see below), a person will lose any right to bail if new proceedings are brought whilst s/he is already on bail.

Clients who are placed on bail, especially if it is for the first time, should have a very clear explanation given to them as to the meaning and effect of bail. Magistrates' courts are increasingly likely to take action on even minor breaches of bail, such as late attendance at court. This may result in prosecution, conviction and the imposition of a relatively small fine. It will, however, have a more significant outcome: it will make the defendant's prospects of getting bail again (in this or subsequent proceedings) much less likely.

Failure to attend in these proceedings or evidence of potential absconding may lead to a custodial remand.

2.2.4 WHAT IS CONDITIONAL BAIL?

If the court has grounds – as set out in 2.2.6 below – for refusing unconditional bail, conditions may be imposed. These can be in any form, as long as they are clear and capable of being enforced by the police. Any conditions should be related in some way to the ground for refusal of unconditional bail. It is important that the meaning and extent of any conditions imposed are unambiguous so that the client is not unwittingly in breach of them. Where a client is in danger of being remanded in custody, s/he may be willing to agree to any condition rather than be incarcerated, but it is still necessary to pay attention to the appropriateness and enforceability of conditions.

2.2.5 WHEN DOES THE CLIENT HAVE A RIGHT TO BAIL?

Prima facie, the client is entitled to unconditional bail, unless a ground for the refusal of bail or for the imposition of conditions is applicable or the allegation is one of murder, manslaughter, rape or attempted murder or rape. In such cases, special provisions apply (see 2.2.13 below). Most of the concern over the granting or witholding of bail arises in relation to imprisonable offences, and normally there is no issue about whether a client charged with or convicted for a non-imprisonable offence should be granted bail. The case will usually be simply adjourned or unconditional bail imposed without discussion. However, there are circumstances in which a defendant charged with a non-imprisonable offence may not be granted bail (see 2.2.10 below).

2.2.6 WHEN CAN THE CLIENT BE REFUSED BAIL?

The client can be refused bail only if a ground for refusal exists: the grounds are laid down in the Bail Act 1976, as amended by the Bail (Amendment) Act 1993 and the Criminal Justice and Public Order Act (CJPOA) 1994. In deciding whether a ground for refusal exists, the court or the police may take account of any relevant matter, but in particular the considerations set out in the Bail Act.

When bail is refused or conditions imposed, the reasons must be given and recorded. These can be very important if there are subsequent applications to challenge or vary the decision.

Clients charged with (or convicted of and awaiting sentence for) an imprisonable offence need not be granted bail if one of the following *grounds* exists:

General right to bail of accused persons and others – section 8 of the Bail Act 1976

(1) A person to whom this section applies shall be granted bail except as provided in schedule 1 to this Act.

(2) This section applies to a person who is accused of an offence when –

(a) he appears or is brought before a magistrates court or the Crown Court in the course of or in connection with proceedings for the offence, or

(b) he applies to a court for bail or for a variation of the conditions of bail in connection with the proceedings.

This subsection does not apply as respects proceedings on or after a person's conviction of the offence or proceedings against a fugitive offender for the offence.

(3) This section also applies to a person who, having been convicted of an offence, appears or is brought before a magistrates court to be dealt with under Part II of schedule 2 to the Criminal Justice Act 1991 (breach of requirement of probation, community service, combination or curfew order).

(4) This section also applies to a person who has been convicted of an offence and whose case is adjourned by the court for the purpose of enabling inquiries or a report to be made to assist the court in dealing with him for the offence.

Often, charges are reduced or withdrawn: this may well affect the need for bail conditions.

(a) the court is satisfied that there are substantial grounds for believing that the defendant, if released on bail (whether subject to conditions or not) would:
   - fail to surrender to custody; or
   - commit an offence while on bail; or
   - interfere with witnesses or otherwise obstruct the course of justice: schedule 1, Part 1 of the Bail Act 1976, as amended;

(b) the offence is an indictable offence or an offence triable either way; and it appears to the court that s/he was on bail in criminal proceedings on the date of the offence: section 26 of the CJPOA 1994;

(c) the court is satisfied that the defendant should be kept in custody for his/her own protection or, if s/he is a child or young person, for his/her own welfare;

(d) s/he is in custody in pursuance to the sentence of a court or of any authority acting under any of the Services Acts;

(e) the court is satisfied that it has not been practicable to obtain sufficient information for the purpose of taking the decisions required by this part of this schedule for want of time since the institution of the proceedings against him/her (only used in early stages);

(f) having been released on bail in or in connection with the proceedings for the offence, s/he has been arrested in pursuance to section 7 of the Bail Act 1976;

(g) his/her case is adjourned for inquiries or a report; the defendant need not be granted bail if it appears to the court that it would be impracticable to complete the inquiries or make the report without keeping the defendant in custody.

After conviction, except for adjournments for pre-sentence reports and for committal for sentence, which are covered by the Bail Act provisions (as immediately above), the court has a discretion of whether to grant bail.

There are special provisions relating to cases of murder, manslaughter and rape (see 2.2.13 below).

2.2.7 WHAT MATTERS DOES THE COURT TAKE INTO ACCOUNT?

In making decisions on bail, the court must take into account the *considerations* specified in the Bail Act 1976.

It is important for the defendant released on bail to understand the increased dangers of offending in relation to his/her bail status.

It is necessary to consider bail in relation to someone already in custody, if the custodial period is likely to end in the near future, but the effect on release date in the event of conviction should be considered.

This relates to the current proceedings: compare with breaches of bail in earlier matters as a consideration for coming to the conclusion that a ground for refusal exists.

Post-conviction bail is relevant only where inquiries or reports are necessary or where there is to be an appeal against a custodial sentence.

The considerations to be taken into account are:

(a) The nature and seriousness of the offence or default (and the probable method of dealing with the defendant for it).

It should be noted that, *except* for the special cases of murder, manslaughter and rape, the nature of the offence is not of itself a ground for refusal of bail, but merely a matter that the court should take into account in determining whether the accused is likely to re-offend, abscond or interfere with witnesses. The assumption is that the more serious the offence and the heavier the likely penalty, the more likely it is that the offender will decamp or seek to influence the outcome of the trial. This consideration also allows a court to take into account the inherent likelihood of some offences being repeated, eg, drugs offences and burglaries, or carrying a high likelihood of interference with witnesses, such as some sex offences.

(b) The character, antecedents, associations and community ties of the defendant.

Primarily, a court will be looking at the risk of absconding. A person with a settled address, family or job is seen as less likely to abscond. It should be remembered that the term means failing to attend court as ordered, and is not confined to defendants who flee the area. Nevertheless, the assurance that the defendant can be located at a specific address and the imposition of a condition to reside there will often reassure a court. Sometimes, this ground allows the court to consider the likelihood of further offences being committed because of associations with other criminal types, and may be relied upon particularly where the defendant is charged with offences in association with others.

(c) The defendant's record in respect of the fulfilment of his/her obligations under previous grants of bail in criminal proceedings.

A defendant who has absconded before, either by 'disappearing' or failing to attend court when on bail, may lessen his/her prospects of bail on another occasion. It should be noted that this consideration relates to attendance in the present or any other matter with which s/he has been involved. History of absconding in the present proceedings can of itself negate the right to bail. Also relevant under this head will be whether the offender has offended previously whilst on bail or failed to comply with conditions.

(d) Except in the case of a defendant whose case is adjourned for inquiries or a report, the strength

Distinguish grounds and considerations. Grounds are the legal reasons for refusal. Considerations are the matters which the court will take into account in arriving at the grounds.

A court might be willing to impose a condition not to communicate with, or go to the address (home or school) of, a witness in a sex offence.

Many criminal clients have a 'head in the sand' approach to court appearances, hoping they will 'go away'. Others are genuinely disorganised and miss appointments. Although you are not responsible for your client's attendance, you must ensure that the client knows of the need to attend and the consequences of failure. This is, to a certain extent, reflected in the new conditions of bail introduced by the CDA 1998 – seeing a legal adviser (see 2.2.9 below).

Defendants who are late in answering bail or attend and then leave the court before their case is called may well have a Bail Act offence recorded against them. Clients should be fully aware of their obligations.

of the evidence of his/her having committed the offence or having defaulted.

It is assumed that the certainty of conviction will make it more likely that the defendant will seek to avoid the consequences by failing to attend. This consideration is also taken into account by courts in considering the likelihood of further offences.

(e) any other matter which appears to be relevant.

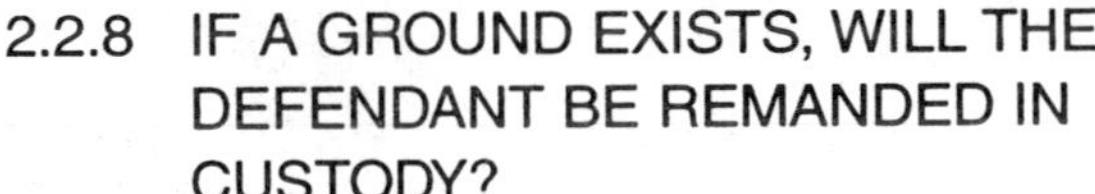

2.2.8 IF A GROUND EXISTS, WILL THE DEFENDANT BE REMANDED IN CUSTODY?

If a condition or conditions can be imposed which will meet the concern of the court or police officer, then conditional bail should be granted.

2.2.9 IF A GROUND EXISTS, WHAT CONDITIONS CAN BE IMPOSED?

Conditions can only be imposed on bail if it appears to the court (or to the custody officer in the case of police bail) that it is necessary to do so for the purpose of preventing the defendant from:

(a) failing to surrender to custody; or

(b) committing an offence while on bail; or

(c) interfering with witnesses or otherwise obstructing the course of justice, whether in relation to him/herself or any other person: para 8(1), schedule 1, Part I of the Bail Act 1976.

Common bail conditions

Conditions can take any form, but the most common are:

(a) *curfew* – ordering the defendant to remain indoors at a certain address between specified hours. This is usually, but not always, imposed in relation to evening or night, where offences have been alleged at that time. It is usually in association with a residence condition;

(b) *residence* – ordering the defendant to live and sleep at a specified address, usually imposed where there is a fear of absconding;

Assessing whether a ground for bail exists

- the nature and seriousness of the offence or default (and the probable method of dealing with the defendant for it);
- the character, antecedents, associations and community ties of the defendant;
- the defendant's record respecting the fulfilment of his/her obligations under previous grants of bail in criminal proceedings;
- the strength of the evidence;
- other relevant matters.

40 What are the grounds for refusal of bail?

41 What matters will the court take into consideration?

42 When can conditions be imposed?

Only if conditions are insufficient to meet the concerns should bail be withheld: *R v Mansfield Justices ex p Sharkey* [1985] QB 613. Justices must perceive a real risk of one of the relevant matters occurring, but need not have substantial grounds for believing they will occur in order to impose conditions. Contrast this with the substantial grounds necessary to refuse bail.

Distinguish curfew as condition of bail and curfew as a sentence under the CDA 1998.

(c) *residence in a bail hostel* – usually imposed where there is no fixed accommodation available to the defendant, or where the accommodation is associated in some way with the allegations. A bail hostel place can only be provided through the probation service and is an expensive resource, so is usually only available if the defendant is in real danger of being remanded in custody without such a place. The condition may included a condition to abide by the rules of the hostel, but in any event, the hostel will provide a measure of control, and failure to comply will usually result in the place and the bail being withdrawn. The defendant will still be able to attend work or education, but will not be allowed to remain if s/he abuses alcohol or drugs (or other residents!);

As this condition involves liaison with the probation service, it cannot be imposed as a condition of police bail.

Having no fixed abode is not *per se* a ground for refusing bail.

(d) *reporting to the police station* – theoretically imposed to prevent absconding or further offending, but it is unclear how such a condition would do either. The condition will specify the day(s) and time at which the client should report to the police station, and specify which station is involved. The reporting times should be arranged so as not to infringe any curfew, or impinge on work or educational commitments;

Although a common condition, it is unclear how reporting can prevent offending. It may give early warning of absconding in the sense of leaving the area, but not of failing to attend court.

(e) *forfeiture of passport or travel documents* – imposed usually if there is a fear of the client leaving the country. This is sometimes allied with a condition not to apply for travel documents;

(f) *non-contact condition* – a condition may be imposed not to contact the complainant or witnesses in the case, where it is thought this might lead to further offending or interference with witnesses. The condition is usually phrased to prevent contact with the person directly or indirectly, which will include contact by visits, telephone or through a third party. The condition may be associated with a condition that the defendant does not visit/go to/ approach the home or workplace of a person involved in the allegations. This type of condition may be considered in many violent offences, including domestic violence cases;

(g) *not to go to a particular place or type of place* – often imposed to prevent re-offending or interference with witnesses in cases of domestic or neighbour violence, or offences involving thefts from shops, violence around public houses, and so on;

43 How can conditions be phrased where allegations of domestic violence have been made against a spouse and your client wishes to have access to children of the family?

44 What are the appropriate grounds, considerations and possible conditions of bail in respect of a persistent shoplifter?

(h) *to attend interview with a legal adviser* – under section 54(2) of the Crime and Disorder Act (CDA) 1998, a court (but not the police) can impose a condition that the defendant must attend an interview with a legal adviser before the next court appearance. This is only possible if the defendant wants to be legally represented, and is a way of hastening that process. If you are already involved, this is less likely to be imposed, as a legal adviser will already have been consulted, but it is envisaged that even in these circumstances, the condition will be imposed in some cases. More likely, however, is the situation where you are contacted by clients who have been given such a condition of their bail. It is, however, difficult to see how such a condition could be enforced;

(i) *to make themselves available for reports* – in a similar vein, a court, but again not the police, may impose a condition on the bail of a convicted person who has been remanded on bail for the preparation of pre-sentence reports, that s/he make him/herself available or that s/he co-operate with the probation service. Again, this is sometimes imposed to hasten the dilatory.

This provision was introduced to attempt to combat delays caused by defendants seeking adjournments, often repeatedly, to 'consult a solicitor'. The defendant's solicitor is not expected to report a breach if the defendant fails to attend a solicitor's appointment.

45 How would you word a condition appropriate for an offender who is alleged to have been involved in town centre violence, who wishes to attend the town centre to obtain regular prescription drugs, to attend the DSS and to see his/her solicitor?

Specifically regulated conditions

There are also two specific conditions referred to in section 3 of the Bail Act 1976, both of which can be imposed to secure attendance.

These are:

(a) the imposition of a surety; and

(b) the taking of security.

A surety is a promise by someone (or more than one person) other than the defendant to pay a sum of money specified by the court if the defendant absconds. The term is also used to refer to the person who undertakes that commitment: s/he 'stands (as) surety in the sum of x'. It should be noted that, in contrast with the security, no money is required to be paid in advance. A court would need to be satisfied that the surety could meet the sum imposed, and that the person is likely to be able to cause the defendant to attend.

Procedure in respect of the taking of sureties

Usually, the person standing surety will be required to attend court, and the court will normally wish to hear from the prospective surety on oath, to establish that s/he understands the obligation and consequences of the defendant failing to attend, and has some form of control over the defendant (section 3 of the Bail Act 1976).

The surety is imposed to ensure attendance, not to prevent commission of offences.

When dealing with a proposed surety, you need to advise that person of the role of a surety, assess the factors that might influence whether a court would accept him/her, and advise him/her as to the consequences if the defendant does abscond.

The consequence for a surety is that some or all of the sum involved may be forfeit (estreated). This is not automatic, but is very often done, bearing in mind:

(a) the means of the surety (though these will have been considered when the surety was imposed);

(b) the amount of blame attaching to the surety.

The presumption is that the full sum will be forfeit, and it is up to the surety to satisfy the court that it should not be so forfeit.

Under s 55 of the CDA 1998, new procedures have been introduced to strengthen this presumption. Whenever a defendant fails to answer bail upon imposition of a surety, the court is required to declare the amount forfeit and summons the surety to court to explain why the sum should not be forfeit. If the surety attends, then the court may, after hearing from him/her, order some, all or none of the sum forfeit. If s/he fails to attend, the court may now proceed in his/her absence, provided they are satisfied that the summons was served properly. The new provisions also allow that if, on the occasion of the non-attendance of the defendant, the surety is actually present, the process can be immediately started without adjourning for the issue of a summons against the surety.

Sureties should not stand unless they are sure that they can pay the amount specified and they trust the defendant to attend.

Although the surety is normally taken by a court, if the person suggested is not available, an order specifying that a surety in a certain sum would be a suitable condition of bail may be specified by the court, and the defendant be kept in custody unless and until a person acceptable to the police or a prison governor is produced to stand as surety in the given sum. The surety is 'taken' by the police or prison governor, and the defendant can then be released.

You need to demonstrate that you have explained in writing the implications of standing as a surety. A security's means may need to be demonstrated to the court by the production of bank or building society documents. Your portfolio must include evidence of having explained the implications of being a surety on at least one occasion.

The surety is imposed to ensure attendance, not to prevent the commissioned offences: *Uxbridge Justices ex p Heward-Mills* [1983] 1 WLR 56.

The taking of security

This involves the deposit of cash or other valuables to secure attendance. This may be done where the defendant is likely to leave the country, eg, in cases where the defendant has strong links with another country, and the imposition of such a condition requires the defendant to produce something of value (whether money or goods) as security against his/her return.

The provision, however, is no longer confined (since the CDA 1998) to cases where the defendant is likely to leave the country. This special condition of the deposit of a security can be imposed in any case to ensure attendance. The means of the defendant or the person given the security must be taken into account.

2.2.10 CAN BAIL BE REFUSED FOR THOSE CHARGED OR CONVICTED OF NON-IMPRISONABLE OFFENCES?

A defendant charged with or convicted of a non-imprisonable offence need not be granted bail, or can have conditions imposed on bail, if:

(a) the court is satisfied that s/he should be kept in custody for his/her own protection;

(b) s/he is already serving a custodial sentence;

(c) s/he has already been bailed in the course of the present proceedings and has been arrested for absconding.

2.2.11 WHEN CAN A BAIL APPLICATION BE MADE?

Theoretically, a decision on bail has to be made on every occasion the client comes before the court, but very often, when a client has initially been given unconditional bail by the police or by a court, there will be no subsequent objection, and on each appearance unconditional bail will be continued. Similarly, if acceptable conditions have been imposed and have not been breached, then they will usually be re-imposed without challenge. The bail matter will, in these cases, normally take place at the end of the day's proceedings in relation to that particular client. However, if an incident such as absconding or further allegations arise, there may be an objection raised by the prosecution to the

Section 8 of the Bail Act 1976

(1) This section applies where a person is granted bail in criminal proceedings on condition that he provides one or more surety or sureties for the purpose of securing that he surrenders to custody.

(2) In considering the suitability for that purpose of a proposed surety, regard may be had (amongst other things) to:

(a) the surety's financial resources;

(b) his character and any previous convictions of his; and

(c) his proximity (whether in point of kinship, place of residence or otherwise) to the person for whom he is to be surety.

(3) Where a court grants a person bail in criminal proceedings on such a condition but is unable to release him because no surety or no suitable surety is available, the court shall fix the amount in which the surety is to be bound ...

R v Bournemouth Magistrates ex p Cross (1989) 89 Cr App R 90.

It might be necessary to consider bail if the accused is already in custody when the period of custody might end before the next hearing.

In the magistrates' court, the time taken for a preliminary hearing will be greatly affected if there is to be a contested bail application. Always liaise with the prosecution and court staff (usher or clerk) to ensure that all are aware of the issue.

continuance of bail. In other cases, the prosecution might object to bail from the outset. It is in these cases that it is most necessary to have full bail information available, but it is good practice to be prepared in all cases.

In other cases, the bail application will itself be the reason for bringing the case before the court.

Bail problems may unexpectedly arise in the event of new charges: the file should always therefore be up to date with relevant information.

2.2.12 IF BAIL IS REFUSED CAN IT BE APPLIED FOR AGAIN AT THE NEXT HEARING?

Schedule 1 to Part IIA of the Bail Act 1976 and *R v Nottingham Justices ex p Davies* [1981] QB 38 established this point.

In some cases, repeated bail applications will be possible, but a client is not permitted to apply for bail on every hearing if it has been previously refused.

A bail application can be made as of right on the first appearance after the one at which bail was refused, so this means that the defendant has a right to make applications on his/her first appearance and the subsequent one. Thereafter, s/he has a right to renew the application only if there has been a change in circumstances, though the court may in its discretion allow for another application to be made, despite the lack of change in circumstances.

R v Dover and East Kent Justices ex p Dean [1992] Crim LR 33; *R v Calder Justices ex p Kennedy* [1992] Crim LR 496: listings in the absence of the defendant or where there is insufficient information on which to base a decision do not count as one of the two opportunities for bail applications as of right.

Where a change in circumstances is relied upon, the court will first need to be persuaded that there is a reason for allowing a renewed application. Therefore, an application to the court to decide whether they can entertain another application may be necessary. A change in circumstances might include any of the following:

- discontinuance of some of the charges/change of charge to a lesser offence;
- availability of a surety;
- availability of employment or accommodation;
- availability of a hostel place.

A decision by the court that circumstances have changed does not mean that they will necessarily accede to the application, however.

2.2.13 CASES OF MURDER, MANSLAUGHTER AND RAPE, OR ATTEMPTED MURDER AND RAPE

Paragraph 9A, schedule 1 to Part I of the Bail Act 1976 and section 56 of the CDA 1998.

There are special provisions in relation to allegations of these offences.

(a) Although there is a presumption in favour of bail in such cases, it is effectively weakened by the provision that, where the prosecution object to bail because of a fear of absconding, committing further offences or interfering with witnesses, then the court must give and record its reasons for giving as opposed to witholding bail.

(b) There is a presumption against granting bail for someone charged for the second time.

The prosecution can appeal against the grant of bail by magistrates in such cases. Although the police may grant bail in these circumstances, it is rare, and is always done with the advice of a senior officer.

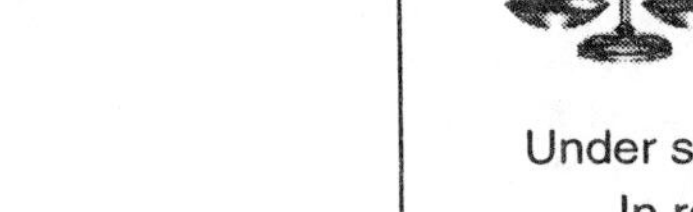

Under section 56 of the CDA 1998:

> In respect of a person who in any proceedings has been charged with or convicted of an offence of:
>
> - murder; attempted murder; manslaughter; rape; or attempted rape; and
> - has been previously convicted for one of those offences,
>
> there is a rebuttable presumption against the granting of bail.

2.2.14 WHAT IS THE PROCEDURE IN A BAIL APPLICATION?

The precise point at which bail is considered will depend on the nature of the proceedings, but will usually be a matter to be determined after the main issue of the hearing. Its determination may affect other issues, such as the length of a remand. In this section we will consider the procedure in the magistrates' court (for police bail, see 2.2.15).

Whenever a question of bail arises and the prosecution objects, the procedure will be similar. First, the prosecution will outline the facts of the case and their objections, based on the grounds in the Bail Act 1976 and the relevant considerations. If the defendant has previous convictions, a list of these will be handed in to the court, but not read out aloud. The defence can then argue why the grounds do not exist, or how they can be met by conditions. It is important that likely objections are explored with the prosecution wherever possible or are anticipated, so that appropriate arguments can be marshalled and appropriate enquiries made. This will be particularly important if alternative accommodation (eg, a condition of residence) or sureties are to be imposed.

In some cases, it will be necessary to forewarn a client that bail is not likely to be granted, though normally, the client will be aware of the problem, as s/he will have been brought to the court in custody.

Outline of proceedings

- Prosecution outlines relevant facts and objections to bail.
- Defence seek to counter objections by:
  - arguing that a ground does not exist; and/or
  - that conditions will meet the problem.
- Magistrates decide.
- Decision recorded and record given to defendant.

It is comparatively rare for bail to be withdrawn in the magistrates' court if it has been previously granted by the police, unless more serious charges or further offences have come to light or the defendant fails to attend, but it can be done. More frequently, it will be a question of negotiating over conditions. The significant bail application in a magistrates' court will involve the seeking of bail, usually with conditions, for the client who has been refused police bail, and care should be taken in such cases to consider the reality and to fully canvass possible conditions. In cases of violence or sexual assault, the obtaining of bail may be assisted if the client can find an address well away from the location of the offence, perhaps with a relative or friend. In these circumstances, it would be advisable to have the person offering such accommodation present in court so that the magistrates can be satisfied that the address is genuine. In some cases, inquiries of the Probation Service to enlist help in obtaining a bail hostel place will be necessary. In some areas, Bail Information Schemes, run under the auspices of the Probation Service, can assist in checking or providing suitable addresses but are usually limited to those in real danger of custodial remands. The Bail Information Scheme is also available in prison and, if requested by a client in prison or his/her solicitor, will make checks on possible bail addresses and on the likelihood of the prisoner observing bail conditions. The scheme will then prepare a report with this information for the CPS and the court.

Where bail is refused or granted subject to conditions, the reasons must be recorded and announced. This is important for explaining the situation to the client, as well as for renewed applications or variations of or appeals against decisions.

2.2.15 POLICE BAIL

When a person who has been arrested by the police is charged, they must be released on bail to attend the magistrates' court at a specific time and date, or brought before a magistrates' court as soon as possible, not later than the next sitting of the court (section 46 of PACE 1984).

Bail can only be withheld by the police if:

- the suspect refuses to give a name and address (or those given are thought not to be true);
- detention is necessary to prevent interference with investigations or justice, to prevent absconding or to prevent commission of further offences (if the arrest was for an imprisonable offence) – the police will apply the same criteria as mentioned above; or

In an early administrative hearing under s 50 of the CDA 1998, the clerk can impose conditions, with the agreement of both sides.

You will need to provide evidence of providing information to at least four relevant agencies; a bail information scheme and probation service are two of them.

In all hearings in the magistrates' court, liaison with the usher can be very valuable. This can be particularly important when waiting for a client on bail or when explaining that there will be a bail application. The usher is one of the agencies listed in the above criteria.

Police grounds for withholding unconditional bail are consistent with the court grounds.

- detention is necessary for the defendant's own protection.

In the case of non-imprisonable offences:

- detention is necessary to prevent injury to someone else or damage to property.

2.2.16 MAY THE POLICE APPLY CONDITIONS?

The police can impose the same conditions on bail as a court, on the same basis, except for the imposition of a condition to reside at a bail hostel, to attend an interview with a legal adviser or for the defendant to make him/herself available for reports. Reasons have to be given and recorded. Whilst this new power of the police to impose conditions has prevented many remands in custody to the magistrates' court, it is clear that conditions are sometimes imposed by the police where a court would not require them. Also, terminology is sometimes unclear. Care should be taken, and a judgment made about whether to accept otiose or unclear conditions pending clarification or removal by a court, or whether an appeal should be made to a second police officer at the police station.

A judgment has to be made about acceding to non-troublesome conditions when these are not strictly applicable in legal terms.

Section 3A of the Bail Act 1976

Where a constable grants bail to a person, no conditions shall be imposed under subsections (4), (5), (6) or (7) of section 3 of this Act unless it appears to the constable that it is necessary to do so for the purpose of preventing that person from:

(a) failing to surrender to custody, or

(b) committing an offence while on bail, or

(c) interfering with witnesses or otherwise obstructing the course of justice, whether in relation to himself or any other person.

(6) Subsection (5) above also applies on any request to a custody officer under subsection (8) of section 3 of this Act to vary the conditions of bail.

2.2.17 CAN THE DEFENDANT CHALLENGE POLICE CONDITIONS?

Appeals to a second custody sergeant: a second officer can be asked to vary the conditions imposed at the time of charge.

Appeals can be made to a court to vary the conditions imposed by a police officer.

Section 3A(8) of the Bail Act 1976

Where a custody officer has granted bail in criminal proceedings he or another custody officer serving at the same police station may, at the request of the person to whom it was granted, vary the conditions of bail; and in doing so he may impose conditions or more onerous conditions.

2.2.18 RECORDS

Reasons for the withholding of bail or the imposition of conditions on bail must be announced in court and formally recorded, and the record given to the defendant. Police reasons for imposing conditions must be recorded in the custody record. This will, of course, be important in order to help advise the client on the extent of any conditions and in the event of any challenge to the terms.

See Documents 2, 3 and 4 in Appendix 6.

2.2.19 CAN THE CONDITIONS BE VARIED?

As mentioned above, police bail can be varied by a second officer or on application to the court. It may also be necessary to seek a variation of court bail. It is important that clients understand the implications of breaching bail in any way whatsoever.

Courts may take differing approaches to temporarily or permanently lifting conditions of bail. Decisions will be affected by the same considerations as generally apply in bail matters: the defendant who has successfully observed his/her bail conditions for a considerable period is more likely to be permitted some leeway. This may involve a reduction in curfew hours or reporting, or the lifting of a ban on visiting an area, or permission to stay at a different address for a short time, for a valid reason.

The court's willingness to temporarily amend bail conditions, for example, for attendance at a birth, a significant family occasion or other matter, will be determined by the nature of the offence and the grounds for withholding unconditional bail.

2.2.20 CAN THE DEFENDANT APPEAL AGAINST THE REFUSAL OF BAIL

A defendant who is refused bail by a magistrates' court may apply:

- again to the magistrates' court (see 2.2.12 above);
- to the Crown Court under section 81(1) of the Supreme Court Act 1981:
  - if the magistrates remanded the defendant in custody after a fully argued bail application;
- to the High Court under section 22 of the Criminal Justice Act (CJA) 1967:
  - against refusal of bail or the imposition of conditions.

Appeal to the Crown Court is the most usual channel of challenging a magistrate's refusal of bail, and legal aid will usually be available (see 2.3 below), but either or both methods can be used.

See Document 5 in Appendix 6.

Appeal to the Crown Court is to the judge alone, who will decide on the same grounds as the magistrates.

2.2.21 CAN THE PROSECUTION APPEAL?

Since the Bail (Amendment) Act 1993 (section 1), the CPS and certain other specified bodies have a limited right to appeal against the granting of bail, and have a right to ask the court to reconsider the granting of bail if further information comes to light (such as the discovery of previous offences).

The prosecution may appeal where bail is granted to a person accused or convicted of:

- an offence punishable by a term of five or more years' imprisonment; or
- an offence of taking a vehicle without authority or an aggravated vehicle taking offence,

if the prosecution:

- object to bail at the hearing;
- give oral notice at the hearing of their wish to appeal at the end of the proceedings; and
- give written notice to the court, within two hours, of their wish to appeal.

The procedural difficulties prevent this power from being often used, but in appropriate cases it can be used – usually to the disruption of the court.

2.2.22 RECONSIDERATION OF DECISIONS GRANTING BAIL

Where the magistrates grant bail in a case involving an indictable (including a TEW) offence, the court may be asked by the prosecution to reconsider their decision in the light of fresh information that subsequently becomes available, and to:

- vary bail; or
- withold bail; or
- impose conditions on bail,

on the same grounds as in a normal bail matter.

If the person whose bail is reconsidered in this way is not before the court, they can be ordered to surrender and may be arrested without warrant.

It is not necessary to use this power where *new offences* have come to light, as they will be separately considered for bail.

Section 5B of the Bail Act 1976

(1) Where a magistrates' court has granted bail in criminal proceedings in connection with an offence, or proceedings for an offence, to which this section applies or a constable has granted bail in criminal proceedings in connection with proceedings for an offence, that court or the appropriate court in relation to the constable may, on application by the prosecutor for the decision to be reconsidered:

(a) vary the conditions of bail,

(b) impose conditions in respect of bail which has been granted unconditionally, or

(c) withhold bail.

(2) The offences to which this section applies are offences triable on indictment and offences triable either way.

2.2.23 CHECKING INFORMATION

Opposed bail applications will depend for their success on putting forward reliable information to the court. It will often be necessary to support and verify information through liaison with:

- probation;
- co-accused's representatives;
- mental health or other social service and health professionals;
- those who are to provide residence or sureties for the client.

The amount of work should be in relation to the likelihood of custody.

2.2.24 HOW LONG CAN THE CLIENT BE REMANDED IN CUSTODY?

The maximum period of remand in custody is eight clear days, unless the defendant has already been remanded in custody for this matter, in which case, a remand of up to 28 clear days is possible (section 128A of the Magistrates' Courts Act (MCA) 1980). No consent from the defendant is needed. If, however, s/he does consent, s/he can be remanded up to three times in custody in his/her absence if s/he has a solicitor acting for him/her.

The above refers to individual remands. Under the Prosecution of Offences Act 1985, there are maximum time limits laid down for defendants to be held in custody between various stages of the proceedings:

(a) for indictable offences, the maximum period between first appearance and committal is 70 days;

(b) for TEW cases being tried in the magistrates' court, 70 days from first appearance to start of trial, unless the mode of trial hearing takes place within 56 days, in which case that is the maximum;

(c) after committal, the maximum from committal to arraignment is 112 days.

If the time limit expires, the defendant must be granted bail unless the court dealing with the case has granted an extension. This can only be done if there is good reason and the prosecution have acted expeditiously.

The extension must be applied for before its expiry, as there is no power to back date the extension of time.

(3) No application for the reconsideration of a decision under this section shall be made unless it is based on information which was not available to the court or constable when the decision was taken.

(4) Whether or not the person to whom the application relates appears before it, the magistrates' court shall take the decision in accordance with section 4(1) (and schedule 1) of this Act.

(5) Where the decision of the court on a reconsideration under this section is to withhold bail from the person to whom it was originally granted the court shall:

   (a) if that person is before the court, remand him in custody, and

   (b) if that person is not before the court, order him to surrender himself forthwith into the custody of the court.

(6) Where a person surrenders himself into the custody of the court in compliance with an order under subsection (5) above, the court shall remand him in custody.

(7) A person who has been ordered to surrender to custody under subsection (5) above may be arrested without warrant by a constable if he fails without reasonable cause to surrender to custody in accordance with the order.

(8) A person arrested in pursuance of subsection (7) above shall be brought as soon as practicable, and in any event within 24 hours after his arrest, before a justice of the peace for the petty sessions area in which he was arrested and the justice shall remand him in custody.

In reckoning for the purposes of this subsection any period of 24 hours, no account shall be taken of Christmas Day, Good Friday or any Sunday.

As the client has an absolute right to bail if the period expires without renewal, it is, of course, important to keep accurate records of the remand dates.

CHECKLIST FOR TAKING BAIL PROOFS

Personal details

name and normal address

telephone number if applicable

age

suggested bail address if different

name and address of any proposed surety

details of surety

Home circumstances of client

marital status

dependents

property ties

employment ties

other family ties

Offending history

any previous for similar offence

for other offences

dates

sentences

compliance with sentences?

fines paid/CSO completed, etc

Employment details

job

income

length of employment

prospects

Previous history on bail

any previous for absconding?

has the client always attended as requested?

If unemployed

prospects of employments

length unemployed

benefit income

Special factors

was the offence alleged to be committed on bail?

is it an offence of murder, manslaughter rape or attempt?

Offence details

has the defendant admitted guilt?

does s/he contest it?

is the evidence against him/her strong?

is it an offence that is likely to merit imprisonment?

consider effect of previous history on likely sentence

In respect of possible conditions

any factor that would make conditions particularly onerous, such as work needs?

Are others charged together with client

is their likely bail position known?

age of co-accused

If there is to be a restrictive condition,

does it need exceptions?

DEALING WITH THE FUNDING OF CASES

RANGE

Achievement must cover the following contexts.

Environment

Police station, court, office, prison.

Nature of funding

Claim 10, legal aid, ABWOR, private funding, police station legal advice, insurance cover, party funding.

Agencies and third parties

DSS, court, CAB, employers, accountants, financial institutions.

EVIDENCE

You will need to produce the specific pieces of performance evidence listed below. In addition, you will need to demonstrate that you have achieved the objectives specified at the beginning of this unit. You may do this by producing further pieces of evidence from real and simulated performance, by answering questions posed by your assessor or by passing a written examination.

You will need to provide evidence of:

1 having discussed the various **Natures of funding** detailed in the **Range** with two clients;
2 having successfully applied for legal aid for a client on at least three occasions;
3 having appealed against refusal of legal aid through the courts on at least one occasion;
4 having documented investigations of three clients' possible sources of funding and explained in writing to them the practicalities of legal aid and private funding.

CRITERIA

You will demonstrate achievement if:

(a) an assessment of clients' financial position is made;
(b) clients are advised on eligibility, availability and extent of funding;
(c) all necessary documentation for legal aid application is completed accurately and in full and submitted with due expedition;
(d) where legal aid is not available the implications are explained to clients and the source of funding established before proceeding with cases;
(e) clients' financial and personal situations are kept under constant review throughout cases;
(f) applications for all necessary extensions, authorities and assignments are prepared;
(g) in the event of legal aid being refused by the court, all review and appeal procedures are followed.

2.3.1 LEGAL AID SCHEME

Legal aid is a system of government funding for those who cannot afford to pay for legal advice, assistance and representation. The primary source of the law in this matter is the Legal Aid Act 1988. Part V (sections 19–26) relates to legal aid in criminal proceedings. The detailed law is contained in Regulations made under the Act as follows:

(a) the Legal Advice and Assistance Regulations 1989 (The Advice Regulations);

(b) the Legal Aid in Criminal and Care Proceedings (General) Regulations 1989 (The General Regulations);

(c) the Legal Aid in Criminal and Care Proceedings (Costs) Regulations 1989;

(d) the Legal Advice and Assistance (Duty Solicitor) (Remuneration) Regulations 1989.

The Act, Regulations, Duty Solicitor arrangements, notes for guidance and relevant case law are contained in the Legal Aid Handbook, which is published annually in July. Other useful sources of information include *Practice Notes on Legal Aid* by Susan Spencer, London: Cavendish Publishing, and the major practitioner works have chapters on legal aid.

The details of legal aid eligibility change very frequently, hence the annual publication of the handbook. Your firm will have the 'cards' for quick computation.

2.3.2 ADMINISTRATION

Legal aid is administered by the Legal Aid Board, members of which are appointed by the Lord Chancellor. The Police Station and Court Duty Solicitor Schemes are administered by local Duty Solicitor committees appointed by the Board.

Applications for legal aid in the magistrates' court and in the Crown Court before committal or transfer are made to the Clerk to the Justices. When a case has been committed or transferred to the Crown Court, an application must then be made direct to the Crown Court. Legal aid for representation in the Court of Appeal is granted by the court itself, which also grants legal aid for appeals before the House of Lords.

The Legal Aid Board have set out transaction criteria for criminal work, to which you must adhere in order to meet the NVQ criteria (see Document 4 in Appendix 1).

2.3.3 FRANCHISING AND THE PROPOSED REFORMS OF LEGAL AID

The Board states: 'The purpose of franchising is to work in partnership with the profession to provide an accessible and quality assured legal aid service to clients, giving improved value for money to the tax payer.' The Board is in the process of running pilot schemes for contracting criminal legal aid and it is probable that, within a fairly short period, legal aid work in both civil and criminal proceedings will be

A Criminal Defence Service was proposed in 1998 and is expected to be set up shortly.

limited to firms with a contract with the Legal Aid Board. It will almost certainly be necessary to have a franchise in order to apply for such a contract.

2.3.4 POLICE STATION LEGAL ADVICE

A solicitor is defined as including accredited representatives in this instance.

A suspect who is under arrest and in detention is entitled to consult a solicitor privately and at any time, upon request. Any such request must be noted in the custody record. This right may only be delayed if the suspect has been detained for a serious arrestable offence and an officer of the rank of Superintendent or above authorises the delay (see Unit 1). The delay may only be authorised if the officer has reasonable grounds for believing that, if a solicitor is contacted:

Section 58 of PACE 1984.

- suspects not yet arrested may be alerted;
- property obtained as a result of an offence may not be recovered; or
- in drug trafficking cases, recovery of the suspect's proceeds from drug trafficking may be hindered,

or for similar such reasons. The reason are set out in detail in the Act and Code C, Annex B.

Legal advice under the Police Station Scheme is available to any person who:

(a) is arrested and held in custody at a police station or other premises;

(b) is being interviewed in connection with a serious services offence; or

(c) is a volunteer. A 'volunteer' is defined as a person who, for the purpose of assisting with an investigation, attends voluntarily at a police station.

Your ability to give legal assistance at the police station is affected by the Police Station Duty Solicitor Scheme.

This Scheme is not subject to any financial eligibility test. The Board will only pay for advice if it is given by a solicitor with a valid practising certificate, by an accredited duty solicitor representative or by a probationary representative registered with the Board.

2.3.5 DUTY SOLICITORS AND OWN SOLICITORS

Remember that only accredited and probationary representatives can act as duty solicitor police station advisers for payment.

Advice and assistance can be given by the suspect's own solicitor or by the duty solicitor. The duty solicitor and any duty solicitor representative are appointed by the local Duty Solicitor Committee on behalf of the Board (Legal Aid Duty Solicitor Arrangements 1996). There is no application form for police station advice and assistance. The advice can include advice on the telephone, advice in private at the police station or other premises, and representation in any application before the magistrates for a warrant for further detention. It also extends to representation before a police inspector in connection with any review of custody time limits or extension of the limits, and representation before the custody officer in connection with an application for bail following charge.

2.3.6 PAYMENT FOR POLICE STATION ADVICE AND ASSISTANCE

A claim is made by completion of form CLAIM 14. This must be submitted to the local regional office within three months of the advice. Although later claims can be accepted for good reason, they may be reduced and, if there is no good reason, claims will be refused. A claim by a duty solicitor for a standby payment must be submitted on form CLAIM 15. Fees allowable are at a fixed hourly rate, with separate rates for telephone calls, depending on whether they are routine or advice calls. A duty solicitor is paid at a higher rate for work done during unsocial hours, and for travelling and waiting time.

2.3.7 LEGAL ADVICE AND ASSISTANCE (THE GREEN FORM SCHEME)

The Legal Advice Scheme is means tested and the eligibility criteria are very low. It is available for advice and assistance on any question of English law, subject to financial eligibility.

Eligibility

There is no contributory system. Legal Aid form 10 must be completed.

Income

The client must be on:

(a) Income Support;

(b) Family Credit;

(c) Disability Working Allowance; or

(d) have a disposable income of £80 per week or less.

The relevant income is the client's gross income over the last seven days, combined with the gross income of their spouse (providing they are living together) or cohabitee. Allowances, full details of which are set out on the Green Form Key Card, are deducted from the total gross income in order to calculate disposable income.

Those on benefit are always eligible under the means criteria.

Capital

The client must also fall within the limits for disposal capital. In calculating disposal capital, certain items are disregarded, including the value of the main house up to a limit of the first £100,000 net equity:

- household effects;
- clothes;
- tools and implements of trade;
- the value of the subject of the dispute.

The maximum disposal capital for a client with no dependants is £3,000.

If a client falls within the eligibility levels, a solicitor can give advice and assistance up to the financial limit of two hours' work. This can be extended, subject to reasonableness in the case of a franchised practice by self-certification, or, in the case of a non-franchised practice, by application on form DS3 to the Legal Aid Board.

46 What is the Green Form used for?

2.3.8 HOW THE LEGAL ADVICE FORM IS USED IN PRACTICE

In criminal cases, the Legal Advice Form can be used for advising a client who knows s/he is facing a possible criminal investigation for preliminary advice. After charge or summons, it can be used for advice, and in a case where legal aid is refused or is unlikely to be granted, it can be used for advice on the law and on plea. If the client decides to plead not guilty, it can also be used for advice on the conduct of the defence. In a guilty plea, it can be used for the preparation of a letter in mitigation, combined with advice to seek the assistance of the duty solicitor if available at court. In a more serious case, it can be used in connection with preparing an application for legal aid, doing essential preliminary work before legal aid is granted and assisting with an appeal against the refusal of criminal legal aid. It can also be used after conviction, in connection with assisting preparation of an application to the Criminal Cases Review Commission.

You must show evidence of having discussed the various nature of funding with two clients, have documentary evidence of considering three clients' possible sources of funding, and explaining in writing to them the practicalities of legal aid and private funding.

2.3.9 CRIMINAL LEGAL AID

Criminal legal aid is available for advice, assistance and representation in all criminal courts. Unlike Green Form advice, there is both a merits test and a financial eligibility test. In the case of proceedings before the magistrates' court, an application is made on form CRIM 1 to the court. Unless the client is exempt from completing a means form because, eg, s/he is receiving Income Support or Income Based Job Seeker's Allowance or Family Credit, then form

5 has to be completed and the supporting evidence of means provided, unless it is impractical to do so. If the latter is the case, reasons must be given. The Government wishes to remove the financial eligibility test for criminal legal aid in the magistrates' court.

You must show evidence of successfully applying for legal aid for a client on three occasions.

2.3.10 CRITERIA FOR REPRESENTATION

This is governed by sections 21 and 22 of the Legal Aid Act 1988. There are certain proceedings where legal aid must be granted (mandatory legal aid):

- murder;
- where the prosecutor appeals or applies for leave to appeal to the House of Lords for the proceedings on the appeal;
- where a person is brought before the court pursuant to a remand in custody when s/he may be again remanded or committed in custody;
- where a person is to be sentenced or otherwise dealt with for an offence by a magistrates' court or a Crown Court, and is to be kept in custody to enable enquiries or a report to be made to assist the court, before proceeding to sentencing or otherwise dealing with him/her.

47 When must legal aid be granted in criminal cases?

Section 21(2) provides that representation may be granted (discretionary legal aid) where it appears to the court to be desirable to do so in the interests of justice: this is further defined under section 22. Further, section 21(7) states that where a doubt arises as to whether representation should be granted to any person, the doubt should be resolved in that person's favour. The detailed criteria for the granting of representation for trial proceedings may include the following:

- the offence is such that, if proved, it is likely that the court would impose a sentence which would deprive the accused of his/her liberty, or lead to loss of his/her livelihood or serious damage to his/her reputation: section 22(2)(a);
- the determination of the case may involve a substantial question of law: section 22(2)(b);
- the accused may be unable to understand the proceedings or to state his/her own case because s/he does not have an adequate knowledge of English, or has mental illness or other mental or physical disability: section 22(2)(c);
- the nature of the offence is such as to involve the tracing and interviewing of the witnesses or expert cross examination of a witness for the prosecution: section 22(2)(d);

48 List the main and the detailed criteria for granting discretionary legal aid.

- it is in the interest of someone other than the accused that the accused be represented: section 22(2)(e).

The CRIM 1 form lists the criteria with a box for you to complete if relevant to your client's case. It is important that the form is completed fully with sufficient information to enable the clerk who considers the application to make an informed decision on the merits. The following practical points may be relevant in deciding whether the person may lose his liberty:

- Reference to the Magistrates' Courts Association Sentencing Guidelines will always be helpful, and is a good starting point.
- A person of previous good character pleading not guilty will always be able to claim the possibility of serious damage to reputation.
- An offence of dishonesty may also lead to the loss of livelihood for a person involved in any position of trust.
- Many cases involve complex cases of law. Self-defence is an obvious example.
- If a case involves tracing and taking proofs of evidence from witnesses, it is always a strong argument that the client, due to his/her age, is too young to undertake this task by him/herself.
- The age of the defendant is also relevant to expert cross-examination of a witness for the prosecution. This is particularly relevant in a case in which the witnesses are police officers.
- The obvious case where it is in someone other than the accused's interests that the accused is represented is a sexual offence of any nature, but it may also be relevant in a case of domestic violence or a serious assault.

2.3.11 FINANCIAL ELIGIBILITY

Unless the client or his/her spouse, or the appropriate contributor in the case of a child under 16, is receiving Income Support, Income Based Job Seeker's Allowance, Family Credit or Disability Living Allowance where legal help would be free, form CRIM 5 must be completed in full. The assets of a spouse/cohabitee will not be taken into account if s/he is living apart from the client, has a contrary interest to the client or if it would otherwise be inequitable to do so.

2.3.12 DISPOSABLE INCOME

This is based on income for the three months prior to the date of the application. If the client is

***Benham v UK* (1996) 22 EHRR 29; (1996) *The Times*, 24 June**

In this important case, the European Court of Human Rights held that a case in the magistrates' court for non-payment of Council Tax were criminal proceedings, and that, as the applicant risked imprisonment, the interests of justice called for legal representation. Although this is of persuasive authority only, pending the implementation of the Human Rights Act 1998, it can be used as an argument in support of legal aid in any case where conviction or sentence is likely to lead to imprisonment.

***R v Gravesham Magistrates' Court ex p Baker* (1997) *The Times*, 30 April**

The Divisional Court held that, where a tenant intends to raise a special reason for non-disqualification from driving on conviction of driving with excess alcohol, for example, a suggestion that his drink had been laced, it is in the interests of justice that he is granted legal aid and that it should extend to the instruction of an expert witness.

***R v Scunthorpe Magistrates' Court ex p S* (1998) *The Times*, 5 March**

In the Divisional Court, a refusal to grant legal aid to a 16 year old charged with obstruction of a police officer in the execution of his duty was quashed as irrational where there was an issue as to whether the officer was acting in the execution of his duty. The court held that the expertise required for the purpose of cross-examination and for proofing defence witnesses was beyond that of a 16 year old. Further conviction would have damaged a young man of good character on the threshold of his life.

49 Is a client on Income Support entitled to legal aid?

employed, it will be necessary to produce payslips for the previous 13 weeks. This requirement often causes problems in practice. Sometimes, clients only have one or two pay slips. If, as is normal, these show their cumulative pay for the financial year, the court would almost certainly accept this as evidence of means. Sometimes, clients are not given payslips at all, in which case they may be prepared to ask their employer to provide evidence of their means. If the client appears in custody, it is extremely unlikely that they will have any payslips with them, and of course, if they do not obtain bail they will probably have lost their job. In these circumstances, the court will normally accept the fact that they are in custody as the reason for their inability to produce the documentary evidence, and grant legal aid if they are further remanded in custody. If bail is granted, normally the court will require the client to produce evidence of earnings. A self-employed client will have to produce his/her latest set of accounts. If the client has become self-employed within the last year or so, no accounts will be available, and it will be necessary for you to ask the client to produce books or whatever records they have.

In addition to income from earnings and profits, other sources of income must be declared, including maintenance payments, Child Benefit, and income from investments. The total gross income must be worked out on a weekly basis, and outgoings are then included on the CRIM 5 form. The deductions taken into account in calculating disposable income are the following:

- Income Tax, National Insurance;
- housing costs, eg, board and lodging (it will be necessary to obtain a letter from a parent if the client is living at home), rent (less any housing benefit received), mortgage payments, including payments towards an endowment up to the maximum monthly instalment on a £100,000 mortgage;
- fixed allowances for dependants. These are normally reviewed annually. Documentary evidence has to be provided to the court. Again, this rule is strictly observed and can often lead to delay in the form being submitted.

In respect of regular outgoings, such as mortgage payments, Council Tax, etc, the court will normally accept one or two monthly bank statements, provided the regular outgoings are identified on the statement. If the client cannot find details of Council Tax, eg, the court may be prepared to accept a bank statement in lieu, provided the regular outgoing is identified on the statement.

2.3.13 DISPOSABLE CAPITAL

This again means the capital of the client, any spouse or partner and, in the case of a child under 16, the appropriate contributor, that is, the parents, and includes:

- savings all types; and
- the value of valuable chattels, including jewellery, racehorses, caravans, furs, antiques and paintings.

The most important asset excluded is the main or principal house, but only the first £100,000 net equity is now excluded, following an amendment in 1996. Also excluded are furniture (excluding valuable antiques) personal clothing, tools and trading equipment.

2.3.14 CALCULATION OF THE CONTRIBUTION

Criminal legal aid, unlike civil legal aid, does not set down the upper limits of income or capital, beyond which a person is ineligible for criminal legal aid. Nevertheless, the court will refuse an application for criminal legal aid unless it decides that the client needs help to pay the costs of his/her case. Also to be taken into account are whether the case is proceeding in the magistrates' court or Crown Court and the complexity of the case.

If the average weekly disposable income of the defendant exceeds £50, a weekly contribution of £1 for every £3, or part of £3, by which the disposable income exceeds £50 per week is payable. Further, if the disposable capital exceeds £3,000, the amount of the contribution is the excess of capital over £3,000.

The court will make a Contribution Order on forms CRIM 6 (income) and CRIM 7 (capital) and notify the client at his/her home address as well as the solicitor. It is open to the client to refuse the offer of legal aid. In practice, in a simple case in the magistrates' court, if the contribution is in excess of £25 per week, the court will almost certainly decide that the client can pay for the cost of his/her own defence. Further, unless disposable capital is only just over £3,000 and the client has no disposable income contribution, the court will almost certainly refuse legal aid, because it would require the client to pay a substantial sum to the court (probably far in excess of the costs). If, however, the client is facing a complex case, perhaps involving expensive evidence or a Crown Court trial, then the court would clearly take a different approach as to whether a client could afford to pay the costs. Although each court will have guidelines, the clerk considering the application has to assess each application on its own merits.

There is one further additional discretionary power which has been introduced throughout the country for applications made on or after 1 June 1996, which allows the assets of persons other than the applicant for legal aid and his/her spouse/partner to be taken into account. This regulation may be applied where the other person has transferred resources to the applicant or has been maintaining the applicant in the proceedings, or where any of the resources of the other person have been made available to the applicant. If this happens, the resources of the other person can be treated as though they were those of the applicant. This discretionary power was introduced as a result of concern over certain special and very expensive fraud cases.

2.3.15 CHANGES IN THE CLIENT'S MEANS

If, after being granted legal aid, the client's means change, s/he must inform the court, or ask the solicitor to do so on his/her behalf. If there is an increase in disposable income of more than £750 per annum, an increased contribution will be payable. If there is a decrease in disposable income of £300 or more, contributions will be reduced appropriately. An increase in disposable capital of more than £750 will also lead to reassessment.

It is a requirement of franchising that the client is told in writing by the solicitor of his/her duty to report any change in his/her means to the court.

You may become aware of a change in your client's means, eg, if s/he receives redundancy or compensation payments. Remember your duty to the legal aid fund (see 2.1.3 above).

2.3.16 REFUSAL OF LEGAL AID – RIGHTS OF REVIEW AND APPEAL

If legal aid is refused, the court will write to the client, giving the reason for refusal. On an application for a review, a court clerk has no power to refuse legal aid. The clerk must either grant the application or pass it to a single magistrate for consideration. It is normally more effective for the advocate to make an oral application before the justices at the next hearing.

Under section 50 of the CDA 1998, legal aid and legal representation matters can be resolved at an Early Administrative Hearing in the magistrates' court.

2.3.17 APPEAL TO AREA COMMITTEE

You must produce evidence of appealing against refusal of legal aid through the courts on at least one occasion.

In an indictable only or TEW offence, there is a right to appeal to the Area Committee of the Legal Aid Board against the refusal. An appeal must be made within 14 days of refusal of legal aid, and not less than 21 days before the date fixed for trial. A client or his/her advocate can ask the court to review refusal of legal aid without prejudice to the right of appeal to the Area Committee. An appeal can only be against refusal on the merits.

2.3.18 CO-DEFENDANTS AND THE EFFECT ON A LEGAL AID ORDER

Remember to identify potential conflicts of interest at an early stage (see 2.1.3 above).

In any case where a client is jointly charged with others, or there are separate charges but the case is connected, the court has power to grant legal aid but assign the same solicitor to act for all defendants, unless in the interests of justice it would not be right to do so. It is therefore important that, if there is a possible potential conflict of interest between your client and a co-defendant, this is set out fully when CRIM 1 is completed.

2.3.19 LEGAL AID IN THE CROWN COURT

Normal practice is to apply orally to the magistrates for legal aid in the Crown Court, upon committal for trial, transfer or sentence. If legal aid has not been granted by the magistrates' court, an application can be made to the Crown Court using the CRIM 1 and CRIM 5 forms, as in the magistrates' court. The application is made to the Chief Clerk. Alternatively, an oral application can be made to the Crown Court judge.

2.3.20 LEGAL AID FOR CHILDREN AND YOUNG PEOPLE UNDER 18

An application for a child under 16 should normally be made by a parent on the child's behalf. The same merits test applies, although the court should be more ready to grant legal aid to a child because of the difficulty involved in a child organising his/her own defence. In the case of a client under the age of 16, the General Regulations (regulation 23(3)) state that the court may require either the applicant or the appropriate contributor, or both, to submit a statement of means and documentary proof. In practice, this means that the parent must complete the form as the appropriate contributor. In the case of a 16 or 17 year old, the application will be assessed on the financial means of the client.

2.3.21 REVOCATION OF A LEGAL AID ORDER

If a contribution is made and a client wilfully refuses to pay the contribution order, the order will be revoked.

2.3.22 WHAT DOES THE LEGAL AID ORDER PAY FOR?

Magistrates' court

The order must be for a solicitor only, unless the client is charged with an indictable offence and the court takes the view that the case is unusually grave or difficult and representation by both solicitor and counsel would be desirable. (See Part V of the General Regulations, specifically regulation 44(3).) In practice, legal aid is normally granted for counsel and solicitor in cases of murder and highly complex fraud. In the normal case where legal aid is granted for a solicitor, only a solicitor can use counsel, but the total remuneration to which defence lawyers would be entitled is calculated on the basis that only a solicitor needs to attend court.

What is your firm's policy on the use of counsel in the magistrates' court?

Crown Court

Legal aid is normally granted for solicitor and counsel. Under regulation 48 of the General Regulations, a legal aid order may provide for the services of two counsel if the proceedings are in the Crown Court, Court of Appeal or House of Lords, *and* either the charge is one of murder or the case appears to be one of exceptional difficulty, gravity or complexity so that the interests of justice require two counsel.

Court of Appeal

A legal aid order for the Crown Court includes counsel advising on appeal and drafting the grounds of appeal, if appropriate. If leave is granted by the single judge to appeal against either conviction or sentence, the Registrar of Criminal Appeals will normally grant legal aid for counsel only, unless, in the case of an appeal against conviction, further solicitors' work is required. This would include cases where witnesses have to be traced or additional forensic experts have to be instructed.

2.3.23 PRIOR AUTHORITY FOR EXCEPTIONAL EXPENDITURE

Under regulation 54 of the General Regulations, when a legally aided client's solicitor considers it to be necessary for the conduct of proceedings, either in the magistrates' court or at the Crown Court, to incur costs by taking any of the following steps:

(a) obtaining a written report or opinion of one or more experts;

(b) employing a person to provide a written report or opinion (otherwise than as an expert);

List five situations in which an expert might be required in a criminal case.

(c) obtaining transcripts of shorthand notes or of tape recordings of any proceedings, including police questioning of suspects;
(d) when, in the Crown Court, the legal aid order provides for the services of solicitor and counsel instructing a QC alone without junior counsel; or
(e) performing an act which is either unusual in its nature or involves unusually large expenditure,

the solicitor may apply to the appropriate Area Committee for prior authority to incur these costs. An application should be made on CRIM 10, with an estimate for the costs which will be incurred. If the Area Committee grant authority, they must fix the maximum fee payable.

If the solicitor incurs the expenditure without prior authority, s/he runs the risk that when his/her costs are assessed in the magistrates' court either by the Legal Aid Board or taxed in the Crown Court by the Court Taxing Officer, the sums incurred may be disallowed or reduced and s/he will have to find the difference out of his/her own pocket. A further reason for applying for prior authority is that if it is refused, regulation 55 provides that the solicitor may be paid by the assisted person privately for this item of work. This is an exception to the general rule that once a legal aid order is granted the solicitor can only be paid for the work done by the Legal Aid Fund.

2.3.24 MAGISTRATES' COURT DUTY SOLICITOR SCHEME

Nearly all magistrates' courts will have a Duty Solicitor Scheme organised by the local Duty Solicitor Committee. A busy, large town court will probably have one, or possibly two, solicitor(s) who attend each day on a rota basis to deal only with duty solicitor cases. A less busy court may be organised during the week on a call-in basis with a rota to cover weekend courts and bank holidays. The services to be provided are set out in the Legal Aid Board Duty Solicitor Arrangements and are as follows:

- advice to a defendant who is in custody;
- the making of a bail application, unless the defendant has received such assistance on a previous occasion;
- representation of a defendant who is in custody on a plea of guilty where the defendant wishes the case to be concluded on that occasion, unless the duty solicitor considers that the case should be adjourned in the interests of justice or of the defendant;

The concept of Duty Solicitor of Choice was introduced by the Legal Aid Board under the Narey reforms and has been in place since 1 November 1999. This enables a client to choose to be represented by his/her own solicitor at an Early First Hearing or Early Administrative Hearing.

- advice and representation of a defendant who is before the court as a result of a failure to pay a fine or other sum ordered on conviction, or to obey an order of the court, and such failure will lead to the defendant being at risk of imprisonment;
- advice and, where appropriate, representation for any other defendant who is not in custody, where, in the opinion of the duty solicitor, such defendant requires advice or representation;
- help to a defendant to make an application for a legal aid order in respect of any subsequent appearance of the defendant before the court. In making such an application the duty solicitor has to ask the defendant whether the s/he wishes to instruct another solicitor to act for him/her, in which case the duty solicitor puts the name of that solicitor on the form.

Restriction on services to be provided:

- a duty solicitor cannot provide representation in committal proceedings or on a not guilty plea, nor, except in circumstances which the duty solicitor considers exceptional, advice or representation to a defendant in connection with a non-imprisonable offence;
- on an adjourned hearing, the duty solicitor shall not, as duty solicitor, represent a defendant to whom s/he, or any other duty solicitor, has provided advice or representation in the same case, except in connection with defendants being at risk of imprisonment for non-payment of the fine, etc, or failure to obey a court order. The general rule that (with limited exceptions) the duty solicitor can only represent a defendant on one occasion is designed to prevent a abuse of the legal aid scheme by defendants who might otherwise have to pay a contribution towards criminal legal aid or pay for the cost of their own defence privately. The Magistrates' Court Duty Solicitor Scheme, like the Police Station Scheme, is free to all defendants who qualify, regardless of their means.

50 Is the court Duty Solicitor Scheme available to those charged with:

(a) being drunk and disorderly?

(b) driving with excess alcohol?

(c) assaulting a police officer?

If so, on what basis?

2.3.25 PAYMENT OF CRIMINAL LEGAL AID

Magistrates' court

A claim for payment must be submitted within three months from the conclusion of the case to the area office covering the court where the client has appeared. There is a standard fee system in operation for magistrates' court work. A claim must be made on the relevant form, depending on whether the claim is for the lower standard fee (CLAIM 7) or the higher standard fee (CLAIM 8).

CLAIM 8 is also used if the claim is above the higher limit for a higher standard fee when the costs are paid at an hourly rate.

Payment in the Crown Court

A claim for costs is sent to the Crown Court Taxing Officer. The court will have supplied a standard form for completion. Again, a strict three month time limit applies for submitting the bill. Most Crown Court cases are paid by a standard fee (either a lower standard fee or a principal standard fee) for the preparation element together with a daily fee for attendance by a solicitor or representative. If the amount of preparation is over the upper fee limit, then, provided the work can be justified, the bill is taxed at an hourly rate depending on the seniority of the fee earner involved. There are provisions for review of Taxing Officers' decisions and appeals. The full procedure is set out in the Legal Aid Handbook and is governed by the Legal Aid in Criminal Care Proceedings (Costs) Regulations 1989.

2.3.26 PRIVATE FUNDING

It is a solicitor's duty to check whether a client is eligible for legal aid. If s/he is not and has no available insurance cover (see below), the solicitor will have to agree with the client how the work is to be paid for.

You must have regard to Law Society Practice Rule 15 (Client Care) and the Solicitors' Costs Information and Client Care Code 1999. The standards are set out in full in the Guide to Professional Conduct of Solicitors, published by the Law Society. The Code provides that, on taking instructions, the client should be given the best possible information about the likely costs of the matter. As a matter of good practice, you should either:

(a) agree a fixed fee for the work;

(b) if this is not practical, give as accurate an estimate as you can, together with the hourly rate which will be charged, the cost of any counsel's fees to be incurred, and any other disbursement, such as expert evidence. Any estimate needs to be prepared with great care, because it can only be exceeded for good reason if prior notice that it will be exceeded has been given to the client.

In practice, most straightforward magistrates' court cases are undertaken on the basis of a fixed fee agreed with the client and paid in advance. In Crown Court cases and more complex magistrates' court cases, particularly where there are other defendants whom you are not representing present, there is

You must be familiar with your firm's client care procedure and your scales of costs.

more difficulty. While, in a straightforward case where a client is pleading guilty, an accurate estimate can be obtained of counsel's brief fee and a fixed fee given to the client, in a more complex case it will almost certainly be necessary to give an estimate. For the estimate to be accurate, it will be necessary to agree the level of counsel's brief fee with counsel's clerk in advance and obtain fixed estimates for any disbursements. In many more serious cases, the extent of the evidence against the client will not be known until at least advance disclosure has been served, or more probably when the committal bundle is served. In this type of case, it must be made clear to the client at the outset why a detailed estimate cannot yet be given, and one should be provided once the information necessary to do so is available. The client should be informed of any development that is likely to increase the cost.

Information concerning costs and estimates should always be given or confirmed in writing to the client. Your firm will almost certainly have a standard letter which complies with the requirements of rule 15 concerning client care, and which then goes on to deal with costs. The firm should also have a procedure for agreeing costs, and will have standard hourly rates for the various categories of fee earner. It will probably be a condition that a cost estimate in anything but the most straightforward of matters must be approved by a partner.

Are you fully aware of your firm's client care procedure?

Finally, the letter giving information concerning costs should reserve the right to render interim bills at stated intervals. It should also reserve the right to ask for money on account of all counsel's fees, expert's fees and, normally, in a criminal case, on account of all the costs of the trial in advance.

2.3.27 INSURANCE COVER FOR COSTS

The standard car insurance policy will almost certainly cover the costs of a driver who is prosecuted for a breach of road traffic law which results in an accident. This will include charges of careless driving, dangerous driving and causing death by dangerous driving, and breaches of the Construction and Use Regulations which relate to an accident. Car insurance policies usually exclude paying for the cost of a defence for a driver who fails to stop or to report an accident and for excess alcohol or speeding, unless they result in an accident. If a driver is unsure about whether to plead guilty or not guilty, then normally an insurance company would pay for the cost of a solicitor for giving advice on plea. In a serious case where death has resulted or there is a substantial civil claim, the insurers may well be prepared to pay for the cost of expert evidence which will clearly be relevant to both any subsequent civil claim as well as the criminal proceedings. Insurance policies for cycles, boats, etc, may provide a similar level of cover.

2.3.28 MEMBERSHIP OF A UNION OR PROFESSIONAL ASSOCIATION

This will often provide cover for legal expenses arising out of criminal proceedings taken against a member in connection with their work activity. For example, the Police Federation provides extensive cover, including legal advice at the police station and, if appropriate, subsequent representation for any police officer who is arrested.

In road traffic cases, some cover may be available for members of the AA and RAC.

2.3.29 COSTS AND THE ACQUITTED DEFENDANT

If a client is found not guilty, the position depends on whether s/he was legally aided or not.

The legally aided defendant

Under regulation 35 of the General Regulations, contributions which have already been paid should be returned to the defendant and future contributions should be remitted.

The private defendant

The law is contained in section 16 of the Prosecution of Offences Act 1985, and guidance is provided by the Lord Chief Justice's *Practice Direction (Costs in Criminal Proceedings)* [1991] 1 WLR 498. Courts with jurisdiction to make a defendant's costs order are as follows.

Magistrates' court

Under section 16(1) of the Act if:

- the prosecution decide not to proceed with information;
- the magistrates decide not to commit for trial and discharge the defendant; or
- the defendant is acquitted after a summary trial.

Crown Court

Under section 16(2) of the Act if:

- a person is not tried for an offence for which s/he has been indicted or committed for trial;

- a Notice of Transfer is given under a relevant transfer provision, but the person in whose case it is given is not tried on a charge to which it relates; or
- any person is tried on indictment and acquitted on any count in the indictment.

Under section 16(3) where:

- a person convicted of an offence by a magistrates' court appeals to the Crown Court under section 108 of the MCA 1980, and either his conviction is set aside or a less severe punishment is awarded.

Court of Appeal

Under section 16(4) where:

- the Court of Appeal grants an appeal against conviction or reduces sentence.

2.3.30 THE EFFECT OF A DEFENDANT'S COSTS ORDER

The effect of a defendant's costs order is that the reasonable costs of a defence are paid out of central funds. A solicitor will prepare a bill and submit the bill and the file in a magistrates' court case, to the clerk to the justices in a Crown Court case, to the taxing officer at the Crown Court, and to the Registrar of Criminal Appeals in a Court of Appeal case.

The court may well call for a copy of the client care letter and information about costs provided to the defendant. The question for the court in assessing the costs is whether the defendant acted reasonably in incurring the costs, bearing in mind the information available to him/her and his/her lawyers at the time the costs were incurred. See *R v Dudley Magistrates' Court ex p Power City Stores Ltd* (1990) 154 JP 654.

51 When can an acquitted defendant get their legal costs paid other than under the legal aid scheme?

52 What will this cover?

RESEARCHING THE LAW

RANGE

Achievement must cover all the following contexts.

Resources

Office library, law library, court library, ILEX, Law Society, LEXIS, colleagues.

Sources

Precedents, statute law, case law, periodicals, digests, encyclopaedias, reference works, indexes and citations, policy documents.

EVIDENCE

You will need to produce the specific pieces of performance evidence listed below. In addition you will need to demonstrate that you have achieved the objectives specified at the beginning of this unit. You may do this by producing further pieces of evidence from real and simulated performance, by answering questions posed by your assessor or by passing a written examination.

You will need to provide evidence of having used four of the **Resources** in the **Range**, to make a full investigation of the pertinent law from the **Sources** in the **Range**, to produce two papers which could be used for the basis of a brief to the client and/or advocate.

CRITERIA

You will demonstrate achievement if:

(a) all literature relevant to the alleged offences is consulted, the information is efficiently collated and authorities' significant points are identified;

(b) the relevant law is applied to the facts of cases to the advantage of clients;

(c) results of the search are presented to clients and advocates in a clear, useful and concise form.

2.4.1 INTRODUCTION

It is a cliché to state that those who work within the law may not always know what the law is, but should know how and where to find it out.

2.4.2 WHEN WILL I NEED TO CARRY OUT RESEARCH?

Although you will, or should, know many legal rules and procedures almost as second nature, there are many situations where research will be necessary. This does not necessarily mean that you will be required to discover abstruse rules or seek out arguments to push back the boundaries of legal interpretation. Of course, that might be required, but on an everyday level, you might need to 'check' something or 'find out ...'.

Thus, you might need to:

- find out a particular aspect or application of the law,
  - eg, to check what sentencing guidelines exist for a certain offence;
- (when the law has changed significantly) discover its implications and any relevant commencement dates,
  - eg, the coming into force of sections of the CDA 1998;
- update on the latest case applying the law in a given situation,
  - eg, case law on mortgage fraud;
- find out what the law is in an area previously unknown to you,
  - eg, when a client has been charged with an offence under legislation unfamiliar to you, or when they wish to know the implications of new law, eg, in trading matters.

You will need to be familiar with, and confident in, investigating new areas and updating and exploring familiar ones, and be aware of how case law affects other decisions by virtue of the principles of precedent. You will need to be able to appropriately explain the results of your research to a client or advocate involved. You will also need to be able to make the best use of resources available to you with the most efficient use of your time and effort.

Consider the situations where you have needed to do legal research.

2.4.3 RESOURCES

Resources you may be able to use include the following.

Your own office library

The extent of this resource will, of course, vary from firm to firm. Nevertheless, as this will normally be your first port of call, it is essential that you are familiar with its extent, strengths and weaknesses, and in particular the manner in which it is arranged and updated. It may indeed be that you have some responsibility in that regard: if so, there is no excuse for not making the best use of it. Larger firms may have a formal law librarian: that individual should be able to help you discover its limits. In other firms, the resources may be somewhat limited and perhaps not arranged in any coherent group, but scattered through the firm's offices. You may need, therefore, to find out who has the books you may need and who has the most up to date copies.

Law library

If you are fortunate enough to work in a town which has a university with a law faculty, there may well be arrangements allowing local practitioners to use the facilities. This may be limited to research and copying access to works, but it is an extremely valuable resource if available. Contact your local university or your local Law Society for information.

Large public libraries may have extensive legal resources, particularly on matters of application to the general public and to high street practitioners. You may find information on matters such as the Fair Trading Act 1973, and such libraries are often well stocked on matters relating to drink driving and drugs offences.

The court library

In some areas, access may be available to the court library, but this is rare. The magistrates' court will have a very limited stock of books and periodicals, but will normally have practitioner works available which can usually be consulted briefly on visits to the court, usually by advocates. Nevertheless, if a difficult point arises, most court staff are helpful.

ILEX

If you are a member of ILEX, you will be able to consult their library.

The Law Society

Some local Law Societies have libraries, and your own firm will have information on this. In addition, or alternatively, it may be that local firms share their own library resources on a reciprocal basis.

The Law Society Library is large and comprehensive. It is open to members of The Law Society and their staff. It also provides a postal or fax service, details of which can be obtained from the library on tel: 020 7242 1222, or fax: 020 7831 0057.

Colleagues

Do not underestimate the value of this resource: you will probably not be the only person who has needed to investigate a point, and discussing the issue with a colleague may in any event clarify the point in your own mind and throw open fruitful lines of enquiry, or responses like, 'I've got an article on that very point on my desk ...'.

However you gain access to research materials, your purpose is the same: to obtain accurate, up to date information as to the state of the law and its application to the matter in issue.

2.4.4 WHAT SOURCES WILL YOU CONSULT?

There are a number of sources you may need to consult.

Primary sources of law

Legal rules emanate from either statutory sources or common law (case law) sources, or often a mixture of the two, as the cases decided in courts will interpret and apply the laws enacted by Parliament.

You will need to be familiar with finding, reading and interpreting both of these primary sources, but there are many other sources which will help you to both locate and understand them and discover the latest legal developments. Major statutory provisions will normally be consulted in reference works or textbooks: it is unlikely that you will need to consult the HMSO version of an Act, but that might be necessary if, eg, a business client seeks advice on how new regulations will affect him/her. If your office has internet access, many primary sources can be located on the web sites of Parliament and of relevant government departments (see 2.4.11 below).

Ponder on four statutory sources and two statutory instruments you have consulted.

2.4.5 WHERE CAN YOU CONSULT STATUTE LAW?

The full text of a statute as originally enacted is contained in the HMSO copy, available from The Stationery Office and most booksellers. There is, of course, no facility for incorporating amendments.

Halsbury's Statutes is a comprehensive, annotated, full text version of all statutes in force. It is arranged in subjects alphabetically, has a loose leaf current statutes service and an annual 'Is it in Force?' volume. Halsbury's thus incorporates amendments, additions and repeals to the original Act.

The internet provides access to many Bills and Acts of Parliament via the government websites (see 2.4.11 below).

2.4.6 WHERE CAN YOU CONSULT STATUTORY INSTRUMENTS (SUBORDINATE LEGISLATION)?

Halsbury's Statutory Instruments provides access to the full text of a statutory instrument (SI), which can be searched by its name, subject matter, reference (SI) number or by reference to the Act under which it was made. The internet (see 2.4.11 below) provides, usually within 15 days, access to SIs.

2.4.7 WHERE CAN YOU CONSULT CASE LAW?

The official law reports include a number of general or specialist series. The most well known are the Weekly Law Reports (WLR) and the All England Law Reports (All ER), issued in periodical form, for later binding. Only a selection of cases are reported: the ones that are deemed to be of most significance. Other cases may be found in the Law Report section of *The Times* and *The Independent*. Care should be taken in the use of cases reported in other legal periodicals and on LEXIS (an electronic database), as these may not be sufficiently detailed or authoritative to use in litigation. House of Lords cases appear on the internet (see 2.4.11 below) on the day judgment is delivered.

A note on precedent

When considering how case law will affect your client's situation, you will need to be aware of the doctrine of precedent. This refers to how the decision of a higher court affects and 'binds' a lower one. Thus, the decision of the House of Lords must be followed by all courts; a decision of the Court of Appeal must be followed by all courts below *it*; and so on. Technically, decisions of the Crown Court do not bind the magistrates' court but, in practice, they will usually be followed.

Only the reasoning of the decision (the *ratio decidendi*) relevant to the case constitutes a precedent. Hypothetical points canvassed in the judgment are called *obiter dicta*, and are persuasive but not binding. This means that the point can be used in argument, but a court is not compelled to follow it.

Distinguish the use of the term 'precedent' in this sense from the terms used to refer to standard or template drafts for pleading and forms, as in an encyclopaedia of forms and precedents.

2.4.8 SECONDARY SOURCES: EXPLAINING THE PRIMARY SOURCES

Textbooks

Conventional student textbooks can be useful to explain the basics of an unfamiliar area, or indeed to confirm or refresh an area, but are unlikely to be appropriate in terms of many practical problems. However, texts designed for the Bar Vocational Courses and the Legal Practice Course and this series, where the topic is covered, are angled towards practitioner problems, in particular, dealing with practical and procedural matters, and are therefore often useful.

Practitioner works

For criminal procedure, there are three major practitioner works that you should be familiar with and use as your primary source of criminal law and practice:

- *Archbold's Criminal Pleading, Evidence and Practice,* for many years the standard work, now published by Sweet & Maxwell in a single annual volume, with three updating supplements per year, 10 issues per annum of *Archbold News,* and also available on CD-ROM. As this work has recently been compressed from three volumes, it tends to be fairly dense reading, but is invaluable as a starting (and sometimes finishing) point for most points of procedure in the Crown Court and for matters of general application in criminal law.
- *Blackstone's Criminal Practice* is published annually by Blackstone Press and is also available on CD-ROM. It covers magistrates' court matters, including driving matters, as well as Crown Court matters. Again, the answer to most common points of procedure or criminal law will be found therein. It is not as comprehensive in Crown Court matters as *Archbold,* but includes summary matters. In some ways it is more accessible.
- *Stone's Justices Manual,* published by Butterworths, is also an annual publication containing all the provisions relevant to the magistrates' court in licensing, family and criminal matters. It is in three volumes and is issued annually.

Using *Archbold*, *Blackstone's* or *Stone's*, find the powers of the court to deal with contempt of court in:

- the magistrates' court;
- the Crown Court.

In addition, the following works may be helpful in a criminal practice:

- *May on Criminal Evidence;*
- *Wilkinson on Road Traffic Law;*
- *Current Sentencing Practice.*

2.4.9 HOW CAN YOU BE SURE YOUR RESEARCH IS UP TO DATE?

Citators can be used to check the latest position in regard to statute or case law.

Current Law is perhaps the most useful publication, and provides reassurance in many areas. It is comprised of a number of different elements:

- *Current Law Case Citator* lists all the citations of reported cases and includes references to the sections of the *Current Law Yearbook* where a case is first referred to and where it is given subsequent consideration. This will usually give you sufficient information to decide which cases you need to look at fully in the law reports;
- *Current Law Legislation Citator* covers Acts passed in the period, how they are affected by statutory instrument, reference to cases dealing with the legislation and details of amendments and repeals;
- *Current Law Monthly Digest* is a very useful publication and one to which many firms subscribe: it includes references to legislation, case law, articles and tables of statutes and statutory instruments. It has a good cumulative index;
- *Current Law Week* is a recent publication designed to update practitioners generally on new cases legislation and policy developments.

Current Law is also available on CD-ROM and via the internet (see 2.4.11 below).

Periodicals, by their nature, are a useful updating tool, as the information is usually very recent, but are not designed to systematically update all the areas of law. The monthly *Legal Journals Index* provides references to items in all UK law journals:

- *Criminal Law Review* is a monthly publication containing topical articles and case reports. The monthly index is cumulative, so a search of the latest issue will cover matters canvassed in the months since the year end;
- *Justice of the Peace* is a publication which, as its name suggests, is concerned with the magistrates' court, and again is useful for topical issues and latest developments;
- *The Times* and *The Independent* carry law reports almost daily, and are useful sources of immediate updating on practice directions and

case law, but it is unlikely that you will have copies of the published versions in your firm: careful filing of the daily reports is therefore essential if they are to be relied upon. Most will eventually be reported in the official law reports;

- professional publications, such as *The Law Society's Gazette* and *The Lawyer,* are a useful way of keeping up to date with developments in the law as they arise, but are less useful to actually conduct research, unless you have a very good memory and an efficient filing system. Otherwise, you will be left merely with an uneasy feeling: 'I am sure there's been a new case/Act of Parliament about ...'

Professional journals are particularly useful sources of information on new matters, but it is unlikely, except in procedural matters, that you will be immediately involved. Read and file the information.

2.4.10 OTHER SOURCES

- Precedents are documents setting out commonly drafted matters. In a criminal practice, these are of limited value, but may include indictments, disclosure statements under the CPIA 1996, and so on. You will find that your office precedents, rather than commercially produced ones, are the most useful in the criminal field. Your office should have a system including standard attendance notes for use at the police station, in the office and at court, a standard sheet for bail information, standard letters to the client, police station, CPS, court and draft precedents for application to the Crown Court for bail, notice of appeal from the magistrates' court to the Crown Court, and alibi notice and defence statement under the CPIA 1996.
- Indexes and encyclopaedias may be available within your office or in any of the locations listed above, dealing either generally with legal matters or with a very specific area.
- Policy documents issued by the Lord Chancellor's Department, the CPS and the Home Office may well give guidance, not only on forthcoming legislation, but also on the details of how existing law is being dealt with in practice. Particularly relevant in a criminal practice may be statements about CPS prosecution practice, prison arrangements, probation, etc.

Locate the CPS Charging Standards.

2.4.11 A NOTE ON ELECTRONIC SOURCES

If your firm has access to electronic sources of information retrieval, this can be a very useful resource, whether they have specific legal databases or not.

LEXIS is an electronic legal database which is constantly updated with the latest cases, even otherwise unreported ones.

JUSTIS is a series of law reports on CD-ROM. Its advantages over a paper-based law report, other than its size, are the search facilities.

Books on CD, such as *Archbold* and *Blackstone*, contain all the information in the paper versions and sometimes additional material, and have powerful search and print facilities.

Internet access: the world is your oyster

Searching such sources can save hours of time – or waste them if you are unfamiliar with their proper and efficient usage. It is time well spent to explore any electronic source and familiarise yourself with its proper usage, before you need to do so in a hurry.

If you have access to the internet, there are many useful sites which you can bookmark for frequent visiting, including sites where copies of legislation and law reports can be found. The following are useful addresses:

Law Commission:
http://www.open.gov.uk/lawcomm

The Law Society:
http://www.lawsoc.org.uk

Home Office:
http://www.homeoffice.gov.uk

Lord Chancellor's Department:
http://www.open.gov.uk/lcd

Cavendish Publishing:
http://www.cavendishpublishing.com

Current legislation

Bills:
http://www.parliament.the-stationery-office.co.uk/pa/pabills.htm

Acts of Parliament:
http://www.hmso.gov.uk/acts.htm

Statutory Instruments:
http://www.hmso.gov.uk/stat.htm

UK Parliament:
http://www.parliament.uk

If you have access to electronic sources, list useful websites you have found other than those opposite.

Consider what resources are generally available to you for checking the latest position on:

(a) case law development;

(b) statutory development.

Legal 'gateways'

The use of what are called 'gateways' enable you to search for a variety of legal sources by means of 'hypertext' links.

Visit http://www.venables.co.uk

and http://www.infolaw.co.uk.

2.4.12 STAGES IN YOUR RESEARCH

Your research may be a simple matter of looking up an individual, straightforward point, but may be a much more complex problem. You will need to develop research strategies. The detail of implementation is adaptable to your own particular style, but should cover four stages:

1 planning the research;

2 carrying out the research;

3 presenting the research;

4 recording the results.

You will see that, in the checklist at the end of this section, a list of questions is set out to enable you to consider the issues at various stages.

Planning

The first task is to identify the problem which you wish to research. This may involve analysing both the legal context and the factual context, and the circumstances in which it arises. You may also need to consider the precise purpose of your research, the time you have available, the relative importance of finding the answer, and its consequences. The answer to these points will direct the form your research will take.

Legal context

We are assuming for the purpose of this activity that you have already concluded that the matter involves a question of criminal law or procedure. You may have to narrow the matter down further in order to consider research avenues.

Factual context

Are there specific facts that are material to the resolution of the question in respect of the client?

What is the purpose of the research: is it for the preparation of and briefing for an advocate's court appearance, or to inform the client as to his position? Or is it to enable him/her to make a decision or to negotiate with the prosecution or a co-accused?

What is the time scale? The time available to find the answer will, of course, affect the type of research you can do.

What is the importance and what are the consequences? Recognition of the consequences of failing to find the answer, or of finding an incorrect answer, is important not merely in order to promote anxiety in the researcher, but in order to arrange priorities and to recognise that the consequence of appearing inept may at times be less significant than costing the firm money or even a client his liberty or reputation.

Therefore:

- what do I need to find out?
- what are my available resources?
- what resources will I use?

Carrying out your research

Having considered the preceding issues and the available resources described above, you will then be able to implement your research plan, ensuring that you:

- consult a reliable source;
- verify the latest position;
- identify any uncertainties.

Presenting the results of your research

Your research may be required for your own use, for a colleague's use, for the client's information or for use of a colleague or other advocate in court. In order to present the information in the best possible way, it is necessary to consider the context in which the information is required. Ask yourself the following questions:

- who is my audience?
- what is their need?

If the audience is a legal professional, you will need to give the information in a way that can be readily applied to the problem in hand. This will usually involve:

- stating the rule with the authority from which it is derived;
- applying the rule;
- indicating any ambiguities or uncertainties;
- isolating the issue;
- concluding with a view, if appropriate.

You need not start from first principles, but you must be clear, accurate and concise. You should have an appreciation of how you or the recipient of your research is to use it: to inform, to negotiate, to persuade or to demand.

You will need to demonstrate achievement by the presentation of two papers, using four of the sources specified in the **Range**, for a brief to the client or advocate.

If the audience is a lay client, you will need to consider their circumstances and the context in which the information is to be given.

- Circumstances:
  - are they familiar with criminal proceedings?
  - or nervous about the procedure?
  - are they worried about publicity, their family, the prospect of a sentence?
  - are they protesting their innocence?
  - or accepting guilt?
  - are they unsure of what to do or expect?
- Context: does the client want:
  - information about process or law?
  - information upon which to make a decision?
  - information about likely outcomes?

Having considered the above points, you will need to make a decision about the best way of presenting your results to your audience in terms of format, content, structure, tone and style.

Very often, the context will dictate whether you use a letter memorandum or other format. The content will be formed from your findings, and the tone and style by the needs of your audience and purpose of communication.

Recording your results

Do not forget to keep and file the results of your research for subsequent use. Simple points might well be filed in your head, but the lengthier and more complex the search, the more important it is that you retain the knowledge and information gained of the relative merit of the method you used. Useful addresses or publications should be retained as a firm's resource.

Record the date of your research and the source(s) of information.

Recording date and source allows for quick up-dating as necessary.

CHECKLIST

Planning your research

what is the factual nature of the problem?

what is the legal nature of the problem?

is there more than one area or approach involved?

what is the context of the problem?

what is the purpose?

what is the time scale?

what is the importance?

what are my areas of research?

Carrying out your research

what is the problem?

what sources exist?

what resources have I available?

how can I best use them?

are they up to date?

how do my findings apply to my problem?

are other issues raised?

Presenting your research

who is my audience?

what are their requirements?

what is the most appropriate form of presentation?

how can I explain the application of my findings most appropriately?

do I have to warn of uncertainties?

do I have to explain advantages or disadvantages?

do I have to provide information on which a decision has to be made?

do I need to provide information as to what will (or might) happen?

do I need to provide information on which an argument to persuade someone else into a course of action is based?

is my method and style of communication appropriate?

Learning from and storing the results of your research

is this an issue that will re-occur?

is it a matter which I now know?

will I need to refer again to my findings?

is my note sufficient?

should I store/disseminate the information?

have I acquired any useful research tools that I can use again or share with others?

ADVISING CLIENTS ON AVAILABLE AND LIKELY PROCEDURES AND PLEA

RANGE

Achievement must cover the following contexts.

Considerations

Credit for guilty plea, bail status following guilty plea, ancillary orders, admissibility of evidence, costs, client's previous convictions, publicity, nature of tribunal representation, rights of appeal.

EVIDENCE

You will need to produce the specific pieces of performance evidence listed below. In addition, you will need to demonstrate that you have achieved the objectives specified at the beginning of this unit. You may do this by producing further pieces of evidence from real and simulated performance, by answering questions posed by your assessor or by passing a written examination.

You will need to provide evidence of:

1 having advised two clients who had the option of a jury or a summary trial of the **Considerations** in the **Range**;

2 having obtained the necessary documents from clients following a guilty plea on two occasions.

CRITERIA

You will demonstrate achievement if:

(a) clients are informed of the choice of venue, if any, in a way which they are able to understand;

(b) practical and tactical considerations are summarised to enable clients to make informed choices regarding venue and plea;

(c) clients are advised in those cases where there is or may be a need to give evidence or produce documents following a guilty plea;

(d) the nature and implications of the 'burden of proof' are explained to clients.

2.5.1 INTRODUCTION

A client will often need advice on whether to plead guilty or not, and on venue of trial. These decisions may well be interlinked. Although the ultimate decision, where there is a choice, is the client's, it is important that they receive full and understandable information about the considerations on which their choice should be made. The client will also need to be fully informed as to the procedures that will apply, and as to any consequences of decisions.

2.5.2 WHERE CAN THE CASE BE TRIED?

All offences are categorised in terms of whether they can be tried summarily only, are triable either way (TEW) or are triable only on indictment. This categorisation dictates the procedures applicable. There are many issues and considerations that arise regardless of the category of offence, which will be considered as appropriate below, but the context and timing for making the decisions, particularly those on plea and venue, are naturally affected by the nature of the case itself.

Sections 17 to 25 of the MCA 1980 are subject to the Interpretation Act 1978, schedule 1, which defines the terms as follows:

(a) 'indictable offence' means an offence which, if committed by an adult, is triable on indictment, whether it is exclusively so triable or triable either way ...

'Summary offence' means an offence which, if committed by an adult, is triable only summarily.

'Offence triable either way' means an offence, other than an offence triable on indictment only by virtue of section 40 or section 41 of the Criminal Justice Act (CJA) 1988 (see 2.5.18 below) which, if committed by an adult, is triable either on indictment or summarily.

The terms 'indictable', 'summary' and 'triable either way', in their application to offences, are to be construed accordingly.

Although the term 'indictable' thus covers all offences which *may* be tried on indictment, the term is often used to indicate offences that can *only* be tried on indictment. Care must be taken to use the context to indicate which is meant.

2.5.3 SUMMARY OFFENCES

Summary offences can only be tried in the magistrates' court and are the least serious offences including, but not limited to, many traffic matters. Cases with which you might be involved which are summary only include:

- assault on a police officer;
- criminal damage where the damage is valued at less than £5,000 (see 2.5.4 below);
- common assault contrary to section 39 of the CJA 1988;
- taking a vehicle without the owner's consent contrary to section 12 of the Theft Act 1968 (but aggravated taking is TEW);
- driving whilst disqualified by court order;
- driving with excess alcohol.

2.5.4 TRIABLE EITHER WAY OFFENCES

TEW offences are those which can be tried either in the magistrates' court or the Crown Court. These include the vast majority of cases with which you will be involved:

- all thefts;
- all burglaries, other than aggravated burglary, burglary in a dwelling where someone was

Offences are made triable either way by the statute creating them or by being included in schedule 1 to the MCA 1980 (see section 17). Summary offences are all made so by statute. *Oke's Magisterial Formulist* contains a useful list of penalties in the magistrates' court.

subjected to the threat of or actual violence, or burglary involving the commission of or intent to commit an offence such as rape, which are triable only on indictment;

- assault occasioning actual bodily harm contrary to section 47 of the Offences Against the Person Act (OAPA) 1861;
- grievous bodily harm contrary to section 20 of the OAPA 1861;
- criminal damage where the damage is £5,000 or over (other than damage by arson and with intent to endanger life, which are triable only on indictment (see below)).

2.5.5 OFFENCES TRIABLE ONLY ON INDICTMENT

These can only be tried in the Crown Court, and comprise the most serious offences, such as rape, blackmail, robbery, grievous bodily harm, wounding with intent and criminal damage by fire.

2.5.6 WHAT MATTERS SHOULD A CLIENT TAKE INTO ACCOUNT ON DECIDING ON PLEA GENERALLY?

For many clients, the decision on plea will be straightforward: they will know whether they are guilty or not guilty of the charge, and will want to plead accordingly. However, in many cases there are other matters to take into consideration.

- What is the client's version of events?
  - There may be a complete denial of involvement, or an explanation.
- Is the client's version of the facts consistent with guilt in law?
  - There may be a point of law involving a valid defence that the client is unaware of.
- Is the prosecution's case sufficient to establish guilt of the offence charged beyond reasonable doubt on the basis of admissible evidence? It is the lawyer's duty to prevent the client being convicted save on the basis of admissible evidence.

For example, the client may have been acting in self-defence in an assault case, or not acting dishonestly in a theft case.

You must consider the burden of proof and the elements of the offence that must be proved (see 2.5.21 below and Table 1 in Appendix 1).

The decision to prosecute and cautioning

When advising a client who has been charged, it is useful to understand the CPS approach to proceedings. Not all cases in which a defendant has been charged will result in prosecution, as the CPS has a continuing duty to assess the appropriateness of prosecution and often may withdraw charges. The

Code for Crown Prosecutors governs the decision to prosecute. The CPS has a twofold test to apply to the decision to prosecute:

(a) is there sufficient evidence to have a realistic prospect of success?

(b) secondly, and only if the first test is satisfied, is it in the public interest to prosecute?

The Code sets out a list of factors which militate for and against prosecution. These are reproduced below.

Where the offender is a first, minor or juvenile offender, it may be possible to persuade the CPS that a caution will suffice. A caution is a formal, recorded warning which carries no punishment, but is only possible if the offender admits guilt. Where a guilty plea is decided upon, but it is thought that a caution might be given, this is always the better course of action for your client. Cautioning policy changes from time to time, but similar criteria are used as in the decision to prosecute. Consult the cautioning guidelines. Recent practice means that repeat cautions are unlikely.

Cautioning is preferable for all subjects of a court case, as long as they accept their guilt.

Extract from the Code for Crown Prosecutors

1 Introduction

1.1 The decision to prosecute an individual is a serious step. Fair and effective prosecution is essential to the maintenance of law and order. But even in a small case, a prosecution has serious implications for all involved – the victim, a witness and a defendant. The Crown Prosecution Service applies the Code for Crown Prosecutors so that it can make fair and consistent decisions about prosecutions.

1.2 The Code contains information that is important to police officers, to others who work in the criminal justice system and to the general public. It helps the Crown Prosecution Service to play its part in making sure that justice is done.

2 General Principles

2.1 Each case is unique and must be considered on its own, but there are general principles that apply in all cases.

2.2 The duty of the Crown Prosecution Service is to make sure that the right person is prosecuted for the right offence and that all relevant facts are given to the court.

2.3 Crown Prosecutors must be fair, independent and objective. They must not let their personal views of the ethnic or national origin, sex, religious beliefs, political views or sexual preference of the offender, victim or witness influence their decisions. They must also not be affected by improper or undue pressure from any source.

3 Review

3.1 Proceedings are usually started by the police. Sometimes they may consult the Crown Prosecution Service before charging a defendant. Each case that the police send to the Crown Prosecution Service is reviewed by a Crown Prosecutor to make sure that it meets the tests set out in this Code. Crown Prosecutors may decide to continue with the original charges, to change the charges or sometimes to stop the proceedings.

3.2 Review, however, is a continuing process so that Crown Prosecutors can take into account any change in circumstances. Wherever possible, they talk to the police first if they are thinking about changing the charges or stopping the proceedings. This gives the police the chance to provide more information that may affect the decision. The Crown Prosecution Service and the police work closely together to reach the right decision, but the final responsibility for the decision rests with the Crown Prosecution Service.

4 The Code Tests

4.1 There are two stages in the decision to prosecute. The first stage is the evidential test. If the case does not pass the evidential test, it must not go ahead, no matter how important or serious it may be. If the case does pass the evidential test, Crown Prosecutors must decide if a prosecution is needed in the public interest.

4.2 This second stage is the public interest test. The Crown Prosecution Service will only start or continue a prosecution when the case has passed both tests. The evidential test is explained in section 5 and the public interest test is explained in section 6.

5 The Evidential Test

5.1 Crown Prosecutors must be satisfied that there is enough evidence to provide a 'realistic prospect of conviction' against each defendant on each charge. They must consider what the defence case may be and how that is likely to affect the prosecution case.

5.2 A realistic prospect of conviction is an objective test. It means that a jury or bench of magistrates, properly directed in accordance with the law, is more likely than not to convict the defendant of the charge alleged.

5.3 When deciding whether there is enough evidence to prosecute, Crown Prosecutors must consider whether the evidence can be used and is reliable. There will be many cases in which the evidence does not give any cause for concern. But there will also be cases in which the evidence may not be as strong as it first appears. Crown Prosecutors must ask themselves the following questions:

Can the evidence be used in court?

(a) Is it likely that the evidence will be excluded by the court? There are certain legal rules which might mean that evidence which seems relevant cannot be given at a trial. For example, is it likely that the evidence will be excluded because of the way in which it was gathered or because of the rule against using hearsay as evidence? If so, is there enough other evidence for a realistic prospect of conviction?

Is the evidence reliable?

(b) Is it likely that a confession is unreliable, eg, because of the defendant's age, intelligence or lack of understanding?

(c) Is the witness's background likely to weaken the prosecution case? For example, does the witness have any dubious motive that may affect his or her attitude to the case or a relevant previous conviction?

(d) If the identity of the defendant is likely to be questioned, is the evidence about this strong enough?

5.4 Crown Prosecutors should not ignore evidence because they are not sure that it can be used or is reliable. But they should look closely at it when deciding if there is a realistic prospect of conviction.

6 The Public Interest Test

6.1 In 1951, Lord Shawcross, who was Attorney General, made the classic statement on public interest, which has been supported by Attorneys General ever since: 'It has never been the rule in this country – I hope it never will be – that suspected criminal offences must automatically be the subject of prosecution.' (House of Commons Debates, Vol 483, col 681, 29 January 1951.)

6.2 The public interest must be considered in each case where there is enough evidence to provide a realistic prospect of conviction. In cases of any seriousness, a prosecution will usually take place unless there are public interest factors tending against prosecution which clearly outweigh those tending in favour. Although there may be public interest factors against prosecution in a particular case, often the prosecution should go ahead and those factors should be put to the court for consideration when sentence is being passed.

6.3 Crown Prosecutors must balance factors for and against prosecution carefully and fairly. Public interest factors that can affect the decision to prosecute usually depend on the seriousness of the offence or the circumstances of the offender. Some factors may increase the need to prosecute but others may suggest that another course of action would be better.

The following lists of some common public interest factors, both for and against prosecution, are not exhaustive. The factors that apply will depend on the facts in each case.

Some common public interest factors in favour of prosecution

6.4 The more serious the offence, the more likely it is that a prosecution will be needed in the public interest. A prosecution is likely to be needed if:

(a) a conviction is likely to result in a significant sentence;

(b) a weapon was used or violence was threatened during the commission of the offence;

(c) the offence was committed against a person serving the public (eg, a police or prison officer, or a nurse);

(d) the defendant was in a position of authority or trust;

(e) the evidence shows that the defendant was a ringleader or an organiser of the offence;

(f) there is evidence that the offence was premeditated;

(g) there is evidence that the offence was carried out by a group;

(h) the victim of the offence was vulnerable, has been put in considerable fear, or suffered personal attack, damage or disturbance;

(i) the offence was motivated by any form of discrimination against the victim's ethnic or national origin, sex, religious beliefs, political views or sexual preference;

(j) there is a marked difference between the actual or mental ages of the defendant and the victim, or if there is any element of corruption;

(k) the defendant's previous convictions or cautions are relevant to the present offence;

(l) the defendant is alleged to have committed the offence whilst under an order of the court;

(m) there are grounds for believing that the offence is likely to be continued or repeated, eg, by a history of recurring conduct; or

(n) the offence, although not serious in itself, is widespread in the area where it was committed.

Some common public interest factors against prosecution

6.5 A prosecution is less likely to be needed if:

(a) the court is likely to impose a very small or nominal penalty;

(b) the offence was committed as a result of a genuine mistake or misunderstanding (these factors must be balanced against the seriousness of the offence);

(c) the loss or harm can be described as minor and was the result of a single incident, particularly if it was caused by a misjudgment;

(d) there has been a long delay between the offence taking place and the date of the trial, unless:
- the offence is serious;
- the delay has been caused in part by the defendant;
- the offence has only recently come to light; or
- the complexity of the offence has meant that there has been a long investigation;

(e) a prosecution is likely to have a very bad effect on the victim's physical or mental health, always bearing in mind the seriousness of the offence;

(f) the defendant is elderly or is, or was at the time of the offence, suffering from significant mental or physical ill health, unless the offence is serious or there is a real possibility that it may be repeated. The Crown Prosecution Service, where necessary, applies Home Office guidelines about how to deal with mentally disordered offenders. Crown Prosecutors must balance the desirability of diverting a defendant who is suffering from significant mental or physical ill health with the need to safeguard the general public;

(g) the defendant has put right the loss or harm that was caused (but defendants must not avoid prosecution simply because they can pay compensation); or

(h) details may be made public that could harm sources of information, international relations or national security.

6.6 Deciding on the public interest is not simply a matter of adding up the number of factors on each side. Crown Prosecutors must decide how important each factor is in the circumstances of each case and go on to make an overall assessment.

The relationship between the victim and the public interest

6.7 The Crown Prosecution Service acts in the public interest, not just in the interests of any one individual. But Crown Prosecutors must always think very carefully about the interests of the victim, which are an important factor, when deciding where the public interest lies.

Youth offenders

6.8 Crown Prosecutors must consider the interests of a youth when deciding whether it is in the public interest to prosecute. The stigma of a conviction can cause very serious harm to the prospects of a youth offender or a young adult. Young offenders can sometimes be dealt with without going to court. But Crown Prosecutors should not avoid prosecuting simply because of the defendant's age. The seriousness of the offence or the offender's past behaviour may make prosecution necessary.

Police cautions

6.9 The police make the decision to caution an offender in accordance with Home Office guidelines. If the defendant admits the offence, cautioning is the most common alternative to a court appearance. Crown Prosecutors, where necessary, apply the same guidelines and should look at the alternatives to prosecution when they consider the public interest. Crown Prosecutors should tell the police if they think that a caution would be more suitable than a prosecution.

7 Charges

7.1 Crown Prosecutors should select charges which:

(a) reflect the seriousness of the offending;

(b) give the court adequate sentencing powers; and

(c) enable the case to be presented in a clear and simple way.

This means that Crown Prosecutors may not always continue with the most serious charge where there is a choice. Further, Crown Prosecutors should not continue with more charges than are necessary.

7.2 Crown Prosecutors should never go ahead with more charges than are necessary just to encourage a defendant to plead guilty to a few. In the same way, they should never go ahead with a more serious charge just to encourage a defendant to plead guilty to a less serious one.

7.3 Crown Prosecutors should not change the charge simply because of the decision made by the court or the defendant about where the case will be heard.

8 Mode of Trial

8.1 The Crown Prosecution Service applies the current guidelines for magistrates who have to decide whether cases should be tried in the Crown Court when the offence gives the option. (See the 'National Mode of Trial Guidelines' issued by the Lord Chief Justice.) Crown Prosecutors should recommend Crown Court trial when they are satisfied that the guidelines require them to do so.

8.2 Speed must never be the only reason for asking for a case to stay in the magistrates' courts. But Crown Prosecutors should consider the effect of any likely delay if they send a case to the Crown Court, and any possible stress on victims and witnesses if the case is delayed.

9 Accepting Guilty Pleas

9.1 Defendants may want to plead guilty to some, but not all, of the charges. Or they may want to plead guilty to a different, possibly less serious, charge because they are admitting only part of the crime. Crown Prosecutors should only accept the defendant's plea if they think the court is able to pass a sentence that matches the seriousness of the offending. Crown Prosecutors must never accept a guilty plea just because it is convenient.

10 Re-starting a Prosecution

10.1 People should be able to rely on decisions taken by the Crown Prosecution Service. Normally, if the Crown Prosecution Service tells a suspect or defendant that there will not be a prosecution, or that the prosecution has been stopped, that is the end of the matter and the case will not start again. But occasionally there are special reasons why the Crown Prosecution Service will re-start the prosecution, particularly if the case is serious.

10.2 These reasons include:

(a) rare cases where a new look at the original decision shows that it was clearly wrong and should not be allowed to stand;

(b) cases which are stopped so that more evidence which is likely to become available in the fairly near future can be collected and prepared. In these cases, the Crown Prosecutor will tell the defendant that the prosecution may well start again;

(c) cases which are stopped because of a lack of evidence but where more significant evidence is discovered later.

2.5.7 HOW WILL THE CLIENT KNOW THE CASE AGAINST HIM/HER?

- In a summary matter, the defendant has no right to know the state of the evidence against him/her, though the CPS may voluntarily provide information. However, in TEW and indictment only cases, the defence will have advance knowledge of the evidence. In those cases, the client should be advised on the strength of the case against him/her. The burden of proving the case is generally on the prosecution, except for defences of insanity or where statute places the burden on the defendant. They will need to prove every element of the offence charged, so that the magistrates or jury are satisfied beyond reasonable doubt of the defendant's guilt. Whilst the court must not be misled, the defendant and his/her legal adviser are entitled to test the evidence against him/her.
- Therefore, in summary matters, although the prosecution might voluntarily disclose the state of the evidence, very often it will be a case of anticipating what the evidence is. Much of this will be information in which the client can assist. Was there an interview? What did the client say? What were the circumstances of any arrest?
- In TEW offences, the situation will be clearer, and it is often in such matters that consideration of issues of plea and the state of the evidence may lead to what is often called plea bargaining. This is the term given to situations where a guilty plea is offered by the defence and (in return) certain of the charges are withdrawn or no evidence offered. This can happen in three different situations:
  - when there are alternative charges;

A solicitor is not professionally permitted to assist a defendant to advance a defence which s/he has been told is untrue, but may allow the defendant to plead not guilty and put the prosecution to proof.

Alternative charges are charges where two different interpretations can be placed on the defendant's actions, where the defendant cannot be guilty of both offences. This can include two levels of the same offence (eg, common assault or actual bodily harm) or alternative methods of involvement (eg, theft or handling).

- when there are a number of charges of varying severity, such as careless driving and driving with excess alcohol; and
- where the defendant is willing to plead guilty to a lesser offence than the one charged.

Furthermore, since the introduction of the CPIA 1996, a new regime of disclosure is introduced in certain situations for material in the possession of the prosecution that might assist the defence, and for the defence in turn to disclose its case.

The rules affect both prosecution and defence and apply:

- to all cases in the Crown Court (whether the defendant is pleading guilty or not guilty);
- to summary trials, ie, when the defendant is pleading not guilty in the magistrates' court, whether the offence is summary or TEW.

Disclosure regime

- The prosecution must disclose to the accused material in their possession that in their opinion might undermine their case (prosecution primary disclosure);
- Then, the defence should (in Crown Court cases) or may (in magistrates' court cases) inform the prosecution of the defence and matters of dispute with the prosecution (defence statement).
- After the defence have given this information, the prosecution must in turn inform the defence of any other prosecution information that may assist the defence argument now that they are aware of it (prosecution secondary disclosure).

2.5.8 WHAT IF THE CLIENT WISHES TO PLEAD NOT GUILTY AGAINST THE WEIGHT OF THE EVIDENCE?

Although the client who wishes to plead not guilty has the right to do so, and the lawyer may defend him/her, clients should be warned of the difficulties. If the prosecution case is overwhelming, it is right that the client should be made aware of these factors and of the possible disadvantages of pleading not guilty.

These are primarily:

- loss of discount or credit for guilty plea. Courts will usually give some credit in their sentence to a defendant who enters his guilty plea at an early stage: the earlier the plea, the greater the discount. This will be lost if the defendant is

In the magistrates' court, the defence may voluntarily disclose the nature of the defence, or information on matters on which they do not agree with the prosecution case. This must be done, if at all, within 14 days of the prosecution primary disclosure.

The defence statement should contain a statement of:

- the general nature of the accused's defence;
- matters on which issue is taken with the prosecution; and
- the reasons why.

Failure to provide one within the required (or any extended) period may result in adverse inferences being drawn.

Remember that you must not allow the defendant to advance a defence you know to be untrue.

Section 39 of the CJPOA 1994.

convicted after a trial. In the magistrates' court, magistrates will normally give credit for an early guilty plea and cut approximately one-third off any fine or prison sentence imposed. In other sentencing decisions, such as discharges and community sentences, they may take account of a guilty plea in general mitigation, without it being possible to specifically shorten a period;
- cost of a trial if the defendant has not been granted full legal aid (see 2.3 above);
- delay. Many clients want to get the case over with, but for others, putting off the inevitable is an advantage;
- in TEW cases, indication of a guilty plea will ensure that the case will be initially, and possibly finally, dealt with in the magistrates' court.

2.5.9 WHAT IF THE CLIENT ACCEPTS THAT S/HE IS GUILTY OF THE OFFENCE BUT DISPUTES THE FACTS IN THE PROSECUTION VERSION OF EVENTS?

Often, clients disagree with details of the prosecution case: the exact number of blows, or the language used in a public order incident, which are not material to the case and will not affect the outcome. At other times, challenge to details may be used to challenge the reliability of the main aspects of the case. There are cases however, where the client is clear that s/he committed the offence charged both factually and legally, but disputes the magnitude of his/her guilt. For example, s/he might agree that s/he stole form the supermarket, but stole goods only to the value of £25, not the £500 alleged, or s/he might accept that s/he occasioned actual bodily harm to a person, but that this was caused by hitting the victim with a clenched fist, not by kicking him/her whilst on the ground. Where the difference may affect the sentence, then either a *Newton* hearing must be held or the defence basis of the plea must be the factual basis for sentencing. A *Newton* hearing is a hearing, with evidence being called exactly as in a trial, on the sole issue of the disputed facts. The court will make a judgment or finding on the basis of what the facts are, and will sentence accordingly.

If, after advice, the client wishes to plead guilty but on a limited acceptance of guilt, then it must be made plain, after the prosecution have outlined the facts (see 2.5.10 below), if any significant part of the facts is disputed, and the sentencer alerted to the difference. It is then a matter for the court to determine whether the difference will affect sentence, and if so, to adjourn for the trial of that

R v Newton (1982) 77 Cr App R 13 gives its name to the *Newton* hearing. You should distinguish this situation from putting the prosecution to proof of the offence when the state of the evidence is unclear, and from pleading guilty to a lesser offence. A *Newton* hearing is a trial – or hearing – of the limited facts, after a guilty plea, and can take place in the magistrates' court or Crown Court.

issue (ie, the *Newton* hearing). Occasionally, the prosecution may indicate that it will accept the defence version and not rely on aggravating features, but this is likely to be rare.

2.5.10 WHAT IS THE PROCEDURE IN SUMMARY CASES?

Whether a case is triable only summarily or it is TEW and a decision has been made to try it summarily, the procedure is the same.

Once the name and address of the accused has been verified, the charge will be put and the defendant asked if s/he pleads guilty or not guilty.

Guilty pleas

If s/he pleads guilty:

- the prosecution will outline the facts of the case, including any response made in police interview;
- explain any matters that the defendant wishes to be taken into consideration (TIC);
- hand in a list of any previous convictions;
- the magistrates will ask for any to be read that they are likely to take into account in sentencing;
- ask for costs and any ancillary orders such as forfeiture, confiscation etc;
- the clerk will put to the defendant any breaches of existing orders, so that these can be dealt with;
- the defence will then make a plea in mitigation;
- the magistrates will sentence or adjourn for the preparation by the probation service of a pre-sentence report. If this is done, sentencing will take place on a later occasion and the same steps followed as set out above.

A TIC is an offence which the defendant admits, usually of a similar nature, and which is taken account of in sentencing but not separately sentenced.

Not guilty pleas

If the defendant pleads not guilty, there will initially be an adjournment to a day for trial or to hold a pre-trial review. If the latter course is taken the pre- trial review will be the time at which decisions about expected length of trial, numbers of witnesses, etc, will be decided upon. The defendant will normally be required to attend unless specifically excused.

At the trial itself, once the name and address of the accused has been verified, the charge will be put and the defendant asked if s/he still pleads not guilty:

Section 9 of the CJA 1967 provides:

(1) In any criminal proceedings, other than committal proceedings, a written statement by any person shall, if such of the conditions mentioned in the next following subsection as are applicable are satisfied, be admissible as evidence to the like extent as oral evidence to the like effect by that person.

- The prosecution will then usually outline the case, setting out the main allegations and probably referring briefly to the witnesses they propose to call.
- They will then call their witnesses in turn, who will give evidence and be cross-examined upon it from the witness box.
- The evidence of witnesses which is not challenged may, by agreement with the defence, be tendered and read in the form of section 9 witness statements.
- The witnesses will be examined-in-chief by the prosecution:
  - and then can be cross-examined by the defence.
- At the end of the prosecution case, the defence may make a submission of no case to answer.
- If that is not made or does not succeed, the defence case starts.
- The defence does not normally make an opening speech but commences by calling the defendant.
- The defendant and any other defence witness will be examined-in-chief by the defence. If the defendant gives evidence, s/he must do so first, before any other witness as to the fact:
  - and then can be cross-examined by the prosecution.
- The defence can then make a closing speech:
  - to which the prosecution can reply only on a point of law.
- The magistrates will then consider their verdict, usually retiring to do so.
- If the verdict is guilty, they will move to the sentencing stage as above.

If not guilty, the defendant will be acquitted.

(2) The said conditions are –

(a) the statement purports to be signed by the person who made it;

(b) the statement contains a declaration by that person to the effect that it is true to the best of his knowledge and belief and that he made the statement knowing that, if it were tendered in evidence, he would be liable to prosecution if he wilfully stated in it anything which he knew to be false or did not believe to be true;

(c) before the hearing at which the statement is tendered in evidence, a copy of the statement is served, by or on behalf of the party proposing to tender it, on each of the other parties to the proceedings; and

(d) none of the other parties or their solicitors, within seven days from the service of the copy of the statement, serves a notice on the party so proposing objecting to the statement being tendered in evidence under this section.

Provided that the conditions mentioned in paragraphs (c) and (d) of this subsection shall not apply if the parties agree before or during the hearing that the statement shall be so tendered.

(8) A document required by this section to be served on any person may be served –

(a) by delivering it to him or to his solicitor; or

(b) by addressing it to him and leaving it at his usual or last known place of abode or place of business or by addressing it to his solicitor and leaving it at his office; or

(c) by sending it in a registered letter or by the recorded delivery service or by first class post addressed to him at his usual or last known place of abode or place of business or addressed to his solicitor at his office; or

(d) in the case of a body corporate, by delivering it to the secretary or clerk of the body at its registered or principal office or sending it in a registered letter or by the recorded delivery service or by first class post addressed to the secretary or clerk of that body at that office.

The defendant does not have to give evidence, but if s/he fails to do so, adverse inferences can be drawn, which means effectively that the court may (not must) infer guilt if it seems that the reason for the failure to give evidence is because of guilt.

2.5.11 WHAT IS THE PROCEDURE IN TEW CASES?

In order that the defendant can make an informed decision on plea and venue, in TEW cases s/he is entitled to advance disclosure of the prosecution evidence or a summary of it. After this has been given, and an opportunity provided for legal advice, if required, the defendant will be asked whether s/he is willing to indicate his/her plea. The consequences of his/her indication will be explained to him/her by the clerk.

Do not forget defence costs after an acquittal.

Changes are being proposed in relation to the defendant's right to choose jury trial in TEW cases.

Where a guilty plea is indicated

If the defendant indicates that s/he wishes to plead guilty, that will be accepted as a plea of guilt by the magistrates, and they will proceed as if s/he had pleaded guilty to a summary offence, except that they retain the power to commit for sentence to the Crown Court. Under the procedure introduced under section 4 of the CPIA 1996, there is no clear role for the prosecution to address the magistrates on seriousness. This means that the magistrates and their clerk must be aware of sentencing practice and consider whether their powers are sufficient, or whether the matter should be committed, under section 38 of the MCA 1980, to the Crown Court.

Increasingly, courts are asking the CPS to take a role at this stage. Practice varies. Nevertheless, the procedure does allow for more serious matters than hitherto to be dealt with in the magistrates' court, with a subsequent lessening of risk at sentencing.

Otherwise, if the defendant indicates a not guilty plea or is unable or unwilling to indicate a plea at this stage, a mode of trial decision must be made. In the mode of trial procedure, an evaluation is made by the magistrates as to where the case will most suitably be tried. Effectively, this means that the magistrates assess whether their powers of punishment would be sufficient were the defendant to be found guilty. If they feel that their powers of punishment are sufficient, then the defendant him/herself is asked whether s/he consents to summary trial or whether s/he would wish to have the matter dealt with in the Crown Court.

The stages in this procedure are mandatory, and any deviation will render any subsequent action invalid.

Section 18 of the MCA 1980 sets out the procedure for determining mode of trial in TEW offences for adult offenders (not applicable to juveniles):

- the charge must be written down if this has not already been done;
- the prosecution will outline the facts and make representations as to the most suitable venue;
- the defendant or his solicitor may make representations;
- the court then considers which method of trial appears more suitable, having regard to:
  - (i) the representations made at the first two points above;
  - (ii) the nature of the case;
  - (iii) whether the circumstances make the offence one of a serious character;
  - (iv) whether the punishment which a magistrates' court would have power to inflict for the offence would be adequate; and
  - (v) any other circumstances which appear to the court to make the offence more suitable for it to be tried in one way rather than the other.

The Mode of Trial Guidelines were reissued in 1995 with the endorsement of the Lord Chief Justice, with the intention of keeping more cases in the magistrates' courts. They include general advice, starting from the presumption that summary trial will be appropriate unless there is reason for Crown Court trial. Advice is also given on particular features that are relevant to the decision in specific cases. Although they are drafted in terms of advising magistrates to commit cases to the Crown Court only if one or more of the specified criteria are present *and* their sentencing powers are insufficient, their general tenor is such that they are read as meaning 'in which case your sentencing powers will be insufficient'. When considering this aspect, which is the main criterion for the magistrates' decision, consideration should also be given to the Magistrates' Association sentencing guidelines, which provide guidance as to the likely sentence in most common offences, and the aggravating and mitigating factors. Both of these should be considered when assessing where a case should be tried and the possible sentence, and can properly be referred to in court.

If the defendant is going to elect trial, there is little point in making representations. If the prosecution suggest Crown Court trial and the defendant wants to be tried in the magistrates' court, there is purpose in seeking to persuade the magistrates to accept jurisdiction. However, if the case is clearly within or outside the court's jurisdiction, the defence may simply concur with the prosecution or make no representations.

The magistrates' jurisdiction is to impose a maximum of six months' imprisonment for one offence and 12 months for two or more TEW offences.

53 What is the purpose of the Mode of Trial Guidelines?

54 How would you make use of them?

The Magistrates' Association Sentencing Guidelines can be found in practitioner works or can be obtained from the Association.

For the mode of trial decision, the prosecution version of events as outlined by them is taken as accurate, but no consideration of the defendant's previous convictions is taken. What is in issue is the appropriate venue for a case of this nature, irrespective at this stage of the defendant's past (which may make the likely sentence heavier), and thus is taken out of the lower court's jurisdiction. This could then be dealt with by committal to the Crown Court for sentence (see 2.5.17 below).

The National Mode of Trial Guidelines can be found in Document 1 in Appendix 6.

If the court's decision is that summary trial is appropriate (ie, if they accept jurisdiction), this will be explained to the accused, and s/he will be asked where s/he wants the case tried. S/he should indicate personally whether s/he consents to summary trial or elects jury trial. It is sufficient (depending on the formulation of the question by the clerk or the magistrate) to say 'here', 'magistrates' court', or alternatively 'Crown Court' or 'judge and jury'.

But see *Kent Justices ex p Machin* [1952] 2 QB 355: the Divisional Court made no express complaint about the consent to summary trial being given in the defendant's presence by solicitor.

If there are more than one accused, the mode of trial decision needs to be made in respect of each of them.

The defendant's choice

In making his choice, it must be explained to the defendant that, if convicted, s/he could still be committed for sentence to the Crown Court, under section 38 of the MCA 1980, if the magistrates are of the opinion that greater punishment should be inflicted than they have power to inflict (section 20(1) and (2)).

If the defendant consents to summary trial, the court will proceed and ask for plea, which (unless the client has changed his/her mind in the last five minutes) will be not guilty. The case will then be adjourned for trial or pre-trial review.

If the defendant elects jury trial, the case will be adjourned for committal proceedings to take place.

If the court decides that the case is more suitably dealt with at the Crown Court, the accused is told this, and there will be an adjournment for committal proceedings.

In either case, bail will need to be considered.

Criminal damage cases pose particular issues: if the value of the damage is less than £5,000 (unless the damage involves arson or danger to life), the matter is treated as summary only, with a maximum sentence of three months' imprisonment or a £2,500 fine. There is thus no mode of trial decision. If the damage is above this level, it is TEW and the procedure is as for any other TEW offence, and the maximum sentence if dealt with in the magistrates' court is as for a level 5 offence. Where the sum involved is not known, the defendant can be asked if s/he is prepared for the matter to be treated as summary only, and if s/he agrees, the matter proceeds on that basis.

The special procedure also applies to aggravated vehicle taking where the only aggravating feature is vehicle damage not exceeding £5,000.

2.5.12 WHAT HAPPENS WHEN THE DEFENDANT FACES A NUMBER OF CHARGES?

The mode of trial decision is taken in respect of each of the TEW offences, but where a number of offences are linked, it may be the case that this will be a factor that would suggest that summary trial is inappropriate. If a TEW matter is associated with a summary matter, there will be a mode of trial decision on the TEW matter or matters and, if the decision is made to commit the case for trial, then the summary matters will be dealt with in the magistrates' court or committed with the TEW charge if covered by section 41 of the CJA 1988 (see also 2.5.18 below).

55 Is there a relationship between plea and venue of trial in TEW cases?

Section 41 of the CJA 1988

(1) Where a magistrates' court commits a person to the Crown Court for trial on indictment for an offence triable either way, or for a number of such offences, it may also commit him for trial for any summary offence with which he is charged and which:

  (a) is punishable with imprisonment or involves obligatory or discretionary disqualification from driving; and

  (b) arises out of circumstances which appear to the court to be the same as or connected with those giving rise to the offence, or one of the offences, triable either way, whether or not evidence relating to that summary offence appears on the depositions or written statements in the case; and the trial of the information for the summary offence shall then be treated as if the magistrates' court had adjourned it under section 10 of the Magistrates' Courts Act 1980 and had not fixed the time and place for its resumption.

(2) Where a magistrates' court commits a person to the Crown Court for trial on indictment for a number of offences triable either way and exercises the power conferred by subsection (1) above in respect of a summary offence, the magistrates' court shall give the Crown Court and the [accused] a notice stating which of the offences triable either way appears to the court to arise out of circumstances which are the same as or connected with those giving rise to the summary offence.

(3) A magistrates' court's decision to exercise the power conferred by subsection (1) above shall not be subject to appeal or liable to be questioned in any court.

2.5.13 WHAT ARE THE ADVANTAGES AND DISADVANTAGES OF THE DIFFERENT COURTS?

Speed/delay

The case will usually be dealt with sooner in the magistrates' court and may take a shorter time actually in court. If the client is in custody pending trial and is expecting a custodial sentence, it may be in his/her interests to remain unconvicted for as long as possible, and thus to delay the trial. The period on remand will be deducted from any custodial sentence.

Cost

The magistrates' court is much cheaper for the client, which will be a consideration if s/he is not fully legally aided.

Publicity

It is difficult always to anticipate which type of trial will attract most local publicity, as much will depend on the nature of the offence and on those involved. However, for an offence of ordinary newsworthiness, not involving anyone who will attract attention to the case, the magistrates' court will normally gain less publicity. It can, however, be a matter of luck in such cases whether a local reporter is in court or not.

Form of representation

Generally, representation in the magistrates' court will be by a solicitor who has been dealing with or is associated with the case. Where representation is a matter of concern to the client, s/he should be advised who will represent him/her in court, as s/he may prefer someone with whom s/he is familiar. Unless a solicitor has higher rights of audience, s/he will not represent the client at Crown Court trial. Representation will usually be by counsel, who will by and large be unknown to the client.

Form of tribunal

The formality of the Crown Court is a factor that should be canvassed with clients. The magistrates' court is less formal and, therefore, less daunting. It may also be more convenient to reach, though this should be of less importance to a client's decision than other factors.

Likelihood of acquittal

It is thought that there is a higher chance of acquittal in the Crown Court for a variety of reasons. Local knowledge is a factor in your advice.

Complex matters of law or involving disputed admissibility of evidence are usually thought to be dealt with more appropriately in the Crown Court.

Sentence

Perhaps the most significant feature for clients with a choice of venue is the differing sentencing powers. Magistrates can only sentence for up to six months' imprisonment and/or a £5,000 fine for one TEW offence, with an overall maximum of 12 months for two or more TEW offences heard together. Local knowledge will be of value in assessing likely sentences in borderline cases. It should also be remembered that the magistrates' court can commit for sentence if they feel that their powers of punishment are insufficient (usually because of hearing about previous convictions or, in serious TEW cases, after a guilty plea). The client should be advised of this.

In advising on sentence and whether it should affect the choice of venue, consideration should also be given to:

- effect of previous convictions;
- sentencing guidelines;
- credit for early guilty plea.

Difficult points of evidence

Where there is a dispute, perhaps over the admissibilty of a confession, the matter is often dealt with more appropriately in front of a judge at the Crown Court.

The general maximum sentences are stated opposite. The magistrates do have greater power in some trading cases (such as Sunday trading, environment and similar matters).

The Magistrates' Association Sentencing Guidelines give the likely sentence for average offences and guidance for increasing or decreasing the sentence. *Always* consult them.

Checklist

Differences between summary trial and trial on indictment:

- Summary trial is trial in the magistrates' court:
  - three lay magistrates or one stipendiary;
  - magistrates decide on facts and law;
  - assisted by clerk;
  - solicitors or barristers appear for prosecution and defence;
  - defendant may represent him/herself.
- Trial on indictment is at the Crown Court:
  - judge decides law;
  - judge decides sentence;
  - jury decides facts, including guilt;
  - usually, barristers appear for both sides;
  - defendant is usually represented by a barrister.

Appeals

If a case is dealt with in the magistrates' court, the client has an automatic right of appeal to the Crown Court against any conviction or sentence; whether this is likely to succeed is of course dependant on the grounds of objection: a Crown Court can also increase the sentence passed by the magistrates. Appeals against Crown Court decisions need leave to appeal and lie to the Court of Appeal (Criminal Division).

No one of the above factors will usually stand alone to influence the defendant's choice. In many cases, not all will be relevant. What matters is that the client is properly and fully advised on the relevant matters, so that s/he can make an informed decision.

2.5.14 CAN THE DEFENDANT CHANGE HIS/HER PLEA?

At any time, the defendant can change his/her plea from not guilty to guilty, and may change it from guilty to not guilty at any time up until the verdict.

2.5.15 CAN THE DEFENDANT CHANGE HIS/HER DECISION AS TO VENUE?

The magistrates have a discretion to allow the defendant to retract his/her consent to summary trial, when s/he has pleaded not guilty, or now wishes to change to a not guilty plea. The test to be applied in determining whether or not to allow the change is whether the defendant understood the meaning (the nature and significance) of his/her earlier decision. Having no legal representation on the earlier occasion is a factor that might help persuade the magistrates to allow a change of election, but is not conclusive.

2.5.16 APPEALS

It is rare, but possible, to appeal by way of judicial review against a mode of trial decision. It is unlikely to be used by the defendant, as the sentence in the Crown Court would demonstrate the correctness or otherwise of the committal. Appeal by way of case stated is not available for non-final matters.

56 List the advantages and disadvantages in general cases of summary trial.

You must produce evidence of having advised two clients on a TEW charge of the considerations involved in choosing a venue.

A late change of plea will not, of course, allow the defendant the full advantage of the 'discount' for an early guilty plea under s 39 of the CJPOA 1994.

2.5.17 COMMITTAL FOR SENTENCE

The defendant can be committed for sentence under section 38 of the MCA 1980 to the Crown Court where the magistrates' powers of punishment are insufficient, either as a result of their hearing about previous convictions or because, on hearing the detail of the case, it seems more serious than they first thought.

The number of committals for sentence have increased considerably as a result of the plea before venue procedure introduced by the CPIA 1996, but, as stated above, some cases are being dealt with in the magistrates' court after a guilty plea that would previously have been refused by the magistrates.

2.5.18 ANCILLARY ORDERS

In order to tidy up outstanding matters, there are other powers of committal to the Crown Court.

Section 40 of the CJA 1988 allows for the defendant to be committed for trial on any offence of:

- common assault;
- taking a motor vehicle without consent;
- criminal damage under £5,000;
- driving whilst disqualified;
- assaulting a prison officer,

which is founded on the same facts as, or forms part of, a series of offences with an indictable offence.

This allows offences that are summary only but linked with an indictable matter to be sent for trial with them.

Section 41 provides that, where a defendant is committed for trial on TEW offences, s/he may also be committed for plea (not trial) for any offence punishable by imprisonment or disqualification arising out of the same circumstances as the TEW offence.

This procedure allows for committal for sentence after a guilty verdict on the major matter.

Section 56 of the CJA 1967 allows for committal to the Crown Court of other offences, including those which are summary only in association with other committals for sentence, etc.

57 In what circumstances can a summary case be tried in the Crown Court?

2.5.19 OFFENCES TRIABLE ON INDICTMENT ONLY

As with summary offences, there is no decision to be made as to venue: whatever the plea, the case must go to the Crown Court.

Under the CDA 1998, when it is fully implemented, indictment only cases will go straight to the Crown Court.

2.5.20 THE BURDEN OF PROOF

When advising the client on plea, you should remember that, in all cases other than:

- where the defendant is relying on the defence of insanity; and
- where statute provides otherwise,

the prosecution has to prove the case. This means that it is up to the prosecution, by relying on admissible evidence, to prove every element of the offence.

The elements of the offence are its constituents parts (see Unit 1).

Evidence might be available but be excluded because:

- it is inadmissible by rule of law; or
- it is excluded in the exercise of the court's discretionary powers.

Examples of inadmissible evidence are evidence of:

- the previous convictions of the defendant:
  - except where permitted under the Criminal Evidence Act 1898, section 27 of the Theft Act 1968 or the similar fact rule;
- hearsay evidence, except where permitted under section 76 of PACE 1984 or sections 23 and 24 of the CJA 1988.

Unfairly obtained evidence can be excluded under the judge's discretionary powers by virtue of section 78 of PACE 1984.

If the prosecution case depends on evidence that is or may be inadmissible, then that is a factor to take into account in advice on plea and, in a TEW case, on choice of venue. When the prosecution evidence does not include evidence of one or more elements of the offence, then the client should be so advised, and a not guilty plea considered.

Remember that the prosecution have to prove every element of the offence beyond reasonable doubt.

The prosecution carries the burden of proof except:

- in the case of insanity and allied defences;
- where a statute provides an exception expressly;
- where there are implied statutory exceptions.

The leading case is *Woolmington v DPP* [1935] AC 462, in which Lord Sankey said: 'Throughout the web of the English Criminal Law one golden thread is always to be seen, that it is the *duty of the prosecution to prove the prisoner's guilt ... subject to the defence of insanity and to statutory exceptions*.'

For example, in the Prevention of Crime Act 1953, the burden is expressly placed on the defence, as section 1 makes it an offence for someone to have with him/her in a public place, without lawful authority or reasonable excuse, *the proof of which shall lie with him,* an article made or adapted to cause injury.

58 When is the plea first investigated in a TEW offence?

59 What is the effect of an indication of a guilty plea in a TEW case?

60 What is the procedure for the decision on venue where no plea is indicated for a TEW offence?

If an argument to exclude evidence is likely to succeed, you should consider how that will affect the prosecution case. If the case is TEW, you should consider whether the argument should take place before a judge.

ASSISTING CLIENTS WITH ANCILLARY MATTERS

RANGE

Achievement must cover all the following contexts.

Ancillary matters

Return property seized, deportation notices, welfare benefits, prison visiting arrangements, limits of non-legal assistance, remand status of prisoners.

Agencies and third parties

DSS, courts, CAB, the Home Office, employers.

EVIDENCE

You will need to produce the specific pieces of performance evidence listed below. In addition, you will need to demonstrate that you have achieved the objectives specified at the beginning of this unit. You may do this by producing further pieces of evidence from real and simulated performance, by answering questions posed by your assessor or by passing a written examination.

You will need to provide evidence of:

1 having provided assistance to clients with three of the **Ancillary matters** in the **Range**;

2 having obtained and reviewed copies of search records in at least two cases.

CRITERIA

You will demonstrate achievement if:

(a) all relevant correspondence is sent to appropriate agencies and copies filed;

(b) any search records are reviewed and sustained efforts made to recover property and documents;

(c) clients are fully informed of wider implications of their arrest for their business or personal life;

(d) in dealing with non-nationals, you enquire whether deportation notices have been served, and you establish their immigration status.

2.6.1 SEIZURE BY THE POLICE

The police's power to search and seize property are largely set out in PACE 1984 and its Codes of Practice A (stop and search) and B (search and seizure).

Stop and search

Section 1 of PACE 1984 allows a police officer to search any person or vehicle for stolen or prohibited articles. Prohibited articles are defined as an offensive weapon or an article made or adapted for use in:

(a) burglary;
(b) theft;
(c) taking away a motor vehicle;
(d) obtaining property by deception.

An officer must have reasonable grounds for suspecting that stolen or prohibited articles are being carried.

Entry, search and seizure

Sections 8–23 of PACE 1984 set out police powers of entry, search and seizure. There are circumstances where the police can exercise these powers without a warrant, but a warrant issued by a justice of the peace (JP) to the police is usually required.

Entry with a warrant

Section 8 of PACE 1984 allows a JP to issue a warrant if s/he is satisfied that there are reasonable grounds for believing that:

(a) a serious arrestable offence has been committed;
(b) there is material specified in the warrant which is likely to be of substantial value to the investigation of the offence;
(c) the material is likely to be relevant evidence;
(d) it is not practicable to communicate with any person entitled to grant access to the premises, or entry will not be granted unless a warrant is produced, or a search may be frustrated or seriously prejudiced unless the police can obtain entry to the premises.

The police may seize and retain anything for which a search warrant has been authorised, under section 8(1) above.

Entry without a warrant

The main provisions are under sections 17 and 18 of PACE 1984. Under section 17 (entry for the purpose of arrest), the police may enter and search for the purpose of:

(a) exercising a warrant of arrest;
(b) arresting a person for an arrestable offence;
(c) recapturing a person unlawfully at large;
(d) saving life and limb or preventing unlawful damage to property.

Under section 18 of PACE 1984, the police may enter and search any premises occupied or controlled by a person who is under arrest for an arrestable offence, if they have reasonable grounds for suspecting that there is, on the premises, evidence relating to that offence or some other arrestable offence connected or similar to the offence for which the person has been arrested.

Search upon arrest

Under section 32 of PACE, the police have the power to search any premises in which a person was when s/he was arrested, or immediately before s/he was arrested, for evidence relating to the offence for which s/he was arrested. Further, the police have a general power of seizure when they are lawfully on premises, if they see anything which they have reasonable grounds for believing has been obtained in consequence of the commission of an offence, and they believe that it is necessary to seize it in order to prevent it being lost, damaged or destroyed.

The police may also seize anything if they have reasonable grounds for believing that it is evidence relating to an offence which they were investigating or any other offence and it is necessary to seize it in order to prevent the evidence being concealed, lost or destroyed.

61 While leaving a house, John is arrested for handling stolen goods. Can the police search the house and seize three televisions and one kilogram of cocaine found there?

2.6.2 RETURN OF SEIZED PROPERTY

Detailed provisions for the carrying out of all searches under warrant or otherwise are set out in Code B. Code B, para 6 relates to seizure and retention of property.

What steps can be taken to get property seized by the police returned?

It is first necessary to consider the statutory or other provision under which the material has been seized. The type of case in which a large amount of documentary and computerised information is seized will normally be a fraud case, drug offence or cases analogous to fraud, such as corruption or a conspiracy to evade tax or excise duty. The police may remove a large quantity of documents from a business, together with computers and computer disks.

Under Code C, para 7, the officer in charge of a search must:

(a) make a record of the search, including a list of any articles seized or a note of where such a list is kept; and

(b) if not covered by a warrant, include the reasons for their seizure.

Code B, para 6.8 also provides that, if property is retained, the person who had custody of it prior to its

You must provide evidence of having obtained and reviewed copies of search records in at least two cases.

seizure must, on request, be provided with a list of description in a reasonable time. It is this list which you are required to review, and you should attempt to get back for the client as much of the material as possible.

There are particular practical difficulties when the police execute a search warrant and seize a large number of computer disks. Under Code B, para 6.5, when an officer considers a computer to contain information, s/he may require the information to be produced in a form which can be taken away and which is visible and legible. In practice, the police may simply remove the computer together with all the disks, because of the time that would be required to print out all the information contained on the computer.

If, on reviewing the search records, they include documents which clearly do not appear to be relevant evidence, then, if the police refuse to return the documents, an application can be made to the magistrates' court under section 1 of the Police (Property) Act 1897 for the return of the documents. Power to make such an application is specifically preserved by section 22(5) of PACE 1984.

Material seized may be relevant evidence but may still be required by an individual or business for the purpose of carrying on legitimate activities. In these circumstances, an approach should be made to the police to discover whether a copy of the document would be sufficient for the purpose of any prosecution, and the police should be referred to the provisions of para 6.7, which provides that property shall not be retained if a photograph or copy would suffice for the purpose of evidence. If the police unreasonably refuse either to return original material or to allow copies to be taken of it, then the remedy will be a civil action by way of judicial review: *Allen v Chief Constable of Cheshire Constabulary* (1988) *The Times*, 16 July (CA).

2.6.3 ARREST OF NON-NATIONALS: DEPORTATION AND REMOVAL

The consequence of conviction of a non-national for an offence punishable with imprisonment is that the non-national may become liable for deportation. This applies irrespective of whether the offence is an Immigration Act 1971 offence or not. In practice, the police rarely prosecute people for Immigration Act offences because it is easier and less expensive for the Home Office to use its administrative powers of detention and removal or deportation. For this reason, we will first deal briefly with the Home Office's administrative powers of deportation, and then the courts' power to recommend deportation of a non-national.

Where computers and software are seized, it is often important to have these returned to enable a business to continue. Immediate action by the defendant's solicitors or the solicitor instructed by a business may be necessary to secure the return of the computers and disks to enable the business to continue trading a soon as possible. The first approach is to negotiate with the police for the return of the documents, computerised information, etc, on the basis that either the police print out the disks urgently and then return the original disks to the business, or that the business be allowed to take copies under the provisions of Code B, para 6.9 and PACE 1984, sections 21 (access and copying of documents) and 22 (retention of evidence).

See *R v Southampton Justices ex p Newman* (1988) 88 Cr App R 202. This case related to the return of property required by a client for the conduct of his defence. The defendant was arrested by customs officers. Customs retained eight address books The defendant's solicitors asked for the return of the address books, on the ground that they were necessary for the preparation of their client's defence. As property had been seized and was being held by customs, there was no power for the magistrates to order the return of property under section 1 of the Police (Property) Act 1897. The court held that PACE 1984, sections 21 and 22, dealt with access to, copying of, and retention of documents seized. Section 22(5) indicated the availability of the procedure under section 1 of the Police (Property) Act 1897. In a case involving Customs, this remedy was not available. The magistrates' court did have inherent jurisdiction, and had the power to adjourn a case until the prosecution handed over copies or original documents in the interests of justice.

Removal and deportation under Home Office's administrative powers

It is important to distinguish between removal and deportation.

Removal

The Home Office can enforce removal from the UK of an alleged illegal immigrant. Examples of illegal entry are:

(a) failure to obtain leave to enter when this is required;

(b) entering with false documents;

(c) entering by misrepresentation or deception.

There is no formal right of appeal of illegal entrants until they have been returned to their country of origin, unless they are asylum seekers (see below).

Deportation

This applies to non-nationals who have entered legally but have overstayed their leave to remain or have been in breach of a landing condition, eg, a student who has worked full time.

The Immigration Rules require the Home Office to take into account all relevant factors before serving a deportation notice. The relevant factors are:

(a) age (eg, a child supported by parents or an elderly person being supported by his family would be less likely to be deported);

(b) length of residence in the UK (eg, the longer the residence, the less likely it is that the deportation notice will be served);

(c) strength of connections with the UK;

(d) personal history, including character, conduct and employment record;

(e) criminal record;

(f) details of any offence for which the person was convicted;

(g) domestic circumstances (eg, a long term relationship and children will make deportation less likely);

(h) compassionate circumstances;

(i) any representations received on a person's behalf.

Right of appeal against a decision to deport

A deportation notice must be given in writing and in a standard form, stating a decision, the reasons for it and an explanation of the non-national's right to appeal within 14 days of the date of the notice. Appeal forms are sent with the letter and must be returned to the Home Office within 14 days. The right of appeal varies, depending on whether the person has been in the UK for more than seven years.

A person in the UK for less than seven years

The appeal is limited to where there was in law a power to make a deportation order for reasons set out in the Notice. Compassionate circumstances cannot be taken into account by the immigration adjudicator.

A person in the UK for more than seven years

The appeal can consider all aspects of a person's situation. These will, of course, include compassionate grounds and family ties.

2.6.4 ALTERNATIVES TO DEPORTATION

Voluntary departure

A person quickly leaves at his/her own expense. The advantage of this is that a deportation order is not made, but there is subsequent prohibition on re-entry. However, if a person wishes to return to the UK, s/he will be in a better position to obtain leave if s/he has not been formally deported.

Supervised departure

The Immigration Service pays for the ticket. This is appropriate when a person is willing to leave and has signed a formal disclaimer of appeal rights. The advantages of supervised departure are that it is quicker than formal deportation and the client will not spend a lengthy period possibly in custody. This can be negotiated by a solicitor on the client's behalf.

2.6.5 DEPORTATION FOLLOWING A CRIMINAL CONVICTION

Section 3 of the Immigration Act 1971 provides that a person who is not a British citizen shall be liable to deportation from the UK if, after s/he has attained the age of 17, s/he is convicted of an offence which is punishable with imprisonment and, on his/her conviction, is recommended for deportation by a court. Notice has to be given to a person in writing, seven days before a court makes such a recommendation. If a recommendation is made by the magistrates' court, there is a right of appeal to the Crown Court within 21 days.

The criteria for exercise of the power to make a recommendation are set out in the case of *R v Nazari* (1980) 71 Cr App R 87 (CA). The most important criterion is whether the person's continued presence in the UK is to the UK's detriment. In *Nazari,* Lawton LJ held that the courts were not concerned with the political situation in the country to which the person is likely to be deported. However, a different view was taken by the Court of Appeal in the case of *R v Thoseby and Krawczyk* (1979) 1 Cr App R(S) 280.

It is important to appreciate that the court only *recommends* deportation. The recommendation is then considered by the Home Office, taking into account the factors in the Immigration Rules set out above, and, if the Home Office decides to serve a deportation notice, there is a right of appeal, as in the administrative procedure.

2.6.6 PRACTICAL CONSIDERATIONS IN IMMIGRATION CASES

Establishing immigration status

If you are advising a person in the police station where there is, or may be, an immigration issue, it will be necessary to establish the following matters:

(a) nationality (check passport if available);

(b) date and place of birth;

(c) nationality of each parent at time of person's birth;

(d) date and place of arrival in the UK;

(e) travel document used;

(f) whether entry clearance was obtained abroad;

(g) reasons given to Immigration Service for visit;

(h) type of leave granted;

(i) length of stay granted;

(j) restrictions on stay;

(k) applications to Home Office for extension of leave;

(l) what person has done since arrival.

It will also be necessary to try and establish whether there has been any deception of the Immigration Service on arrival.

If a person is awaiting interview by an immigration officer, it will be necessary for you to see the immigration officer and try to establish as much information from that officer as possible, in order to assist you in assessing the immigration status of your client.

It will also be necessary to find out from your client his/her reasons for wanting to remain in the UK. The main considerations will include the following:

(a) husband/wife/partner who is British or settled in the UK;
(b) British-born child;
(c) health problems;
(d) desire to complete course if a student;
(e) fear of persecution in country to which the person would be returned.

Immigration interview

If a client is being interviewed by the immigration officer, then it would not be appropriate to remain silent because the decision on whether to serve a deportation notice is discretionary. Therefore, it is important that the client co-operates fully with the immigration officer and puts forward, in particular, reasons for remaining in the UK. An interview would take place under caution and be tape recorded.

Political asylum

If your client wishes to make an application for political asylum, s/he should have specialist advice before being interviewed at length about this. You should make it clear at the beginning of the interview that your client wishes to apply for political asylum but needs to take specialist advice before being interviewed.

Your client should be advised to answer questions and give any reason for overstaying or illegal entry, and that s/he should say that s/he wishes to apply for political asylum for reasons which will be explained fully after having had access to specialist advice. If you are not in a position to give that specialist advice, it may be possible (if your firm has an immigration practice) to obtain this from a colleague. Alternatively, the client should be referred urgently to a firm of solicitors or specialist agency who can provide him/her with the necessary advice. The name of a suitable firm for this purpose can be obtained from:

(a) Council for Welfare of Immigrants, 115 Old Street, London EC1V 9JR. Tel: 020 7251 8708;
(b) Immigration Law Practitioners Association, 115 Old Street, London EC1V 9JR. Tel: 020 7250 1671.

If a person has a fixed address and has applied for asylum, s/he may be released with conditions. Alternatively, once a notice of appeal has been lodged against the deportation notice, an application for bail can be made to an adjudicator. Sureties are normally required from British citizens.

The adjudicator, in deciding whether to grant bail subject to surety, will have to consider whether the proposed surety is suitable. This will mean that the surety must satisfy the adjudicator that s/he can pay the sum promised if the detained person does not answer bail. This is normally done by producing evidence of savings, by means of bank statements, building society books, etc. The amount of the surety will depend on the likelihood of the person absconding and the means of the proposed surety or sureties. If the detained person fails to answer bail, then the surety can forfeit some or all of the amount the s/he stands surety in. Specialist advice should be obtained in connection with bail and the private conduct of an appeal against deportation.

2.6.7 WELFARE BENEFITS: CRIMINAL CLIENTS GENERALLY

Your client may already be in receipt of welfare benefits. Clients may also seek your advice on the effect upon their benefits of a possible prison sentence.

Adults in legal custody

Legal custody is defined as imprisonment in connection with criminal proceedings, as opposed to civil proceedings. It includes a period of remand in custody. It does not include residence in a bail hostel or a period of release on licence from prison. As a general rule (Social Security Contributions and Benefits Act 1992, section 113(1)(b)), while in prison, an individual is not entitled to benefit, but there are several very important exceptions.

Job Seeker's Allowance

A person will be disqualified from Job Seeker's Allowance while in prison because s/he is not available for work.

Other benefits

A number of other benefits are suspended for a person who is in prison on remand awaiting trial. These include: Incapacity Benefit, Attendance Allowance, Disability Living Allowance, Severe Disablement Allowance, Maternity Allowance, Widows' Benefits, Retirement Pensions, Disablement Benefit, Reduced Earnings Allowance and Retirement Allowance. However, if a person is acquitted or convicted and not sentenced to imprisonment (which includes a suspended sentence), then, on release from custody, s/he would be paid arrears of benefit.

Children in legal custody

Child Benefit ceases after a child has been in custody for eight weeks. However, if the child is remanded in custody but not sentenced to a custodial sentence, arrears will be paid at the end of the period of remand.

Housing Benefit and Council Tax Benefit

If a person is remanded in custody awaiting trial, Housing Benefit and Council Tax Benefit are payable for 52 weeks, provided that the home has not been rented out to someone else and the prisoner intends to return there.

It is payable for 13 weeks for a person sentenced to a period of imprisonment. This provision is very important, as it will cover the great majority of custodial sentences imposed by magistrates' courts.

Assistance with the cost of visiting a close relative in prison

The family of your client, especially if on benefit, may find it difficult to afford to visit. Assistance may be obtained from the Home Office for close relatives. A close relative is defined as a husband, wife, an established unmarried partner, brother, sister, parent or child.

Assistance normally covers the travel costs, including meals and, if necessary, accommodation for a maximum of 26 visits in a 12 month period, if the claimant is receiving Income Support or Family Credit. There is also discretion to pay part of the costs if the client's means are limited but s/he is above Income Support level. An application must be made on form F2022, obtainable from the local Welfare Benefit Office or from the Assisted Prison Visits Unit, PO Box 5152, Birmingham B15 1SD, telephone 0121 626 2797.

You need to provide evidence of having provided assistance to clients with three of the ancillary matters specified within the **Range**.

Discharge Grant

A prisoner who is eligible for Income Support and is travelling to an address within the UK is entitled to apply for a Discharge Grant. The purpose of this is to provide a prisoner with sufficient money on release to meet immediate needs. In addition, a prisoner will obtain a travel warrant to an address within the UK.

Further advice

This outlines some of the provisions of welfare benefit law relevant to prisoners themselves. Any firm which has a legal aid franchise must have a person within the firm responsible for giving welfare benefit advice, and s/he must consider referring any criminal client or, if appropriate, his/her family, to specialist advice. Alternatively, if you do not have specialist provision within your practice, a referral should be made to a Citizens' Advice Bureau, a law centre or another firm of solicitors which can provide that advice.

Further reading

- *Professional Welfare Benefits Handbook*, published by Child Poverty Action Group.
- *Rights Guide to Non-Means Tested Benefits*, published by Child Poverty Action Group.

The two books above are updated and published on an annual basis.

- *Disability Rights Handbook*, published by Child Poverty Action Group.

63 What are the effects of a custodial sentence on Housing Benefit, Council Tax Benefit, Job Seeker's Allowance, etc?

2.6.8 VISITS TO PRISONERS AND CORRESPONDENCE

If a client is sentenced to or remanded in prison, s/he may be concerned about keeping in touch with family and friends. Additionally, you may be contacted by relatives as to how the prisoner can be visited.

Prison law is largely governed by the Prisoners Act 1952 (as amended), the Prison Rules 1999, Home Office Advice and Instructions to Prison Governors, and court judgments. This unit covers the rights of both remand and sentenced prisoners to receive visitors and to receive and send correspondence. For other matters, you should refer to the Prison Rules.

Remand prisoners

Visits

Unconvicted prisoners are entitled to receive as many visits as they wish 'within such limits and subject to such conditions as the Home Secretary may direct': Prison Rules, rule 35(1). At present, the entitlement is up to 90 minutes per week. Some prisons will allow a visit almost every day up to 15 minutes, although it is becoming more common for visits to be limited to three each week.

Correspondence

Correspondence is covered by rule 35(1) of the Prison Rules, which allows unconvicted prisoners to send and receive as many letters as they wish, but within such limits and such conditions as the Home Secretary may direct. There is now no automatic opening and checking of correspondence, but random checks may be carried out.

Solicitors' letters may not be opened. See also below on correspondence between legal advisers and inmates.

Telephone calls

Prisons now have card phones. These will only take cards issued by the Prison Service, which can be bought by prisoners, usually at the canteen. Prisoners' telephone calls are monitored, and these could include calls to legal advisers, although Home Office policy documents state that, in those circumstances, the calls should not be taped, and if they are inadvertently taped, they should not be listened to.

Other privileges of remand prisoners

While on remand, a prisoner cannot be required to work. Remand prisoners are also allowed to wear their own clothes. Relatives can bring clothes to the prison for prisoners to wear. These will be searched before they are given to the prisoner.

Correspondence between legal advisers and inmates

This is now dealt with under rule 39. This rule reflects decisions in a number of European Court of Human Rights and High Court cases which resulted in ensuring confidentiality in correspondence with legal advisers, subject to certain security safeguards.

All letters to clients in prison should be marked 'Rule 39 applies – Solicitor's letter'. If the letter is so marked, it should only be opened by a Prison Governor and read if there is reasonable suspicion that it contains an illegal enclosure or that its contents might endanger prison security or are of a criminal nature. In these circumstances, a prisoner should have the right to be present when the letter is opened. Rule 39 applies to both remand and convicted prisoners.

In these cases, of major importance to prisoners, the European Court of Human Rights decided that it was a breach of Article 8 of the European Convention for a prisoner's correspondence with his lawyer to be read as a matter of routine.

Article 8 provides that:

(1) Everyone has a right to respect for his private and family life, his home and his correspondence.

(2) There shall be no interference by a public authority with the exercise of this right except such as in accordance with the law and is necessary in a democratic society in the interests of national security, public safety or the economic well being of the country, for the prevention of disorder or crime, for the protection of health or morals, for the protection of the rights and freedom of others.

Convicted prisoners

Social visits

Convicted prisoners are entitled to receive two visits in every four week period: rule 35(2). A visitor on a social visit must be in possession of a valid visiting order. The prisoner is provided with visiting orders to send to those s/he wishes to visit him/her. Under the relevant standing orders, the normal people entitled to visit are defined as close relatives, which would include spouses, common law partners, parents, brothers and sisters. Social visits are also allowed from friends.

Normally, up to three visitors are permitted at any one time. There are provisions which allow prisoners to accumulate visits, but there are circumstances where, if a prisoner is in a prison far from home, s/he may be moved to a prison nearer home for the visits.

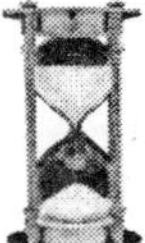

64 Your client has been imprisoned. His wife rings to ask whether she and the teenage children of the family will be able to visit.

Correspondence

Detailed provisions about this are in rules 34 and 35 of the Prison Rules. The matter is also dealt with by Standing Order 5(b), which includes the following statement of principle:

> The policy of the Prison Service is to encourage inmates to keep in touch with the outside world through regular letter writing, to respect the privacy of correspondence to and from inmates as far as possible and to ensure that it is transmitted as speedily as possible.

Under rule 35(2)(a) of the Prison Rules, convicted prisoners are allowed to send one letter a week at public expense. In practice, under the provisions of Standing Order 5B, prisoners are usually allowed to send as many privilege letters as they wish, subject to the overriding right of the Governor pursuant to rule 34 to prevent correspondence in the interests of good order and discipline.

A privilege letter is any letter which the prisoner is allowed to send in excess of the one letter a week that s/he is allowed under rule 35 of the Prison Rules.

2.6.9 PRACTICAL CONSIDERATIONS: CORRESPONDING WITH AND VISITING CLIENTS IN PRISON

Correspondence

As you will be aware, clients who have been remanded in custody in connection with a sexual offence or an assault on a child present particular problems. They will usually be well advised to ask for rule 45 (removal from association with other prisoners).

If they are in fact sharing a cell, it is not uncommon for correspondence to be read by the

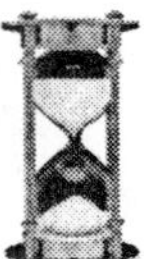

65 What is the difference between convicted and remand prisoners' rights in respect of communicating with friends?

prisoner's cell mate and other people. Great care should, therefore, be taken not to include much detail in any letter that might exacerbate your client's situation. Further, prosecution advance disclosure or committal papers which will contain statements from victims must not be given to your client to retain in prison or sent through the post. This is partly to protect your client, but also to prevent the material from being passed on to other sexual offenders.

Visits to a prisoner

Visits to a prisoner have to be arranged by appointment in advance and, when you attend, you will need evidence of identity and a letter on your firm's headed notepaper confirming the appointment. When visiting a prisoner, the degree of security in a prison will vary dramatically from a local category B or C prison to a high security prison. Your position as a solicitor's representative does not exempt you in any way from being searched or from your papers and briefcase going through the metal detector and x-ray machine.

Smuggling drugs or contraband

You should exercise the greatest caution if a prisoner's family asks you to deliver clothing to a prison for your client, in case you are being used to inadvertently smuggle in drugs.

All clothing is, of course, searched before being handed over to a prisoner, but even a very small quantity of cannabis inadvertently left in a pocket may be sufficient for you to be arrested.

Further reading

Creighton, S and King, V, *Prisoners and the Law*, 1996, London: Butterworths.

APPENDIX 6: DOCUMENTS

DOCUMENT 1: NATIONAL MODE OF TRIAL GUIDELINES

General mode of trial considerations

Section 19 of the Magistrates' Courts Act 1980 requires magistrates to have regard to the following matters in deciding whether an offence is more suitable for summary trial or trial on indictment: (1) the nature of the case; (2) whether the circumstances make the offence one of a serious character; (3) whether the punishment which a magistrates' court would have power to inflict for it would be adequate; (4) any other circumstances which appear to the court to make it more suitable for the offence to be tried in one way rather than the other; (5) any representations made by the prosecution or the defence.

Certain general observations can be made: (a) the court should never make its decision on the grounds of convenience or expedition; (b) the court should assume for the purpose of deciding mode of trial that the prosecution version of the facts is correct; (c) the fact that the offences are alleged to be specimens is a relevant consideration; the fact that the defendant will be asking for other offences to be taken into consideration, if convicted, is not; (d) where cases involve complex questions of fact or difficult questions of law, the court should consider committal for trial; (e) where two or more defendants are jointly charged with an offence each has an individual right to elect his mode of trial; (f) in general, except where otherwise stated, either way offences should be tried summarily unless the court considers that the particular case has one or more of the features set out in the following pages and that its sentencing powers are insufficient; (g) the court should also consider its powers to commit an offender for sentence, under section 38 of the Magistrates' Courts Act 1980, as amended by section 25 of the Criminal Justice Act 1991, if information emerges during the course of the hearing which leads them to conclude that the offence is so serious, or the offender such a risk to the public, that their powers to sentence him/her are inadequate. This amendment means that committal for sentence is no longer determined by reference to the character or antecedents of the defendant.

Features relevant to the individual offences

Note: Where reference is made in these guidelines to property or damage of 'high value' it means a figure equal to at least twice the amount of the limit (currently £5,000) imposed by statute on a magistrates' court when making a compensation order.

[Note: Each of the guidelines in respect of the individual offences set out below (except those relating to drugs offences) are prefaced by a reminder in the following terms 'Cases should be tried summarily unless the court considers that one or more of the following features is present in the case and that its sentencing powers are insufficient. Magistrates should take account of their powers under section 25 of the Criminal Justice Act 1991 to commit for sentence'.]

Burglary

1 Dwelling-house

(1) Entry in the daytime when the occupier (or another) is present.

(2) Entry at night of a house which is normally occupied, whether or not the occupier (or another) is present.

(3) The offence is alleged to be one of a series of similar offences.
(4) When soiling, ransacking, damage or vandalism occurs.
(5) The offence has professional hallmarks.
(6) The unrecovered property is of high value [see above for definition of 'high value'].

Note: Attention is drawn to para 28(c) of schedule 1 to the Magistrates' Courts Act 1980, by which offences of burglary in a dwelling cannot be tried summarily if any person in the dwelling was subjected to violence or the threat of violence.

2 Non-dwellings

(1) Entry of a pharmacy or doctor's surgery.
(2) Fear is caused or violence is done to anyone lawfully on the premises (eg, nightwatchman; security guard).
(3) The offence has professional hallmarks.
(4) Vandalism on a substantial scale.
(5) The unrecovered property is of high value [see above for definition of 'high value'].

Theft and fraud

(1) Breach of trust by a person in a position of substantial authority, or in whom a high degree of trust is placed.
(2) Theft or fraud which has been committed or disguised in a sophisticated manner.
(3) Theft or fraud committed by an organised gang.
(4) The victim is particularly vulnerable to theft or fraud (eg, the elderly or infirm).
(5) The unrecovered property is of high value [see above for definition of 'high value'].

Handling

(1) Dishonest handling of stolen property by a receiver who has commissioned the theft.
(2) The offence has professional hallmarks.
(3) The property is of high value [see above for definition of 'high value'].

Social security frauds

(1) Organised fraud on a large scale.
(2) The frauds are substantial and carried out over a long period of time.

Violence (sections 20 and 47 of the Offences against the Person Act 1861)

(1) The use of a weapon of a kind likely to cause serious injury.
(2) A weapon is used and serious injury is caused.
(3) More than minor injury is caused by kicking, head-butting or similar forms of assault.
(4) Serious violence is caused to those whose work has to be done in contact with the public or who are likely to face violence in the course of their work.
(5) Violence to vulnerable people (eg, the elderly and infirm).
(6) The offence has clear racial motivation.

Note: The same considerations apply to cases of domestic violence.

Public Order Act offences

1 Cases of violent disorder should generally be committed for trial

2 Affray

(a) Organised violence or use of weapons.
(b) Significant injury or substantial damage.
(c) The offence has clear racial motivation.
(d) An attack upon police officers, prison officers, ambulancemen, firemen and the like.

Violence to and neglect of children

(a) Substantial injury.
(b) Repeated violence or serious neglect, even if the physical harm is slight.
(c) Sadistic violence (eg, deliberate burning or scalding).

Indecent assault

(1) Substantial disparity in age between victim and defendant, and the assault is more than trivial.
(2) Violence or threats of violence.
(3) Relationship of trust or responsibility between defendant and victim.
(4) Several similar offences, and the assaults are more than trivial.
(5) The victim is particularly vulnerable.
(6) Serious nature of the assault.

Unlawful sexual intercourse

(1) Wide disparity of age.
(2) Breach of position of trust.
(3) The victim is particularly vulnerable.

Note: Unlawful sexual intercourse with a girl under 13 is triable only on indictment.

Drugs

1 Class A

(a) Supply; possession with intent to supply: these cases should be committed for trial.
(b) Possession: should be committed for trial unless the amount is consistent only with personal use.

2 Class B

(a) Supply; possession with intent to supply: should be committed for trial unless there is only small scale supply for no payment.
(b) Possession: should be committed for trial when the quantity is substantial and not consistent only with personal use.

Dangerous driving

(1) Alcohol or drugs contributing to dangerousness.
(2) Grossly excessive speed.
(3) Racing.
(4) Prolonged course of dangerous driving.
(5) Degree of injury or damage sustained.
(6) Other related offences.

Criminal damage

(1) Deliberate fire-raising.
(2) Committed by a group.
(3) Damage of a high value [see above for definition of 'high value'].
(4) The offence has clear racial motivation.

Note: Offences set out in schedule 2 to the Magistrates' Courts Act 1980 (which includes offences of criminal damage which do not amount to arson) must be tried summarily if the value of the property damaged or destroyed is £5,000 or less.

DOCUMENT 2: RECORD OF DECISION TO GRANT UNCONDITIONAL BAIL

RECORD OF DECISION TO GRANT UNCONDITIONAL BAIL (CRIMINAL CASES)

(Bail Act 1976, s 5; Magistrates' Courts Rules 1981, rr 66, 90)

.... Magistrates' Court

(Code:)
Date:

Accused:

Date of birth:

Alleged offence[s]: [short particulars and statute]

Decision: The accused is granted bail with a duty to surrender to the custody of [place] Magistrates' Court on [date] at [time] am/pm [or [the Crown Court at the time and place for the time being appointed by that court]].

Signature ....
Justice of the Peace
[Clerk of the Court present during these proceedings]

DOCUMENT 3: RECORD OF DECISION TO GRANT CONDITIONAL BAIL

RECORD OF DECISION TO GRANT CONDITIONAL BAIL (CRIMINAL CASES)

.... Magistrates' Court (Code:)

Date:

Accused:

Date of birth:

Alleged offence[s]: [short particulars and statute]

Decision: The accused is granted bail, with a duty to surrender to the custody of [place] Magistrates' Court on [date] at [time] am/pm or [the Crown Court at the time and place for the time being appointed by that court]; the bail being subject to the following conditions:

Conditions: Conditions to be complied with before release on bail

To provide suret[y][ies] in the sum of £ [each] to secure the accused's surrender to custody at the time and place appointed.

†

Conditions to be complied with after release on bail

†

* Reasons: The above conditions were imposed on the grant of bail for the following reason(s):

Signature ....

Justice of the Peace

DOCUMENT 4: RECORD OF DECISION TO WITHHOLD BAIL

RECORD OF DECISION TO WITHHOLD BAIL (CRIMINAL CASES)

(Bail Act 1976, s 5; Magistrates' Courts Rules 1981, rr 66, 90)

.... Magistrates' Court (Code:)

Date:

Accused:

Date of birth:

Alleged offence[s]: [short particulars and statute]

Decision: The court, having found that the exception(s) to the right to bail specified in the first column of the Schedule hereto applies [apply] for the reason(s) specified in the second column of the said Schedule, withholds bail.

The accused is [remanded in] [committed to] custody for appearance before [place] Magistrates' Court on [date] at [time] am/pm] lor [the Crown Court at the time and place for the time being appointed by that court]].

Signature ....

Justice of the Peace

[Clerk of the Court present during these proceedings]

SCHEDULE

Exception(s) to right to bail (Include relevant Part and paragraph number(s) of Schedule I to Bail Act 1976)	Reason(s) for applying the Exception(s) specified in first column

DOCUMENT 5: CERTIFICATE AS TO HEARING A FULL ARGUMENT ON APPLICATION FOR BAIL

CERTIFICATE AS TO HEARING A FULL ARGUMENT ON APPLICATION FOR BAIL (CRIMINAL CASES)

(Bail Act 1976, s 5; Magistrates' Courts Rules 1981, rr 66, 90)

.... Magistrates' Court (Code:)

Date:

Accused:

Date of birth:

Alleged offence[s]: [short particulars and statute]

I hereby certify that, at a hearing this day, the court heard full argument on an application for bail made [by] [on behalf of] the accused, before refusing the application and remanding the accused in custody under section [ ] of the Magistrates' Courts Act 1980.

[The court has not previously heard full argument on an application for bail by or on behalf of the accused in these proceedings] [The court has previously heard full argument from the accused on an application for bail, but is satisfied [that there has been the following change in his circumstances:] [that the following new considerations have been placed before it:]]

Signature ....

Justice of the Peace

[or By order of the Court

Clerk of the Court]

APPENDIX 7: ANSWERS TO THE SELF-ASSESSMENT QUESTIONS

SAQ ANSWERS: 2.1

35 The client's age, anxiety level, mental health and criminal record may affect the way you deal with him/her. S/he may be dishonest, violent, a drug abuser or a sex offender.

36 You may have to take instructions from your client in a court or prison. It is important to bear in mind that:

- there may be a lack of privacy;
- time may be limited, especially if you are using a non-designated interview room, and access to your client may also be limited;
- the client may experience more stress in these surroundings than s/he would in a police station. Stress, privacy, time, access.

37 Your responses will depend on whether you have your client's authority to divulge the information. Often, this can be inferred from what you know of the relationship. Are the family members living together, estranged, in contact? Are you sure that the person, in any event, is the mother or spouse as claimed?

The information in the two examples is public information, and can be gained from the court involved, so your inquirer could be asked to address the question to the court if you are unsure of your professional duty.

38 You have no duty to correct the information, but must not rely on, or allow an advocate to rely on, the client's good character in a bail application or plea in mitigation. It may be that, in order to sensibly address the court, the conviction will need to be revealed: the client's permission should be obtained.

39 No – you can probe the prosecution case and put the prosecution to proof, but you cannot advance a positive defence.

SAQ ANSWERS: 2.2

40 Grounds:

- fear of failure to surrender:
- commission of further offences;
- interference with witnesses;
- TEW offence, and already on bail;
- already in custody;
- for own protection.

41 Considerations:

- nature and seriousness:
- character and antecedents;
- record on bail;
- strength of evidence;
- any other relevant matter.

42 Conditions can be imposed where grounds exist for refusal.

43 Examples might be not to visit (the address) save by prior arrangement to arrange access to children or not to communicate with spouse save through solicitors to arrange access to children. In circumstances such as these, the arrangements for access might involve a third person; where the risk of further offences is deemed high, access may not be allowed for by the court.

44 The ground would be risk of further offences. The considerations would be previous history of offending, including any offending on bail, and possibly the strength of the evidence. The conditions might state that the defendant should not go to/enter one of the following:

- a designated shop;
- a specified shopping area the town centre (which must be specified as to extent);
- all supermarkets;
- shops belonging to a specific retailer.

45 Not to go to (designated area) save:

- to see his/her solicitor, by prior appointment;
- to attend the DSS (usually a day and time would be specified);
- to visit (specified chemist) on (specified times).

NB: a court may be willing to consider such exceptions, but it may call into question whether the exclusion is necessary in the first place; alternatively, the number of exceptions may concern a court as to whether any exceptions should be made at all.

SAQ ANSWERS: 2.3

46 Legal aid for advice and assistance on any matter of English law for two hours work.

47 In cases of:

- murder;
- prosecution appeal to the House of Lords;
- appearances in custody, where a custodial remand is again likely, remands in custody for reports.

48 Client falls below the means threshold, and it is in the interests of justice, which includes:

- fear of loss of liberty or livelihood;
- involvement of difficult questions of law;
- client has inadequate English or a disability;
- tracing, etc, of witnesses;
- the interest of a third person.

49 Yes, if it is in the interests of justice.

50 Subject to the restrictions on the stage of proceedings set out in 2.3.26 above:

(a) if the defendant is in custody or has difficulty in representing himself, otherwise not;

(b) if the defendant is in custody or is in danger of a custodial sentence or there is a technical legal defence, otherwise unlikely;

(c) yes.

51 When the prosecution is abandoned or the defendant is acquitted or an appeal is successful.

52 Reasonable costs of the defendant, unless his/her own action brought the cases on him/herself.

SAQ ANSWERS: 2.5

53 The Guidelines indicate where a TEW offence should be tried, depending on the circumstances.

54 The listed factors can be used to argue for trial in the magistrates' court in a case where the court might consider refusing jurisdiction, and the defendant wishes for summary trial.

55 If the defendant definitely wishes to plead guilty, there is no reason to seek a Crown Court hearing. If the plea is to be not guilty, a variety of factors arise (see 2.5.13 above). Indicating a guilty plea in the magistrates' court will mean that the case is not committed for trial.

56 Consider: sentence; speed; publicity; likelihood of acquittal; form of representation; cost (see 2.5.13 above).

57 Section 40 of the CJA 1988 provides for trial of certain summary offences, if founded on the same facts or if part of a series with a TEW offence.

58 In the magistrates' court.

59 The case will not have a mode of trial hearing – it will proceed in the magistrates' court.

60 There is a full mode of trial hearing.

SAQ ANSWERS: 2.6

61 Yes, under section 32. The police have power under section 32 of PACE 1984 to carry out an immediate search. If they have reasonable grounds for believing that the three televisions have been stolen, they can seize them. The cocaine can be seized on the ground that it is an illegal substance. The power under section 32 can only be exercised if the police carry out the search at the time of arrest or immediately thereafter, but they could rely on section 18 of PACE 1984 to seize the goods if they returned some hours later.

62 It is not affected. A condition of residence at a bail hostel does not in any way affect your client's right to claim Job Seeker's Allowance.

63 They are suspended during custody. Housing Benefit and Council Tax Benefit are payable for 13 weeks to a person sentenced to a period of imprisonment. Job Seeker's Allowance is not payable to a person serving a custodial sentence.

64 Yes, with a visiting order. The prisoner's spouse and two of his children would be allowed to visit. You should explain that, normally, two visits are allowed per month and that a visiting order will be sent by the prisoner to his spouse.

65 Unconvicted prisoners have unlimited access. A remand prisoner can receive and send an unlimited number of letters. Convicted prisoners are allowed to send one letter per week at public expense but, in practice, they are normally allowed to send additional letters at their own expense, subject to the right of the Governor to prevent correspondence in the interests of good order and discipline.

APPENDIX 8: SELF-ASSESSMENT TESTS

WRITTEN TEST 1

Gerald has been arrested in connection with an allegation of assault occasioning actual bodily harm on his wife. The injuries to his wife involved severe bruising about the head and shoulders. He was interviewed, and made full admissions. There has been a history of acrimonious relations between the couple, usually when drink has been involved, but the police have never been involved before. He has no previous convictions:

(a) On what grounds may unconditional bail be refused?

(b) Are there conditions that might be imposed?

(c) If bail were refused, how could Gerald challenge that decision?

(d) How would the position differ if the charge were manslaughter?

WRITTEN TEST 2

Richard Ransome appears for the first time in the magistrates' court today, having been arrested last night and kept in police custody. He is charged with burglary of a dwelling house.

The prosecution allegation is that, on the night before the court appearance, a burglary took place at the home of Janet Hutchinson in Priory Road, Southall. She returned home at midnight to find her front door ajar. She called out, and a white male dressed in denim jeans and a dark jumper rushed past her and down the street.

Richard Ransome was arrested at 12.10 am in the street leading from Priory Road. When asked by the police what he was doing, he said he was walking home. He was dressed in clothes fitting Miss Hutchinson's description.

He tells you he has always attended in answer to bail and has complied with the Community Service Order. He denies the offence. He says he had been out with friend and was walking home. He is aged 26. He lives alone in rented accommodation at 32 The Mansions, Ealing. He is unemployed, but sometimes does casual work on a building site. His last casual work was one month ago. His parents (in their 50s) live in Ealing and he is on good terms with them. His father is a delivery driver and his mother is an office cleaner.

Previous record:

March year before last:	Ealing Mags	TWOC x 3 offences	Probation 1 year
December last:	Ealing Mags	Burglary dwelling	CSO 180 hrs
February this year:	Ealing Mags	Theft (from shop)	fine £150

(a) On what grounds may unconditional bail be refused?

(b) Are there conditions that might be imposed?

(c) If bail were granted could the prosecution challenge the decision?

(d) Is Richard Ransome likely to be eligible for legal aid? On what grounds?

(e) What will be the procedure for deciding on mode of trial?

(f) When will plea be entered?

(g) What information will you need from your client before advising on plea?

APPENDIX 9: ANSWERS TO THE SELF-ASSESSMENT TESTS

WRITTEN TEST 1

Your answers should deal with the following:

(a) Fear of further offences.
(b) To live at another address; not to communicate directly or indirectly with his wife.
(c) By application to the Crown Court.
(d) Grounds must be given for allowing trial.

WRITTEN TEST 2

Your answers should deal with the following:

(a) Fear of further offences; interfering with witnesses; absconding.
(b) Possibly a curfew, together with conditions not to contact the witness and to report to a police station at specified dates and times.
(c) Yes, if they objected at the trial.
(d) Subject to means, yes, because the sentence may lead to a loss of liberty.
(e) If a guilty plea, it will be dealt with in the magistrates' court. If not guilty, as in 2.5.11 above.
(f) In the magistrates' court.
(g) His version of events and instruction on plea.

CHECKLIST SUMMARY OF UNIT 2

At the end of this unit, you should know:

- when information must be disclosed by and to your client;
- when the client can be arrested and searched;
- when bail can be withheld;
- when and how legal aid can be obtained;
- how to research the law;
- what information is required before giving preliminary advice;
- how to challenge bail decisions;
- how to advise clients on the procedure that might affect them;
- how to advise clients on mode of trial and plea;
- how to advise clients on matters relating to property seized, welfare benefits and deportation issues;
- how to advise clients and their families on prison visits.

UNIT 3

DEALING WITH COURT APPOINTMENTS

OVERVIEW

There are seven activities making up this unit:

3.1 liaising with clients, agencies and third parties;

3.2 briefing advocates;

3.3 supporting advocates;

3.4 taking proofs of evidence;

3.5 disclosing evidence;

3.6 exploring areas for agreement;

3.7 advising clients on post-disposal matters.

OBJECTIVES

To become fully competent in this unit, you will need knowledge and understanding of:

Criminal justice agencies

- describe the hierarchy and organisation of the police, courts and prosecution authorities.

Client knowledge

- describe the main types of clients likely to be encountered in criminal litigation work and how they would be handled;
- describe the consequences of taking inconsistent instructions from clients.

Representative's role in court

- describe the main features of the court rules and good practice related to clients' and clients' supporters' attendance of court;
- describe the paralegal's role in liaising between client, advocate, witnesses and clients' supporters.

Case management

- describe the principal elements of good practice in relation to the management of cases.

Procedure

- describe the main aspects of the restrictions on reporting in the media;
- describe the different types of pre-trial hearings (including plea and directions hearings) and their purposes.

Bail

Explain statutory provisions for bail in relation to:

- police station:
  - appeals against imposition of conditions/ variations to a second custody sergeant;
- magistrates' court:
  - appeals against police conditions;
  - applications for unconditional bail;
- Crown Court:
  - appeals against refusal from a magistrates' court (defence);
  - appeals against grant of bail (prosecution);
- High Court:
  - appeals against refusal from the Crown Court;

- applications to vary bail conditions imposed in a magistrates' court.

Home Office production orders

- describe the procedures for obtaining Home Office production orders.

Witnesses

- describe the procedures to be followed when warning witnesses to attend.

Time limits

- describe the dangers inherent in failing to observe time limits, court requirements and other professional obligations.

Briefs

- describe the function, contents and layout expected in a brief.

Evidence

- describe the main points in the rules related to admissibility of evidence for:
  - defence evidence;
  - prosecution evidence;
- describe the function, contents and layout expected in a proof of evidence;
- explain why it is important to try to agree evidence pre-trial.

Disclosure

- describe the circumstances in which evidence must or can be disclosed;
- describe the rules related to format and time scales for disclosure including when it is appropriate or necessary to serve a defence statement under the Criminal Procedure and Investigations Act 1996.

Appeals

- describe the broad rules pertaining to appeals regarding entitlement, time limits, bail, funding and consequences (including costs).

Sentences

- describe the implications of sentences in relation to:
- confiscation of property;
- forfeiture of property;
- destruction of property;
- fingerprints and DNA samples;
- rehabilitation;
- custodial sentences;
- non-custodial sentences and orders;
- describe the rules pertaining to destruction, retention and return of property and materials created within the proceedings.

LIAISING WITH CLIENTS, AGENCIES AND THIRD PARTIES

RANGE

Achievement must cover all the following contexts.

Contacts
Clients in custody, clients on bail, alternative contact points.

Witnesses
Witnesses of fact, expert witnesses, character witnesses.

Agencies
Counsels' clerk, prosecuting authorities, witnesses, probation service, prison authorities, court authorities, witness service, process server, co-accuseds' legal representatives, interpreters, sureties.

Professional and ethical standards
Duty to clients, standards of care, protection of interest, conflicts of interest, obligations to the court, client confidentiality.

EVIDENCE

You will need to produce the specific pieces of performance evidence listed below. In addition, you will need to demonstrate that you have achieved the objectives specified at the beginning of this unit. You may do this by producing further pieces of evidence from real and simulated performance, by answering questions posed by your assessor or by passing a written examination.

You will need to provide evidence of:

1 having explained to three **Contacts** in the **Range**, verbally and in writing, their duties while in custody and on bail, and on the consequences of not meeting those duties;
2 having explained in writing to at least one potential surety what his/her role is and having ensured his/her attendance at court (see 3.1.1 below).

CRITERIA

You will demonstrate achievement if:

(a) clients are kept informed of progress;
(b) clients' obligations and roles in their own defence are emphasised;
(c) choice of approved advocates is agreed with clients;
(d) clients and witnesses are advised on acceptable court behaviour and etiquette;
(e) clients and witnesses are informed in writing of forthcoming hearings at which they are required to attend;
(f) in the event of a guilty plea, probation officers are informed;
(g) court office is informed immediately of any difficulties in the progress of cases or any characteristics of cases requiring specific action;
(h) the need for any necessary Home Office production orders is identified at an early stage;
(i) sureties are informed of the requirement for them to appear at court or the police station.

3.1.1 INTRODUCTION

This unit will deal with communication with your client both verbally and in writing. It is most important that communication with your client be in terms and in language that s/he can understand.

Your clients will almost certainly include children, people with learning difficulties of all ages, and people who cannot read or write, or have great difficulty in doing so. It is important that there be genuine communication with the client, so that what you are saying is clearly understood. It is equally important that letters be written in language which the client can understand, and that they be kept simple and as short as possible.

3.1.2 LEGAL AID BOARD TRANSACTION CRITERIA

Your firm will almost certainly have a system in place with standard checklists and letters to ensure that the Legal Aid Board requirements for franchising are covered. You will soon become aware that, while the majority of criminal cases can be adequately prepared by completing the requirements of the checklist system, a substantial minority of cases need far more thought and a more proactive approach if your client is to receive an adequate defence.

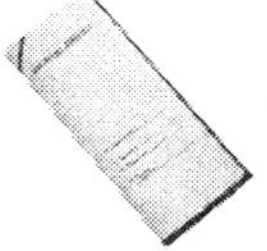

You will find a copy of the Transaction Criteria in Document 4 in Appendix 2.

Requirements of the Transaction Criteria

The Transaction Criteria require you to advise your client on:

(a) what the prosecution will have to prove before the offence is made out;

(b) how the client should consider pleading;

(c) which court could deal with the matter and, if relevant, the advantages and disadvantages of trial in the magistrates' court and Crown Court.

When your client first comes to see you, it may be that you or your firm have acted for the client in the police station. In those circumstances, you will probably have a reasonable idea of the strength of the prosecution's case and, if your client has answered questions in his/her interview, what your client's response is. Alternatively, you may see a client who has been interviewed in the police station, and the only information you have when s/he first sees you is his/her own account of what happened and perhaps a copy of the charge sheet.

It is always helpful to explain to a client at an early stage what the prosecution has to prove before the offence is made out, and confirm that advice in writing. This puts in context the issue for the client to consider if s/he has told you that s/he wishes to plead not guilty. It would almost certainly be sensible to delay advising a client how s/he should consider pleading in an either way matter until you have received advance disclosure, obtained the tapes of any police interview and listened to them. Some clients will of course come to you saying that they wish to plead guilty because they were caught stealing from their employers and have made a full admission to the police. In those circumstances, subject to checking that the client's version of events is correct and that s/he has not made an admission because of improper pressure applied by the police, advice on plea is not really necessary and you can concentrate on preparing mitigation.

In any case, where the client tells you that s/he wishes to plead not guilty, you clearly need as much information as possible about the strength of the prosecution's case and about what evidence there is. The matters the client will have to consider in deciding on his/her plea and on which court to deal with the matter are set out fully in 2.5 above.

3.1.3 WHAT INFORMATION SHOULD YOU GIVE TO A CLIENT?

All information supplied by the prosecution to the defence and any expert evidence obtained by the defence should, in general, be forwarded as soon as possible to the client for his/her consideration.

There are, of course, exceptions to this. If you are acting for a child, then it may be better and more appropriate to see the child with an appropriate adult, summarise the evidence, and go through it with them in the office. Copies of statements could subsequently be supplied to the child and appropriate adult.

In the case of an offence involving sexual assault upon a child or an adult, witness statements should not be posted to a client in custody. Such material should be taken by you to the accused in prison for a meeting to obtain the client's instructions and should be removed afterwards.

The role of the appropriate adult is to help communication with the young person, to act as an independent person and to safeguard the interests of the child or young person.

Prison inmates accused or convicted of sexual offences are very vulnerable. Witness statements may be seen by cell mates, which would increase risk to the client. Statements containing sexually explicit material may be circulated in prison for the purpose of sexual gratification.

3.1.4 WHAT ARE THE CLIENT'S OBLIGATIONS AND ROLE IN HIS/HER OWN DEFENCE?

It is difficult to generalise about this because it will depend very much on the nature of the charge and your client's intelligence and ability to help him/herself.

Whether the charge relates to an incident which lasted only five minutes (eg, an affray where your client was present but claims s/he took no part), or to a complex fraud stretching over months or years, it is essential, if the defence is to be successful, for you to obtain as much positive input from the client as possible. There is always a tendency among some clients to adopt a 'head-in-the-sand' attitude to a trial and leave matters entirely in the hands of their lawyers. You should emphasise that an effective defence involves the client's full concentration and effort. You will, in particular, need your client's assistance in:

(a) preparing the detailed proof of evidence for him/her (see 3.4 below);
(b) tracing witnesses;
(c) going through the prosecution's witness statements;
(d) going through any unused material;
(e) making observations or comments on the prosecution statements or unused material;
(f) following up leads disclosed by the prosecution's witness statements and unused material.

It is not unusual for criminal clients to miss appointments and fail to attend conferences with counsel. It is, therefore, important that, at the outset of the case, if necessary, you make clear to the client that the successful defence of the charges s/he faces is going to depend in part on full co-operation from him/her and, if you are having a conference with counsel in another town, it may be sensible to travel with your client or give him/her a lift to make sure that s/he arrives.

3.1.5 CHOICE OF ADVOCATE

This decision is one for the client to make and, although in most cases the client will leave it to you to make the choice for him/her, it is important that s/he accepts your choice. It is a franchising requirement that a firm have a list of approved advocates from the Bar that it uses, and there may also be in-house solicitor advocates.

Sometimes, a client will wish you to brief a solicitor advocate or barrister who has represented him/her in the past, and you must, if possible, follow your client's wishes. If the advocate the client requires is not on your approved list, then the reason for using that advocate must be noted on the file. In the magistrates' court, where fixed dates are given for trials, it will usually be possible to ensure that the chosen advocate is available. The position is unfortunately very different in the Crown Court. Although trials involving expert witnesses and lengthy trials are normally given fixed dates, the majority of trials are simply placed in the 'Warned List' with effect from a certain date. This means that the parties are warned that they must be available to proceed any time after the date first appears in the list. The normal practice is for the Crown Court listing office to telephone the parties between 2 and 3 pm on the day before the case is due to be listed. The chance of a chosen advocate who may have had a conference with the client being available at such short notice is probably, at best, 50%. The fact that 50% of the CPS briefs are not dealt with by the advocate of choice is not going to be any consolation to your client, who may have confidence in the advocate s/he has already met in conference and who perhaps has represented him/her at a plea and directions hearing.

A plea and directions hearing is a pre-trial procedure in the Crown Court, where a plea is entered and and arrangements for and length of trial are determined.

It is, therefore, important when you discuss choice of advocate with your client, that you make clear to him/her that you cannot guarantee that the chosen advocate will be available to represent him/her, because of the court listing system. It will then be necessary for you to liaise with counsel's clerk to provide an acceptable substitute of a similar level of seniority to the advocate originally briefed. Most counsel's clerks, particularly if you use their chambers regularly, will go to great pains to provide an adequate substitute. Provided the case has been well prepared and there is a detailed brief and a note of any conference with the papers, it should be possible for your client to be competently represented.

3.1.6 COURT BEHAVIOUR AND ETIQUETTE

Should I instruct my client on court behaviour and etiquette?

It is easy to forget how frightening and alien an environment a court can be to both inexperienced clients and defence witnesses. How your client behaves in court affects his/her case. This is extremely important at remand hearings, where an unco-operative and aggressive attitude may jeopardise the likelihood of bail. Similarly, the laid-back attitude adopted by some young males may give the impression that they do not take the proceedings seriously. The bench may form the impression that any bail conditions imposed are likely to be ignored.

The nature of the advice you give to your client will depend on his/her own nature and temperament. It is important to make clear to the client that the key to acceptable court behaviour is politeness. It helps all clients to be made aware of the formalities that they will be expected to adhere to in court, such as standing when the member(s) of the bench enter and leave and when addressed by the court.

The client should also be made aware of what will actually occur at the hearing. The client should be told what is wrong (if anything), where s/he should stand, and so on. For many defendants, the notion of orderly conduct, with participants taking turns at speaking, is a novel one.

In an application for bail, the client should be told that the prosecution will outline its case first, and that the defence advocate will have a chance to address the prosecution's objections to bail when the prosecution advocate has finished speaking. The client should be told that any interruptions by him/her from the dock will not assist his/her bail application.

Instruct witnesses on court behaviour and etiquette

It is equally important that both the client and any defence witnesses of fact be told about the procedure at the trial. If possible, any defence witnesses should be brought into the court when it is not sitting, so that they can be shown where the witness box is, the layout of the court, and familiarise themselves with it. They should be told to address the bench or jury, not the advocate asking the questions, and to speak clearly and slowly.

You should always give your witnesses a chance to go through statements before giving evidence, so as to refresh their memory. You will already have explained to them that they cannot read from their statements in court, although in certain cases, they may be allowed to refer to a contemporaneous statement to refresh their memory.

Not only does this indicate politeness, it will also help the client to be at ease by understanding the procedure.

A contemporaneous statement, such as information contained in a police officer's notebook, can be referred to in court to refresh a witness's memory if it was made or verified by the witness personally and was made soon after the incident, when matters were fresh in the witness's mind. In certain cases, it has been held that it is open to a trial judge, in the exercise of his/her discretion and in the interests of justice, to permit a witness to refresh his/her memory from a statement made soon after the events (although not falling within the definition of contemporaneous). See *R v Da Silva* (1990) Cr App R 233 (CA).

Witnesses of fact have to be told that they will remain outside court until called to give evidence. You must explain to them about the purpose of cross-examination and how to deal with it. Finally, and most importantly, both your client and his/her witnesses should be told that, if the court adjourns during the course of their evidence, neither you nor the advocate can discuss the case with them until their evidence has been completed.

Expert witnesses

It is likely that any expert witness you rely on is familiar with court procedure and will not need guidance from you about it. However, if the expert does not attend court regularly, either you or possibly the advocate in the case should explain the procedure. An expert witness will normally remain in court throughout the prosecution and defence cases because s/he is giving his/her expert opinion on facts arising from the evidence. It is clearly essential that, at the very least, a defence expert witness hears the testimony of the prosecution's expert witness, so that s/he can comment on any points arising from it.

Checklist for defence witnesses

Prior to the hearing

(a) Has a full proof of evidence been taken and signed by the witness?

(b) Is it necessary to apply for a witness summons to ensure attendance by the witness?

At the hearing

(c) Has the witness read through the proof to refresh his/her memory?

(d) Does s/he know roughly when s/he will be called?

(e) Does s/he know the method of question and answer?

(f) Has s/he been advised to address answers to the magistrates/jury; to speak slowly and clearly; to ask for clarification if a question is unclear; and that you will intervene if improper questions are asked?

3.1.7 FORTHCOMING COURT HEARINGS

The dates of forthcoming hearings should be confirmed in writing by you to your own client. If the client is on bail, the client must be warned about the consequences of failing to attend court. You must also confirm any trial date to your witnesses in writing and ask them to contact you to confirm that they have received notification. It is obviously a wise precaution to apply for witness summonses to be issued and served on any witness of fact or expert witness you wish to rely on, if their attendance may be in doubt.

An application for a witness summons now has to be accompanied by an affidavit in support, setting out the grounds for the summons in detail. If an expert is very busy, s/he may be asked to attend court in two different cases at the same time. You can safeguard your position by serving a witness summons, and many experienced experts will ask you to do this to prevent arguments arising over which court they should attend. The reasons for this are that, if a witness decides not to come to court, it is going to be very difficult to obtain an adjournment of the trial, it will protect your client's interests and will also prevent any difficulty arising with an employer refusing to allow a witness to have time off work. The best practice is always to write to either the magistrates' court or the Crown Court, depending on where the trial is taking place, to apply for a witness summons to be issued, and then arrange to serve it on the defence witnesses.

66 What are the consequences of a client failing to attend court?

67 What are the consequences of a witness failing to attend court, having been served with a witness summons?

Trials in the magistrates' courts will be for a fixed day, and if you have served a witness summons, the only further action you will probably need to take is to telephone the witnesses two days before the hearing to remind them about the trial, especially if there has been a long gap between your letter and the date.

The position in the Crown Court is different. Lengthy cases, very serious cases and cases involving expert evidence are normally given fixed hearing dates at the plea and directions hearing, or shortly afterwards. The majority of Crown Court cases are not given a fixed date, but are given a date when the case will appear in the Warned List. As mentioned above, the Warned List indicates that the case may be listed at any time after it first appears in that list.

The normal method of notification from the Crown Court list office is a telephone call between 2 and 3 pm on the previous day. It is, therefore, essential that you have a telephone number at which you can reliably contact your client. If your client is not contactable by telephone, which is not uncommon, you should arrange with your client for him/her to telephone the office at a particular time every afternoon, from the date when the case first appears in the Warned List. You also have to notify your witnesses by telephone or, if necessary, by someone from the office going to see the witness.

Your portfolio should show evidence of having explained to three contacts (specified in the **Range**) their duties whilst in custody and on bail and the consequences of not meeting them. Advice should be given both orally and in writing.

In practice, it will be unusual for defence witnesses to be required on the first day of a Crown Court trial, and you will normally arrange a provisional timetable with the trial advocate so that you can keep in contact with your witnesses once the trial starts to make sure that they are in court in good time to give evidence. You will obviously need to give both your client and witnesses the number of the court and a meeting place at court.

3.1.8 WHEN SHOULD YOU INFORM THE PROBATION OFFICER OF YOUR CLIENT'S PROPOSED PLEA?

In the magistrates' court, a *pre-sentence report* will only be prepared if it is ordered by the court after your client's conviction. Your liaison with the probation service before that stage would normally only arise if there was a need for help in finding a place in a bail hostel for a client who does not have a fixed or suitable address, or, if possible, for assistance in diverting the case away from the criminal justice system. Diversion would be appropriate where your client is suffering from a handicap or mental illness which would be better dealt with by treatment than by processing the case through the criminal justice system. In many courts, there is now a criminal justice mental health team attached to the probation service which includes psychiatric social workers, psychiatric nurses and a psychiatrist, who perhaps attend court on a particular day each week.

In the Crown Court, you should always notify the Crown Court probation liaison officer in advance of your client's proposed guilty plea. Most Crown Court probation officers will write to you, asking for a simple form to be completed.

3.1.9 LIAISON WITH THE COURT

In magistrates' courts, trial dates are normally fixed some weeks ahead. If a problem arises due to non-availability of a witness or a health problem affecting your client, it is important that you write as soon as possible to the listing office at the magistrates' court, sending a copy of your letter to the CPS, asking for an adjournment. If there is no objection from the CPS and there is evidence to support the reason for the adjournment, then, provided it is not made at the last moment, this will normally be agreed without any need for a hearing.

If an application has to be made for a hearing date to be adjourned in the Crown Court, you should fax or write to the listing officer, and send a copy of your letter to the CPS. As Crown Court cases are more serious and involve a greater use of resources, Crown Courts will be less ready to grant an adjournment without the need for the matter being relisted before the judge. The willingness of any court to grant an adjournment will obviously depend on how soon before the proposed hearing date you make your application and whether court time is going to be lost or other matters can be fixed to prevent this happening. Ultimately, the court will be governed by what it considers to be in the interests of justice. However, even if you do obtain an adjournment, there may be an issue of costs to be resolved.

Reforms were introduced on 1 November 1999 to reduce delay in the criminal justice system. As a result, courts will be less willing to allow adjournments (see 2.3.24 above).

3.1.10 THE CLIENT WHO IS SERVING A PRISON SENTENCE

If your client is already a serving prisoner, you must notify the CPS in good time before any trial date or hearing date, so that the CPS can apply for a Home Office production order for the prison to produce the client in court. Sometimes there is difficulty, particularly in the magistrates' court, if notice is short.

3.1.11 WHAT DO YOU TELL A SURETY WHO HAS TO APPEAR AT THE POLICE STATION OR AT COURT?

You must explain to any surety that s/he stands to forfeit all or some of the money s/he stands surety in if your client fails to answer his/her bail. Sureties must also be told to take with them to the police station, or to bring to court, evidence that they have access to the money they are prepared to stand surety for.

This is often done by production of a building society book or some kind of share certificate. If a client is relying on the equity in a property, the court will obviously be concerned about the interests of other people living in the property and will require your client to produce some evidence of what the equity is, normally by producing a building society statement or a document of similar nature.

It is important that responsibilities of the surety be explained to him/her before s/he goes into the witness box or attends at the police station, because any surety who seems half-hearted about his/her responsibilities and duties is likely to be rejected by the court.

You must produce evidence of having explained in writing the role of the surety and having ensured the surety's attendance.

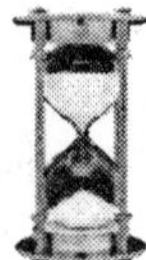

68 What are the responsibilities of the surety?

BRIEFING ADVOCATES

RANGE

Achievement must cover all the following contexts.

Court

Crown Court, magistrates' court.

Advocates

Barrister, solicitor-advocate.

Relationship to candidate

Solicitor, agent, principal.

EVIDENCE

You will need to produce the specific pieces of performance evidence listed below. In addition, you will need to demonstrate that you have achieved the objectives specified at the beginning of this unit. You may do this by producing further pieces of evidence from real and simulated performance, by answering questions posed by your assessor or by passing a written examination.

You will need to provide evidence of:

1 having organised and delivered to two **Advocates** files and synopses in good time in three different types of case;

2 having identified gaps in the papers and reasons why and communicated this to the advocate in two cases.

CRITERIA

You will demonstrate achievement if:

(a) files or documents are delivered to advocates in a timely fashion;

(b) files, documents and information are collated and organised in a logical sequential order, which can be easily assimilated by the advocate;

(c) summaries are provided as to the main issues;

(d) any outstanding information is identified and its omission accounted for;

(e) duplicates are retained of all documents which leave your control or the control of principals;

(f) notice of any further steps to be taken are obtained from advocates;

(g) contact with advocates' clerks is handled in such as way as promotes effective working relationships.

3.2.1 INTRODUCTION

The purpose of a brief is to provide the advocate with a summary of the facts and issues, and to provide copies of all the documents in the case. This part of the unit will therefore explain the type of summary which will assist an advocate, and what documents should be sent with the brief. When you prepare a brief, particularly for a Crown Court trial, you must remember that the chosen advocate may be unavailable at the last minute before the trial and someone else may have to prepare the case at short notice. The brief must thus be complete in itself, be quick and easy to assimilate and easy to refer to.

We will begin by dealing with a Crown Court brief for trial, and then discuss a Crown Court brief on committal for sentence under section 38 of the Magistrates' Court Act (MCA) 1980. We will then go on to deal with a magistrates' court brief.

3.2.2 CROWN COURT BRIEF FOR TRIAL

A Crown Court brief will normally be prepared immediately after committal by the magistrates' court for trial. The brief should be marked on the outside page with 'Legal Aid', or space should be left for a brief fee, which will be agreed with counsel's clerk after delivery of the brief.

The normal convention is that the brief starts with the list of the contents. These should be prepared sequentially, and the normal order is as follows:

(a) draft indictment;

(b) CPS summary of the issues in the case;

(c) committal bundle, consisting of the prosecution's witness statements and exhibits;

(d) the prosecution's schedule of unused material which, in the opinion of the prosecutor, might undermine the prosecution's case, or a statement that there is no such material, pursuant to section 3(1) of the Criminal Procedure and Investigations Act (CPIA) 1996;

(e) list of client's previous convictions;

(f) copies of prosecution plans, photographs, videos, etc;

(g) the client's custody record or records;

(h) tapes of interviews in the police station;

(i) any notices of additional evidence served by the CPS;

(j) the defence case – client's own proof of evidence;

Disclosure under the CPIA 1996 must be considered very carefully. After delivery of the defence statement, further disclosure may follow from the CPS, or should be pressed for, if there are issues arising in the defence statement which may well be the subject of other evidence or information in the hands of the CPS or police.

(k) the client's observations on the prosecution's evidence;

(l) the client's defence statement, served pursuant to section 5(5) of the CPIA 1996 (in a complex case, this might be prepared in draft and left to be settled by counsel at a conference);

(m) the statements of fact by the witnesses for the defence;

(n) the character statements for the defence, if any;

(o) the statements by the expert witnesses for the defence, together with exhibits, plans, photographs, etc, if any;

(p) relevant correspondence with the CPS, witnesses, etc;

(q) a copy of the legal aid order.

If the papers are of any volume, they will normally be included in a folder, using subject dividers for various classes of document.

Conventions used

There are certain conventions relating to the style of a brief.

When sending a brief to a barrister, s/he is always addressed as 'counsel' in the third person, eg, 'Counsel is asked to appear at X court to represent the defendant Kelly Smith'.

Solicitors also refer to themselves in the third person: 'Instructing solicitors have written to the CPS following disclosure of the Defence Statement to press for further disclosure under the CPIA 1996 ...'

The front of the brief should include the name of the fee earner in charge of the case and their telephone, fax and emergency telephone numbers. When instructing a solicitor advocate or solicitors to act as agents in any court, the same information will be needed, but the instructions and brief are set out in the form of a letter to that other solicitor's firm, with enclosures as in the brief.

The amount of detail necessary in the summary of the facts and analysis of the issues will of course depend on the complexity of the case. What is not needed is a very lengthy, word for word recital of what each and every prosecution witness says, and of what the defendant and his/her witnesses will say. This will not assist the advocate, who will turn to the actual statements themselves.

What is helpful is a summary of the main facts in date and time order, followed by an analysis of the issues in the case. If your client has any particular characteristics which could cause problems at court, such as an extremely aggressive temperament or a history of psychiatric illness, this should be mentioned in the brief so that counsel is warned

Your portfolio should provide evidence of having organised and delivered to two advocates files and synopses in good time in three different types of case.

beforehand of the type of problems s/he may face in discussing matters with the client. It will assist counsel in an assessment of the strength and weaknesses of the defence witnesses to be included.

Missing information

It happens very frequently that, when the brief is prepared, exhibits have not yet been served by the CPS. If this is the case, letters asking for service should be included in the bundle of correspondence sent to counsel, and counsel's attention should be drawn to the fact that they have not yet been served.

Equally, at the time the brief has been prepared, experts may have been instructed but may not yet have completed their reports, and this too should be brought to counsel's attention, and copies of the letters of instruction should be included with the brief.

Your portfolio should include evidence of having identified gaps in the papers, the reasons for such gaps and having communicated this to the advocate.

Initial conference with counsel

A conference in prison will be arranged by the defence solicitors, who first have to find out the counsel's availability from their clerk, and then arrange a prison appointment with the prison, which should be confirmed in writing. The fee earner attending the prison will need a letter on the firm's headed writing paper confirming the appointment to take with him/her to the prison.

In any case where a client is pleading not guilty, at least one conference with counsel should be held. If the client is in custody, the logistics of trying to arrange this before the plea and directions hearing may be difficult, but nevertheless every effort should be made to have a conference before the first hearing in the Crown Court.

At this stage, neither the prosecution nor the defence cases may be complete, and the purpose of the conference is:

(a) for the client to receive advice from counsel on his/her plea;

(b) for counsel to go through the evidence with the client in detail; and

(c) for counsel to advise on further steps that should be taken by the defence solicitors to prepare for trial.

Issues relating to what the prosecution's witnesses say can be agreed; which witnesses must be warned to attend trial can also be dealt with at this stage. It is important that a careful note is made by the representative of the defence solicitors who attends the conference, and this should subsequently be sent to both counsel and the client.

The note should record information, advice given by counsel, requests for further information and a list of action to be taken by counsel, instructing solicitors and the client.

Similarly, after the plea and directions hearing, a copy of the order made by the judge at the plea and directions hearing should be sent to counsel, and all notices of further evidence or further unused material disclosed in response to the defence statement should be forwarded to counsel as soon as they are received.

3.2.3 BRIEF ON COMMITTAL FOR SENTENCE TO THE CROWN COURT BY THE MAGISTRATES' COURT

The most common reason for a committal for sentence is when the magistrates' court is of the opinion that its own powers of punishment are insufficient in respect of an either way offence. It may then commit an adult to the Crown Court for sentence under section 38 of the Magistrates' Courts Act (MCA) 1980. The number of such committals has increased substantially, following the introduction of the plea before venue procedure on 1 October 1997.

When the magistrates' court commits a defendant for sentence to the Crown Court, no committal file is prepared by the CPS. The prosecution documents to be included in the brief will, therefore, be the charge sheet and those prosecution statements disclosed as a result of advance disclosure, together with a summary of the interview and the tapes. The defence documents should include a signed proof from a client and any character evidence and any medical report obtained for the purpose of mitigation. The brief itself should summarise the facts of the offences to which the client has pleaded guilty, and then concentrate on issues of mitigation, drawing counsel's attention by reference to any sentencing guidelines or factors which may make the offence more or less serious.

If the defendant pleaded guilty at the first appearance, remember to include this fact, as this is a significant mitigating factor in most cases. Where the client has previous convictions, information which may make these appear less significant than otherwise should be included.

3.2.4 BRIEF IN THE MAGISTRATES' COURT

The principles for a brief in the magistrates' court are obviously the same, whether counsel or solicitor agents are instructed. The contents of the brief or letter of instruction in the case of a solicitor agent will, of course, depend on the nature of the hearing.

Advocates may be instructed to make a bail application, to apply for an adjournment, to deal with a formal committal to the Crown Court, for the purpose of a magistrates' court trial or to represent the client on a sentencing hearing or trial.

These briefs will often have to be prepared at short notice and be sent by fax.

In the case of a brief to make an application for bail, the advocate should be provided with the client's previous convictions, if available, and instructions as to the grounds for applying for bail, answering any anticipated objections by the prosecution, as well as giving details of a fixed address, any suggested conditions, and the name and address of any possible surety.

For the legal background to bail issues, see 2.2 above.

The information needed to instruct counsel or agents in connection with a magistrates' court trial or magistrates' court sentencing hearing is basically similar in nature to that needed to instruct an advocate in the Crown Court. The main difference is that, in a case which is triable only summarily, there is no obligation on the prosecution to serve any statements at all. However, the CPS may make voluntary disclosure in such cases, and very often any information gained is obtained informally (if at all) and may be on the basis of discussions with the CPS. Prosecutors will normally summarise statements on the telephone or lend the prosecution papers to look at during or before a hearing in court. The attitude of the CPS to supplying voluntary advance disclosure will depend on the policy and resources of the particular office you are dealing with.

At Early First Hearings under the Narey provisions, the CPS will provide basic disclosure in summary as well as TEW offences, provided that the defendant has been charged, not summonsed. (Proceeding by way of summons is normally reserved for less serious matters.)

3.2.5 INSTRUCTION OF AN ADVOCATE IN YOUR OWN FIRM

When an outside advocate is used, the practice is to copy all the necessary documents and keep the originals, except photographs and exhibits which cannot easily be copied in the file. If you are briefing an advocate in your own firm, you would normally send the advocate a memo, together with the file.

If the advocate is representing 10 or 15 of the firm's clients in court, s/he will be greatly assisted by a summary of the facts and a notification of the issues, such as you would provide to counsel in a brief. In addition, it is important for the file to be well organised, with the relevant types of documents kept together, as this will assist the advocate in his/her preparation and in finding the papers at court. You should ensure that there are sufficient copies of any character letters, medical reports or any photographs or plans to be put before the bench, so that there is a copy for each magistrate and, in the case of a summary trial, additional copies for the prosecution and witnesses.

A brief chronology of court appearances will be invaluable in showing the advocate the stage which the case has reached, particularly where the advocate is attending on an interim matter and the case will not be finally resolved. This is often recorded in a progress sheet inside the file.

69 Why is it important to send counsel well organised briefs?

SUPPORTING ADVOCATES

RANGE

Achievement must cover all the following contexts.

Venue

Office, prison, court, counsel's chambers, site visits.

Agencies

Counsels' clerks, prosecuting authorities, witnesses, probation services, expert witnesses, prison authorities, court authorities, witness service, process server, co-accused's legal representatives, interpreters.

EVIDENCE

You will need to produce the specific pieces of performance evidence listed below. In addition, you will need to demonstrate that you have achieved the objectives specified at the beginning of this unit. You may do this by producing further pieces of evidence from real and simulated performance, by answering questions posed by your assessor or by passing a written examination.

You will need to provide evidence of:

1 having documented advocates' requests or advices and having taken action on them promptly in two cases;

2 having identified occasions when conferences with the advocate are necessary, and having made arrangements to ensure all parties concerned attend at the **Venue** arranged;

3 having made full notes of two court hearings.

CRITERIA

You will demonstrate achievement if:

(a) all requests from advocates are acted on promptly and a sustained effort is made to fulfil their requirements;

(b) the need for a conference with advocates is assessed and those required to attend are identified;

(c) conferences are arranged at times and places acceptable to all parties;

(d) full, detailed notes are taken of all discussions, advice is given and decisions are made;

(e) clients and witnesses are provided with adequate directions to court and are introduced to the court environment and personnel;

(f) clients are encouraged to arrive at the court in good time;

(g) full notes are taken of all evidence, submissions, decisions of hearings and reasons given by the court.

3.3.1 INTRODUCTION

Effective teamwork with the advocate is the key to good preparation of the client's defence. It is important that you understand your responsibilities as case manager, as compared to those of the advocate, particularly when counsel is used. If advice by the advocate is not properly recorded or points are not followed up adequately, the client's defence will suffer. Reference to counsel's clerk was briefly made in 3.1.5 above. All arrangements for appointments for conferences and briefs to appear in court are made through the clerk or clerks in the set of chambers to which the barrister belongs. If the matter is privately paid rather than funded by legal aid, it is the clerk with whom you negotiate the brief fee.

3.3.2 RECORDING COUNSEL'S ADVICE

As we saw in 3.2 above, in any case in the Crown Court where a client wishes either to plead not guilty or to seek counsel's advice on his/her plea, then, as a matter of course, a conference should be held shortly after committal. If the client is on bail, this would normally be held in counsel's chambers or possibly in your firm's office. If the client is in custody, arrangements will have to be made for a conference in prison.

Arranging a conference

When a conference is to be held with a client in custody, you will need to book an appointment with the prison at a time convenient to counsel and to yourself. When you attend prison, you will need a letter on your firm's headed writing paper confirming the appointment. You must take some means of identity with you, as well as the letter, to show at the prison gate. A cheque card or credit card would normally be acceptable.

The limited prison visiting hours may make such a conference difficult to fix before a plea and directions hearing. The time limits are such that if the client is in custody, the conference may have to be held in the Crown Court, although every effort should be made to have a conference in prison before the day of the plea and directions hearing.

Committals for trial only take place for cases in which:

(a) the offence can only be tried on indictment;

(b) the case is triable either way and the defendant has indicated a plea of not guilty or has not been able to indicate any plea; and

(c) the case is either not suitable for summary trial or the defendant has elected Crown Court trial.

NB: under the Crime and Disorder Act 1998, indictment only cases will go straight to the Crown Court.

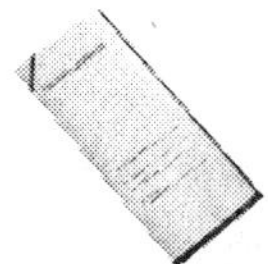

A model letter to a prison governor is provided in Document 1 in Appendix 10.

A plea and directions hearing is a hearing in the Crown Court for all either way or indictment only cases that are committed for trial. At this hearing, the judge will give directions on a variety of matters regarding length of trial (due to the number of witnesses, etc), the nature of the case and arrangements for video evidence, and s/he will make orders concerning experts' reports if these are relevant. It is, therefore, important that counsel

The conference

Counsel's approach to a conference will obviously vary, but normally you would expect counsel to go through the evidence with the client and consider with him/her their account of the events. S/he will do this by reference to a transcript of any interview and the client's proof of evidence, in order to identify and discuss with the client the important issues in the case and give the client advice on his/her plea.

Considerations regarding the plea

Counsel should always draw the client's attention to the fact that credit can be given for an early guilty plea (section 48 of the Criminal Justice and Public Order Act (CJPOA) 1994). The effect of this is that a client who pleads guilty to an offence rather than contesting the charge will usually be given credit for this in sentencing. It is usual for the length of any prison sentence to be reduced by as much as one-third as a result of the entry of a guilty plea, with consequent saving of time and costs.

Additional evidence, witnesses and disclosure

Counsel will advise on the additional evidence which s/he considers should be obtained for the trial, including any expert evidence. Counsel will normally advise at this stage on which prosecution witnesses can be agreed so that their statements can be read out at trial and those who need to attend trial can be warned. The prosecution witnesses' statements supplied by the prosecution at committal are deemed to be accepted by the defence and the witness not required to attend the trial, unless notice is given by the defence within 14 days of committal (section 68 and schedule 2 of the CPIA 1996). The objection has to be made in writing to the prosecutor and the Crown Court. The Crown Court has discretion to permit an objection to a statement is aware of such matters before the plea and directions hearing, which will normally be fixed by the magistrates' court on the day of the committal, usually four to five weeks after committal.

The earlier the plea is entered, the greater the 'discount'. Where an offence is TEW, the plea can be entered when plea before venue is considered in the magistrates' court. If a client at plea before venue indicates a not guilty plea or refuses to indicate a plea and the matter is committed to the Crown Court, it is likely to reduce the 'discount' available. In the case of a matter triable only on indictment, the earliest effective time a guilty plea can be indicated is at the plea and directions hearing.

being read at trial outside the 14 day time limit. In practice, it is very important that consideration is given, at or immediately after committal, to whether objections should be taken to the reading of the statement. Any evidence which is disputed should be objected to within the 14 day limit. If it is possible to have a conference with counsel before the expiry of the 14 days, then counsel will obviously consider these issues.

Although objection is made to the prosecutor and to the Crown Court against the reading of statements at trial, it is always possible to change your decision at a later date if it is decided that it is not necessary to hear live evidence from that witness. By the time of the conference, the defence statement will either have been served or, if 14 days from primary disclosure by the prosecution has not expired, it will be available for counsel to consider in draft. At the conference, counsel may well ask for you to press the CPS to provide further disclosure of unused material.

If the case involves expert evidence, then at some stage you will need a conference with your expert, although it is unlikely that his/her evidence will be complete before the plea and directions hearing. This will probably be left to a second conference.

Your note of the conference

While some counsel may even produce an agenda for a conference in a criminal case, this is unusual. The purpose of your note of the conference is to put into a coherent form all points arising from it. It is likely that there will be a list of matters which both you and the client have to deal with after the conference. It may well be helpful to prepare a separate checklist to pin on the inside of the file cover, to make sure that all counsel's requirements are carried out. The client should always be sent a note of the conference and a letter listing any further information needed from him/her or other action for him/her to undertake.

If, at the conference, you do not fully understand counsel's advice on some particular point, do not hesitate to ask him/her to explain it fully.

As a matter of good practice, a copy of the typed note of the conference should be sent to counsel to be placed with the brief. A copy should also be sent to the client as mentioned above. If you are attending the conference on behalf of another fee earner in the firm, you should obviously provide that fee earner with a copy, and discuss any points arising from the conference. It is even more important that a client understands counsel's advice. It may be that, after the conference, the client has to make some

If no objection is made, these witnesses will not be called at trial and their statements will be read.

The disclosure regime under the CPIA 1996 means that some, but not necessarily all, of the information the prosecution has will be disclosed. It is important to press the prosecution in all cases where it may have further information which may assist the defence. Remember that the defence statement should trigger secondary prosecution disclosure of any matter that might assist the defence as set out in that statement.

70 How detailed should the note of the conference be? To whom should you send copies and why?

decisions, including a decision on his/her plea in the light of that advice, perhaps in consultation with you or someone else in your firm. Sometimes, a decision by a client on his/her plea may be made during the conference. It is clearly essential that this is documented. You will have to ensure that the steps agreed on in the conference are undertaken speedily.

You will need to produce evidence of having documented the advocate's requests or advice and having taken prompt action on them in two cases.

Follow-up of requests for further information

All requests for further information, or the need to obtain further witness evidence, should be diarised and followed up if the information is not forthcoming from the police or CPS. It is very common to have to chase the CPS to provide information. The reason for this is that the CPS may be waiting for the information to be provided by the officer in the case. It is important that, at the plea and directions hearing, the advocate who represents your client is in a position to tell the judge what requests for information have been made and when, and the judge may then make an order that the CPS provide information within a certain amount of time. If the CPS fails to do so, this must then be followed up, and as a last resort you can apply to the Crown Court for the matter to be listed for a mention so that you can seek a further order from the judge. Normally, the threat to apply to list the matter for a mention is sufficient to get a response from the CPS.

If counsel has asked you to obtain expert evidence, it is prudent to ask him/her to confirm the advice in writing, so that you can send the advice with your request for prior authority to incur the expense to the Legal Aid Board area office. Apart from this occasion, it is unusual for counsel to provide written advice in a criminal case, except in a complex matter.

71 What steps should you take if the CPS fail to respond to your request for disclosure of unused material?

Where expert evidence is required, there are several matters that will need to be resolved. You will first need to select a competent expert. You will have a list of approved experts, which is of course a condition of franchising. If the expert needed is not on your own list, you will have to make further enquiries and justify the decision to instruct the expert. Counsel may have suggestions as to an appropriate expert. Alternatively, you may be able to obtain a recommendation from another criminal practice. If the case is funded by legal aid, you will need to get authorisation from the local area office. In order to obtain authorisation, you will have to obtain an estimate from your proposed expert and make enquiries about his/her availability (see 3.4 below for further discussion of information to be provided to an expert). The issue of expert evidence will be discussed at the plea and directions hearing, and the judge may give directions as to when the substance of the expert's report is to be disclosed to the prosecution. In a complex case, the plea and directions hearing may have to be adjourned so that further directions can be given on these issues.

3.3.3 THE NEED FOR A CONFERENCE

In any potential not guilty case in the Crown Court, a conference with the trial advocate should be held. It is important for the client to receive advice from his/her advocate on their chance of success, the possible sentence s/he may receive if convicted or, if a guilty plea is made, on the evidence which should be obtained for him/her to contest the case or on supporting information for a plea in mitigation. Equally, it greatly assists the trial advocate to have discussed the case with the client beforehand and to have tested the strength of his/her account by questioning him/her.

You will need to show that you have identified occasions when conferences with the advocate are necessary and have made arrangements to ensure that all parties attend at three venues in the **Range**.

Summary and non-complex cases

In a summary case which goes for trial, if the trial advocate is a member of your firm, s/he will probably wish to see the client in order to go through the evidence before the day of the trial. Alternatively, in a simple case, a meeting 45 minutes before the trial is due to start may be sufficient. If an outside advocate is to be used in a legal aid case, either as solicitor agent or counsel, a conference before the day of the trial would usually be impractical.

A guilty plea in the Crown Court

Even where your client is pleading guilty in the Crown Court, a conference may well be advisable for a very serious case, or in any case where the client is a person of previous good character and there is a chance of avoiding a custodial sentence. In a more straightforward matter, provided you have fully prepared mitigation and there are no exceptional circumstances, it is probably satisfactory to have a conference on the morning of the sentencing hearing.

Vulnerable clients

If the client is vulnerable due to mental illness or mental incapacity, this is an additional reason for having a conference. In the cases of clients under 18, where serious matters may be subject to trial in the youth court (particularly in cases where an adult in the same position would be tried in the Crown Court), a conference should always be held with the trial advocate well before the day of the hearing, so that the case can be properly prepared. It is important, particularly when acting for children who may be facing serious charges at the age of 13 or 14, that careful consideration is given to the selection of an advocate who can deal sensitively with the client and in whom the client will have confidence.

Cases involving expert witnesses

Witnesses of fact should not attend a conference with counsel. However, in any case involving an expert whose evidence conflicts with an expert called by the prosecution, a conference is clearly of the greatest possible benefit to the trial advocate, as it will enable him/her to understand fully the expert's report and to be in a position to cross-examine the prosecution's expert effectively.

3.3.4 ATTENDANCE BY CLIENTS AND WITNESSES AT COURT

You must give your client directions to the court if s/he is not already familiar with its location, and you must encourage him/her to arrive in good time before the hearing commences. If the client has no previous court experience, an opportunity should be found to take the client into court (when the court is not sitting) to familiarise him/herself with the layout, explain where the witness box is, where the advocates will stand, and emphasise the importance of addressing his/her replies to the magistrates (in the magistrates' court) or the jury (in a Crown Court).

A client should also be told how to address the magistrate(s) or, in the Crown Court, the judge. A client will, of course, have a chance to get used to the atmosphere and procedure in court while the prosecution's case is being presented. Lay witnesses, however, will not have this advantage, so it is important that they too are familiarised with the court layout if possible and are taken into the court at a time when it is not sitting. The procedure for giving their evidence and for being cross-examined also needs to be explained to them. Witnesses should be provided with a plan showing the location of the court if they do not know it, and you should explain how to claim travel costs and expenses for loss of earnings.

In the magistrates' court, it is usual to address the chairman as 'Sir' or 'Madam'. A stipendiary magistrate should be called 'Sir' or 'Madam'. It will not assist your client's case to address the stipendiary magistrate as 'mate', as one of the writer's clients did during the course of a bail application. Crown Court judges, Recorders or Assistant Recorders should be called 'Your Honour'. High Court judges are addressed as 'My Lord' or 'My Lady', as the case may be. Those who practice in the Old Bailey will know that circuit judges there are always called 'My Lord' or 'My Lady', and the Honorary Recorders of Liverpool, Manchester and Cardiff are also addressed as 'My Lord' or 'My Lady'.

3.3.5 NOTE OF COURT HEARING

The requirements of any note are that it is both accurate and legible. It will be necessary to use abbreviations in preparing a note in order to keep up with the speed of the witnesses' speech. You will work out your own abbreviations, but it is important that what you record is clear and intelligible. This is important because it may be relied upon by the advocate in the case, both during the trial and in considering any appeal. This is particularly so when the advocate is engaged in examination-in-chief of the defence witnesses or cross-examination of the

You will need to provide evidence of having made notes at two court hearings.

prosecution witnesses. S/he may well want to refer to an answer, either when dealing with a later witness or in the closing speech to the jury. When counsel is not standing up and asking questions, s/he will be taking his/her own notes. Your familiarity with the case will alert you to which points are of particular importance and whether a particular word, phrase or time may have significance. It is also important to record the situation in which it is said: in evidence-in-chief or in cross-examination.

You can show this in your note by 'X in ch' for evidence-in-chief, 'XX' for cross-examination and 'Re X' for re-examination.

Summing up and sentencing remarks

A very careful note should be made of the judge's summing up, and of the judge's sentencing remarks if your client is convicted.

Appeals against conviction are usually based on errors in the judge's direction, that evidence has been referred to inaccurately, that the jury has been wrongly guided on the law, or that the jury has not been guided at all. It is therefore important that, at an early stage, an assessment of whether such mistakes have been made is undertaken. A transcript of the summing up will have to be obtained at a later stage. Appeals against sentence are not often based on the judge's remarks, but these will give a clear indication of his/her approach to the sentence, which may be appealable, and occasionally will reveal in themselves an error of law or practice.

3.3.6 ENSURING ATTENDANCE BY WITNESSES AT COURT

It is your responsibility as case manager to ensure that witnesses attend court at the correct time. It will always be necessary to consider whether a witness summons should be issued requiring a witness to attend and give oral evidence and/or produce documentation.

Witness summons

The law relating to the issue of witness summonses is now contained in section 66 of the CPIA and rule 23 of the Crown Court Rules. You should refer to the full provisions of the Act and the Rules, but matters to bear in mind are that any application for a witness summons should be issued as soon as possible after transfer to the Crown Court and should be supported by an affidavit, which must:

(a) set out any charge on which the proceedings are based;

(b) specify any stipulated evidence, document or thing in such a way as to enable the directed person to identify it;

(c) specify grounds for believing that any stipulated evidence is likely to be material evidence;

(d) specify grounds for believing that any stipulated document or thing is likely to be material evidence.

It is possible for the witness to apply to the Crown Court and, if s/he satisfies the Crown Court that s/he cannot give any evidence likely to be material or produce any document or thing likely to be material, the court may direct that a summons shall be of no effect.

In the magistrates' court, the procedure is governed by section 98 of the MCA 1980. It is necessary to satisfy a judge that the witness:

- is likely to be able to give material evidence or produce a document likely to be material evidence at summary trial; and
- will not attend voluntarily as a witness. Again, an application for a witness summons must be made as soon as is practicable after a defendant has pleaded not guilty.

It is always a wise precaution to issue a witness summons against a witness who is giving important factual evidence. It is very unusual for witnesses to fail to attend court if they have been summoned. It will also help to prevent difficulty with employers if a summons has been issued. In the case of an expert witness, it may also be wise to issue a witness summons in case they become double booked.

72 What is the likely consequence if an important defence witness fails to appear at trial and you have not issued and served a witness summons upon him/her?

TAKING PROOFS OF EVIDENCE

RANGE

Achievement must cover all the following contexts.

Environment

Office, court, prison.

Agencies

Defendants, defence witnesses, prosecution witnesses, enquiry agents, court office, agents (solicitors), interpreters.

Third parties

Expert witnesses, character witnesses, witnesses of fact, support agencies.

Disabilities

Mental disabilities, physical disabilities, clients without English as their first language.

EVIDENCE

You will need to produce the specific pieces of performance evidence listed below. In addition, you will also need to demonstrate that you have achieved the objectives specified at the beginning of this unit. You may do this by producing further pieces of evidence from real and simulated performance, by answering questions posed by your assessor or by passing a written examination.

You will need to provide evidence of:

1 having produced at least four proofs of evidence;

2 having arranged medical or specialist assistance in at least one case.

CRITERIA

You will demonstrate achievement if:

(a) clients are given the opportunity to consider prosecution evidence;

(b) factual issues in dispute are identified;

(c) any disabilities or potential disabilities are identified and medical or specialist assistance requested;

(d) clients' proofs of evidence contain their accounts of events, their observations on the prosecution evidence and their personal history;

(e) witness statements in section 9 of the Criminal Justice Act (CJA) 1967 form are taken from any relevant third parties who can support clients' cases;

(f) information in proofs of evidence is correct, complete, produced in a format easily assimilated by advocates and is dated and signed;

(g) copies of clients' or witnesses' own proofs of evidence are made available and opportunity is given to amend and sign them.

3.4.1 INTRODUCTION

The ability to take a good proof of evidence from your client or a witness of fact is an essential skill for the criminal litigator. The purpose of taking a proof is to record the client's instructions in writing for the use of the advocate. This can be for the purpose of applying for bail (see 2.2 above), making a plea in mitigation or conducting a defence in the magistrates' court or Crown Court. This unit will deal first with the client, including the vulnerable client and the client without English as a first language. It will then deal with taking proofs for witnesses of fact (including prosecution witnesses), expert witnesses and character witnesses.

You need to show that you have produced four proofs of evidence.

3.4.2 TAKING A PROOF FROM A CLIENT

Preliminary points

It is important that you emphasise to a client that everything s/he says to you is on the record. Although it may seem surprising, it is still possible to meet the occasional client who believes that the job of a defence solicitor is to invent an appropriate account which will get him/her off the charge. You should explain to the client the purpose of the proof, and make it clear that to get a clear and detailed account may take some time. The proof should be in the first person and should use a client's own words. It should contain only admissible evidence. Finally, it is good practice to prepare a proof in section 9 form. The reason for this is that a degree of formality will perhaps make the witness reflect carefully on what s/he is saying.

See the example of a witness statement, Document 2 in Appendix 10.

3.4.3 THE CLIENT'S PROOF

If you or a member of your firm have represented a client at the police station, you may already have a considerable amount of material. This will have been gathered from taking your client's instructions in private at the police station and from questions (if any) that s/he has answered in police interview. It is obviously important that you have this information to hand when you take your client's proof of evidence. However, it is very unlikely that your client was actually shown any prosecution statement in the police station. Further, it is probable that additional evidence may have been obtained by the police after charge.

If your client has made it clear that s/he intends to plead not guilty to an either way offence, it would be sensible to wait for advance disclosure of the prosecution case, so that your client can consider the detailed allegations made by the prosecution witnesses and deal with these in his/her proof. It will be essential for you to obtain your client's detailed comments or observations on the prosecution witness statements, and the easiest time to do this is clearly at the same time as the proof is prepared. Comments can be included in the proof, although it is probably simpler and easier for the advocate if they are put into a separate document.

You should be patient and sympathetic to your client, but it may well be necessary to press him/her for further information on some points of detail. It is important that you put to your client, in a positive way, some of the points which the prosecution are likely to press him/her on. If you see your client for the first time after s/he has been interviewed and charged, you will need to record his/her initial instructions at your first meeting. It is important that you give your client a chance to explain the story in his/her own words. As this will be your first meeting, it is sometimes best to ask him/her to explain the circumstances without taking detailed notes, and then go through the matter again more slowly so that you can record what is said. Most clients will welcome the opportunity to give their account and this will help you to identify the important issues. You can then direct your questioning to those points of the story.

You should explain to the client, particularly in an either way offence, that you will receive advance disclosure at a later stage, that you are taking a preliminary statement and that this will have to be expanded on and detailed allegations dealt with when you have further information from the prosecution, including your client's interview with the police and the tapes of that interview. The proof should deal with the events in chronological order

It is important to consider the issue of professional conduct which will arise in the case of a client who instructs you that s/he is guilty but intends to plead not guilty. Professional conduct will require you to advise the client that, in view of their instruction that they admit the offence, you can only act for him/her on the basis that you do not put forward a positive defence of not guilty but simply test the strength of the prosecution's case. In practice, this is unlikely to achieve anything for your client or for you, and if s/he insists on pleading not guilty, it will be sensible to advise him/her to seek advice from another firm (see Unit 1).

and, so far as possible, a separate paragraph should be devoted to each event.

3.4.4 OTHER INFORMATION FOR THE PROOF

A client's personal history and other matters for use in litigation should be included in the proof. The best way to obtain this information may be by use of a pro forma. An example of such a pro forma is shown opposite. Information can then be taken from the pro forma and incorporated in the proof. Matters to be included in the proof should include the following:

- address and telephone number;
- education and qualifications;
- employment history;
- if employed for a lengthy period why did s/he become unemployed and what are his/her job prospects;
- health – if any health problems are relevant to the offence, take full details of any physical or mental illness with a view to considering whether a report may be necessary (see 3.4.7 below);
- medication taken;
- family relationships and dependants;
- earnings, other income, savings, ability to pay any fine;
- previous convictions, in particular, whether the client is current subject to any court order, community service, probation, conditional discharge or bind over;
- interests and any involvement in voluntary work, etc.

Criminal attendance note

Full name

DOB

Address

Telephone number

Marital status

Dependants

Education and qualifications

Employment

Unemployment history

Offence

Details of charge

Has client already appeared in court?

Events of the alleged offence

Proposed plea

Witness

Name

Address

Date of arrest and appearance at police station

Statement or interview to police officer

Did s/he receive advice from the duty solicitor at the police station?

Existing court order and name of any probation officer or social worker involved

Any relevant medical condition

Advice

1 Plea
2 Has client been advised of credit for early guilty plea?
3 Probable sentence if convicted, including liability for costs
4 Legal aid
5 If not guilty in an either way offence, advice on mode of trial
6 Application for:
   (a) Advance disclosure
   (b) Custody record
   (c) Tapes of police interview
   (d) List of previous convictions
   (e) Unused material
7 Date of letter of advice to client on plea

3.4.5 PROOF FOR A GUILTY PLEA

If your client instructs you that s/he wishes to plead guilty, and you are satisfied that this is the correct plea, you still need to obtain your client's account of what happened. As your client is admitting the offence, you must try to include in the proof the following:

- the reason or reasons why your client committed the offence;
- his/her attitude to the offence and to any victim;
- the likelihood of the offence being repeated;
- the client's ability to pay compensation if appropriate.

The other background information, set out in 3.4.4 above, should also be included.

3.4.6 YOUNG PEOPLE AND CHILDREN

It is important, indeed essential, that when you take a proof of evidence from an adult client, you see him/her alone, so that you are getting the client's instructions and not those of a friend or parent. It is equally important with young people and children that you ensure that you obtain their instructions. In the case of a young child, it may be easier to take their instructions if a parent or appropriate adult is present. There can be no absolute rule and it obviously depends on the nature of the offence and the relationship of the child and appropriate adult.

When taking instructions for a proof of evidence for a child, it is very important that you explain clearly to them what the purpose of the meeting is and that you speak to the child in language which you are satisfied they can understand. The benefit of having a parent or other adult present is that they will know the child far better than you will and can assist in communication.

Some parents clearly have a good relationship with their children and will sit patiently, allowing you to build up trust with the child and obtain the child's instructions. Other parents may be very overbearing and highly critical of their children. This may make it almost impossible to establish any trust with the child or to be satisfied that you are obtaining the child's truthful instructions. A proof from a child must be prepared and contain the same information as a proof for an adult, whether it is for a guilty or not guilty plea. If the events took place over a lengthy period of time, it may be necessary to have more than one meeting to obtain the child's full instructions.

73 What additional problems and responsibilities do you have when taking a proof of evidence from a child under 14?

3.4.7 VULNERABLE ADULTS

Refer to 1.5 above, which deals with taking instructions from vulnerable clients in the police station. The same principles obviously apply when taking a proof of evidence from an adult who is either mentally handicapped, with a level of understanding lower than his/her physical age, or suffering from a mental illness. Custody officers are usually quick to recognise vulnerable clients and, in the case of a person with limited understanding, will arrange for social services to attend, who normally arrange for legal representation as a matter of policy. A client who is severely mentally disabled may have a social worker who will be able to assist you, as far as your client's level of understanding is concerned. When taking a proof of evidence from a person with a mental disability, you will obviously concentrate particularly on the question of a client's guilty knowledge (*mens rea)* and their level of understanding. When you are taking a proof, you will obviously be considering carefully whether the client falls within the category of cases that should be dealt with by diversion from the criminal justice system.

Such a person may be cautioned or diverted to social services for help, or no further action may be taken. Ideally, this happens in the police station, but if it has not, the CPS will always consider representations made on behalf of a person with a mental disability if there is a real doubt as to whether or not they had the necessary criminal intent. You may well consider it necessary to obtain an assessment from a psychologist of the client's level of understanding.

If a client is suffering from a mental illness, this presents particular problems. You may find it very difficult to obtain clear and precise instructions. A client may have difficulty discussing the matter rationally, or may have problems with concentration. Often, such a client may have a fixed view of what occurred, or may be suffering from an obsession which makes taking instructions time consuming and difficult. In these circumstances, you have to take the best instructions you can, and then consider with the advocate the best way you can help the client. It may be necessary to obtain a psychiatric report. Many courts now have a psychiatrist who attends court once a week, and cases can be adjourned for a psychiatric assessment. The psychiatrist will assess whether your client is fit to plead and, if s/he is fit to plead, whether s/he is suffering from a mental illness or from necessary conditions for a Hospital Order under section 37 of the Mental Health Act 1983. In the case of an offence which carries a prison sentence, a magistrates' court may deal with a defendant and make a Hospital Order, provided it is satisfied that the defendant did the act or made the omission charged, without convicting the defendant. You will have to discuss with your client, if possible, what s/he wishes you to do in his/her best interests if a Hospital Order seems a possible disposal.

74 What particular considerations do you have to bear in mind when taking a proof from a person who suffers from a mental illness?

3.4.8 CLIENTS WITHOUT ENGLISH AS A FIRST LANGUAGE

It is important that you use an interpreter with a professional qualification and (preferably) some knowledge of the legal system. You should always discuss with the interpreter where s/he would like to sit and how best to proceed. Normally, it is best for the interpreter to sit next to the client and for you to sit opposite. It is very important that you explain the purpose of the meeting and the reasons for obtaining a proof of evidence fully and clearly. If you have advance disclosure, the interpreter may have to translate the statements to the client, and then translate their comments back to you. In a complex case, it may be better for you to obtain authority from the Legal Aid Board to ask the interpreter to translate the more important pieces of evidence into the client's language so that they can consider the statements in detail, as this may save time. You will obviously have to have the proof prepared in English, and then send it to the interpreter to translate into the relevant language for the client to check and sign.

Interpreters should interpret, not advise.

3.4.9 PREPARATION AND SIGNATURE OF A WITNESS STATEMENT

In all cases where you take a witness statement, whether it is from a client, a witness of fact or a character witness, the statement must be typed and then sent to the client to check, amend and alter as necessary, and sign. If the amendments are substantial, then obviously the statement (which will be on the computer) should be re-typed to incorporate them. It is very important that the statement is signed, in case the witness is unable to attend court (for whatever reason). The witness should always be told not to show the witness statement to anyone and not to discuss its contents with other witnesses.

You should also explain to the witness that s/he will not be able to read from the statement in court: its purpose is for the advocate to know what the witness is going to say, so questions can be phrased accordingly. The witness statement should be available at court, so that the witness can read it outside the witness box before giving evidence.

Refreshing memory: the issue of whether witnesses should be allowed to refresh their memory in the witness box has been the subject of a number of Divisional Court and Court of Appeal decisions. In *AG's Reference (No 3 of 1979)* (1979) 69 Cr App R 411 (CA), it was held that a witness giving evidence may refresh his/her memory by reference to any writing concerning the facts to

3.4.10 WITNESSES OF FACT

There are two matters which should be considered before taking a statement from a witness of fact. The first is that it may well be necessary to see the witness at their own house, or outside normal office hours, or both. Witnesses may be more or less willing to assist, but they will certainly be reluctant to give up work time to come and see you. It is also important that you ask any witness of fact whether or not they have any criminal convictions. The importance of this is that, except in certain limited circumstances where the defendant has attacked the character of a prosecution witness or put his/her own good character in issue, the prosecution cannot cross-examine the *defendant* about previous convictions. There is no such restriction on cross-examining a *witness*. If you take a statement from a witness in a public order offence and s/he has convictions him/herself for similar types of matters, it

which he testified, made or verified by him/herself at a time when his/her memory was clear: this is the principle which allows police officers to refer to their notebook containing contemporaneous notes.

The rule of contemporaneity has been diluted in *R v Da Silva* (1990) 90 Cr App R 233 (CA), where it was held that it was open to the trial judge, in the exercise of his discretion in the interests of justice, to permit a witness who had begun to give evidence to refresh his/her memory from a statement made near to the time of the events in question, even though it did not come within the definition of contemporaneity. This was subject to the judge being satisfied of the following matters:

(a) the witness said he could not now recall the events because of the lapse of time;

(b) s/he had made a statement much nearer the time of the events, when his/her memory was clear;

(c) s/he had not made a statement before coming into the witness box; and

(d) s/he wished to have an opportunity to read the statement before s/he needed to give evidence.

In the case of *R v South Ribble Magistrates' Court ex p Corcoran* (1996) 2 Cr App R 1994, the Divisional Court held that there was no difference between a witness who had not made his/her statement before coming into the witness box and a witness who had had that opportunity and failed to take in what s/he was reading, for whatever reason.

is not going to impress the court or assist your client's defence if you call that person as a witness and his/her credibility is then attacked by the prosecution on the grounds of their previous convictions. It is therefore important that the information is available in the proof of evidence, so that the advocate can decide whether, notwithstanding the convictions, it is worth the risk of calling the witness to support your client's case, or whether it is likely to do more harm than good. If you explain the reason for having to ask the witness this, they will normally understand the position and will be happy to give you the information you require. Statements of witnesses of fact should be prepared in chronological order, in the same way that you would prepare a proof for your own client. It should obviously be sent to the witness to check and sign.

If a *prosecution* witness's character is attacked by the defence, previous convictions of the defendant may be cross-examined by the prosecution, pursuant to the section 1(f) of the Criminal Evidence Act 1898.

3.4.11 PROSECUTION WITNESSES

The principle is that 'there is no property in the witness' and you are therefore free to interview a prosecution witness if you think this is necessary to help prepare your client's case. The purpose of interviewing a prosecution witness would be to try to obtain further information or evidence which you thought was essential to the preparation of your client's defence. The potential problem you face in interviewing a prosecution witness is that if, at trial, the witness departs from the statement s/he gave to the police and gives evidence which favours your client, you may find yourself accused of interfering with the witness or attempting to pervert the course of justice. It is therefore essential that you safeguard yourself and your client against any such accusation. The correct procedure is to inform the officer in the case and the CPS of your intention to approach a prosecution witness and give the officer in the case the opportunity to be present when you interview the witness. You should also keep careful attendance notes of contact with any prosecution witness.

This means that either side may interview any witness and call them – apart from the defendant, who cannot be called by the prosecution.

3.4.12 EXPERT WITNESSES

An experienced expert witness will normally prepare their own statement in a section 9 form. On occasions, you may need to obtain statements from expert witnesses, such as GPs, who do not regularly appear before the criminal courts. In those circumstances, the normal way to proceed would be to commission a medical report, if appropriate, from a GP, and then for you to convert that into the form of a section 9 statement and ask the witness to check it carefully against his/her own report, before filing and dating it in the normal manner. It is

You need to produce evidence of having arranged specialist or medical assistance in at least one case.

obviously important that you give full details of the expert's professional qualifications and experience in the first paragraph of the statement, so as to establish him/her as an expert. Alternatively, you can obviously give guidance to a witness you are using who is not familiar with criminal evidence or the court's requirements, and give them the necessary guidance, in so far as the formalities of their statements are concerned.

3.4.13 CHARACTER WITNESSES

If a person of good character is facing trial, particularly in connection with an offence of dishonesty, character evidence may be called on his/her behalf. A character witness cannot express any view on whether the defendant has or has not committed the offence with which s/he is charged, as that is clearly a matter for the jury or the magistrates (as the case may be). S/he is, however, entitled to comment on the general reputation of the defendant.

Obviously, a character witness is of more use to the defendant if s/he is him/herself of excellent character and standing.

Character evidence is most commonly used at a sentencing hearing. The normal way of obtaining character evidence is to write a letter to the prospective witness, requesting character evidence. At a sentencing hearing, an advocate will normally put about three or four letters from character witnesses before the court, and possibly call one witness if they can speak particularly well of the defendant's character. For the purpose of a sentencing hearing, a letter would be accepted by the court, but if you are calling character evidence at a trial, the letter should be put in a the form of a section 9 statement and served on the CPS. It may well then be accepted by the prosecution without the need to call the maker of the statement.

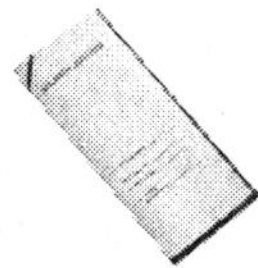

See the example of a letter to a character witness in Document 3 in Appendix 10.

Note that it is important that the potential character witness is informed, at least in outline, of what your client is facing trial for or has been convicted of.

3.4.14 USE OF ENQUIRY AGENTS

It may be necessary, particularly in a case where there are a large number of potential witnesses or they are widely scattered, to use an enquiry agent to trace witnesses and take statements from them. Your firm will have an enquiry agent who it uses regularly, and who will be aware of the need to prepare statements in section 9 form. It is important that you obtain prior authority from the Legal Aid Board to instruct an enquiry agent in these circumstances. This requires you to obtain an estimate from the enquiry agent or at least a maximum figure as to his/her fees. It is also essential that the work which the enquiry agent does is directly relevant to the conduct of your client's defence.

DISCLOSING EVIDENCE

RANGE

Achievement must cover the following contexts.

Documents

Witness statements in admissible form, alibi notices, section 9 statements, section 10 admissions, witness summonses, expert evidence, defence statements.

EVIDENCE

You will need to produce the specific pieces of performance evidence listed below. In addition, you will need to demonstrate that you have achieved the objectives specified at the beginning of this unit. You may do this by producing further pieces of evidence from real and simulated performance, by answering questions posed by your assessor or by passing a written examination.

You will need to provide evidence of:

1 having identified the difference between disclosable and non-disclosable **Documents** for three cases;

2 having prepared and produced at least two lists of disclosable **Documents** which disclose the documents in a way useful to the advocate;

3 having identified cases where primary and secondary disclosure apply and when a defence statement must or ought to be served.

CRITERIA

You will demonstrate achievement if:

(a) all the information which is required to be disclosed is identified to advocates;

(b) the information which paralegals are instructed to disclose is formulated and disclosed within the required time scales;

(c) privileged material is identified and not disclosed to opponents.

3.5.1 INTRODUCTION

This unit will deal with the duties and responsibilities of both prosecution and defence to disclose information and evidence to each other. The CPIA 1996 for the first time created a statutory framework to govern the duties of prosecution and defence. The CPIA applies to all offences in which the criminal investigation was commenced on or after 1 April 1997.

The common law rules will continue to apply to cases where the investigation began before 1 April

1997. Today, these form only a very small minority of cases, and will normally be extremely serious offences, such as murder or rape, where a defendant is arrested long after the offence has been committed or where s/he appeals against conviction. It is important that your firm retains in its library the 1997 editions of *Archbold* or *Blackstone,* which deal with the 1997 rules in detail. The common law rules pre-1997 relate to prosecution disclosure, since defence disclosure was only required where the defence relied on an alibi or if the defence proposed to rely on expert evidence when the substance of the report had to be disclosed to the prosecution.

The CPIA 1996 was based in part on the recommendations of the Royal Commission on Criminal Justice 1993, which was set up after the successful appeal of the 'Guildford Four'. Only the broad approach of the Royal Commission became law and the main purpose of this Act was to reduce what was regarded as an undue burden on the prosecution to disclose unused material following the decision in *Keane*. The Act also places increased obligations on the defence to disclose the nature of its case. Part I (sections 1–21) of the CPIA creates a staged approach to disclosure, which can be summarised as initial prosecution disclosure, followed by defence disclosure, followed by additional prosecution disclosure. The detailed provisions will be considered below. Section 23 of Part II of the Act provides for a Code of Practice to ensure, *inter alia*, that information which is obtained in the course of a criminal investigation and which may be relevant is recorded, that any record is retained, and that any other material which is obtained in the course of a criminal investigation is retained.

The pre-CPIA 1996 law was contained in a number of important Court of Appeal decisions. The duty of the prosecutor under the common law was to disclose relevant material. In the case of *R v Keane* [1994] 1 WLR 746, Lord Taylor CJ held that unused material should be disclosed if it:

(a) is relevant or possibly relevant to an issue in the case;
(b) raises or possibly raises a new issue whose existence is not apparent from the evidence the prosecution proposes to use; or
(c) holds out a real, as opposed to fanciful, prospect of providing a lead on evidence which goes to (a) or (b).

3.5.2 MAGISTRATES' COURT AND YOUTH COURT

Section 1 of the CPIA 1996 provides that the Act applies to the magistrates' court and youth court, where they proceed to summary trial and an accused pleads not guilty, and to all cases in the Crown Court. We will first deal with the position in the magistrates' and youth court.

Primary disclosure by the prosecutor

Under section 3 of the CPIA, the prosecutor must:

(a) disclose to the accused any prosecution material which has not previously been disclosed to the accused and which, in the prosecutor's opinion, might undermine the case for the prosecution against the accused; or

(b) give to the accused a written statement that there is no such material. Section 3 goes on to define prosecution material as material which is in the prosecutor's possession and which came into his/her possession in connection with the case against the accused, or which is in pursuance of the code s/he has inspected in connection with the case for the prosecution against the accused.

Voluntary disclosure by the accused

Under section 6(2) of the CPIA 1996, the accused can (but need not) give a defence statement to the prosecutor and, if s/he does, s/he should also give a copy of the statement to the court. This must be done within 14 days, beginning on the day when the prosecutor complies with section 3 of the CPIA 1996. It is possible for the defence to apply to the magistrates' court for an extension of time: the application should be made before the time expires. The purpose of voluntary disclosure by the defence in the form of a defence statement is to trigger secondary disclosure by the prosecution. The contents of a defence statement will be discussed below.

Secondary disclosure by a prosecutor

Section 7 of the CPIA 1996 states that this applies where the accused gives a defence statement in the Crown Court under section 5 or a voluntary defence statement under section 6. Under subsection (2), the prosecutor must disclose to the accused any prosecution material which has not previously been disclosed to him/her and which might be reasonably expected to assist the accused's defence, as disclosed by the defence statement given under sections 5 or 6. Alternatively, the prosecutor must give the accused a written statement stating that there is no such material.

3.5.3 DISCLOSURE IN THE CROWN COURT

The procedure in the Crown Court is similar, with the exception that disclosure by the accused of his/her defence is compulsory in the sense that adverse

Defence disclosure in the magistrates' court is voluntary and should only be made if it assists the client's case.

75 An accused is charged with threatening behaviour contrary to section 4 of the Public Order Act 1986. The prosecution case is that s/he threatened a police officer, who then sprayed him/her on three occasions with CS gas, as a result of which s/he became more violent. S/he was then arrested. The officer informs the accused at the police station that the incident has been captured on CCTV video. The accused instructs the defence that s/he did not threaten the officer, and only clenched his/her fists in self-defence after the officer had for no reason sprayed him/her with CS gas.

What steps would you take to force the prosecution to disclose the video to the defence?

76 The accused is charged with driving with excess alcohol. There is reason to believe that the intoximeter had not been working correctly, and the defence seeks disclosure of the service record and log book after taking expert evidence on the point.

What steps would you take to force the prosecution to disclose the service record and log book?

consequences may flow from failure to do so (see 3.5.5 below). The prosecutor must give primary disclosure under section 3 of the Act. In practice, this is normally given to the defence on the committal hearing, or shortly afterwards.

Compulsory defence disclosure

Within 14 days from the date at which the prosecutor gives primary disclosure, the defence must serve their defence statement – see section 5 of the CPIA 1996. It is important to note that this section does not apply unless the prosecutor has served on the accused a copy of the indictment and a copy of the set of documents containing the evidence which is the basis of the charge, ie, the committal bundle.

The defence statement must be a written statement:

(a) setting out in general terms the nature of the accused's defence;

(b) indicating the matters on which s/he takes issue with the prosecution; and

(c) setting out, in the case of each such matter, the reason why s/he takes issue with the prosecution.

Further, under subsection (7), if the defence statement discloses an alibi, the accused must give particulars of the alibi in the statement, including:

(a) the name and address of any witness the accused believes is able to give evidence in support of the alibi, if the name and address is known to the accused when the statement is given;

(b) any information in the accused's possession which might be of material assistance in finding any such witness, if his/her name is not known to the accused when the statement is given.

You must produce evidence of having identified the difference between disclosable and non-disclosable documents in three cases.

Alibi

An alibi is evidence that, because of the presence of the accused at a particular place or area at a particular time, it is likely s/he did not commit the offence charged (ie, s/he was somewhere other than the place where the offence was committed, at or close to the relevant time).

It is important to note that, although a defence statement is voluntary in the magistrates' court, if the defendant does decide to serve a defence statement under section 6, the provisions of section 5, relating to the details of any alibi relied on, must be included.

You need to provide evidence of having prepared and produced at least two lists of disclosable documents which disclose the documents in a way that is useful to the advocate. Remember the documents to be listed in the brief (see 3.2.2 above).

3.5.4 TIME FOR SERVICE OF THE DEFENCE STATEMENT

This is governed by the Criminal Procedure and Investigations Act 1996 (Defence Disclosure Time Limits) Regulations 1997. These provide that the relevant period for sections 5 and 6 of the CPIA 1996 is a period beginning with the day on which the prosecutor complied with section 3 of the Act, ending with the expiration of 14 days from that day. The court may extend the period of time for serving a defence statement, but only if the accused makes an application before the expiration of the period of 14 days. Any such application shall state that the accused believes, on reasonable grounds, that it is not possible for him/her to give a defence statement under sections 5 or 6 within the 14 day period, specify the grounds for so believing, and specify the number of days by which s/he wishes that period to be extended. The practical effects of this short time limit are that detailed preparation of your client's defence will probably have to commence before the committal proceedings and, most importantly, you will need a detailed proof of evidence from your client before or immediately after the committal proceedings to enable you to prepare the defence statement and serve it in time with your client's approval.

Increased pressure for speed in the courts means that thorough, early preparation is ever more vital.

3.5.5 FAULTS IN DISCLOSURE BY THE ACCUSED

The consequences of failing to comply with the disclosure provisions are set out in section 11 of the CPIA 1996. If an accused does any of the following, section 11 applies:

- the accused fails to give the prosecutor a defence statement under section 5;
- the accused gives the prosecutor a defence statement under the subsection but does so after the end of the prescribed period;
- the accused sets out inconsistent defences in the defence statement given under section 5;
- at trial, the accused puts forward a defence which is different from any defence set out in the defence statement given under that section;
- at trial, the accused adduces evidence in support of an alibi without having given particulars of the alibi in a defence statement given under that section; or
- at trial, the accused calls a witness to give evidence in support of an alibi without having complied with section 5 as regards the witness in giving a defence statement under that section.

Failure to disclose properly means the court may draw an adverse inference against your client. This means the jury may be invited to consider why your client did not disclose the defence. Was it that s/he made it up in court?

Section 11(3) provides that:

(a) the court or, with the leave of the court, any other party may make such comment as appears appropriate;

(b) the court or jury may draw such inferences as appear proper, in deciding whether the accused is guilty of the offence concerned.

Section 11(4) provides that, where the accused puts forward a defence which is different from any defence set out in the defence statement, the court, in doing anything under subsection (3) or in deciding whether to do anything under that section, shall have regard to:

(a) the extent of the difference in the defences; and

(b) whether there is any justification for it.

Under section 5, a person shall not be convicted of an offence solely on an inference drawn under subsection (3). This means that there must be some other evidence against your client, as an inference cannot be the sole basis of conviction.

If a defendant decides to give a voluntary statement under section 6 of the CPIA 1996, the same consequences apply as when the defendant gives a statement under section 5. The terms of section 11(3) of the CPIA are similar to those contained in sections 34–38 of the Criminal Justice and Public Order Act 1994, and therefore the arguments in case law under that Act appear relevant to any fault in a defence statement.

3.5.6 DRAFTING A DEFENCE STATEMENT

The short time limit for filing a defence statement with the court and serving a copy on the CPS (14 days from the date the prosecutor gives primary disclosure) means that the responsibility for this will normally fall on the defence solicitors. This was certainly the view of the Bar Council, who gave guidance on counsel's involvement in drafting defence statements in 1997. The guidance makes it clear that, if counsel is asked to draft a defence statement, they must only do so if they are in full possession of all the relevant information relating to the prosecution and defence cases, including, in particular, a signed proof of evidence from the defendant. In practice, counsel would normally only be asked to draft a defence statement in a particularly complex or difficult matter. If this is the case, you might need to apply for an extension of time (see 3.5.4 above).

It is most important that the accused approves the contents of the defence statement. It would certainly be a wise precaution, having drafted the defence statement and amended it in the light of any comments by the defendant, to ask him/her to sign the draft to signify his/her approval. When drafting a defence statement, you must be in possession of a detailed signed proof of evidence from your client. You must then consider how detailed the defence statement should be and what information it should contain. You must bear in mind that, in order to prevent an adverse inference being drawn, the defence statement should:

- set out in general terms the nature of the accused's defence, eg, self-defence, no intention to use an object as an offensive weapon, no dishonest intention;
- indicate the matters on which the accused takes issue with the prosecution, eg, 'I did not raise my fists or threaten the officer before s/he sprayed me with CS gas';
- give, in respect of each matter, the reason why the accused takes issue, eg, 'The police officer could not have seen me clench my fists until s/he had sprayed me with CS gas'.

Your client should be made aware of the consequence of serving an inaccurate defence statement.

One factor you will consider in drafting a defence statement is whether there is likely to be unused material which could assist your client's defence. If so, the defence statement must contain sufficient detail to enable this material to be identified. If the purpose of the defence statement is essentially defensive, however, in order to prevent an adverse inference being drawn, it would be a mistake to include too much detail.

An example of a case in which you might believe that the prosecution are likely to have material which could assist you is where your client is charged with causing death by dangerous driving as a result of driving on the wrong side of a road with a single carriageway in each direction, when s/he believed s/he was on a dual carriageway. It would be important to establish whether any similar incidents had occurred and to obtain full details of the accident statistics for that stretch of road. In such a case, a detailed defence statement might well result in substantial secondary disclosure being made of other similar types of accident which could assist your client's defence.

An example of the minimum content of a defence statement where a husband is alleged to have indecently assaulted his estranged wife, having telephoned the police and reported that his wife had caused him actual bodily harm, is as follows:

(a) the nature of the accused's defence is that no indecent assault of any nature took place;

(b) the matter on which the accused takes issue with the prosecution is the allegation that he touched the complainant on her breast without her consent;

(c) the reason why the accused takes issue with the prosecution about this matter is that the allegation is untrue. Furthermore, the allegation was made after the accused had telephoned the police to complain that his wife had assaulted him by hitting him on the head with a teapot, causing him substantial bruising and abrasions.

3.5.7 SENSITIVE MATERIAL

In the case of sensitive material, a court can order material not to be disclosed to the extent that the court, on an application by the prosecutor, concludes that it is not in the public interest to disclose it and orders accordingly. (section 7(5) of the CPIA 1996). Examples of sensitive material are the names of informers and details of police surveillance techniques. A prosecutor is only obliged to make an application to the court if s/he considers that disclosure of the material might undermine the prosecution case. The principles set out in the case of *R v Davis, Johnson and Rowe* (1993) 97 Cr App R 110 apply:

(a) the prosecution must give notice to the defence that they are applying for a ruling by the court;

(b) the prosecution must indicate to the defence the category of the material held;

(c) the defence must be given the opportunity of making representations to the court.

However, where the Crown contends that it would not be in the public interest to disclose even the category of material in question, different considerations apply. Although the Crown should still notify the defence that an application will be made, the category of material need not be specified and the application will be without notice. If the judge hearing the application considers that the normal procedure ought to have been followed, s/he will order this. If not, s/he will rule on the application.

This is an application of the principle of public interest immunity, where a party is prevented from seeing disclosable material due to the supervening public interest in secrecy.

There are occasionally exceptional and rare cases where the material is regarded as being so sensitive that even the fact that the application is being made need not be revealed to the defence. This applies when the fact of the application would itself reveal the existence of the material in question. It is then open to the court, if it considers it appropriate, to order that the defence should be made aware that the application has been made, or even to order a hearing on notice.

3.5.8 APPLICATIONS TO THE MAGISTRATES' COURT OR CROWN COURT

It is open to the defence to apply to a magistrates' court or Crown Court, pursuant to section 8 of the CPIA 1996, when the accused has given a defence statement under section 5 or 6 and the prosecutor either complies with section 7 by making a secondary disclosure, purports to comply with it or fails to comply with it.

If the accused has reasonable cause to believe that:

(a) there is prosecution material that could be reasonably expected to assist the accused's defence as disclosed by the defence statement given under section 5 or 6; and

(b) the material has not been disclosed to the accused,

the accused may apply to the court for an order requiring the prosecution to disclose such material to the accused.

There is, further, a continuing duty of the prosecutor to disclose until the accused is acquitted or convicted. If any material comes to light at any stage, the prosecutor must disclose it to the accused as soon as is reasonably practicable.

3.5.9 DISCLOSURE OF EXPERT EVIDENCE

The Crown Court (Advance Notice of Expert Evidence) Rules 1987, made pursuant to section 81 of PACE 1984, require a party to proceedings before a Crown Court to give advance notice of any expert evidence that s/he proposes to adduce. The Rules prohibit that party from adducing such evidence without prior disclosure unless the court gives leave. Similar provisions have been made in the Magistrates' Court (Advance Notice of Expert Evidence) Rules 1997, pursuant to section 20 of the CPIA 1996. These Rules apply to both prosecution and defence but have little relevance to the prosecution because, in the Crown Court, all prosecution evidence, including expert evidence, will normally be disclosed as a result of committal proceedings. In the case of a summary offence in the magistrates' court, where there is no requirement for the prosecution to disclose their case, the rules are equally relevant to prosecution and defence.

The Rules provide that any party intending to rely on expert evidence, whether of fact or opinion, must provide the other with a written statement of any finding or opinion that s/he proposes to adduce by way of such evidence. Further, on request, s/he must also supply a copy of the record of any observation, test, calculation or other procedure on which the finding or opinion is based, or s/he must allow reasonable opportunity to examine such a record. These provisions are important because they enable a defence expert in a dangerous driving case, eg, to inspect the working documents of the prosecution expert.

An expert's report should be prepared in section 9 format (see 3.4 above), and the Rules provide that in a Crown Court case it should be served as soon as is practicable after committal. In the magistrates' court, a case which may involve expert evidence is usually adjourned to a pre-trial review, where the court will give directions as to when the defence expert evidence should be served. This must provide the prosecution with a reasonable opportunity to obtain their own expert evidence, if they wish.

3.5.10 WITNESS SUMMONSES

If you are concerned that your witness may not attend court voluntarily, you should consider issuing a witness summons. This may be a sensible precaution in the case of a very busy expert witness, in case there is a clash of court appointments. Experience will soon show you that, although a potential witness may be prepared to give a statement, very few lay witnesses are keen to attend court. This is both because of the sometimes regrettable amount of hanging around at court that they have to do and because giving evidence in any court, particularly the Crown Court, can be intimidating.

Magistrates' court procedure is contained in section 97 of the MCA 1980 and rule 98 of the Magistrates' Courts Rules 1981. The defence should write to the Clerk of the Justices, requesting the issue of a witness summons. They should give the full name of the witness and confirm whether or not they have a statement from him/her and that they are satisfied that the witness can give relevant evidence. The letter should also explain why a summons is needed and specify the amount of conduct money to be tendered to the witness. Conduct money is for travelling expenses to and from court.

The court, provided you have applied in sufficient time, will then normally issue a summons and send two copies to you for service. You must arrange for this to be served personally on the witness. It is usual to instruct an enquiry agent to do this and at the same time tender the conduct money.

The procedure in the Crown Court has recently been changed, as a result of the amendment of section 2 of the Criminal Procedure (Attendance of Witnesses) Act 1965 by the CPIA 1996 and the associated Crown Court Rules. Under the Act, any witness summons can require a person to attend before the Crown Court at the time and date stated in the summons, and give evidence or produce a document or thing. An application for the witness summons should be made as soon as possible after committal and should normally be supported by an affidavit setting out the following information:

(a) details of the charge;

(b) any evidence, document or thing the witness needs to produce, to be set out in such a way as to enable the directed person to identify it;

(c) the grounds for believing that the directed person is likely to be able to give any evidence or produce any document or thing;

(d) the grounds for believing that any stipulated evidence is likely to be material evidence;

If the defence witnesses fail to attend court, your client risks having the case proceed in their absence. A court is more likely to grant an adjournment if you have taken all steps to secure the witnesses' attendance. Increased concerns about delays are obvious in the courts – they are less willing to grant adjournments.

(e) the grounds for believing that any document is likely to be material evidence.

The Crown Court Rules also provide that, in certain cases, notice of the application shall be served on the person to whom the witness summons is proposed. It is then open to the witness to appear or satisfy the court that s/he cannot give material evidence or produce and material document.

The penalty for any witness who fails to obey a witness summons served upon them, whether in the magistrates' court or in the Crown Court, is that they can be found guilty of contempt of court and be punished accordingly.

EXPLORING AREAS FOR AGREEMENT

RANGE

Achievement must cover all the following contexts.

Environment

Conference, court, meetings with experts, formal pre-trial discussions, office, prison.

Agencies

Advocate, co-accused, prosecution, experts, court.

EVIDENCE

You will need to produce the specific pieces of performance evidence listed below. In addition, you will need to demonstrate that you have achieved the objectives specified at the beginning of this unit. You may do this by producing further pieces of evidence from real and simulated performance, by answering questions posed by your assessor or by passing a written examination.

You will need to provide evidence of having agreed facts with two **Agencies** in the **Range** in two different cases.

CRITERIA

You will demonstrate achievement if:

(a) facts common to parties are identified and consideration is given to the benefit of agreeing these facts in advance of trial or sentence;

(b) clients are advised of the merits of agreeing with such facts and their instructions are obtained and recorded in advance of any further action;

(c) liaison and communications are conducted in a manner which promotes good will and trust.

3.6.1 INTRODUCTION

This unit discusses the way in which facts can be agreed with the prosecution, in connection with both trials and sentencing hearings, and the benefit to your client in attempting to do so. It also explains the way in which, by identifying the issues and agreeing as many non-disputed facts as appropriate, court time can be saved and your client's chances of a fair trial increased. It begins by dealing with issues relating to sentencing and continues with issues relating to trials.

3.6.2 SENTENCING

If your client admits to committing an offence and wishes to plead guilty, either to the offence for which s/he is charged or perhaps to a less serious offence, it is very important that the case proceeds on the basis of an agreed version of facts, if possible. An example of this would be a domestic dispute where your client is charged with making threats to kill and assaulting his/her partner. S/he may deny making any threats to kill, but admit that an argument took place in which there was a lot of shouting and further admit to pushing his/her partner. In this case, s/he clearly would not have a defence to common assault, but *would* have a defence to making threats to kill.

You can only advise your client to plead guilty to an offence which s/he admits to. It may well be possible, in such a situation, to reach agreement with the prosecution that, in return for a plea of guilty to common assault, the charge of threatening to kill will be withdrawn. It might be possible for an advocate to achieve this at court, but an alternative is to write to the prosecution with your client's version of events, suggesting that a plea of common assault would be acceptable.

This is usually the better course, as the CPS representative at court may not have authority to plea bargain, but, even if s/he has, s/he may not have time to consider your representations fully. The CPS will then consult the officer in the case, who may speak to the victim, and the matter could then proceed on the basis of an agreed version of events. You would clearly need your client's instructions before making any such approach to the prosecution and these must be carefully recorded in an attendance note.

There are other occasions when it may not be possible to reach agreement. An example is where a client is charged with possessing a prohibited weapon, eg, a can of pepper spray. S/he instructs you that s/he bought the can at a car boot sale and kept it in the back of his/her car. The prosecution case is that, when stopped for driving with excess alcohol, your client pulled out the can, pointed it at the officer and attempted to fire it. Your client denies this and says that all s/he did was throw it away so that it would not be found in his/her possession. In this type of situation, it is obviously worth trying to persuade the prosecution to proceed on the basis of your client's version of events. If they are not prepared to do so, then, because the effect on sentence could be considerable, there may be no alternative but to have a *Newton* hearing on the issue of exactly what your client did with the pepper spray. Sometimes, *Newton* hearings are inevitable, but the defence should always try to avoid them, if possible, by trying to agree a version of events with the prosecution which is acceptable both to your own client and to the prosecution.

A *Newton* hearing is a 'trial' of an issue relevant to sentence. See 2.5.9 above.

77 Why is it important for the defence to avoid the need for a *Newton* hearing?

In a relatively minor offence, where your client is a person of previous good character and perhaps did not have the benefit of advice at the police station, it may be worth considering the possibility of persuading the CPS that a caution would be more appropriate than proceeding with a hearing. This would apply to a case where a client was perhaps charged with being drunk and disorderly, but, having considered the matter further and taken advice, has accepted that s/he was likely to be convicted. In such a case, if s/he is a person of previous good character, the CPS might be prepared to agree to the police dealing with the matter by way of a caution, which will save your client both money and the stigma of a conviction.

A caution involves acceptance of guilt by the client and will be recorded and can be referred to in court in any subsequent proceedings.

3.6.3 TRIALS

It helps the court if the issues in the case can be agreed between the parties and identified to the court. An example of this is where there is clearly no issue on causation in a case of causing death by dangerous driving. In other words, if it is obvious from the circumstances that the deceased died as a result of injuries received in a collision with your client's car, it would be in your client's interest to indicate to the prosecution that you are prepared to make a section 10 admission that the deceased died as a result of injuries received in the accident.

You need to show evidence of having agreed facts with two agencies specified in the **Range** in two different cases.

The effect of this will be that the jury and the relatives of the deceased will not have to hear evidence from the pathologist as to the injuries suffered and the cause of death in court; the trial will be accordingly shortened and the jury will be better able to focus on the real issue, which is the manner of your client's driving. You will clearly need your client's instructions before any such admission is made. This is the type of issue that can be considered at a conference held between committal and the plea and directions hearing. Your client can be advised of the advantage of trying to agree as much of the non-controversial evidence as possible, and if you receive instructions to that effect, a formal admission can be made at the plea and directions hearing. Under section 10 of the CJA 1967, the admission is recorded in writing and is signed by the advocates for prosecution and defence.

In the magistrates' court, more complex cases are adjourned for a pre-trial review, and one purpose of pre-trial review is to try to agree issues, so far as possible, in the same way that the plea and directions hearing in the Crown Court operates. This may mean agreeing about facts, or it may mean agreeing that certain witness statements can be read.

3.6.4 SUMMARY OF POLICE STATION INTERVIEWS

Summaries prepared by police officers, particularly in less serious cases, are often extremely short and totally inadequate. It is for this reason that, except in a case in which you were present for the interview and feel it is not necessary, or the client makes a clear admission of guilt to you, it is always essential to obtain a copy of the tape recorded interview and listen to it.

If you are not satisfied with the prosecution summary, the procedure is that the defence prepare their own transcript of the interview, which is served on the prosecution, and the prosecution and defence agree on a version to go before the court. One difficulty with summaries produced by the police is that they often obtain inadmissible evidence, especially evidence relating to other offences which are prejudicial but not relevant to the matters before the court.

As an alternative to preparing a transcript, you may be prepared to agree the summary, provided certain parts are deleted before they go before the court. Both the magistrates' court and Crown Court will expect this to be done by you, in agreement with the prosecution, before the case starts. In the magistrates' court, you do not want the magistrates who have to rule on both law and fact to hear the prejudicial information, nor do you want to annoy the court by wasting time. The task of preparing a summary is often left to the trial advocates to sort out, either at the pre-trial review or shortly before the trial starts. There is however, no reason why, having discussed the matter with the trial advocate, you should not try to get this resolved before that stage.

If you want a tape to be played to the jury or magistrates' court, it is again essential to prepare a transcript, so that the tape can be fully edited and inadmissible evidence removed before it is played to the court.

3.6.5 EXPERT EVIDENCE

In civil cases, there has for some time been provision after exchange of expert reports, for experts to meet to try to agree the key issues between them and identify the extent to which they can agree. There is no reason why such a meeting cannot take place in a criminal case with your client's instructions, if it is considered that it would be helpful to do so. It may well be necessary for the defence expert to visit the prosecution expert in any event, to check working documents and other evidence. Discussion at that stage without prejudice on either

Practice Direction (Crown Court: Plea and Directions Hearings) [1995] 1 WLR 1318 sets out rules establishing plea and directions hearings in the Crown Court. The Direction states that, in contested cases, prosecution and defence will be expected to assist the judge in identifying the key issues and to provide any additional information required for the proper listing of the case. Rule 10 sets out a list of matters where the prosecution and defence will be expected to inform the court. These are lengthy, but include:

(a) the issues in the case;

(b) the issues of evidence of any medical condition of the defendant or witnesses;

(c) facts which are to be admitted in accordance with section 10(2)(b) of the CJA 1967;

(d) exhibits and schedules which are to be admitted;

(e) any point of law which it is anticipated will arise at trial;

(f) any application to be made for evidence to be made through live television links.

side may well help to narrow the issues and may also secure a degree of concession from the prosecution expert on the strength of his/her evidence.

3.6.6 CO-OPERATION WITH CO-DEFENDANT'S SOLICITORS

The degree to which you can co-operate with a co-defendant's defence team will obviously depend on the nature of your client's defence. If s/he is running a cut-throat defence, ie, s/he is blaming the other party, no co-operation will be possible. In the more common case where, although there are issues between the defendants, their defence in general terms is the same, co-operation may well be beneficial. This can take the form of co-operating in interviewing witnesses and passing on copies of signed witness statements. It may be helpful to exchange transcripts of interviews, which are going to go before the court in any event.

It is obviously important that you obtain your client's clear instructions before any degree of co-operation takes place. You may also be acting for a defendant who does not appear to be as heavily involved as other parties in, say, a violent disorder. In those circumstances, it may be helpful for your client if the jury distance your client from his/her co-defendants, and this would be a reason for exercising caution in the degree of co-operation with the co-defendant's legal advisers.

ADVISING CLIENTS ON POST-DISPOSAL MATTERS

RANGE

Achievement must cover all the following contexts.

Environment

Court, prison, office.

Agencies

Court, prosecution, probation service, police.

Property

Fingerprints, photographs, property seized in the investigation, DNA.

EVIDENCE

You will need to produce the specific pieces of performance evidence listed below. In addition, you will need to demonstrate that you have achieved the objectives specified at the beginning of this unit. You may do this by producing further pieces of evidence from real and simulated performance, by answering questions posed by your assessor or by passing a written examination.

You will need to provide evidence of:

1 having obtained an advice on appeal from the advocate, and having explained it orally or in writing to the client, within the time limits allowed;

2 having met with two clients after judgment to explain whether an appeal is available or not and, if it is, the procedure for appeal; the latter should then be confirmed in writing;

3 having met with two clients to explain how their sentence could be served;

4 having successfully assisted the client in obtaining the return of his/her **Property** seized in the investigation on at least one occasion.

CRITERIA

You will demonstrate achievement if:

(a) advice is given on procedures for appeal against conviction, sentence or any other order against clients;

(b) implications of sentence are explained to clients;

(c) clients are assisted in seeking return of property;

(d) advice given is accurate in law and in fact;

(e) liaison and communication with clients are conducted in a manner which promotes good will and trust.

3.7.1 INTRODUCTION

Dealing with a client after the case has been disposed of can involve a variety of situations.

Acquittal

You may be dealing with a client who has been acquitted (or against whom the case has been withdrawn or discontinued). Such a client may be very grateful for the assistance from you and your firm, or may consider that the acquittal was no more than s/he deserved (whether or not that is an accurate reflection on the circumstances).

An acquitted defendant will usually be entitled to reimbursement of his costs and the repayment of any legal aid contribution already made.

There may be matters to finalise with such a client: recovery of costs and return of legal aid contribution may be necessary and should have been considered in court (see 2.3 above). Property or samples and fingerprints may have been taken during the investigation, which should now be returned or destroyed. Such clients may nevertheless have other matters outstanding, and the immediate euphoria should not allow you to forget them.

Accurate recording is important in all cases, but it may be particularly important where some but not all matters have been dealt with, or where the client has a long history of offences, as a complex history may lead to confusion and mistakes. The court or Crown Prosecution Service (CPS) record may contain omissions or duplications, or may simply be unclear at times, so make sure yours is correct.

Your files will need to be finalised with a record of the outcome, together with the settling of any fees, costs and legal aid matters.

Conviction

At other times, and probably in the majority of cases, you will be dealing with a convicted client, after either a guilty plea or after a trial. The client may be relieved or disgruntled about the sentence imposed, but in any case you will need to explain the consequences of any sentence to your client. You may also have to canvass the possibility of appeal where you or your client feel that the decision was inappropriate. Even after a trial where the client strongly asserted his/her innocence, many clients will accept the conviction as proper. Others will, rightly or wrongly, consider that they have been the subject of a grave injustice, either in the conviction or in the sentence that followed. Some of them will blame you or your firm.

It will be very rare for a prison or a community sentence to be imposed in the magistrates' court without a prior adjournment for a pre-sentence report; in the Crown Court, this may happen. The seriousness of the offence, however, will indicate that a prison sentence is expected if there is a conviction. The defendant will often have been in custody in any event, awaiting trial.

You may have to advise clients at court immediately after the sentence or in prison. All clients should be seen at court after sentence, and arrangements should be made for any post-sentence discussion that cannot be dealt with at court.

It is especially important that you see those clients who are given an immediate custodial sentence in the court cells before they are taken to prison. Although the client should have been made aware of the possibility of a prison sentence, some defendants adopt a 'head-in-the-sand' attitude. Occasionally, it will fall to you to break the news to a spouse or parent, but, in any event, common humanity and professional conduct demand that you visit the client and deal with any immediate advice. You should, in such circumstances, be aware of the location of the prison involved, visiting and contact arrangements and, of course, know the expected release date.

Clients with non-custodial sentences may only need advice if an appeal is considered.

It is a very difficult task to prepare a client appropriately for the likely outcome. You should seek a balance between an indication of what you think is likely, whilst indicating that it could be worse – or better. Exaggerating a sentence so that the client thinks your firm has worked a miracle or underplaying so that the client is unprepared is in no one's interests.

You may not be able to calculate the release date precisely, taking account of days on remand in custody and so on, but you should be able to explain the broad thrust of the sentence, and confirm release date at a later stage.

3.7.2 DEALING WITH CLIENTS AFTER CONVICTION

As mentioned above, clients may react very differently to conviction or sentence. Much may depend on how they have been prepared for the possible outcomes, but, as stated above, clients may shut their eyes even to an inevitable result.

The most difficult situation is naturally that of the client who is given a prison sentence, but some clients may be appalled or outraged about other sentences and of course conviction itself. You may therefore have to advise an upset, angry or frightened client, who may consider that your advice 'got him into this'. You may also have to consider a number of post-disposal matters with the client, including the possibility of an appeal.

3.7.3 EXPLAINING THE SENTENCE

Whenever a client is sentenced, you should make sure that s/he understands the effect of the sentence. Sometimes, this will be clear to the client, especially if s/he is a regular offender. For community sentences, the probation officer must also explain the sentence and implementation of the order, but in all cases you should make sure that the client understands what has happened, and what s/he should do next. Even where the magistrates or judge have explained what is to happen in great detail (as they will when imposing a custodial or community sentence), you should ensure that the client understands his/her situation fully.

There may be other questions in relation to the consequences of the sentence that your client is unclear about. Set out below are some of the particular matters which might concern your client in relation to particular sentences (see Appendix 1).

When imposing a custodial sentence, by virtue of sections 1(4) and 2(3) of the CJA 1991, the court must explain in ordinary language why such a punishment has been imposed and the reason for its length. The court will also explain in great detail the reasons for and the effect of a community sentence.

A note on bind overs

A bind over is not strictly a sentence, as it is usually imposed after an application that the defendant show cause why s/he should not be bound over. If this procedure has been canvassed, you will have explained to your client the consequences of agreeing to the bind over.

These are that if s/he fails to 'keep the peace and be of good behaviour' in the period specified, s/he will forfeit some or all of the amount in which s/he was bound over. A bind over can be breached by committing any offence, but normally action is taken only where the conduct is of the same or a similar nature as the complaint that gave rise to the binding over, especially if it involves the same aggrieved person or class of persons. Bind overs are often imposed in neighbour disputes and in minor domestic incidents.

Consideration of a bind over is a serious matter, though it is preferable to being prosecuted. It does recognise guilt, and if a bind over is decided on by the court, consent must be given by the subject of it. Failure to give consent can only result in imprisonment. It is vital, therefore, that the implications and consequences of a bind over be fully explained before the court is invited (by the prosecution) to follow that route.

Discharges

Absolute discharge

If your client has been given an absolute discharge, s/he may be rather confused. You should explain that the court has found them guilty but has imposed no punishment (however, costs and compensation may be imposed with a discharge). It is a conviction, and will thus appear on the client's criminal record.

An absolute discharge is 'spent' six months after imposition under the Rehabilitation of Offenders Act 1974.

Conditional discharge

A conditional discharge may need more explanation. You should explain that, provided no further offence is committed within the period of the conditional discharge, no action will be taken (though there may be costs and compensation awarded and, in driving matters, points may be endorsed on the licence). But, if any further conviction (ie, after a guilty plea or a trial in any court) occurs within the specified period, the court dealing with the subsequent offence may impose any sentence that the original court had power to impose, bearing in mind the normal criteria.

The magistrates' courts cannot deal with breach of a Crown Court conditional discharge order.

If a person who has been discharged re-offends, this is normally dealt with by a fine or by no action being taken. However, even if the subsequent court takes no action specifically on the breach, it will probably take account of the previous matter when arriving at its sentence for the new offence, because failure to respond to previous sentences is seen as an aggravating feature of a case.

A common sentence for first (comparatively trivial) offenders is a one year conditional discharge. A conditional discharge is rehabilitated after one year or the length of the order, whichever is greater.

If the subsequent offence is punished only by a discharge, this does not count as a conviction in order to activate the earlier conditional discharge.

78 What is the sole 'condition' under a conditional discharge?

79 What happens if the condition is not adhered to?

3.7.4 FINES, COSTS AND COMPENSATION

Fines and costs

In the magistrates' court, the most common disposal is the fine. Some level of costs towards the cost of bringing the case is very often ordered against the convicted defendant, whether pleading guilty or not guilty, unless s/he is given a custodial sentence. The CPS asks for a standard rate of costs according to the type of case involved, eg, summary or TEW offence, guilty plea or trial. This increases from time to time, and you will soon become aware of the current rates.

Costs are rarely imposed if someone is given a custodial sentence.

Compensation

The court must consider the award of compensation whenever a victim of an offence has suffered physical harm, property loss or damage (other than in driving offences). Compensation can stand alone as a sentence or be allied with others, as can a fine. Like fines, compensation levels will depend on the financial means of the offender, but will rank ahead of fines or costs. Care should be taken to challenge requests for compensation that are inadequately supported or seem to be inflated, but recognition of and offering compensation may be taken as a sign of remorse and, therefore, a mitigating factor.

A client who is sentenced to custody should not have additional financial matters imposed, but s/he may already have some fines outstanding: s/he can ask via the prison authorities for these to be remitted by virtue of serving days in lieu.

All financial orders are paid into the court or its collecting office, and the court will pass on compensation to the aggrieved. When a number of financial orders are made against one offender, the compensation takes priority in payment. If a financial order is made against a client, you should have already taken instructions about whether s/he is able to pay any fine immediately or whether there should be a request for 'time to pay'. The order, if not immediate, will specify a weekly or monthly sum to be paid, or a period within which the amount should be discharged.

You should ensure that the client fully understands when and where payment is to be made (the court will usually provide written information of the address and mechanisms, and many courts now accept credit cards), and the client must be aware that if payment is not made as directed, enforcement proceedings will inevitably follow. Although in some places enforcement will take some time, the client should not be under the illusion that s/he will not eventually be chased. Indeed, as courts are arranging enforcement more efficiently, long delays are becoming less common.

3.7.5 COMMUNITY SENTENCES

A client who receives a community sentence will normally have seen a probation officer for the preparation of a pre-sentence report, which is required before the imposition of most types of community order and is obtained for all orders as a matter of practice. The officer will therefore have explained the effect and consequences of the orders in question. Before the court sentences, the advocate will usually have explained the recommendations in the report to the client and should have canvassed any alternative course the court might take. The client, therefore, should have a good idea of the effect of any possible order. However, it is good practice to ensure that s/he is aware of the practical effect of the order, of the effect of breach and of the effect of the commission of further offences during the currency of the order.

It is not your responsibility to see that the client observes the terms of his/her order, but it is part of your duty to ensure that s/he understands what his/her responsibilities are.

The client should be reminded not only to attend any interviews or other appointments, but also to keep the Probation Service informed of any change of address. Often, s/he will be required to see a probation officer to arrange an appointment before leaving court; in other cases, s/he will be notified as to when s/he should attend.

Curfews are now available as a community sentence throughout the country.

3.7.6 CUSTODIAL SENTENCES

A client will normally be well aware that a custodial sentence is a possible outcome, because of the seriousness of the offence itself, because of the seriousness after taking account of the client's record, or because it is an offence of sex or violence where the protection of the public from future offending is an issue. Again, there will usually have been an adjournment for a pre-sentence report, required before a custodial sentence is imposed, unless the court deems it unnecessary (section 3(2) of the CJA 1991), and the client should have been aware of the possibility of custody at that stage, if not before. There are, however, various practical matters that you will need to explain to your client.

What was the sentence exactly?

Particularly where a number of offences are dealt with by a custodial sentence, the client may became confused as to totality. This is even more the case where some sentences are consecutive or concurrent. What matters immediately to the client is the total sentence, but it is proper that they should be aware of the breakdown of the sentences, especially is there is the possibility of appeal against one or more convictions.

What is the length of time that will be served?

The court is now required to tell offenders sentenced to custody that:

(a) part of their sentence will be served in the community;

(b) any period already spent on remand in custody awaiting trial or sentence will be deducted from the sentence given (section 67 of the CJA 1967).

However, you should again explain this to the client.

Where will the sentence be served?

You should be aware of the prison to which sentenced adults are initially taken in your area. If you are not sure, seek advice from the court gaoler.

80 What are the possible consequences of failing to comply with a community service order?

81 What are the maximum number of hours under a community service order and in what period must they be served? (See Unit 1.)

Concurrent sentences are served simultaneously; consecutive sentences are served one after the other.

For sentences up to 12 months: the offender is released after half the sentence.

For sentences from 12 months to four years: the offender is released after half, but on licence up to the three-quarter point.

For sentences of over four years: early release is at the discretion of the Parole Board (sections 33–36 of the CJA 1991).

A complicated computation might arise where the offender is sentenced for a number of matters in respect of some of which s/he has been on bail and some in custody: take advice.

You must provide evidence of having met clients on two occasions to explain how their sentence could be served.

3.7.7 DEFERRED SENTENCES

Occasionally, a court will defer a sentence for up to six months (section 1 of the Powers of Criminal Courts Act (PCCA) 1973), which means that they do not immediately make a decision. This is not merely an adjournment, and the procedure is used where there is expected to be a significant alteration in the defendant's behaviour, perhaps associated with treatment for addiction, counselling, the making of compensation or a change of job or lifestyle. The ultimate sentencing court has power to sentence in any way available to the deferring court, but the expectation is that, if the defendant does what is expected of him/her, the sentence will be as indicated, but if s/he fails to respond, the sentence will usually be custodial.

It is therefore very important that the client understands the consequences of failing to comply with the court's expectations. Obviously, the commission of further offences during the deferred period will mean that a custodial sentence is almost inevitable.

R v George [1984] 1 WLR 1082. If the defendant has conformed to the court's expectations, s/he can legitimately expect a non-custodial sentence.

3.7.8 PROPERTY ORDERS

There are a number of orders that a court may make in addition to the main sentence, which will or may affect property in the possession of, or even belonging to, your client. These include confiscation, forfeiture, destruction and restitution orders.

Confiscation orders

Under the Drug Trafficking Act 1994, the Crown Court can make orders in relation to the confiscation of the profits of drug trafficking offences. Under the CJA 1988, this power applies also to all indictable offences where the offender has benefited financially from the crime.

Where a confiscation order is sought, the prosecution must serve a written notice on the court indicating this.

Although this power is applicable to confiscate the proceeds of any indictable offence, it tends to be used mostly in financial fraud and drug trafficking, where the powers are more extensive and the profits are often greater and somewhat easier to identify.

Forfeiture

Under section 43 of the PCCA 1973, an order can be made in respect of the forfeiture of property seized from offender, if the purpose of the property was for committing or facilitating the commission of an offence. Property may have been seized in the course of an investigation as part of the evidence of the offence, such as tools that were used in burglary.

Where an offence is punishable with imprisonment and is committed involving the use of a car and the offender was driving or in charge of the car, this can result in the confiscation of the car (section 43(1) of the PCCA 1973). This will be an inappropriate disposal if it has a disproportionate effect, considering the magnitude of the offence.

The forfeiture order can also be used where the offence consists of the possession of property which is in itself unlawful and which is seized from the offender, or is under his/her control at time of arrest or summons. This would include things such as drugs, weapons or obscene material.

Destruction order

A destruction can be ordered of items that are themselves illicit, and this order is often allied with forfeiture. This order is often made in cases involving drugs, weapons, obscene items and the products of counterfeiting, thus allowing the police to destroy these items. In other cases involving forfeited items (under a forfeiture order, above), the police, acting under the Police Property Act 1897, will sell the items (the proceeds go mainly to criminal justice charities).

Restitution

This can be ordered in respect of items which have been the subject of a conviction for theft or an allied offence, and can thus be ordered to be returned to their rightful owner. This will usually arise where there has been a dispute over whether the goods were in fact stolen.

Occasionally, where stolen goods have passed into other hands after the offence, civil proceedings may follow to determine the legal owner of items, but this tends to be confined to high value items such as motor vehicles.

3.7.9 EFFECT OF VERDICT ON SAMPLES TAKEN

If the defendant client is convicted, s/he has no right to have samples and fingerprints destroyed.

3.7.10 EFFECT OF VERDICT ON PROPERTY RETAINED BY POLICE

As stated above, the sentence may allow the police to dispose of items of property in a variety of ways. Where property has been seized which was not involved in a crime, the client will be entitled to its return unless there is a dispute over ownership, in which case there may need to be a civil application in the magistrates' court for the determination of ownership.

You must provide evidence of having assisted the client in the return of property seized in the investigation on at least one occasion.

3.7.11 REHABILITATION

The Rehabilitation of Offenders Act 1974 provides that offences are spent (ie, they need not be disclosed in non-sensitive job applications, should not be disclosed in the press and will not usually be referred to in court) after a specified period in relation to the sentence imposed. The period is re-activated if a subsequent conviction takes place within that period.

The periods set out below are those in respect of adult offenders. For offenders under 18, the period is shorter:

(a) life imprisonment and sentences over 30 months are never spent;

(b) a sentence of imprisonment from six months to 30 months is spent after 10 years;

(c) for sentences of imprisonment under six months, the period is seven years;

(d) for community service orders, probation orders and fines, the period is five years;

(e) in respect of conditional discharges, the period is one year or the length of the order, whichever is the longer;

(f) absolute discharges are spent after six months.

3.7.12 APPEALS AGAINST DECISIONS OF THE MAGISTRATES' COURT

To the Crown Court

The most usual appeal route against magistrates' decisions is to the Crown Court (section 108 of the MCA 1980). The defendant can always appeal:

(a) against the sentence imposed by the magistrates;

(b) against conviction, if s/he pleaded not guilty.

You must provide evidence of having met with two clients after judgment to explain whether an appeal is available or not and, if it is, the procedure for appeal. The latter should be confirmed in writing.

There is no appeal against conviction after a guilty plea because, of course, the defendant brought about his/her own conviction. The only exception to this is if the plea was equivocal (see 3.7.21 below). Thus, if the defendant thought that pleading guilty indicated that s/he had a defence and, therefore, that the magistrates should have refused to accept the guilty plea, s/he may appeal against conviction. The same applies if the guilty plea was entered as a result of duress (ie, pressure from others).

To the High Court

It is possible to appeal on a point of law to the High Court:

- by way of case stated; or
- for judicial review,

but both of these are comparatively rare.

A case can be stated (under section 111 of the MCA 1980) where the decision was wrong in law or was in excess of jurisdiction, and only lies when a final determination of the case has been made.

Judicial review lies where there has been error of law on the face of the record (ie, the court had no power to do what it did), where there has been an excess of jurisdiction (eg, a procedure was not carried out correctly) or where there has been a breach of the rules of natural justice, because of bias or the failure to hear both sides. An interim decision can be the subject of judicial review.

3.7.13 CAN THE PROSECUTION APPEAL?

The prosecution cannot appeal to the Crown Court against an acquittal or sentence, but they may appeal to the High Court on a point of law, as above.

3.7.14 APPEAL TO THE CROWN COURT

The hearing in the Crown Court of an appeal against conviction will take the form of a rehearing: evidence will be given and the tribunal will be a judge sitting with two magistrates. There is thus no argument to establish a ground for the appeal, nor do written grounds need to be provided. Nevertheless, thought will need to be given as to the reasons for appealing, as there is no merit in appealing merely to have a second bite at the cherry if the outcome is likely to be the same.

Your client may wish to appeal if:

(a) the conviction was against the weight of the evidence;
(b) there was a decision on a point of law that may be decided differently in the Crown Court;
(c) the defence case is likely to be more persuasive in the Crown Court;
(d) a point could be argued or evidence adduced that was not presented at the magistrates' hearing.

An appeal against sentence is also heard before a judge and two magistrates, and again will take the form of a rehearing with a plea in mitigation being given by the defence after the facts have been outlined. Additional facts or factors which were not

The main consideration in advising on appeal is the prospect of success. Other factors include the stress to the client, the costs if relevant and any dangers, such as a possible increase in sentence.

As the appeal will take the form of a rehearing, it will not be necessary to demonstrate formally that the lower court made a wrong decision, but naturally, there is no point in appealing unless it did.

dealt with in the magistrates' court can be argued before the Crown Court. As the Crown Court can increase as well as reduce sentence, a defendant should not appeal unless there are good grounds for doing so, eg, because the magistrates clearly failed to take account of some important mitigating factor, or sentenced on the wrong basis, or the sentence was clearly excessive.

Although the defendant and legal adviser may take issue with the fact of conviction, it may be that the sentence is of such a nature that your advice might be not to appeal. The fact that the period for appeal runs from sentence enables this to be taken into account in cases where sentence is later than the date of conviction, perhaps because of the need for reports.

3.7.15 TIME LIMIT FOR APPEAL TO THE CROWN COURT

A notice of appeal must be served within 21 days of the date of sentence, even where the appeal is against conviction only.

The period within which the notice must be served can be extended by the Crown Court, but this is usually done only when the defendant was unaware of the conviction (because it was heard in his/her absence, possible only for minor matters) or the possibility of appeal, or where the case is complex. As the grounds for appeal need to be given at the time of serving the notice, it is not usually necessary for there to be a delay in order to obtain legal advice. The Crown Court will take account of the merits of the case and the reasons for delay when determining whether to extend the period.

3.7.16 PROCEDURE FOR APPEAL TO THE CROWN COURT

The procedure for appealing to the Crown Court from the magistrates' court is that a notice of appeal must be sent to the clerk to the magistrates and to the prosecutor within 21 days of sentence.

No leave is required for appeal, and the grounds need not be specified on the notice. The hearing itself will take the form of a rehearing with the adduction of evidence (not limited to evidence adduced in the magistrates' court) before a judge and two lay magistrates, who will be from a bench other than the convicting/sentencing bench. No jury will be involved.

3.7.17 APPEALING AGAINST ANCILLARY MATTERS

There is no appeal against legal aid contribution orders to the Crown Court. Legal aid matters can be challenged before the area committee.

3.7.18 BAIL PENDING APPEAL

Where custody is imposed and the defendant is appealing against conviction or against the custodial sentence, bail pending appeal may be granted by the magistrates. If they refuse, application for bail pending appeal can be made to the Crown Court or a High Court judge in chambers. Bail pending appeal will usually only be granted if the conviction or choice of sentence depends on a disputed point of law or practice, or if the sentence is short and may well have been served substantially or in full (taking account of early release) before the hearing of the appeal.

3.7.19 ENFORCEMENT SUSPENDED DURING APPEAL

Certain other sentences can be ordered not to be enforced pending the determination of an appeal once the appeal has been lodged. Occasionally, this is appropriate in the case of a fine, and community sentences will rarely be enforced pending an appeal. The most significant matter, apart from a custodial sentence, where suspension pending an appeal is often considered, is in relation to disqualification from driving.

3.7.20 ABANDONMENT OF APPEAL

The defendant (now the appellant) may abandon his/her appeal by giving notice to:

(a) the Crown Court;

(b) the magistrates' court; and

(c) the prosecution,

at least three days before the hearing date, although the Crown Court might (and usually will) allow the abandonment even without such notice.

If the appeal is abandoned, the Crown Court cannot increase the sentence imposed by the magistrates. If the appeal was against a custodial sentence imposed by the magistrates' court and bail was given pending appeal, the appellant will have to surrender to the magistrates' court and be taken into custody.

3.7.21 POWERS OF THE CROWN COURT ON APPEAL

On appeal from the magistrates' court, the Crown Court may (Supreme Court Act 1981, section 48):

(a) quash the conviction – the appellant is thereby acquitted of the offence;

(b) send the case back to the magistrates' court for a fresh trial (eg, if the plea was equivocal);

(c) vary the sentence, either by reducing it or increasing it.

An equivocal plea is a plea of guilty where a valid defence is indicated.

The fact that the Crown Court can increase the sentence, though not, of course, beyond the maximum available to the magistrates' court for the offence, should deter most unmeritorious appeals. An appeal against any part of the magistrates' decision means that the Crown Court can alter any other part of the decision. This is particularly important where there are a number of decisions: an appeal against one allows reconsideration of another.

3.7.22 APPEAL AGAINST A DECISION OF THE CROWN COURT

The normal route to appeal against Crown Court decisions is to appeal to the Court of Appeal (Criminal Division). The prosecution can also appeal on an Attorney General's reference against unduly lenient sentences (sections 35–36 of the CJA 1988) and against a tainted acquittal under section 54 of the CPIA 1996.

There are three important differences between appeal to the Crown Court and appeal from the Crown Court to the Court of Appeal (Criminal Division):

(a) leave is required to appeal to the Court of Appeal – appeal lies as of right from the magistrates' court;

(b) appeal to the Court of Appeal is based on an argument that the lower court erred – appeal to the Crown Court is a rehearing;

(c) the Crown Court can increase the sentence imposed by the magistrates. The Court of Appeal cannot impose a sentence which is 'greater overall' than that imposed by the Crown Court.

3.7.23 APPEALS AGAINST CONVICTION

Leave of the Court of Appeal is required before an appeal against conviction is commenced unless the Crown Court judge certifies that the case is suitable for appeal. An appeal must be lodged within 28 days of the conviction (not the date of sentence, which may be later).

The ground of appeal will generally be on the basis of an error in the trial, but occasionally, where there is a novel or uncertain point of law involved, a judge will certify the case.

A barrister should usually be instructed to draft the grounds of appeal. This should be the barrister who conducted the case.

As barristers are directed by their code of professional conduct only to advise an appeal if there are sufficient grounds to do so, this is a protection against the loss of time which may be awarded to penalise an unmeritorious appellant.

3.7.24 LEAVE TO APPEAL

Application for leave to appeal is made to a single judge, who, on a consideration of the papers, will determine whether the case is worthy of argument before the full court. If the judge grants leave, the case will be summarised by the registrar of criminal appeals for the Court of Appeal and counsel will submit a skeleton argument.

If the single judge refuses leave, the appeal can still be pursued, but the appellant risks having a loss of time direction made if leave is again refused by the full court. The client will be protected from this if the renewed appeal was made on the advice of counsel, unless the single judge indicated that it was wholly without merit.

This means that, if the appellant was sentenced to a custodial sentence, a direction can be made that some or all of the time between the beginning of the appeal process and the refusal of leave shall not count towards the serving of the sentence.

Loss of time is not ordered merely because an appeal was unsuccessful, but as a disincentive for pursuing unmeritorious appeals once leave has been initially refused.

Bail pending appeal can be granted by a single judge, or an expedited appeal may be ordered if the defendant has served the sentence before the appeal is heard.

If the appellant was in receipt of legal aid for the original trial, the certificate will cover advice on appeal. Legal aid for the hearing may be granted by the registrar or a single judge. Provided that the appellant satisfies the means criteria, legal aid will be granted, as appeals always involve legal matters where legal advice will be necessary.

3.7.25 GROUNDS FOR APPEAL AGAINST CONVICTION

Under section 2 of the Criminal Appeal Act 1968 as amended by the 1995 Act, there is one ground of appeal against conviction, namely, that the conviction is unsafe. It seems that the meaning to be given to that term is in relation to the previously applied test of whether there is a lurking doubt (at least) that an injustice was done in convicting the defendant. This, however, is not intended to allow the Court of Appeal to overturn convictions with which it happens not to agree.

The reasons for overturning the verdict of the jury will be because of either:

(a) an irregularity in the course of the trial, including the conduct of the judge;

(b) a misdirection by the judge in the summing up, such as failure to direct the jury or an incorrect direction on:
- the burden and standard of proof;
- the relevance of good character evidence;
- the relevance of evidence of the bad character of the accused, where it is admitted;
- identification evidence and its dangers;
- elements of the offence;
- inferences from silence;

(c) an error of law by the judge in the course of the trial, such as:
- the exclusion of evidence that should have been admitted;
- the inclusion of evidence that should have been omitted (eg, character evidence or hearsay);
- a direction on a point of law on the basis of which defence decisions were made;
- a failure to accept a submission of no case to answer.

Appeals are usually on the basis of a misdirection by the judge.

3.7.26 FRESH EVIDENCE

Under section 23 of the Criminal Appeal Act 1968, the Court of Appeal may hear new evidence where:

(a) there is a reasonable explanation for failing to bring the evidence at trial (eg, it has only recently come to light);

(b) it seems capable of belief;

(c) it might provide a ground for appeal.

3.7.27 APPEAL AGAINST SENTENCE

There is no ground laid down by statute for appeals against sentence, but the ground is basically that the sentence is too long in the light of current sentencing law and practice. This is formulated is one of the following ways:

(a) error of law – the judge imposed a sentence which was not permitted (eg, where the age of the offender precluded the sentence);

(b) wrong in principle;

(c) wrong approach;

(d) disparity between co-accuseds;
(e) manifestly excessive;
(f) defendant has a legitimate sense of grievance.

Appeal against sentence must be lodged within 28 days of the sentence.

3.7.28 POWERS OF THE COURT OF APPEAL

Where the court allows an appeal against conviction, it can:

(a) quash the conviction;
(b) order a re-trial if in the interests of justice (or a *venire de novo* when the original trial was a nullity);
(c) substitute a conviction for an alternative offence.

Where the court allows an appeal against sentence, it should not impose a sentence which is overall more severe than the one imposed by the Crown Court (but remember, loss of time can be ordered: see 3.7.24 above).

3.7.29 APPEAL BY THE PROSECUTION

If the defendant is acquitted at the Crown Court, there is no appeal against that acquittal, but the point of law that led to the decision may be taken by the prosecution to the Court of Appeal by way of an Attorney General's reference.

The prosecution can also appeal against a sentence imposed in the Crown Court by way of an Attorney General's reference (under section 35 of the CJA 1988) if:

(a) the offence is triable only on indictment or is an offence of threatening to kill, cruelty to or neglect of children, indecent assault, or serious fraud; and
(b) the sentence was unduly lenient (falling outside the acceptable range of sentences for the offence).

3.7.30 ADVISING THE CLIENT

Care should be taken when advising a client on appeal: you should have taken ensured, before any decision on verdict or sentence is reached, that the client's expectations are realistic. Nevertheless, there will still be times when both you and the client are surprised and disappointed by the verdict or sentence. The client should be advised carefully of the merit and likely outcome of an appeal, bearing especially in mind the possible disadvantages.

For Crown Court cases conducted by counsel, you will seek advice on appeal from the counsel who dealt with the case. Instructing counsel to advise on appeal in these cases will be comparatively straightforward. Where you are seeking advice on appeal on a case not conducted by counsel, most typically one dealt with in the magistrates' court, you will need to set out all the information, in the form of instructions, in order to advise, as in any case when seeking counsel's views.

Do not forget the value of an informal opinion from a colleague on the merits of an appeal, and always be conscious of the time available to begin an appeal.

Costs of the appeal will be covered by any legal aid certificate (see Unit 2).

When you have obtained the advice or considered the position yourself, you will need to explain it carefully to your client, including:

(a) the possibility of success;

(b) the consequences if the appeal fails;

(c) the costs involved, if any;

(d) the time factor;

(e) what will happen if no appeal takes place;

(f) if an appeal is to be made, what will happen until it is heard.

You must provide evidence of having obtained an advice in writing from the advocate, and explained it orally or in writing to your client, within the time limits allowed.

APPENDIX 10: DOCUMENTS

DOCUMENT 1: MODEL LETTER TO PRISON FOR CONFERENCE WITH CLIENT IN CUSTODY

The Governor

HM Prison

Chelmsford

5 January 2000

Dear Madam

Re: David Smith

Prison Number ....

Conference 11.1.00 9.30am

Please admit Miss V Brown of this firm and Counsel Miss Diane Jones of Silversmiths Buildings for a conference with the above client.

Yours faithfully ...

DOCUMENT 2: EXAMPLE OF A WITNESS STATEMENT

WITNESS STATEMENT

(Criminal Justice Act 1967, s 9, Magistrates' Courts Act 1980, s 5A(3)(B) and 5B, Magistrates' Courts Rules 1981, r 70)

STATEMENT OF

AGE (if under 18, if over 18 insert 'over 18')

OCCUPATION

This statement (consisting of – pages, each signed by me) is true to the best of my knowledge and belief and I make it knowing that, if it is tendered in evidence, I shall be liable to prosecution if I have wilfully stated in it anything which I know to be false or do not believe to be true.

DATED THIS DAY OF 2000

(At the end of each page:

SIGNED

SIGNATURE WITNESSED BY)

DOCUMENT 3: EXAMPLE OF A LETTER TO A CHARACTER WITNESS

5 January 2000

Dear Sir/Madam

I understand from Mr A that you have kindly said that you would be prepared to give character evidence on his behalf.

I would be very grateful if you could write a letter addressed to myself. The letter should contain the following information:

(a) the length of time you have known Mr A;
(b) the capacity in which you have known Mr A, ie, friend, neighbour, employer;
(c) your opinion of his character and general behaviour based on your knowledge of him.

I enclose a stamped addressed envelope and look forward to hearing from you as soon as possible. It would be helpful if you could let us have your letter by no later than [in good time for his hearing]. If you are able to come to court on Mr A's behalf, this would also be most helpful, and I would be glad if you could telephone me or my secretary, Ms X, with your telephone number so that we can arrange to contact you with the court number and time.

Yours sincerely ...

APPENDIX 11: ANSWERS TO THE SELF-ASSESSMENT QUESTIONS

SAQ ANSWERS: 3.1

66 If a client fails to attend court, the normal consequence, in the absence of evidence of illness, would be for the court to issue a warrant for his/her arrest. If the client telephones, saying they are too ill to attend, then, in the magistrates' court, the client would normally be bailed in their absence, on condition that a medical certificate is produced before the next hearing. In the Crown Court, particularly if the matter is listed for trial, a judge might issue a bench warrant for the arrest of the defendant with a view to a medical examination by a police surgeon at court.

67 If a witness fails to attend court in answer to a witness summons, then, provided the court is satisfied that a witness summons has been personally served on the witness, the witness is technically in contempt of court and could be arrested and punished for this. In practice, the party relying on the witness would usually be reluctant to press for this, as their object is getting the witness to court to give evidence on their client's behalf. Every attempt should, therefore, be made by the defence to follow up the witness summons and to try to get the client to court, provided the defence are still satisfied that the client will give reliable evidence.

68 The responsibilities of the surety are to ensure attendance by the defendant at court.

SAQ ANSWERS: 3.2

69 A lucid and well organised brief will not only assist the advocate originally briefed to advise your client to the best of his/her ability, but also, in the event of the advocate who is briefed not being available, it is very important that the substitute is able to prepare fully for the trial at short notice, relying on the brief and enclosures you have prepared.

SAQ ANSWERS: 3.3

70 A full and clear note of the conference is important so that all members of the defence team, that is, the advocate, the client and yourself, are fully aware of what they have to do following the conference. It is also important, particularly if advice is given on plea by counsel, that the client is given this information in writing to enable him/her to consider it. Further, if the original counsel is not available when it comes to the trial, then it will be of the greatest possible assistance to anyone taking over the brief to have a clear note of the conference and what decisions were made.

71 If the CPS fail to disclose unused material following your service of a witness summons, then you should follow this up in correspondence and, if necessary, on the telephone. If a reasonable excuse is not given, inform the CPS. Unless the material is supplied within a defined period of time, say, seven days, you should ask the Crown Court to list the matter for a mention. This will usually ensure that the information is provided. If it is not, you should write or fax the Chief Clerk at the Crown Court, asking for the matter to be put in the list for the purpose of seeking an order from a judge.

72 If a witness fails to appear at the trial and their evidence is of crucial importance, you will be faced with the decision whether or not to apply for an adjournment. An adjournment is more likely to be granted by the court if it considers that the defence have taken all reasonable steps to ensure that the witness attends. In practice, it is fairly unusual for a witness to fail to obey a witness summons served on them. The court will make its decision whether or not to grant an adjournment in the interests of justice and fairness to both prosecution and defence; and the more important the witness to the defence case and the less the defendant is at fault in failing to have the witness at court, the more likely it is that an adjournment will be granted.

SAQ ANSWERS: 3.4

73 Difficulty in obtaining a clear proof from a child can be caused by the influence of a parent or parents. If a child, particularly one of previous good character, has been arrested for a criminal offence, this puts a great strain on the relationship between parent and child. If the relationship is a good one, then the parents will be supportive and understanding of your need to see the child by him/herself, if appropriate, to obtain a clear account of what happened. If however, the parents are very angry with the child and are overbearing in their attitude towards him/her, this can make your task of obtaining the child's instructions difficult. It is important that you take time to explain to a parent, before any interview takes place, what the purpose of the interview is and why it is most important that you obtain the trust of the child, ie, so that you can obtain his/her own version of what occurred.

74 Anyone suffering from mental illness who is arrested is clearly going to be very vulnerable, and may well find it difficult to discuss the offence rationally with you or to understand or accept advice. This in itself puts an additional responsibility on that person's legal adviser. If someone is clearly suffering from a mental illness, it is important to try and obtain, by tactful questioning, some understanding of the type of illness and any medication and treatment they are receiving for it. If the client is on bail, then, if your court has a mental health team attached to it, an adjournment for an assessment by the psychiatrist attached to the court may be a sensible and prudent initial step. This may give you grounds for suggesting diversification in the criminal justice system to the CPS. Alternatively, if the client is remanded in custody for an offence of some seriousness, both the Crown Court and magistrates' court have the power to remand an accused person to a hospital, under section 35 of the Mental Health Act 1983, in order for a report to be made.

SAQ ANSWERS: 3.5

75 Threatening behaviour is a summary offence only, and voluntary disclosure by the prosecutor will not take place until your client pleads not guilty, probably not until two or three weeks before trial. Therefore, it would be sensible to write to the CPS, asking for voluntary disclosure of the tape. If you do not receive it, you should press the CPS for primary disclosure and, as soon as this has been made, serve a defence statement identifying the issues and the reason why the CCTV material may be relevant. If you do not succeed in obtaining the tape in this way, or the prosecutor states that s/he has seen it and it does not assist your client's defence, then you should still ask to see it yourself, and also consider making an application under section 8 of the CPIA 1996 to the magistrates' court for an order for disclosure.

76 In this case, the client would almost certainly have pleaded not guilty at his first appearance in court. If the only possible defence open to the defendant was that the intoximeter was not working correctly, then a voluntary defence statement should be served as soon as possible, identifying the grounds upon which disclosure of the intoximeter log book and service record may assist the defence. If the CPS denied access to these or delayed their disclosure, an application to the magistrates' court under section 8 of the CPIA would again be necessary.

SAQ ANSWERS: 3.6

77 The reason for trying to avoid a *Newton* trial if possible is that it is very difficult for a defendant to be successful. The reason for this is that, after a defendant has admitted the offence, the court will inevitably, even if subconsciously, regard any attempt by him/her to minimise his/her part in it as self-serving. It may have the effect of undoing the benefit which the client would receive by pleading guilty. It is most important that you do not put pressure on your client to agree a version of events which is not true, but equally the client must be left in no doubt as to the desirability of trying to avoid a *Newton* trial if at all possible.

SAQ ANSWERS: 3.7

78 The sole condition under a conditional discharge is not to commit further offences in the specified period.

79 If the condition of the discharge is not adhered to, the defendant can be re-sentenced for the original offence together with the subsequent one.

80 Failure to comply with a community service order means that the person who is the subject of the order may be brought before a court for the breach: the magistrates may fine up to £1,000, impose a community service order for up to 60 hours (not to exceed in total the maximum) or revoke the original order and deal in some other way for the original offence (this will normally be custody); if the order was a Crown Court order, there may be a committal to the Crown Court.

81 The maximum number of hours is 240, and these must be served within a year of imposition.

APPENDIX 12: SELF-ASSESSMENT TESTS

WRITTEN TEST 1

Dean has been charged with burglary of shop premises. He has a number of previous convictions for similar offences. He comes to see you two days before his initial court appearance, stating that he denies the offence and wants to elect trial by jury. He claims that he has an alibi, the brief details of which he gave to the police when interviewed. After assisting him in completing an application for legal aid, you arrange for him to apply for an adjournment until legal aid is granted and for you to consider advance disclosure. Advance disclosure makes clear that the prosecution are relying on evidence of glass fragments found in his clothing, which was seized when he was arrested, which the forensic scientist claims are similar to the glass in the window which was smashed at the time of the burglary. A summary of the interview says that Dean claimed that he was at a public house with a group of people whose first names only he knew, in a town 20 miles away on the evening of the burglary.

Once legal aid has been granted, what steps would you take to prepare Dean's defence pending committal to the Crown Court? What issues would you ask counsel to consider when you brief counsel after the committal hearing? How would you proceed to draft the defence statement? If you decided that further time was needed for this, how would you go about obtaining it?

WRITTEN TEST 2

Brendan has been charged with violent disorder jointly with three other defendants, all of whom are friends of his. He is a student in his early twenties and is a person of good character. The incident involved a violent confrontation with another group of five youths, two of whom are in hospital with serious injuries. When interviewed by the police, Brendan admitted he was at the scene, but claimed that he only became involved when one of his friends was being attacked by a youth armed with a iron bar. The police have taken 15 statements from eye witnesses, and at the police station they mentioned that they had seized a private security video which showed part of the incident. Brendan indicates a not guilty plea and the magistrates decide that the case is more suitable to be tried at the Crown Court.

What witness evidence would you try and obtain to assist Brendan? Explain what steps you would take to ensure the attendance of witnesses at the Crown Court. Describe how you would obtain a copy of the private security video if it does not form part of the prosecution case. Brendan was interviewed for a total of 100 minutes on tape, but there is a summary which is six pages long. What steps would you take in relation to the tape recorded interview before briefing counsel?

APPENDIX 13: ANSWERS TO THE SELF-ASSESSMENT TESTS

WRITTEN TEST 1

1 You would need to obtain the custody record and a copy of the tape. You would also need to take a detailed statement from Dean as soon as possible, confirming exactly where he claims he was and with whom; then you must make attempts to trace the people with whom he claimed he was with at the time of the burglary. It will then be necessary to take proofs of evidence from any witnesses who supported the alibi.

2 Counsel should be briefed as quickly as possible after the committal to the Crown Court, and also instructed to advise on evidence, preferably in conference. The issues which you would want Counsel to advise on would include forensic evidence and whether to obtain your own forensic report on the issue of the glass fragments, the strength of the evidence against Dean, and the likely sentence on conviction after a trial, including any discount he might gain by pleading guilty. In addition, it will probably be sensible to draft a defence statement and obtain your client's approval to it, but discuss this in conference with Counsel.

3 If you need further time to draft the defence statement, an application should be made to the Crown Court almost immediately after committal, and you must certainly obtain a hearing date before the expiry of the 14 day time limit. You should apply by letter, giving your reasons for the application and giving a copy of the letter to the CPS. The judge might extend your time without the need for a hearing or, alternatively, the matter would be listed for a mention before the judge at the Crown Court at short notice.

WRITTEN TEST 2

1 Witnesses of fact – you need to obtain the names and addresses of any possible witnesses to the incident who have not already been interviewed by the police, and arrange to go and see them and take statements from them as soon as possible, or instruct a firm of private investigators to do this.

2 You would need to make a formal application to the Crown Court for witness summonses to be issued, and support your application by an affidavit setting out the grounds for believing the witness is likely to be able to give material evidence or that any documents or thing the witness can produce is going to be relevant to the issues in the case.

3 You should write to the CPS, asking for disclosure of the video, once legal aid has been granted. There is also no reason why you should not approach the officer in the case directly and ask for the video, sending a copy of any letter you write to the officer to the CPS. If you have not succeeded in obtaining the video on a voluntary basis, a detailed defence statement should be prepared after committal, stating the basis upon which you consider that the private security video might assist your defence. This should be sufficient for the video to be disclosed. If it is not, an application should be made to the judge at the plea and directions hearing for the video to be given to the defence.

3 Tape recorded interview – in a serious and difficult case such as this, it will be essential for you to obtain the tapes and listen to the tape recorded interview. If the summary is clearly inadequate, then a transcript should be prepared so that this can be sent with the brief to counsel. Tapes of any interview should always be sent to counsel with the brief in any case where the proposed plea is or may be not guilty.

CHECKLIST SUMMARY OF UNIT 3

At the end of this unit, you should be able to:

- advise the client on sentence, appeal and the return of property;
- explain to clients their duties whilst on bail and the consequences of non-compliance;
- explain to a surety their duties and the consequences of non-compliance;
- deal with other agencies that will assist in the client's defence;
- identify how papers should be prepared for advocates;
- support advocates in conference and in court;
- understand how to produce proofs of evidence;
- understand the duties of disclosure of evidence;
- understand the importance of agreeing areas where there is no dispute.

INDEX